1 MONTH OF
FREE
READING

at

www.ForgottenBooks.com

By purchasing this book you are eligible for one month membership to ForgottenBooks.com, giving you unlimited access to our entire collection of over 1,000,000 titles via our web site and mobile apps.

To claim your free month visit:

www.forgottenbooks.com/free91400

ISBN 978-0-332-20867-1
PIBN 10091400

BY THE SAME AUTHOR

A MANUAL OF BIBLE HISTORY

VOL. I., THE OLD TESTAMENT. 660 pages and
7 Maps.

VOL II., THE NEW TESTAMENT. 440 pages
and 2 Maps.

" This is a difficult piece of work exceedingly well done.
The author has succeeded in producing that which he has
aimed at—viz , a book which may be used in class and for
examination purposes, and at the same time serve as an
introduction to Bible study in general. A word of praise
must be given to the lucidity and order which reigns
throughout   This has been secured by the logical sub-
division of the matter, a very full table of contents, well-
chosen running titles, and last (but not least) for the clear
fount of type employed.   A novel feature is found in the
Maps, which Messrs. Washbourne have had specially
printed, with the names given according to the Vulgate
spelling. Altogether an ideal text-book for Bible History
in Catholic schools."—*The Month.*

" Preachers, as well as parents and teachers, will be glad
to possess so handy and so helpful a book."—*Stella Maris.*

THE
STUDENT'S CATHOLIC DOCTRINE

THE STUDENT'S
CATHOLIC DOCTRINE

BY

REV. CHARLES HART, B.A.

ST. CUTHBERT'S GRAMMAR SCHOOL, NEWCASTLE-ON-TYNE
AUTHOR OF "THE INTERMEDIATE ENGLISH GRAMMAR" AND "MANUAL OF BIBLE
HISTORY" (VOL. I.—THE OLD TESTAMENT; VOL. II.—THE NEW TESTAMENT)

"I am the Good Shepherd ; and I know Mine and Mine know
Me. . . . And other sheep I have that are not of this fold: them
also I must bring, and they shall hear My voice, and there shall be
one fold and one Shepherd."—JOHN X. 14, 16.

THIRD EDITION, REVISED

R. & T. WASHBOURNE, LTD.

PATERNOSTER ROW, LONDON
AND AT MANCHESTER, BIRMINGHAM, AND GLASGOW

1919

𝕶ihil 𝕺bstat.

F. THOMAS BERGH, O.S.B.,
Censor Deputatus.

𝕴mprimatur.

EDM. CAN. SURMONT,
Vicarius Generalis.

Westmonasterii,
Die 28 Augustii, 1916.

PREFACE

THE present volume has been written primarily for the use of colleges and prospective teachers, and for private instruction. It is hoped, too, that it will be found especially suitable to put into the hands of the intending convert.

The general arrangement of the book is based, as far · as possible, on the division and order of the Catechism; and the marginal notes to the various paragraphs should not only render catechetical instruction more easy, but should serve a useful purpose in aiding the memory of the student preparing for examinations.

The matter for such a work, from its very nature, has necessarily been selected and compiled from various authors; yet the writer has been at pains so to arrange the ideas, and to explain them in such a way, that the clearness and conciseness at which he has aimed throughout will, it is trusted, enable the student readily to grasp and retain the all-important matter contained therein.

Besides consulting various well-known treatises on the subject, he has especially made use of the learned works of Cardinal Gousset, "Théologie Dogmatique et Théologie Morale" (four volumes), Father Schouppe's "Abridged Course of Religious Instruction," and the Abbé Gaume's "Catéchisme de Persévérance"; while, for the Sacraments, considerable use has been made of Paquet's "De Sacramentis" (two volumes).

Whatever value the present work may possess, it may here be stated that in all probability it would never have been written at all, had it not been for the suggestion and kindly encouragement of the late Canon Pool, Religious

Inspector for the Diocese of Salford, who, up to the very time of his death, took a lively interest in its progress, and read the greater part of the MS.

The author desires to thank all those who have helped him in any way in his delicate task. Especially would he thank the Very Rev. Canon Sutcliffe, Chairman of the Diocesan Inspectors, for his kindness throughout, but particularly for reading the MS., and for his very valuable suggestions; the Very Rev. Dr. Mann, the learned author of the "Lives of the Popes"; the Rev. W. Dunne, B.A., Professor of Moral Theology at Ushaw College; and the Rev. Dr. Leo Hart, all of whom have carefully read the proofs, and have rendered much useful aid to the author.

St. Cuthbert's Grammar School,
Newcastle-on-Tyne,
Feast of Our Lady's Assumption, 1916.

PREFACE
TO THE SECOND EDITION

This edition has been carefully revised and corrected. As the changes that have been made are for the most part merely verbal, it will be found that the pagination has hardly been interfered with. The greatest changes will be found in Chapter LXI., dealing with Fasting and Abstinence; Chapter LXV., concerning the Forbidden Degrees of Marriage; and Chapter LXXXIII., detailing the Diriment Impediments of Marriage.

These modifications have been found necessary through the coming into force of the New Code of Canon Law at Whitsuntide this year (1918), and the work will now be found to be in harmony with the Code as far as the latter touches on these and other points.

Feast of SS. Peter and Paul, 1918.

CONTENTS

PART I

FAITH

CONTENTS

PART II

HOPE

PART III

CHARITY

SECTION I.—THE COMMANDMENTS OF GOD

PART IV

THE SACRAMENTS

CONTENTS

PART V

VIRTUES AND VICES

INTRODUCTION

THE DIVINITY OF JESUS CHRIST

" Who is he that overcometh the world, but he that believeth that Jesus is the Son of God?" (1 JOHN v. 5).

As many who profess to be Christians go so far as to call
Scepticism con-
cerning our
Lord's Divinity.
in question not merely the supreme dignity of our Lord's Humanity, but even doubt His Divinity, it has been thought well to preface this work with an introductory chapter setting forth a few of the Scriptural proofs for that fundamental and central truth of our holy Religion, the Divinity of Jesus Christ.

Some of these so-called Christians are willing to grant that Christ was the most perfect of all *creatures*, but they maintain that He was no more than a creature, that there was a time when He was not, that He was not *properly* God, *i.e.*, that He was not the same God, and had not the same substance and nature as the eternal Father and Creator of all things. They regard Him as a great teacher, it is true, and as one setting us the noblest example of virtue, but they fail to realise in any true sense that He is God, equal to the Father and to the Holy Ghost, and claiming the same Divine honour and worship.

In subsequent chapters we shall see that Faith teaches
The Blessed
Trinity.
us that there are three Persons in God : the Father, the Son, and the Holy Ghost ; that the Father is God, that the Son is God, that the Holy Ghost is God ; that these three Persons are really distinct from one another, but equal in all things, having all one and the

xi

same nature and substance, common to the Father, and to the Son, and to the Holy Ghost. But here we shall confine ourselves to treating only of the Divinity of God the Son.

St. John, we are told, wrote his Gospel for the express purpose of demonstrating the Divinity of Jesus Christ against those heretics of his day who pretended that Jesus was a mere man who had no being or existence before He was born—as they asserted—of Joseph and Mary.

Reason for St. John's Gospel.

Opening, then, this Gospel, we read in the very first chapter: "In the beginning was the Word, and the Word was with God, and the Word was God. The same was in the beginning with God. All things were made by Him; and without Him was made nothing that was made. In Him was life, and the life was the light of men. ... And the Word was made flesh and dwelt among us" (John i. 1-14). According to the Gospel, therefore, the Word *was* at the beginning of things, that is, He existed before anything was created; He is not then a creature. All things were made by the Word; the Word then was not made— He is therefore eternal. The Word was united with God, and formed only one nature with God; He was therefore God Himself, *et Deus erat Verbum.*

Many writers, to prove the Divinity of Jesus Christ, have appealed to prophecy and miracles, yet He Himself refers to these mainly in proof of His Divine *mission* and *work*, and points out to the Jews that He fulfils in His Person and in His work all that has been foretold of the Messias; but this is altogether different from the question of the Divinity of His Person. "Moses," says Father Devivier, "was the *messenger of God*; he also was entrusted with the mission of establishing a more perfect religion than that which preceded it, and yet the Jewish people never thought of considering him as God. Jesus Christ, on the contrary, *is adored as*

Our Lord is adored as God.

God by all who for nineteen centuries have been proud to bear His name and to follow His doctrine. This fact is undoubted ; but does Jesus deserve this adoration—*is He truly God ?* . . .

"We believe in the Divinity of the *mission* of Jesus Christ, because He expressly declared that He was sent by God, and that He confirmed this mission by the most irrefutable proofs. We must believe in the Divinity of *His Person, if He has positively given Himself out as God.*

"Now, it is a fact absolutely certain, attested by a great

Our Lord affirms His Divinity.

number of perfectly clear texts, that Jesus *affirmed Himself to be God.* Without the least ambiguity, and in a multitude of circumstances, He declared that He was God, the Son of God, equal in everything to the Father who had sent Him."*

That our Lord constantly applied to Himself this

Son of God.

supreme title, "Son of God," was indeed a surprising revelation of His true nature. It was a title, too, constantly given to Him by His disciples ; and yet in this Soul, so meek, so humble, it called forth not the slightest astonishment or opposition.

To those who were constantly with Him, who had seen

Peter's confession.

the miracles which He wrought, and who themselves had worked miracles in His name, He on one occasion put the question, "Whom do *you* say that I am ?" Simon Peter answering for all, said : "Thou art Christ, the Son of the living God" (Matt. xvi. 15, 16). And again when speaking for the twelve : "We have believed and have known that Thou art the Christ, the Son of God" (John vi. 70).

Note, too, the expression of Martha's faith just before

That of Martha.

the raising to life of her brother Lazarus : "Lord, I have believed that Thou art Christ, the Son of the living God, who art come into this world" (John xi. 27).

* Devivier, "Christian Apologetics," vol.i., p. 334.

St. Thomas, also, after affirming that he would not
That of St. Thomas. believe that Christ was risen from the dead unless he received the most convincing proofs, is brought to the humble confession, "My Lord and my God" (John xx. 28). He saw the humanity, remarks St. Augustine, and confessed the Divinity.

Yet again : after Christ had stilled the tempest, they
That of many disciples. that were with Him in the ship fell down at His feet and worshipped Him, saying : "Thou art truly the Son of God" (Matt. xiv. 33).

Now what was our Saviour's attitude to all this? Was He fired with indignation, as naturally He would have been, had He been an ordinary man, on hearing applied to Himself the sacred name of God? See how Paul and Barnabas behaved when the enraptured people wished to pay them Divine homage. They indignantly rejected the proffered honours. Rending their garments, they ran among the people exclaiming : "O men, why do you these things? We are mortals, men like unto you" (Acts xiv. 13, 14). And when the disciples of John the Baptist thought that perhaps he was the Messias, John never ceased to disabuse their minds; but pointing to our Lord, he exclaimed : "Behold the Lamb of God, behold Him who taketh away the sins of the world. . . . And I give testimony that this is the Son of God" (John i. 29, 34).

Yet, though our Saviour constantly hears Himself
Our Lord allows the title "Son of God." addressed as the Son of God, the true Son of God, He not only permits such epithets to be applied to Him unchecked, and allows Himself to be adored as God, but He praises Peter for applying them to Him, and, as the reward of his clear and open profession of faith, declares to him the dignity to which he is to be raised : "Blessed art thou, Simon Bar-Jona: because flesh and blood hath not revealed it to thee, but My Father who is in heaven. And I say to thee: That

thou art Peter; and upon this rock I will build My
Church, and the gates of hell shall not prevail against it "
(Matt. xvi. 17, 18). He also rewarded Martha's confession
of His Divinity by raising to life her brother Lazarus who
had been dead four days.

Nay, more: besides accepting the title and declaring
blessed those who gave it to Him, He even
seeks an acknowledgment of it in such as come
to Him for spiritual or temporal favours. To the man
born blind, to whom He had just given sight, He said:
" Dost thou believe in the Son of God?" The man asked:
" Who is He, Lord, that I may believe?" Jesus said to
him: " Thou hast both seen Him, and it is He who
talketh with thee." He answered and said: " I believe,
Lord. And falling down he adored Him " (John ix. 35-38).

He even seeks it.

Jesus Christ Himself, too, directly affirmed His own
Divinity. Speaking to Nicodemus He said:
" God so loved the world as to give His Only-
begotten Son; that whosoever believeth in
Him may not perish, but may have life everlasting "
(John iii. 16). And what He said to Nicodemus in the
secrecy of an intimate discourse, He made the common
subject of His preaching in Jerusalem.* Here He affirmed
His Divine Sonship, absolute and eternal, His essential
unity with the Father, in such terms that the Jews
murmured, were indignant, stopped their ears, and even
took up stones to cast at Him. And when He said to
them: " Many good works I have shown you from My
Father; for which of these works do you stone Me?"
they answered: " For a good work we stone Thee not, but
for blasphemy; and because that Thou, being a man,
makest Thyself God " (John x. 24-33).

He affirms His Divine Sonship.

Neither threats nor entreaties, nor the prospect of a
cruel death, could make Him retract His affirmation of His

---

* See Bougaud, "Le Christianisme," vol. ii., p. 622.

Divinity for a single instant: " If Thou be the Christ, tell
us." Jesus answered : " If I shall tell you, you will not
believe Me." The priests replied: " Art Thou then the
Son of God?" And He said: " You say that I am "
(Luke xxii. 66-70). The High-priest was not content
with this reply. Wishing to have some strong accusation
against Him, he put the question distinctly and with the
utmost religious solemnity. " I adjure Thee," he exclaimed,
" by the living God, that Thou tell us if Thou be the
Christ, the Son of God." Jesus said to him : " Thou hast
said it " (Matt. xxvi. 63, 64).

The leaders of the Jews certainly never mistook His
assertions, but accused Him of having blas-
His claim phemed by saying that God was His Father,
understood by
the Jewish and by making Himself equal to God (John
leaders v. 18). They therefore sought to kill Him ;
and when they brought Him before Pilate, what was
their accusation against Him? " We have a law; and
according to the law He ought to die, because He made
Himself the Son of God " (John xix. 7).

And the people, too, well knew the reason for His
condemnation ; for as He hung upon the Cross,
And people
alike. " they blasphemed Him, wagging their heads
and saying: Vah, Thou that destroyest the temple of
God. . . . If Thou be the Son of God, come down from
the Cross. He trusted in God; let Him deliver Him now
if He will have Him; for He said : I am the Son of God "
(Matt. xxvii. 39-43).

Even the centurion who had to see to the carrying out
of the death sentence, and those that were with him
watching Jesus, " having seen the earthquake, and the
things that were done, were sore afraid, saying : Indeed
this was the Son of God " (Matt. xxvii. 54).

Our Saviour, then, not only accepted the title, Son of
God, true Son of God, and congratulated and rewarded

those who gave it to Him, but took it to Himself in private, in public, in the streets of Jerusalem, before the rulers of the people and before the tribunals. He died rather than give it up; *He died for having taken it.*

Moreover, whatever are the titles that are given to God, Jesus appropriates them; whatever is the homage that is due to God, Jesus claims it; whatever the powers that belong to God, Jesus exercises them. Not only did He take the name of God, of Son of God, but He assumed to Himself the functions, the acts, and the necessary and supreme attributes of God: " All things whatsoever the Father hath are Mine" (John xvi. 15).

Jesus claims Divine prerogatives.

Yet in calling Himself God, Jesus Christ clearly distinguishes Himself from the Person of the Father who has sent Him, and whose work He has come to do: " What things soever the Father doth, these the Son also doth in like manner" (John v. 19). "The Father loveth the Son; and He hath given all things into His hand" (John iii. 35). "Father, the hour is come, glorify Thy Son, that Thy Son may glorify Thee" (John xvii. 1). "If any one love Me, he will keep My word, and My Father will love him, and We will come to him, and will make Our abode with him" (John xiv. 23).

He distinguishes Himself from the Father,

He distinguishes Himself just as clearly from the Person of the Holy Spirit. "I will ask the Father, and He shall give you another Paraclete, that He may abide with you for ever" (John xiv. 16). "But the Paraclete, the Holy Ghost, whom the Father will send in My name, He will teach you all things, and bring all things to your mind, whatsoever I shall have said to you" (John xiv. 26).

And from the Holy Ghost,

Thus Jesus pointedly distinguishes Himself from God the Father and God the Holy Ghost, but never from God' the Son. He never speaks of the Son as of one other than Himself. It is He Himself who is the Son.

But never from the Son.

Moreover, in taking the name of the Son, He takes it in a sense which implies nothing less than absolute equality in power and substance with the Father and the Holy Ghost. " I am the way, and the truth, and the life. No man cometh to the Father, but by Me. If you had known Me, you would without doubt have known My Father also; and from henceforth you shall know Him, and you have seen Him." Philip said to Him : " Lord, show us the Father, and it is enough for us." Jesus answered him : " Have I been so long a time with you ; and you have not known Me ? Philip, He that seeth Me seeth the Father also. . . . Do you not believe that I am in the Father, and the Father in Me ? Otherwise believe for the very works' sake. Amen, amen I say to you, he that believeth in Me, the works that I do, he also shall do ; and greater than these shall he do ; because I go to the Father : and whatsoever you shall ask the Father in My name, that will I do, that the Father may be glorified in the Son. . . . If you love Me, keep My command- ments ; and I will ask the Father, and He shall give you another Paraclete, that He may abide with you for ever, the Spirit of Truth, whom the world cannot receive, because it seeth Him not, nor knoweth Him. . . . If any man love Me, he will keep My word, and My Father will love him, and We will come to him, and will make Our abode with him " (John xiv. 6-23).

In the above we have clearly indicated to us the Three Persons of the Blessed Trinity, as also Their union and Their distinction. And among these Three Persons, Jesus is the Son.

He is God the Son.

Claiming then to be the Son of God, this meek, humble, holy, gentle being never hesitates, in His discourses, to take the rank which becomes a Man-God, to place

Himself above all creatures whether in heaven or on earth; Ranks Himself above patriarchs and prophets; above Abra-
as God.　ham, Moses, David and Solomon; above John the Baptist, the greatest of the children of men; even above the angels: "Thinkest thou that I cannot ask My Father, and He will give Me presently more than twelve legions of angels?" (Matt. xxvi. 53). He affirms His existence to be before the creation, from all eternity: "Amen, amen, I say to you, before Abraham was made, *I am*" (John viii. 58).

He even acts and speaks as God. He commands, He Acts and speaks judges, He absolves, He decides and disposes
with Divine　all things with an absolute authority. To
authority.　Peter He gives the keys of the Kingdom of Heaven; to him and to the other apostles He grants the power of working miracles and of remitting sins. While others work miracles in the name of God, and by virtue of delegated powers, it is as Sovereign Master that Jesus gives His commands to nature, to men, to angels, to demons. To the daughter of Jairus who had just died, He said: "Damsel, I say to thee, arise" (Mark v. 41). To the widow's son who was being carried out for burial, He said: "Young man, I say to thee, arise" (Luke vii. 14). To Lazarus, who had been four days in the tomb: "Lazarus, come forth" (John xi. 43). And in each case the dead rose up in obedience to His call.

Jesus, then, was not content with merely *declaring* His Divinity. In support of His claim He invoked the test of His works, and it was by miracles that He obtained belief in His words; for a miracle worked in favour of a doctrine is a Divine seal impressed upon that doctrine.

As God, He forgives sins. When, on a certain occasion, Jesus forgives the Scribes and Pharisees were scandalised at
sins.　His remitting sins, and charged Him with blasphemy, saying in their hearts: Who can forgive

sins but God? Jesus, knowing their thoughts, said to
them : " Why do you think evil in your hearts ? Whether
is it easier to say, Thy sins are forgiven thee; or to
say, Arise and walk ?   But that you may know that
the Son of Man hath power on earth to forgive sins :
Arise, He said (turning to the man sick of the palsy), take
up thy bed, and go into thy house." Immediately the
man rose up, and went away in the sight of all (Matt.
ix. 2-7).   And in the case of Magdalene, He forgives her
all the sins she has committed against God, as a debt contracted towards Himself, and on account of her great love
for Him : " Many sins are forgiven her because she hath
loved much " (Luke vii. 47).

He declared that He would come to life again *by His
own power.* " Destroy this temple, and in three
days I will raise it up. . . .   But He spoke of
the temple of His body " (John ii. 19, 21).

*He is omni-
potent.*

" No man taketh my life away from Me ; but I lay it down
of Myself ; and I have power to lay it down, and I have
power to take it up again " (John x. 18).   What He
declared He would do, that He did when He raised Himself to life again on Easter Sunday.

Beside taking the titles which belong to God, and
attributing to Himself Divine power, He demands the homage which is due to God alone.
He will be the object of *faith :* " Let not your

*He requires the
homage due to
God alone.*

heart be troubled.   You believe in God, believe also in Me "
(John xiv. 1).   " If I do the works of My Father, though
you will not believe Me, believe the works ; that you may
know that the Father is in Me, and I in the Father "
(John x. 38).   Of *love :* " If any one love Me, he will keep
My word, and My Father will love him, and We will come
to him, and will make Our abode with him " (John xiv. 23).
Of *prayer :* " Whatsoever you shall ask the Father in My
name, that will I do. . . . If you shall ask Me anything

in My name, that will I do" (John xiv. 13, 14). Of *adoration*: "And behold Jesus met them . . . but they came up and took hold of His feet, and adored Him" (Matt. xxviii. 9). And the man who had been born blind said: "I believe, Lord. And falling down, he adored Him" (John ix. 38).

It may be objected, it is true, that certain passages of Scripture seem to represent the Son of God as

Jesus as God and Man.

inferior to the Father; such, for instance, as speak of submission to the Father and doing His Father's will. It should be noted, however, that in these passages it is not a question of the Word considered simply as the Word, that is, of the Son of God considered as God; but of the Word made flesh, of the Son of God made man, of Jesus Christ who has two natures, the Divine nature which He has in common with the Father and the Holy Ghost, and the human nature which He has in common with us. Now, although Jesus Christ—God the Son made man—is inferior to the Father according to His humanity, He is equal to Him according to His Divinity. As Son of God, He is one and the same God with the Father: "I and the Father are One" (John x. 30); that is, one in Divine nature, but not in personality.

Christ, then, clearly claimed to have the nature and prerogatives of God—in fact, was crucified

Conclusion.

because of His claim. Had this claim been false or illusory, it is impossible for God to have supported His mission and teaching by the sanction of miraculous power. But He did so support it. Therefore the claim to it is true and Divinely sanctioned.

THE STUDENT'S CATHOLIC DOCTRINE

PART 1

FAITH

"He that believeth, and is baptised, shall be saved ; but he that believeth not shall be condemned (MARK xvi. 16).

CHAPTER I

THE END FOR WHICH MAN WAS CREATED

"For Thyself, O God, Thou hast made us," says St. Augustine ; "therefore our heart will be rest-less until it rests in Thee." Every man, then, sent by God into this world is sent for one end, and for one end only—viz., that, by knowing, loving, and serving God, he may save his soul and gain heaven. Hence arises that all-important question, "What must I do to save my soul?" The only satisfactory answer to this is to be found in the words of the Catechism : "To save my soul I must worship God by Faith, Hope, and Charity ; that is, I must believe in Him, I must hope in Him, and I must love Him with my whole heart."

The end of man.

To show how empty are all earthly pleasures, and how wanting they are in true happiness, we have Solomon, the wisest of kings, crying out in the bitterness of his heart : "I said, I will go and abound with delights, and enjoy good things. I heaped together for myself silver and gold and the wealth of kings and provinces. And whatsoever my eyes desired, I refused

Pleasure not true happiness.

them not; and I withheld not my heart from enjoying every pleasure, and delighting itself in the things which I had prepared. And when I turned myself to all the things which my hands had wrought, and to the labours wherein I had laboured in vain, I saw in all things vanity and vexation of mind, and that nothing was lasting under the sun " (Eccles. ii. 1-11).

And yet the very things of this world, if only we make a right use of them, may serve as stepping-stones to the attainment of that happiness which alone can satisfy the human heart: " Whether you eat or drink, or whatsoever else you do, do all for the glory of God " (1 Cor. x. 31).

It is of supreme importance, then, for each one of us to know in what way we are to worship God by Faith, Hope, and Charity, since it is in this that the whole religious life of man consists. Speaking of the Spiritual House of the Soul, St. Augustine calls Faith its foundation, Hope its walls, and Charity its roof or covering.

By Faith we worship God in firmly believing all that He has revealed to His Church. It is by Faith that

We worship God by Faith. we honour the veracity of God, get a right knowledge of Him, and submit our reason to His sovereign truth; for when we accept the truths which God has revealed because He, the very Truth, has revealed them, and accept them whether our finite minds can grasp them or not, we honour the Divine veracity by giving to God the homage of our reason.

We worship God by Hope when we expect with con-

By Hope. fidence that He will give us salvation and all the means necessary to obtain it, resting our assurance on the power, goodness, and mercy of God, His fidelity to His promises, and the infinite merits of our Saviour. It is in this way that we pay Him the homage of our confidence and trust.

We worship God by Charity when we love Him above

all things because He is infinitely good, infinitely perfect,
By Charity. and infinitely worthy of our love. It is by
this virtue of Charity that we conform our
own will in all things to the most holy will of God, and
honour him by offering Him the homage of our affections.

And because God is the sovereign Lord of all things,
He requires this service of us, and will cast
Necessity of.
serving God from Him for ever, not only the rapacious, the
unjust, and evil-doers generally, but all such
as refuse to pay Him this triple worship which is His due:
" The unprofitable servant cast ye out into the exterior
darkness. There shall be weeping and gnashing of teeth "
(Matt. xxv. 30). How necessary, too, is this service for
each one of us if we wish to attain eternal happiness!
" For what doth it profit a man if he gain the whole
world, and suffer the loss of his own soul ?" (Matt. xvi. 26).

The three virtues of Faith, Hope, and Charity are called
God the *object* *Theological Virtues*, because they relate directly
of the Theolog- to God, and have God as their immediate end or
ical Virtues. *object*. We believe in God, we hope in God, we
love God. There are, besides, Moral Virtues, so called
because they regulate our conduct in regard to ourselves
and to our neighbour ; and, although they are exercised with reference to the will of God, yet they have
God as their object only indirectly; for example, almsgiving has as its immediate object the relief of want.
But the immediate object of Faith is God Himself and all
the truths which He has revealed ; the immediate object of
Hope is God, who has promised to give Himself to us for
all eternity in Heaven ; the immediate object of Charity is
God Himself as the perfection of all that is good and holy.

God the *motive* God is also the cause or *motive* of the Theo-
of the Theolog- logical Virtues. The proper motive of Faith
ical Virtues. is the Divine veracity : we believe the truths
of Revelation because God, who is the very Truth and who

can neither deceive nor be deceived, has revealed them to us through the infallible teaching of His Church. All possibility of error is therefore excluded. But the decisions of the Church, although they are infallible, are not the motive of our Faith; they are only the sure means of knowing the truths of Faith, which is founded on the Word of God.

The proper motive of Hope is the infinite goodness and power of God, and His fidelity to His promises. In view of the merits of His Divine Son He has promised us eternal life, and all the means necessary to obtain it, if on our part we faithfully observe what He requires of us.

The proper motive of Charity is the infinite goodness of God in Himself, and His infinite goodness to us: for His Divine perfections, too, He is infinitely deserving of our love. Nay, God even commands us to love Him: " Thou shalt love the Lord thy God with thy whole heart, and with thy whole soul, and with thy whole mind, and with thy whole strength " (Mark xii. 30). The love of God, moreover, is the great end for which we were created, as on it depends our happiness or misery for all eternity : " The Lord keepeth all them that love Him; but all the wicked He will destroy " (Ps. cxliv. 20).

CHAPTER II

NATURE, GROUNDS, AND RULE OF FAITH

WE base our judgments and opinions on many grounds.

Grounds of belief.

Some truths, of their very nature, are *self-evident* and necessary: for example, when once we understand the meaning of the terms, we cannot conceive how 3 added to 7 could give us other than 10; or picture to ourselves a circle the radii of which were not equal; or consider the whole as anything but greater than its part. Other things we know to be true from *experience*—that is, from the evidence of our own senses; while, again, there are many things which we do not know of ourselves, but which we accept on the authority of other people. Now, if our belief rests on the testimony of man, who may err, it is *human* or *historical faith;* if it is based on the testimony of God, who cannot err, it is *Divine faith,* or Faith as a Theological Virtue.

Divine Faith. Divine Faith, then, in the words of the Catechism, is " a supernatural gift of God which enables us to believe without doubting whatever God has revealed." It is a virtue infused by the Holy Ghost into our souls at Baptism, by which we believe, firmly and without hesitation, all that God has revealed, and, through His Church, proposes for our belief. " Faith is the evidence of things that appear not " (Heb. xi. 1); and, consequently, knowledge gained by experience, or in any other way, is not Faith, but merely practical wisdom : " For by grace you are saved through faith, and that, not of yourselves, for it is the gift of God " (Eph. ii. 8).

Ground of Divine Faith. The ground or motive of our Faith is the Divine veracity; and what makes our Faith *divine* is believing the truths of Religion because God, who is Truth itself, and who cannot deceive us, has revealed them to us. What He has revealed, then, must be true whether we understand it or not.

Oneness of Faith. The truths of our Faith, as we gather from the words of our Lord Himself, we are to learn from the Church which He came on earth to establish : " Going therefore, teach ye all nations, baptising them in the name of the Father, and of the Son, and of the Holy Ghost: teaching them to observe all things whatsoever I have commanded you : and behold I am with you all days even to the consummation of the world " (Matt. xxviii. 19, 20). " He that heareth you, heareth Me, and he that despiseth you, despiseth Me " (Luke x. 16). And as there is but *one Lord,* there can be but *one Faith :* " One Lord, one Faith, one Baptism " (Eph. iv. 5) ; whence it follows that there can be but one *true*

Church, or exponent of that Faith : "He that holdeth not this unity of the Church, doth he think he holdeth the Faith ?" asks St. Cyprian.   And if at any time other faiths arise, then those who profess them begin by falling away from the one only Faith, and generally end in having no faith at all.

Moreover, to show us that Faith is a matter of supreme importance, and that we cannot afford to **Necessity of** neglect it without the gravest consequences to **Faith.** ourselves, our Lord solemnly warns us : " He that believeth, and is baptised, shall be saved ; but he that believeth not shall be condemned " (Mark xvi. 16). And St. Paul, writing to the Hebrews, tells them : "Without faith it is impossible to please God" (Heb. xi. 6).   If what we believe, or whether we believe or not, were of no consequence, it would not have been necessary for God to reveal a Religion ; but " this is the judgment : because the light is come into the world, and men loved darkness rather than the light" (John iii. 19).   " He that believeth not the Son, maketh Him [*i.e.*, God] a liar " (1 John v. 10).   From what has already been said we can now see the force of those simple words of the Catechism, " I am to know what God has revealed by the testimony, teaching, and authority of the Catholic Church."

And since Faith is necessary for salvation, Christ must have left us a certain means of arriving at a **A Rule of Faith** knowledge of the Truth, a Rule which must **necessary.** enable all, without exception, to come infallibly to the Truth ; for He Himself tells us : " He that believeth not shall be condemned " (Mark xvi. 16). And this Rule that He has laid down for us must be *plain*, that all may understand it ; it must be *universal*, that is, it must extend to every revealed truth ; and it must be *certain*, that all may follow it without hesitation or doubt.

Our Rule of Faith is the teaching of the Catholic Church; and all other Rules of Faith, as we shall presently see, are unsatisfactory. The Catholic Church, which Christ came down from heaven to establish, must be the only true Church, since He, who is Truth itself, could not teach contradictory doctrines. But to take Scripture, or the Written Word of God,* as the only Rule of Faith, as some do, breaks the rule of *plainness*, since in all ages there have been countless numbers who could not read; while, even among the learned, many have been unable to agree as to the true sense of some of the most important passages. St. Peter himself in Scripture tells us that in St. Paul's Epistles there "are some things hard to be understood, which the unlearned and unstable wrest, as they do also the other Scriptures, to their own destruction" (2 Pet. iii. 16). How dangerous, then, is the position of those who rely on their own private interpretations of the Sacred Writings!

Rule of Scripture not plain.

Neither does the Rule of Scripture alone satisfy the second quality, that of *universality*; since the Scriptures do not include every revealed truth. Are we not in Scripture told to observe the *seventh day* of the week, or Saturday, as the day of rest?

Rule of Scripture not universal.

---

* Holy Scripture consists of a number of writings, composed by different persons and at various times. Gathered together they form the Bible (Greek, *biblia*, the books), and they differ from all other books in that their authors were all inspired by the Holy Ghost. Those written before the birth of our Lord form the Old Testament, the others the New. The former contains the history of the Patriarchs and of God's chosen people, the Israelites or Jews, as well as the Psalms, several books of moral teaching, and many prophetical books. The latter consists of the four Gospels, or Lives of our Lord, written by St. Matthew, St. Mark, St. Luke, and St. John, the Acts of the Apostles by St. Luke, many Epistles or Letters, mostly by St. Paul, and the "Apocalypse" or Revelation of St. John. The books of the Old Testament were carefully preserved by the Jews, and the Catholic Church finally gathered together the books of both Testaments, and declared them to be the Written Word of God.

Yet all Christians observe the *first day*, or Sunday. Scripture commands us to abstain from things strangled and from blood (Acts xv. 20); but this command no longer binds.   No mention is made in Scripture of infant baptism.   The Scriptures do not tell us how many Sacred Books there are, nor what Books are authentic: we look to the Church for guidance in all these matters.

Nor is the Rule of Scripture alone a *certain* rule.   Those who follow this Rule often appeal to Scripture to prove contradictory doctrines; and each is satisfied that he alone has hit upon the genuine meaning: hence the innumerable sects that have arisen from following private judgment, exercised on Scripture, as their Rule of Faith.

Rule of Scripture *not certain*.

The Catholic Rule, on the contrary, is suited to all, both to those who cannot read and to those who can.   Such passages in Scripture as are described by St. Peter as " hard to be understood," and from which some wrest a meaning " to their own destruction," are infallibly explained by the teaching of the Church.   The Rule, moreover, is in perfect keeping with the command of our Lord to His Apostles, " Teach ye all nations . . . teaching them to observe all things whatsoever I have commanded you " (Matt. xxviii. 19, 20).

Catholic Rule *plain*.

The Catholic Rule, **too**, comprises the *whole* Word of God, and includes all that God has revealed, whether by Angels, or by the Prophets, or by His own Divine Son, Jesus Christ.   St. John the Evangelist himself tells us in his Gospel that it would require a great many books to record all the various doings and sayings of our Divine Lord: " Many other signs did Jesus in the sight of His disciples that are not written in this book . . . which, if they were written every one, the world itself, I think, would not be able to

Catholic Rule *universal*.

contain the books that should be written " (John xx. and xxi.). But all these things our Lord included in His injunction to His Apostles when He bade them teach the observance of whatsoever He had commanded them.

The Catholic Rule is also a *certain* rule. " I will ask the Father," said our Lord to His Apostles, "and He shall give you *another Paraclete, that He may abide with you for ever; the Spirit of Truth,* whom the world cannot receive . . . but you shall know Him, because He shall abide with you, and shall be in you" (John xiv. 16, 17). " But the Paraclete, the Holy Ghost, whom the Father will send in My name, He will teach you all things, and bring all things to your mind, whatsoever I shall have said to you " (John xiv. 26). In the above words, then, we are promised by our Lord the *perpetual presence* of the Spirit of Truth in His Church ; for it is evident that this Spirit of Truth was promised not only to the Apostles, but also to their successors through all generations. Hence it is that, in every age and clime, the Holy Ghost constantly watches over the Catholic Church, and preserves her both from the open and the secret attacks of her enemies. Now what the Apostles received from Christ they handed on to their successors in the ministry, and so on from generation to generation ; and in this way has come down to us "the Faith once delivered to the saints " (Jude i. 3).

Catholic Rule certain.

But to understand fully the nature of this Rule of Faith, we must first of all clearly grasp the meaning of the term *Tradition* as employed by the Catholic Church. By Tradition is meant the handing down of those revealed truths which the Apostles taught, but which are not contained in the Scriptures : " Therefore, brethren, stand fast, and hold the traditions which you have learned, whether by word or by our epistle " (2 Thess. ii. 14). Hence we see, says

Tradition explained.

St. Chrysostom, that the Apostles did not, by writing, deliver all the things that were to be believed, but many things by word of mouth only, which have been per- petuated by Tradition ; and these traditions (afterwards committed to writing), no less than the writings of the Apostles, are deserving of faith.

Indeed, the Apostles were not commissioned by Christ to write at all, but to go and *preach* the doctrine which He had taught them : " Go ye into the whole world, and preach the Gospel to every creature " (Mark xvi. 15). And St. John : " Many other signs did Jesus in the sight of His disciples, which are not written in this book " (John xx. 30). The Bible, then, does not contain the whole revealed Word of God, nor does it anywhere tell us what Books are Divine, or their number. Indeed, were it not for Tradition, we should not have a Bible at all.

Divine Revelation, then, has come down to us *partly by writing*—that is, by the Holy Scriptures or the Bible ; *partly by word of mouth*—that is, by Tradition. And this Tradition has been handed down by the Church without interruption from the time of the Apostles, who taught what they had received from Christ, and passed it on to their successors. This handing down, too, has been partly by word of mouth, and partly, though not written by the Apostles, by the writings of the Fathers, the Decrees of Councils, and the rites of the Catholic Church. " And the things which thou hast heard of me by many witnesses, the same commend to faithful men, who shall be fit to teach others also " (2 Tim. ii. 2).

Our rule of Faith, then, is *Scripture* and *Tradition*, both infallibly interpreted by the Catholic Church, " the pillar and ground of truth " (1 Tim. iii. 15). The Church tells us what truths God has revealed or made known to us, and we accept them on the authority of God. Nor does the

The Catholic Rule of Faith.

Church ever make a new Article of Faith, but, whenever any of her doctrines have been seriously attacked or called in question, she has declared this or that truth to have been revealed from the beginning and taught in all the ages of the Church.

CHAPTER III

QUALITIES AND ORIGIN OF FAITH

FAITH, as we have seen in the last chapter, embraces all the truths which the Church teaches, and which God has made known to us by the Patriarchs and the Prophets, and last of all by His only Son, our Lord Jesus Christ. Yet Faith to be of value must possess certain

Necessary qualities of Faith. definite qualities: it must be *supernatural*— that is, in addition to its being elicited by the aid of grace, we must believe because God has spoken; it must be *firm* or unwavering, for when God has spoken, reason must be silent, and submit; it must be *entire* or *universal*—that is, it must embrace all revealed truths: "Teach them to observe all things whatsoever I have commanded you" (Matt. xxviii. 20). We cannot doubt or call in question a single revealed truth without at the same time calling in question the Divine veracity, and thereby destroying the very foundation on which our Faith rests.

Our Faith, moreover, should be lively and constant:

Our Faith must be lively and constant. *lively* in the sense that we should live up to it by ever avoiding evil and doing good; for that only, says St. Gregory, is true Faith which does not contradict in works what is believed in words. And St. James: "As the body without the spirit is dead, so also faith without works is dead" (ii. 26). "And if I should have all faith, so that I could remove mountains," says St. Paul, "and have not charity, I am nothing" (1 Cor. xiii. 2). Our Faith is *constant* or steadfast when

we are ready to make any sacrifice rather than lose it :
"Whosoever shall deny Me before men, I will also deny
him before My Father who is in heaven" (Matt. x. 33).

If Faith, then, must possess the qualities we have named,
and if "without Faith it is impossible to
Explicit and please God" (Heb. xi. 6), we naturally ask
Implicit Faith. ourselves the question, How can the Faith of
the poor uninstructed Catholic be as that of the learned
theologian? The difficulty is explained by showing that
there are two ways in which we can believe the truths of
Revelation—viz., either by *Explicit* or by *Implicit* Faith.

Our Faith is said to be *explicit* when the truths which
we believe are known to us distinctly, and we give our
assent to each separate article of our belief *in particular*.
It is said to be *implicit* when we believe *in a general way*
all revealed truths, although we do not know them distinctly and in particular.

Now from the nature of Faith, and from our Lord's instructions to His Apostles, it is evident that we
Implicit Faith are bound to believe, at least with an *implicit*
required of all. Faith, all that the Church believes and teaches ;
for He not only bade them go into the whole world and
teach the observance of *all the things* which He had commanded them, but added : "He that believeth not shall
be condemned" (Mark xvi. 16). Yet all Christians are not
bound to know all the truths of Faith with an explicit
knowledge of each separate truth ; it is enough that their
belief should extend in a general way to all that God has
revealed to His Church.

Explicit Faith   The habit of Faith* infused into the soul
in certain truths at Baptism is sufficient in the case of young
necessary.   children, and all such as never come to the
use of reason. But all those who are capable of making an

---

* The habit of Faith is a supernatural quality permanently
inherent in the soul, enabling us, when we come to the use of
reason, to make supernatural acts of belief.

act of Faith are obliged to believe, *implicitly* at least, all that the Church believes and teaches, and *explicitly* some of the principal truths of Religion of which they cannot be ignorant without danger to their eternal salvation. Thus it is necessary to know, and explicitly believe, that there is a God who is the sovereign Lord of all things; and that there is a future state in which we shall be rewarded or punished according to our works in this life: " Without faith it is impossible to please God ; for he that cometh to God must believe that He is, and is a rewarder of them that seek Him " (Heb. xi. 6).

It is, moreover, held by many theologians that, after the coming of Christ, we are required to believe explicitly, as necessary for salvation, the mysteries of the adorable Trinity (*i.e.*, the Unity and Trinity of God), and the Incarnation, Death, and Resurrection of our Saviour. These are contained in the Apostles' Creed.

We must also know and explicitly believe, at least in substance, the Our Father, the Hail Mary, the Ten Commandments, the Commandments of the Church, and such Sacraments as we are bound to receive.

Seeing, then, the absolute necessity of Faith for salvation, we naturally ask ourselves how we arrive at the possession of it. " By grace you are saved through faith," says St. Paul, " and this not of yourselves; for it is the gift of God " (Eph. ii. 8). It cannot, therefore, be acquired by us, but is infused into the soul at Baptism. Christians at their Baptism receive the habit of Faith, which enables them, when they reach the years of discretion, and are duly instructed in the truths of Revelation, to elicit suitable acts of Faith. It is the beginning, foundation, and root of justification, and the first of all the virtues, since without Faith it is impossible to please God.

Faith infused into the soul at Baptism.

CHAPTER IV

POSITIVE AND NEGATIVE DUTIES OF FAITH

THE duties which Faith imposes on us are both of a *positive* and of a *negative* kind. "We are *commanded*," as the Catechism tells us, "to worship the one, true, and living God by Faith," and are *forbidden* "all wilful doubt, disbelief, or denial of any article of Faith, and also culpable ignorance of the doctrines of the Church."

Positive and negative duties.

›Now we worship God by Faith whenever we make acts of Faith—that is, whenever we acknowledge our belief in the truths revealed by God, and proposed by His Church for our acceptance. It is in this way that we pay direct homage to Him by honouring His eternal Truth. Such acts, moreover, tend to strengthen our Faith, and to keep alive in our hearts love and attachment to our holy Religion.

But our worship of God by Faith may be either *internal*, when it exists merely in the mind and heart ; or *external*, when it is outwardly professed by words and signs. Yet whenever we make an outward profession of our Faith, an internal act of Faith also must of necessity accompany it; and certain definite times or occasions do arise when we are called upon to make a definite act of Faith.

An *internal* act of Faith is necessary :—

Necessity of *internal* Acts of Faith.

1. When we attain the perfect use of reason, and have been sufficiently instructed in the truths of Religion.

2. When temptations arise against our Faith, and the only way to put them to flight is by an act of Faith.

3. From time to time during life, especially when we are about to perform a duty which demands an act of Faith.

4. When we are in danger of death.

In order to fulfil the obligation of making an act of
Faith, however, a fixed formula is by no means always
necessary ; for example, when we make the sign of the
Cross, or hear Mass, or make a visit to the Blessed Sacrament, or practise any of the virtues, by these very acts we
are making a profession of Faith ; and when we recite the
Apostles' Creed, we make an act of Faith more or less
explicit in all the truths of Religion.

There are occasions also when we are in duty bound
Necessity of to make an external declaration of our Faith ;
external Acts and this outward profession must, as we have
of Faith. seen, be accompanied by an internal act of the
same virtue. We are forbidden, under pain of mortal
sin, to deny our Religion either *expressly* or *virtually*.
We must never, then, by our conduct give a reasonable
impression to others, even in appearance, that we are
denying it. Nay, our very silence might even constitute
a real denial. Nor must we be ashamed of our Religion
before men: "Whosoever shall deny Me before men,
I will also deny him before My Father who is in
heaven " (Matt. x. 33). Whenever, then, God's honour,
or the salvation of our neighbour, or the cause of Religion
demands it, we are bound to make an open profession
of our Faith : "Whosoever shall confess Me before men,
I will also confess him before My Father who is in heaven "
(Matt. x. 32).

But if we are never allowed to deny our Faith, we are
Causes may not called upon to manifest it on every
arise for conceal- possible occasion. Grave causes may at times
ing our Faith. arise which justify, not a *denial* of our Religion,
but the concealment of it from others. The mere fact
of not undeceiving people who mistake us for non-
Catholics does not constitute a denial of our Faith, provided we use no improper means to conceal it. But to
be present at the religious ceremonies of non-Catholics

would be altogether unlawful if, by being present, we gave others to understand that we were actually taking part in their worship. Mere curiosity, without danger to our Faith or scandal to others, might be innocent enough.

Sins against Faith. To neglect to make acts of Faith in the circumstances we have named above would render us guilty of sin, more or less grave, yet it would not cut us off from membership with the Church. But there are certain grave sins against Faith which are committed by persons who either neglect the gift of Faith, or who renounce the Faith they have once held. These sins, which are essentially opposed to Faith and imply, for the most part, actual separation from the Church, may be classed under the four headings of *Infidelity, Heresy, Apostasy,* and *Scepticism* or *Doubt.*

Infidelity or Disbelief. Those who do not believe in the doctrines of Christ are said to be in a state of *Infidelity;* but when the infidelity arises from involuntary or invincible ignorance of the doctrines of the Church, it may be termed *negative infidelity.* In such a case it is not a sin : "If I had not come, and spoken to them, they would not have sin ; but now they have no excuse for their sin" (John xv. 22). And St. Paul : "Whosoever have sinned without the law shall perish without the law ; and whosoever have sinned under the law shall be judged by the law" (Rom. ii. 12).

But when a man has well-founded reasons for believing that the Christian religion is the true one, and yet neglects to inquire further into it, he is guilty of what is termed *privative* infidelity, or infidelity in a partial degree, because his action is so far voluntary ; and of *positive* infidelity, or infidelity in the fullest sense, if, after being perfectly convinced, he still refuses to embrace the truth ; for now he is "without excuse for his sin," and his position is one of

great danger: " He that believeth not shall be condemned "
(Mark xvi. 16).

Under Infidelity we rank *Paganism, Judaism,* and
Mahometanism, while Paganism itself embraces

The different kinds of Infidelity. the state of all those who are either in reality
or professedly without faith ; such as *Atheists,*
who do not believe in the existence of God ; *Deists,* who
believe in the existence of God, but deny His providence
and reject all revealed religion ; and *Idolaters,* or those
who adore false gods.

As Infidelity supposes the previous absence of the true
Faith, *Heresy* supposes its pre-existence, but the

Heresy. subsequent rejection of one or more revealed
truths. Heresy, then, may be defined as the obstinate
adherence of a baptised Christian to some error directly
opposed to an article of Faith, to a truth which the
Church proposes for our belief, as being revealed by God.
But if a Christian were unconsciously to hold to an error,
he would be in *material* heresy only ; if he were conscious
of his error, and still persisted in it, his heresy would
then be *formal* and real.

Heresy must not be confounded with *Schism.* The one
is opposed to the infallible *teaching* of the

Schism. Church, the other to her *ruling power.* Schism,
then, which means a cleaving, a rending asunder, is a
separation from the Church by reason of a revolt against
her in her capacity of *Ruler.* Schism, moreover, generally
ends in Heresy.

Apostasy, which always supposes previous faith, is the
entire abandonment of the Christian Faith by

Apostasy. one who has been baptised. It differs from
Heresy in this, that the apostate rejects all the articles of
Faith, whereas the heretic denies only some, yet continues
to profess Christianity. Formal Heresy and Apostasy
are most grievous sins.

2

Even doubts concerning any article of Faith should at once be banished from our minds, since, if they are wilful and deliberately consented to, they become grave sins. Wilfully to doubt what has been revealed by God is virtually to call in question the Divine veracity, and is, in fact, formal Heresy. If our doubts arise from ignorance, we should, without delay, seek the necessary instruction; if they come through our own fault, from listening to false teachers, or reading books dangerous to our Faith, we should at all costs shun the occasions of them.

Scepticism or Doubt.

We are also strictly bound in conscience to secure both for ourselves and for those under our charge sufficient knowledge of the Faith, as culpable ignorance of the doctrines of the Church is always sinful. The true Faith is a most precious jewel, " a pearl of great price, which when the merchant had found, he went his way, and sold all that he had, and bought it " (Matt. xiii. 46).

CHAPTER V

MYSTERIES OF FAITH AND PRINCIPAL CREEDS

THE ground of our Faith, as we have seen, is the Divine veracity : we believe revealed truths, and this without the least shadow of doubt, on the testimony and word of God : " Faith is the evidence of things that appear not " (Heb. xi. 1). When God speaks, His word excludes all possibility of error.

Now God, as St. Paul assures us, has made Himself known to us by revealing Himself to us through the Patriarchs and the Prophets of old, and last of all through His only-begotten Son. "No man has seen God at any time; the only-begotten Son, who is in the bosom of the Father, He

Mysteries of Faith.

hath declared Him'" (John i. 18). The Revelation, then, which God has given us concerning His infinite Being and attributes must contain truths which are above our reason, seeing that it is only finite, and therefore altogether incapable of grasping the infinite. Such revealed truths are what we call the Mysteries of Faith.

And our belief in religious mysteries is reasonable enough, since reason itself compels us to **Mysteries in** admit the truth of many things which we **nature.** cannot fully understand, but of whose existence we can have no doubt. In the order of nature we believe in many facts which do not admit of explanation, and which must ever remain deep mysteries even to the most learned; for example, who can explain the life we know to be in the smallest blade of grass? or how it is that the tiny seed cast into the soil can grow up into a plant and produce fruit a hundred-fold? How much more, then, should we expect to find mysteries in Religion! And if our weak intellects fail to grasp even created things, or can arrive only at an imperfect knowledge of them, how can they possibly understand mysteries of Religion, which are infinitely above all created things? Yet no one considers himself unreasonable in believing many things that he does not understand; on the contrary, he would be regarded as one bereft of reason were he to refuse to believe many of the things around him simply because he could not understand them. It is the same in regard to the mysteries of Faith. • Our intellects are too weak to comprehend God, who is infinite.

We are told in the Catechism that a Mystery of Faith **A Mystery not** " is a truth which is *above* reason, but revealed **contrary to** by God." Now *above* reason does not mean **Reason.** *contrary* to reason; it merely implies that our reason, being finite or limited, is unable to grasp a mystery which is beyond its reach. But God who is the author of reason is also the author of Revelation: He has spoken, and His word is infallible. And as I believe in natural mysteries, although I fail to understand them, so I believe in revealed mysteries, even if I cannot understand them, because they come to me on the authority of God.

What, then, are the chief mysteries of Faith revealed to us by God? Again we find a ready answer in the Catechism: "The chief mysteries of Faith which God has revealed are contained in the Apostles' Creed."

The Apostles' Creed.

The Apostles' Creed (Latin, *credo*, I believe) contains the leading articles of our Faith, and is the most ancient abridgment of the doctrines of the Catholic Church. Tertullian speaks of "A Rule of Faith descending from the tradition of the Apostles," who are said to have composed it before separating "to go into the whole world to preach the Gospel to every creature." Yet the Creed did not assume its present form till many centuries later. By means of this short abridgment, the Apostles' Creed, all Christians were easily able to learn, from the very first, the most important truths of Religion, and to make a clear profession of one and the same Faith: "Hold the form of sound words, which thou hast heard of me in faith, and in the love which is in Jesus Christ" (2 Tim. i. 13).

In the course of the history of the Church heretical doctrines sprang up at different times. Whenever this happens it becomes necessary for the Church to warn the faithful against the prevailing error, to expound and declare the truth in clear and unmistakable language, and to condemn the heresy. And just as the Apostles had once assembled in Jerusalem under the presidency of St. Peter when differences had arisen in regard to Religion, so afterwards their successors, the Bishops of the Church, assembled under the presidency of the Pope, or his delegate, to settle disputes regarding

General Councils.

the truths of Faith. Such an assembly of Bishops, presided over by the Pope, is called a General Council; and the decisions it arrives at in matters of Faith or Morals, when confirmed by the Pope, are infallible, formulated as they are under the guidance of the Spirit of Truth, which Christ promised should remain with His Church for ever.

One of the most famous Councils was that held at Nice in Bithynia, A.D. 325, after Arius had begun to propagate his heresy in which he denied the Divinity of our Lord, by maintaining that Jesus Christ was neither co-equal nor co-eternal with the Father. The Council condemned the heresy, and drew up the Creed called the Nicene Creed.

The Nicene Creed.

In the year 381 a General Council was held at Constantinople to proclaim the Divinity of the Holy Ghost against the false teaching of the Macedonian heresy. The Council confirmed and extended the Nicene Creed, which, thus enlarged, is sometimes spoken of as the Creed of Constantinople, and is that which is used in the Mass.

The Creed of Constantinople.

Another Creed, known as the Athanasian, was for a long time thought to have been drawn up by St. Athanasius, patriarch of Alexandria (d. A.D. 373); but it probably belongs to a later period. It is now commonly admitted to have first appeared in Spain during the first half of the fifth century. The title " Athanasian " may have been given to it from the fact that it sums up the teachings of St. Athanasius against the Arian heresy, since it explains and develops the doctrines of the Blessed Trinity and of the Incarnation, or the twofold nature in the one Divine Person of God the Son, doctrines which were so vigorously defended by this great saint against the Arians.

The Athanasian Creed.

The last of these great summaries of the Catholic Faith, adopted throughout the universal Church, was that of Pope Pius IV.

The Creed of Pope Pius IV.

This Creed was directed against the errors of the Reformation, and was drawn up A.D. 1564 immediately after the Council of Trent.

CHAPTER VI

THE APOSTLES' CREED

THE Apostles' Creed contains the principal mysteries of our Faith, and is an abridgment of what we are to believe in reference to God, to man, and to the world.

In regard to God we are required to believe that there is only one God; that in this one God there are three Divine Persons, distinct from each other, yet each equally God; that these three Persons form but one God, having exactly the same nature; that the Father begot the Son, the eternal *Word*, equal to Himself from all eternity, the same God with the Father and the Holy Ghost; that the Son was made man to redeem us from sin and hell; that in Jesus Christ, God the Son made man, there are two complete natures, the Divine and the human nature, and consequently two wills, the Divine and the human will; that, although there are *two natures* in Jesus Christ, there is only *one Person*, the Person of God the Son; and that the Holy Ghost is equal to the Father and to the Son, yet proceeds from both.

What the Creed teaches us of God.

In regard to man the Creed teaches us that he has been created by God; that he has an immortal soul; that he has sinned and been redeemed; that he will rise again at the last day to be judged; that he will be rewarded or punished eternally according to his works; and that God has given him the means of arriving at the truth, of doing good, and of making atonement for his sins, through the merits of Jesus Christ.

Of man.

In regard to the world, we must believe that it has been created by God out of nothing; that He preserves and governs it by a universal provi-dence; and that one day it will have an end.

Of the world.

The Creed itself contains twelve parts or articles, and, since it has the Blessed Trinity as its founda-tion, these articles may for convenience be divided into three groups, the first of which refers to God the Father and the work of Creation, which is especially attributed to Him; the second to the Son and the work of Redemption; and the third to the Holy Ghost, the Sanctifier, and His work in the Church.

Divisions of the Creed.

From what has already been said of Faith, we have learnt that, by the words "I believe," is not merely meant "I think," "I am of opinion," but "I hold for certain," without a shadow of doubt, as this my certainty rests on the testimony of God Himself, who has revealed to His Church the truths which I believe. My faith, then, rests on an infallible authority; it is founded on the Divine veracity.

I believe.

CHAPTER VII

THE FIRST ARTICLE OF THE CREED

" I believe in God the Father Almighty, Creator of Heaven and Earth."

THE UNITY AND TRINITY OF GOD.

IN this, the first Article of the Creed, we are taught to believe in one self-existent, all-perfect Being, the supreme Spirit who had no beginning, and who will never have an end; a Being possessing every perfection in an infinite degree.

God's Attri-butes.

He is *omnipotent*, in that He possesses infinite power; He is *omniscient*, having a knowledge of all things, even of

our most secret thoughts ; He is *omnipresent*, His presence
reaching to every part of creation : " Whither shall I go
from Thy Spirit ? or whither shall I flee from Thy face ?
If I ascend into heaven, Thou art there ; if I descend into
hell, Thou art present. If I take my wings early in the
morning, and dwell in the uttermost parts of the sea ; even
there also shall Thy hand lead me, and Thy right hand
shall hold me " (Ps. cxxxviii. 7-10).

God, moreover, is infinitely wise, holy, and just ; He is
infinitely good, merciful, and true ; infinitely amiable, faithful, and unchangeable. Independent Himself, all things
depend upon Him for their very existence ; His providence
watches over all the works of His hand ; He takes an exact
account of our thoughts, words, and works ; and, according
as these are good or bad, He will mete out a just reward
or punishment.

This infinite, all-perfect Being is one and single in
nature : " Hear, O Israel, the Lord our God is one Lord "
(Deut. vi. 4) ; yet in the one Divine nature there are three
Persons, the Father, the Son, and the Holy
Ghost, each possessing certain personal quali-
ties which cannot be attributed to the others.

The Blessed Trinity.

Thus, the Father, the First Person of the adorable Trinity,
proceeds from no one : this cannot be said of the Son or of
the Holy Ghost. The Son, the Second Person, derives His
origin from the Father by an eternal generation : " Born
of the Father from all eternity " : this cannot be said of
the Father or of the Holy Ghost. The Third Person,
the Holy Ghost, proceeds—also from all eternity—from
the Father and the Son as from a single principle : this
cannot be said of the First or of the Second Person.

Yet the Three Persons of the Blessed Trinity, though
numerically distinct from one another, are consubstantial ; that is, they have one and the same
indivisible Divine nature and substance. The

The Unity of God.

Father is truly God, the Son is truly God, the Holy Ghost is truly God—and yet these Three Persons are not three Gods, but one God, in every way equal.   As to Persons, then, they are distinct; as to Substance, they are one—" There are three that give testimony in heaven, the Father, the Word, and the Holy Ghost: and these three are one" (1 John v. 7)—consubstantial, co-eternal, and co-equal.

And though, in the language of Scripture, power and the work of Creation are attributed in a special manner to the . Father, wisdom and the work of Redemption to the Son, holiness and the work of our Sanctification to the Holy Ghost, yet power and wisdom and holiness, and all the attributes of the Divine essence, except what constitutes the distinction of Persons, are common, and belong equally to the whole Trinity.

Our finite minds can never grasp this most sublime and profound of all mysteries; God alone, who is infinite, can comprehend Himself: it is enough for us to know that the Blessed Trinity has been revealed.   It is the principal and fundamental doctrine of Christianity, and to deny it would be to reject the Catholic Faith.

CHAPTER VIII

PROOFS FOR THE EXISTENCE OF GOD

God, as we have seen, is a spirit, infinite, eternal, all-powerful, who sees all things, who knows all things, and who is everywhere present.   It is God, too, as we shall see, who created everything, that is, who made everything out of nothing; heaven and earth, as well as Angels and men—in a word, everything that is outside Himself.   It is He who directs all things, governs all things, and, in His wisdom, disposes all things.

Now there are many ways in which God has manifested
Himself, both in a natural and a supernatural
manner; and here we propose to give a few of
the many proofs of this manifestation of His
existence.

God's mani-
festation in
divers ways.

1. *From the visible world.* There is no effect without a
cause. If we see a beautiful picture, we naturally think of
the painter who produced such a work; a house naturally
suggests an architect; an engine supposes an engineer; so
also the visible world supposes a cause for its existence,
and for that regular and perfect order which we observe in
nature; for it cannot be reasonably supposed that the
world made itself, or that the regularity which we observe
in the heavenly bodies, or the wonderful laws of nature,
are things of chance. What we see, then, in the world
around us is a sensible proof of the existence of God. "All
men are vain, in whom there is not the knowledge of God:
and who, by these good things that are seen, could not
understand Him that is; or who, attending to the works,
have not acknowledged who was the Workman" (Wisd.
xiii. 1). And St. Paul, too, in his Epistle to the Romans,
says: "For the invisible things of Him, from the creation of
the world, are clearly seen, being understood by the things
that are made: His eternal power also and divinity: so
that they [who refuse to believe] are inexcusable" (i. 20).
And again: "He left not Himself without testimony,
doing good from heaven, giving rains and fruitful seasons"
(Acts xiv. 16).

(2) *The testimony of the nations.* All peoples, from the
beginning of the world, have believed in the existence of
God, have acknowledged their dependence upon Him, and
worshipped Him: "The fool hath said in his heart: There
is no God" (Ps. xiii. 1).

(3) *The natural law, the voice of conscience.* Our conscience tells us that some actions are morally good, and that

others are unlawful, which goes to show that deep down in man's nature is a law written by the hand of a superior, by God, a law that all are bound to obey. It is this voice of conscience which warns us to fear an Avenger of evil and to trust in a Rewarder of virtue; but this comes not from ourselves, but from God, the Supreme Legislator, who requires us to avoid evil and to do good : "They show the work of the law written in their hearts, their conscience bearing witness to them, and their thoughts within themselves accusing them, or else defending them " (Rom. ii. 15).

(4) *By Revelation.* But it is Revelation that gives us the most complete and certain knowledge of God, a knowledge based ou the veracity of God Himself. And this Divine Revelation includes whatever God at any time has revealed or made known for man's salvation, whether by the Patriarchs, or the Prophets, or by Angels, and at last by His only Son, our Lord Jesus Christ : " God, who, at sundry times and in divers manners, spoke in times past to the fathers by the prophets, last of all, in these days hath spoken to us by His Son " (Heb. i. 1, 2). And again : " No man hath seen God at any time : the only-begotten Son who is in the bosom of the Father, He hath declared Him" (John i. 18). No creature can comprehend the infinite greatness of God, none but His only-begotten Divine Son who is in the bosom of the Father by a union and unity of substance and nature, and He it is that has declared Him.

CHAPTER IX

FIRST ARTICLE OF THE CREED (*continued*)

CREATOR OF HEAVEN AND EARTH.

"GOD," we are told in the Catechism, " is called Creator of heaven and earth, because He made heaven and earth, and all things out of nothing, by His word." Catholic

doctrine tells us that God, the Supreme Spirit, who'
alone exists of Himself, and to whom nothing
God's design in is impossible or difficult, is the Creator and
the Creation.
Sovereign Lord of all things, visible and invisible. Not because He needed it did God create the world,
but because, being infinitely good, He would impart of His
goodness to other beings ; and, though He created the
world for His own greater honour and glory, and stood
in no need of creatures, yet, for the good and happiness
of all rational creatures, He chose to manifest His power
and magnificence in the creation of the world.

Now as by *Creator* we mean one who gives being to what
before was not ; one who causes to exist what
God the   before did not exist ; one who makes a thing
Creator.
out of nothing ; and by *creature* that which is
produced out of nothing ; it follows that an all-powerful,
necessary, self-existing Being, God alone, can create, and
that all things, except God, are creatures : " In the beginning God created heaven and earth " (Gen. i. 1). And
in the first chapter of St. John's Gospel : " All things
were made by Him ; and without Him was made nothing
that was made." Yet again, in the Psalms . " He spoke,
and they were made ; He commanded, and they were
created " (Ps. cxlviii. 5).

It is in the first Book of Genesis that we find recorded
the history of the Creation. Faith, then,
The world   teaches us that the world did not always exist,
created in time.
but was created in time, or in the beginning of
time : " In the beginning God created heaven and earth."
God had only to will it, and all that exists out of Himself
--the beautiful earth which we inhabit, all the visible
universe, the stars of heaven, all living things, plants,
animals, and men, and those invisible pure spirits, the
Angels—all sprang into being : " He spoke, and they were
made." But Man, the last of God's creatures in time,

was, after the Angels, the most perfect of God's works, since he, like them, was endowed with intelligence and free-will.

When the work of Creation was ended, God did not leave it to chance, but, by the same power of His will with which He had created it, He continued to preserve and govern it. By His Divine Providence, He has a care of all things, and in His wisdom and goodness directs all things to the end for which He created them: "God made the little and the great, and He hath equally care of all" (Wisd. vi. 8). "Are not two sparrows sold for a farthing? and not one of them shall fall on the ground without your Father" (Matt. x. 29).

God's Providence.

If, then, God orders and directs all things, how comes it that there is so much sin and misery in the world? Now as regards sin, God wills it not; He forbids it, yet permits it. He gives us grace and abundant help to avoid it; He uses threats to deter us from it, but He will not constrain us, since, having created man with a free will, He leaves him to follow it. Yet He knows how to avail Himself of this evil of sin in order to carry out His eternal decrees: "You thought evil against me; but God turned it into good" (Gen. l. 20).

God forbids, but permits sin.

But as for sufferings, persecutions, afflictions, and misfortunes, these God not only permits, but Himself ordains for our good: "Good things and evil, life and death, poverty and riches, are from God" (Ecclus. xi. 14). "If we have received good things at the hand of God, why should we not receive evil?" (Job ii. 10). Even if our afflictions arise from the perversity of men, it is equally the will of God as far as our sufferings and our personal merit are concerned. He would have the *sinner* acknow-

Sufferings permitted and ordained.

ledge the chastisement and mend his ways, that he may not perish everlastingly; the *just man* He would wean from the world, and purify more and more, that he may abound in merit and receive in heaven the priceless reward of his patient suffering : " Not by your counsel was I sent hither, but by the will of God " (Gen. xlv. 8). " Blessed are ye when they shall revile you and persecute you. . . . Be glad and rejoice, for your reward is very great in heaven ' (Matt. v. 11, 12).

CHAPTER X

FIRST ARTICLE OF THE CREED (*continued*)

CREATOR OF HEAVEN AND EARTH : THE ANGELS.

THE highest and most perfect of all God's creatures, by reason of the excellence of their nature, are the Angels, those pure spirits endowed with power, free-will, and intelligence, who ᠆ surround the throne of, God, " His ministers who do His will " (Ps. cii. 21). The angelic nature is far superior to that of man, having in it nothing material or corporeal. They are unlike the spirit or soul of man, which was formed by God to animate a body, and has a natural tendency to it. But though they have no body themselves, they possess the power of appearing to us under bodily forms.

The Angels.

We know for certain that the Angels were made before the sin of our first parents, since it was one of the fallen Angels who assumed the form of a serpent to tempt Eve; and there are passages in Scripture which go to show that it was before the creation of man, and even before the formation of the world out of chaos. God Himself gives us to understand this in His words to holy Job : " Where wast thou when I laid the foundations of the

Creation of the Angels.

earth? upon where are its bases grounded? or who laid the corner-stone thereof, when the morning stars praised Me together, and *all the sons of God* made a joyful melody?" (Job. xxxviii. 4, 7). Their creation, then, may reasonably be supposed to be expressed in the first verse of Genesis: "In the beginning God created heaven and earth." Some of the Fathers see in the separation of the light from the darkness the rewarding of the good and the punishment of the fallen Angels.

God created the Angels in the state of innocence, happy, and endowed with excellent gifts; but their happy state did not render them incapable of committing sin. He had created them free, and willed that they should undergo a trial in order that everlasting happiness with Him might be the reward of their fidelity. Nor did all remain steadfast under the trial. Many, by pride, rebelled against God, and, being in an instant changed into devils, were cast from Him for ever down into the fires of hell: "God spared not the angels that sinned" (2 Pet. ii. 4). It is even believed that Lucifer, the leader in this revolt, drew after him a third part of the heavenly host.

Trial of the Angels.

Though the exact number of the Angels is nowhere stated in Scripture, it must be very great; and probably vastly surpasses the number of men that will have appeared on the earth from the time of man's creation to the end of the world. It is not difficult to understand this if we consider that Almighty God assigns to each particular soul created by Him a separate Angel as its guardian. And if God created man to fill in heaven the place of the lost Angels, who are supposed to have formed a third part of the heavenly host, we may well wonder at the magnitude of their number. According to the Prophet Daniel: "Thousands of thousands ministered to Him, and ten thousand

The number of the Angels.

times a hundred thousand stood before Him " (Dan. vii. 10).
And St. John, in the Apocalypse, tells us how he saw around
the throne of the Lamb a multitude of Angels: "And
the number of them was thousands of thousands " (v. 11).

The nine choirs. According to the common opinion of the
Fathers, the Angels are divided into *three hierarchies,* and each hierarchy into *three choirs :*

(1) Seraphim, Cherubim, and Thrones.
(2) Dominations, Principalities, and Powers.
(3) Virtues, Archangels, and Angels.

The Angels are thus named from a Greek word meaning
sent, or *messenger,* a name which describes rather
The name Angel. their office than their nature, and which is
common to all the blessed spirits, irrespective
of hierarchies or choirs.   Only three of the heavenly host
are known to us under special names : *Gabriel,* "the strength
of God," announced the Incarnation ; *Michael,* " who is
like unto God," led the faithful hosts against Lucifer and
his rebel Angels; *Raphael,* "the remedy of God," con-
ducted the younger Tobias to Rages and back.

The fallen Angels, though condemned to everlasting
torments, are not always confined to the limits
The bad Angels. of hell, but great numbers, still bearing their
torments with them, are permitted by God to
come upon the earth for the trial of men.   So great is
their malice against us, who have been invited to fill their
places in heaven, that St. Peter bids us " Be sober, and
watch ; because your adversary, the devil, as a roaring
lion, goeth about, seeking whom he may devour; whom
resist ye, strong in faith " (1 Pet. v. 8, 9).   In their envy
and hatred they lay snares for us that, by leading us into
sin, they may drag us along with them in the broad road
to destruction.

Not only do the demons tempt man to sin, but, by

means of *possession*, they are allowed sometimes to affect the body: yet their power is limited, and they can never harm us beyond what God permits, as we see in the example of holy Job. Even their temptations are permitted only for the trial of our virtue, and, if we ask it, God will always give us the grace necessary to triumph over all their attacks: "God is faithful, who will not suffer you to be tempted above that which you are able; but will make also with temptation issue, that you may be able to bear it "(1 Cor. x. 13). If, then, we are overcome, the fault is always our own. Their designs, too, are often defeated by the care of our Angel guardians for us: "He hath given His Angels charge over thee, to keep thee in all thy ways. In their hands they shall bear thee up, lest thou dash thy foot against a stone " (Ps. xc. 11, 12).

The chief occupation of the good Angels is to adore and praise God without intermission for all eternity: "They rested not day and night, saying: Holy, holy, holy, Lord God Almighty, who was, and who is, and who is to come" (Apoc. iv. 8). "And I heard the voice of many Angels, saying: The Lamb that was slain is worthy to receive power, and divinity, and wisdom, and strength, and honour, and glory, and benediction" (Apoc. v. 11. 12).

The good Angels.

Another office of the good Angels is to take part, as God's ministers, in the government of the visible and the invisible world, and especially to execute the Divine commands in regard to what concerns man's salvation. It is by the ministry of Angels that all the greatest events mentioned in the Old and in the New Testament have been brought about: " Are they not all ministering spirits, sent to minister for them who shall receive the inheritance of salvation ?" (Heb. i. 14).

It is the teaching of the Church that every one has a guardian Angel appointed by God as his special protector

3

throughout life; so that the good Angels, besides their office of praising God in heaven and acting as His ministers and messengers, watch over and assist us in our sojourn upon earth: "See that you despise not one of these little ones: for I say to you, that their angels in heaven always see the face of My Father who is in heaven" (Matt. xviii. 10). It is moreover generally believed, and is implied by the Sacred Scriptures, that Churches, provinces, nations, and empires have also their appointed Angel guardians. St. Michael was the special protector of Israel, and is now venerated as the guardian Angel of the Church of God. And in the Acts most interpreters see the guardian Angel of Macedonia in the Macedonian who implored St. Paul, on behalf of the province which he guarded, to pass over and preach to that province (xvi. 9).

Angel Guardians.

Our guardian Angels defend us not only against spiritual evils, but against bodily evils also : " Behold, I will send My angel, who shall go before thee, and keep thee in thy journey, and bring thee into the place that I have prepared" (Exod. xxiii. 20). How we should love them, then, and with what confidence we should recommend ourselves to them in all dangers and temptations! "The angel of the Lord shall encamp round about them that fear Him, and shall defend them" (Ps. xxxiii. 8).

CHAPTER XI

FIRST ARTICLE OF THE CREED (*continued*)

CREATOR OF HEAVEN AND EARTH: MAN.

WE have seen that, next to the Angels, the most perfect of all God's works was man, a being composed of a body and a soul, and endowed with reason and free-will: " And God created man to

Man.

His own image; to the image of God He created him "
(Gen. i. 27). " And the Lord formed man of the slime
of the earth, and breathed into his face the breath of life ;
and man became a living soul " (Gen. ii. 7). Man, moreover, received the additional blessing of lordship over all
the other creatures upon earth, and was capable of knowing,
loving, and serving his Creator.

God sent a deep sleep upon Adam, the first man, and,
Adam and Eve. while he was asleep, took one of his ribs and
built it into a woman, whom He gave to
Adam to be his companion and helpmate. On seeing
her, Adam exclaimed : " This now is bone of my bones
and flesh of my flesh ;" and God blessed them and thus
instituted the ordinance of matrimony, which our Lord
later raised to the dignity of a Sacrament. " And Adam
called the name of his wife Eve, because she was the mother
of all the living " (Gen. iii. 20). Adam and Eve, the first
parents of the whole human race, were, like the Angels,
created in a state of innocence, grace, and happiness, and
enriched with most excellent gifts, destined as they were
to know, love, and serve God on earth, and, in company
with the Angels, to glorify Him and to be happy with
Him for ever in heaven.

The greatest and most excellent gift of God to man was
that of creating him in the state of original
Original justice, or sanctifying grace. Together with
justice. sanctifying grace Adam also received the *sonship*
of God, or the right to an inheritance in the kingdom
of heaven. But these gifts were gratuitous gifts of God,
and supernatural, being in no way, like our natural gifts,
essential attributes of man's nature. God further exempted
man from all infirmities of body and soul, and even death
itself, to which ills he became subject only by rebelling
against his Creator.

Thus gifted with special graces and privileges, our first

parents were placed in a Paradise of pleasure, a garden abounding with delights, which God prepared for their abode. Here they were to remain in happiness and innocence until, without suffering death, they were to be transported to the heavenly Paradise where they were to reign with God for all eternity.

Destiny of man.

Yet Adam and Eve soon lost their innocence by transgressing a simple command which God imposed upon them for the trial of their obedience: "Of every tree of Paradise thou shalt eat: but of the tree of knowledge of good and evil thou shalt not eat; for in what day soever thou shalt eat of it, thou shalt die the death" (Gen. ii. 16, 17). Had Adam continued faithful to God, he would have transmitted to the whole human race not only his natural, but also his supernatural gifts; his children would have been born in the state of innocence, and, like himself, would have been happy and immortal, enjoying freedom from sickness and pain, and destined in due time to be translated to a happier Paradise.

The trial.

Through want of faith in God's word, Adam, at the solicitation of Eve, who had been deceived by the devil in the guise of a serpent, disobeyed God's command, and instead of enjoying greater happiness and of being like God, which the devil had promised, both he and Eve at once experienced a hitherto unknown sense of shame and degradation, and a desire to shun God's presence. In this way they accomplished not only their own ruin, but that of their descendants as well: "By one man sin entered into this world, and by sin death; and death passed upon all men, in whom all have sinned" (Rom. v. 12).

The Fall.

Their punishment was swift and sure, yet tempered with mercy. They were at once driven from Paradise, and deprived of those gratuitous gifts and graces with which we have seen them endowed.

Man's punishment.

With the loss of original justice they lost their innocence and happiness; their minds were darkened, and they became prone to evil. Toil and sickness and pain were to be their lot during life, and then they were to suffer death: "Cursed is the earth in thy work," God said to Adam. "In the sweat of thy brow shalt thou eat thy bread, till thou return to the earth out of which thou wast taken; for dust thou art, and unto dust thou shalt return" (Gen. iii. 16-19). This, moreover, was to be the lot of all their descendants; for those supernatural endowments which God had bestowed upon them were now taken away, and could not be transmitted to their offspring. Thus was the whole human race plunged into the greatest misery: "God created man incorruptible . . . but by the envy of the devil death came into the world" (Wisd. ii. 23, 24).

Sin, with its fatal consequences, was to pass from Adam to all mankind, and all who are born into the world come with its fatal stain upon their souls: "By one man sin entered into this world . . . in whom all have sinned." This sin is called *Original Sin*, and differs from Actual Sin in this, that it does not arise from any act of ours, but is inherited by us from Adam, who was the *origin* and head of all mankind: "We were all by nature children of wrath" (Eph. ii. 3).

Original Sin.

But God's mercy in the punishment of the sin of our first parents was as perfect as His justice, which demanded a satisfaction adequate to the sin. No creature, however, least of all fallen man, was capable of making such atonement. Yet instead of destroying him utterly and at once, as He had a perfect right to do, God left him time for repentance, and even promised him a Redeemer through whose merits he might recover his lost innocence and his title to the kingdom of heaven. And as after the Fall no man could be saved except through the merits of our Saviour, so, even

The promise of a Redeemer.

before His coming upon earth, all who were saved were saved through faith in the Redeemer to come, and by uniting their actions with His merits and atonement.

CHAPTER XII

THE SECOND ARTICLE OF THE CREED

" And in Jesus Christ, His only Son, our Lord."

GOD, then, did not leave our first parents without a gleam of hope, which greatly lightened the burden of their punishment, and comforted them in all their miseries. To the serpent He had said : " I will put enmities between thee and the woman, and thy seed and her seed : she shall crush thy head, and thou shalt lie in wait for her heel " (Gen. iii. 15). In these words we have the *first promise* of a Redeemer to come ; for it was by her seed, Jesus Christ, God the Son made man for us, that the woman was to crush the serpent's head. This promise and its frequent renewal kept up in the hearts of the people before the coming of the Messias a longing desire for its fulfilment, and formed a great part of their religion : " Amen, I say to you, many prophets and just men have desired to see the things that you see, and have not seen them ; and to hear the things that you hear, and have not heard them " (Matt. xiii. 17).

First Promise of a Redeemer.

As man's offence was against a Being of infinite goodness and holiness, the debt which he incurred was one of infinite satisfaction to the offended majesty of God. But no merit of any mere creature could be sufficient to make such a satisfaction, since no creature, however exalted or holy, could offer more than a finite reparation. The Redemption, the reconciliation

A Divine Redeeemer necessary.

of fallen humanity with God offended by sin, needed a being capable of fully atoning for man's sin, and of restoring to man those supernatural gifts and graces that had once been his. For this atonement there was need of a Mediator who should at the same time be both God and man—man, that He might be able to suffer and die for us; God, that an infinite merit might attach to any act of atonement He might will to make. Such a Redeemer, such a Mediator, was given to man by God, and He was none other than the INCARNATE WORD, Jesus Christ, the Second Person of the Blessed Trinity.

Nor could mankind have been saved except by such a Mediator, because such a one alone, being God
Christ our Mediator. and man, was able to atone for the guilt of sin, and to re-establish that supernatural union between God and man which sin had destroyed. And although each and every action or suffering of our Saviour was of infinite value and sufficient to atone for man's guilt, yet His Heavenly Father willed that our Redemption should be effected by the shedding of His most precious Blood, and by His death upon the Cross: "He humbled Himself, becoming obedient, unto death, even to the death of the cross" (Phil. ii. 8). "He was wounded for our iniquities, and He was bruised for our sins: the chastisement of our peace was upon Him, and by His bruises we are healed" (Isa. liii. 5).

To accomplish the work of our salvation, a sublime mystery was needed—the mystery of the In-
Mystery of the Incarnation. carnation, the mystery of the Son of God made man for us. Faith teaches us that the Second Person of the Blessed Trinity, having the same nature with God the Father, became also truly Man by taking a body and soul like ours: "The Word was made flesh." God the Son became the Man Jesus Christ. We therefore believe that Jesus Christ is not only truly God,

born of the Father from all eternity, but is also truly Man, having been Man only from the time of His In-carnation—*i.e.,* from the time of His taking flesh ; that He assumed our human nature and united it to His Divine nature, yet so as to form but one Person : " Being in the form of God, He thought it not robbery to be equal with God : but emptied Himself, taking the form of a servant, being made in the likeness of men, and in habit found as a man " (Phil. ii. 6, 7).

There are then *two natures* in Jesus Christ, the nature
of God and the nature of man, and these two
The Hypostatic natures are inseparably united in the *one Person*
Union.
of God the Son : " In the beginning was the Word and the Word was God. . . . And the Word was made flesh " (John i. 1 and 14). As the soul and body are so united in man as to form but one person, so the Divine and human natures, by means of what is termed the *hypostatic* or personal *union*, constitute the one person of Jesus Christ, who is at the same time true God and true Man. Nor will the hypostatic union ever be dissolved. It was not broken even by death itself. As with us death means the separation of the soul from the body, so the death of Christ resulted from the separation of His soul from His body on the Cross. But when His sacred body lay in the tomb, the person of the Word still remained united to it, just as it remained united to His blessed soul in Limbo. When our Lord uses the words : " I and the Father are one " (John x. 30), He is speaking of His Divine nature ; just as when speaking of Himself as man, He says : " The Father is greater than I " (John. xiv. 28).

And as there are two complete natures in Jesus Christ, the
Divine nature and the human nature, so also
Two wills in there are two wills distinct from each other,
Jesus Christ.
a Divine will and a human will ; yet the human will is ever in perfect harmony with the Divine will. When, in His agony in the garden, His human nature

dreaded all those sufferings which were then presented to His soul for His acceptance, and which in a few hours He was to undergo, it was His human will which prompted Him to pray to be delivered from them: "My Father, if it be possible, let this chalice pass from Me." Yet notice how at once He conformed to the good pleasure of the Divine will by presently adding : ' " Nevertheless, not as I will, but as Thou wilt " (Matt. xxvi. 39).

From what has been said we see that Jesus Christ has not always been both God and Man. Before the time of His Incarnation the Son of God existed in the nature of God only ; but since His Incarnation He exists in two natures, the same person being both God and Man. As God, He is everywhere ; as God made Man, though sitting at the right hand of the Father in heaven, He is nevertheless present on earth in the Blessed Sacrament of the Altar. His promise, "Behold I am with you all days, even to the consummation of the world " (Matt. xxviii. 20), He will ever make good by His Sacramental presence in the Holy Eucharist; by dwelling in the hearts of the faithful ; and by His providential care and constant protection of His Holy Church, which He continually assists by the Holy Ghost. In the words of Father Schouppe, " Christ is living. He lives' always and everywhere, not only in heaven where He ascended, but in the entire world and in the minds and hearts of men. Since His death on Mount Calvary, He has more than ever shown Himself to be the living God, and His living power is specially shown and developed in Christianity ; by it He speaks, He teaches, He commands, He forbids, He combats, and He triumphs. All passes away and dies around Him ; He alone lives and abides for ever, the Soul and the Chief of His Church.". We find the same idea beautifully summed up in the words of St. Paul : " Jesus Christ yesterday, and to-day, and the same for ever " (Heb. xiii. 8).

Where is Jesus Christ?

CHAPTER XIII

THE SECOND ARTICLE OF THE CREED (*continued*)

"And in Jesus Christ, His only Son, our Lord."

As it was to redeem us from sin and hell and to teach us how to gain heaven, the end of our creation, that God the Son became man, we shall next consider how admirably the sacred name Jesus Christ, the name of the Saviour sent to accomplish this work, expresses the office which He came on earth to fulfil.

The Holy Name Jesus. The holy name Jesus means Saviour, and was the name brought down from heaven by the Angel Gabriel when he came to announce to the Blessed Virgin the mystery of the Incarnation : "Behold thou shalt conceive in thy womb, and shalt bring forth a Son, and thou shalt call His name Jesus" (Luke i. 31). Again, in the words of the Angel to St. Joseph, we are told : "That which is conceived in her is of the Holy Ghost. She shall bring forth a Son, and thou shalt call His name Jesus; *for He shall save His people* from their sins" (Matt. i. 20, 21). Before the coming of Christ, the expectations of both Jews and Gentiles were directed towards a Saviour, and the characteristic name of Saviour was peculiar to the Messias.

A name of power and confidence. To show our deep respect for this holy name, it is a pious custom to bow the head whenever we either repeat it ourselves, or hear it pronounced by others. St. Paul, in his Epistle to the Philippians, speaking of our Saviour, says : "God hath exalted Him, and hath given Him a name which is above all other names: that in the name of Jesus every knee should bow, of those that are in heaven, on earth, and under the earth : and that every tongue should confess that the Lord Jesus Christ is in the glory of God the Father"

(ii. 9, 10). It is moreover a name of great *power* to be called upon in time of temptation and danger : " For there is no other name under heaven given to men, whereby we must be saved " (Acts iv. 12). And it is a name of *confidence*, since, through it, God has promised to grant all our requests : " Amen, amen, I say to you : If you ask the Father anything in My name, He will give it you. . . . Ask, and you shall receive, that your joy may be full " (John xvi. 23, 24).

The name Christ signifies " Anointed," and is also applied to God the Son made Man for us :
hrist. " The Messias cometh who is called Christ " (John iv. 25) ; and this because of His threefold character of *Priest, Prophet*, and *King*. In the Old Law the High-priest, and Prophets and Kings were anointed with oil, and specially set apart for the dignity and office to which they were called : " Jesus of Nazareth : you know how God anointed Him with power, who went about doing good, and healing all that were oppressed by the devil " (Acts x. 38). Yet it was not with material oil that our Lord was anointed, or received His consecration, but His anointing is the fulness of the Divinity that dwells in Him.

Jesus Christ is a *Priest* in once having offered Himself on Calvary for the atonement of sin, and in
Priest. continuing to offer Himself daily in the Mass, through the ministry of His priests, in order to apply to our souls the merits of His Passion and Death : " Thou art a priest for ever, according to the order of Melchise-dech " (Heb. v. 6).

He is a *Prophet* in the twofold meaning of the word—
Prophet. as a teacher of the truth and guide to eternal life, and that not only as one foretelling things to come, but as knowing all things. He has revealed to us the mysteries of God ; He has taught us what we are to do to be saved : " A Prophet shall the Lord your God

raise up unto you out of your brethren. . . . Him you shall hear, according to all things whatsoever He shall speak to you " (Acts iii. 22).

Not only is He a *King*, but He is the " King of kings and Lord of lords " (Apoc. xix. 16). He is our King because He came down on earth to establish the Church, a spiritual Kingdom, to which we belong, and over which He rules, and of which He will continue to be Head throughout all eternity : . "Thou sayest that I am a King : for this was I born, and for this came I into the world, that I should give testimony to the truth. . . . My kingdom is not of this world " (John xviii. 36, 37).

King.

As the Second Person of the Adorable Trinity, Jesus Christ is the only true and real Son of God, born of the Father from all eternity : " In the beginning was the Word, . . . and the Word was God " (John i. 1). He is co-eternal with the Father and has one and the same substance with Him, proceeding from Him by an eternal generation : "Thou art My Son, to-day [*i.e.*, the day of eternity] have I begotten Thee " (Heb. i. 5). Jesus Christ, then, is the only Son of God by nature, whereas we are His children by adoption through grace ; but not by nature, nor from all eternity.

His only Son.

The term " our Lord," which we commonly use in reference to God the Son made Man, though equally to be referred to all the Divine Persons by reason of the sovereign dominion which God, as our Creator, possesses over all the works of His hands, is especially applicable to the Second Person, since as God He created us, and is therefore Lord of all ; and as God made Man He redeemed us " at a great price," and restored us to liberty after we had become the slaves of the devil by sin. He is our Lord, too, in a special manner by His Incarnation, and as such was given to

Our Lord.

us by His eternal Father: "By this hath the charity of God appeared towards us, because God hath sent His Only-begotten Son into the world, that we may live by Him" (1 John iv. 9).

How great then should be our love, respect, and obedience for so good a Lord, seeing that to Him we owe all that we possess, whether it be in the order of nature or of grace!

CHAPTER XIV

THE THIRD ARTICLE OF THE CREED

" Who was conceived by the Holy Ghost, born of the Virgin Mary."

IN the Third Article we have the fulfilment of God's promise of a Redeemer, in the Incarnation and Birth of our Saviour: "When the fulness of the time was come, God sent His Son, made of a woman" (Gal. iv. 4). And again, in the words of St. John: "The Word was made flesh, and dwelt amongst us" (i. 14). Even the miraculous circumstances attending His birth had long before been foretold by the Prophet Isaias when he promised a *sign*, or a miracle, to King Achaz: "Behold a virgin shall conceive and bear a Son, and His name shall be called Emmanuel [*i.e.*, *God with us*]" (Is. vii. 14). Conceived and made Man, by the power of the Holy Ghost, in the womb of the blessed Virgin Mary, without having had any man for His father, He was born of her without any detriment to her virginity. After the birth of her Son, Mary was at once both virgin and mother; and thus was Jesus both miraculously conceived and miraculously born into this world.

Fulfilment of the Promise.

When the time decreed by God for sending His Only-begotten Son into the world was come, the Archangel Gabriel was sent from heaven to be the bearer of the glad tidings of Christ's Incar.

The Annunciation.

nation, and of man's salvation, as also to obtain the consent of Mary to become the Mother of the Word made flesh. Coming into Mary's presence, Gabriel saluted her with the words, " Hail, full of grace, the Lord is with thee: blessed art thou amongst women." Mary was troubled in spirit at the Angel's greeting, not knowing what manner of salutation this might be; whereupon the Angel continued, " Fear not, Mary, for thou hast found grace with God : behold thou shalt conceive in thy womb, and shalt bring forth a Son, and thou shalt call His name Jesus. And He shall be great, and shall be called the Son of the Most High; and the Lord God shall give unto Him the throne of David, His father, and He shall reign in the house of Jacob for ever; and of His king- dom there shall be no end." To Mary's question, how this should be done, as she had vowed to live always a virgin, the Angel answered: " The Holy Ghost shall come upon thee, and the power of the Most High shall overshadow thee. And therefore also the Holy One which shall be born of thee, shall be called the Son of God." Then, in all humility, the holy Virgin gave her consent: " Behold the handmaid of the Lord, be it done to me according to thy word. And the Angel departed from her " (Luke i. 28-38). At that moment, without ceasing to remain a spotless virgin, Mary conceived in her womb the Saviour of the world. Then it was that the Second Person of the ever Blessed Trinity, still remaining un- changeably the same God, became united to our human nature.

At this time our Lady and St. Joseph were living, and for some time after continued to live, at Nazareth, and it seemed as though this city must witness the birth of the Messias; yet it had been foretold that Bethlehem was to be His birth- place: " And thou, Bethlehem Ephrata, art a little one

Jesus to be born at Bethlehem.

among the thousands of Juda: out of thee shall He come forth unto me that is to be the Ruler in Israel : and His going forth is from the beginning, from the days of eternity " (Mich. v. 2).

At length, by a special providence of God, a decree was issued by Augustus Cæsar, the Roman Emperor, for a census of "the whole world." In obedience to this decree Mary and Joseph, both being of the family of David, were obliged to go to Bethlehem, the city of David, situated some eighty miles from Nazareth. The country to be traversed was hilly, and it was the depth of winter. Yet the delicate Virgin and her holy spouse set out without delay for Bethlehem. Here they sought in vain for admission to the inns, which were already crowded with travellers more wealthy than they, and were at length compelled to content themselves with no better shelter than that afforded by a poor stable, which was occupied, as is generally believed, by an ox and an ass. Here, exposed to the chilly blasts of a winter's night, Mary gave birth to the Saviour of the world, and, wrapping Him up in swaddling-clothes, laid Him in the manger. Thus, on this first Christmas-day, is the Son of God born into the world.

The Nativity.

We are told that while some shepherds " were watching and keeping the night watches over their flocks," an Angel of the Lord suddenly stood beside them, and they feared with a great fear. But the Angel bade them be not afraid. " For behold," he said, " I bring you tidings of great joy . . . for this day is born to you a SAVIOUR, who is CHRIST THE LORD, in the city of David. And this shall be a sign to you. You shall find the Infant wrapped in swaddling-clothes, and laid in a manger." Then there appeared with the Angel a multitude of the heavenly host, praising God and pro-

An Angel appears to the shepherds.

claiming : "Glory to God in the highest: and on earth peace to men of good will" (Luke ii. 10-14). The shepherds hastened to the stable, and seeing, they believed that He who lay there in such great poverty was their King, the Son of God.

We may truly say then that God was born and that God suffered for us, and consequently that the Blessed Virgin is truly the mother of God, or of Him who is truly God, though not that she is the mother of the Godhead. Mary is the mother of God because Jesus Christ, her Son, who was born of her according to the flesh, is not only man, but is also truly God. Remaining God as He was from all eternity, the Divine Word also became Man by reason of His birth in time.

Mary, Mother of God.

When a child is born into the world, its body alone is formed of its mother's substance, its soul comes straight from the hand of God ; yet, because body and soul are so united in the mother's womb as to form but one person, she is indeed the mother of that person. So, too, in the womb of Mary the Eternal Word was united to our humanity, and became her Son. Mary, then, is truly the mother of God, a fact to which the Scripture is constantly bearing testimony : "There was a marriage in Cana of Galilee ; and the mother of Jesus was there" (John ii. 1). And again, in St. John : " Now there stood by the cross of Jesus His mother" (xix. 25). St. Elisabeth, too, the mother of the Baptist, makes a beautiful and concise profession of her faith in the Divinity of Christ and in the Divine maternity of Mary in her salutation to her cousin : "Blessed art thou amongst women, and blessed is the Fruit of thy womb. And whence is this to me, that the mother of my Lord should come to me ?" (Luke i. 42, 43). Indeed, if Mary is not truly the mother of God, then her Son is not God, and therefore, not being a Person of infinite dignity, the merit of His actions would not be infinite, nor, consequently, sufficient to atone for Adam's sin, which was an offence against an infinite God. The doctrine of the Incarnation is then the bed-rock of Christianity, without which its whole fabric must necessarily fall to the ground.

It· is only from such considerations as the foregoing that we can gather the full meaning of the words, "I believe in Jesus Christ, His only Son, our Lord, who was conceived by the Holy Ghost, born of the Virgin Mary"; and of that beautiful invocation of the Church, guided by the same Holy Spirit, " Holy Mary, Mother of God, pray for us sinners, now, and at the hour of our death."

Before bringing this chapter to a close, let us turn our thoughts for a moment to St. Joseph, the virgin-spouse of Mary, and head of the Holy Family on earth: " Jesus . . . being (as it was supposed) the Son of Joseph" (Luke iii. 23).   He was given by heaven to Mary to be the protector of her virginity, to secure her from calumnies in the birth of the Son of God, and to assist her and her Divine Infant in their flight into Egypt ; and, as guardian or foster-father of the Incarnate Word, he had the Son of God obedient to him: "And He went down with them and came to Nazareth, and was subject to them" (Luke ii. 51).

St. Joseph.

CHAPTER XV

HERESIES ON THE INCARNATION

THE doctrine of the Incarnation has been attacked from every point of view, but, for the sake of clearness and conciseness, we class the chief heresies under three headings, according as they err against " *the Divine Nature*," or "*the Human Nature*," or " *the Union of the Two Natures in the One Person of Jesus Christ*."

(*a*) THE CERINTHIANS AND THE EBIONISTS :

At the end of the first century St. John wrote his

Heresies against the Divine Nature. Gospel against Cerinthus and Ebion and their disciples, who denied the Divinity of Christ, teaching that our Saviour was a mere man who had no existence before He was born of Joseph and Mary, as they held, and that the Son of God came to Him in His Baptism.

(*b*) THE ARIANS :

Arius of Alexandria and his sect, in the beginning of the fourth century, maintained that Jesus Christ had not the nature of God. They allowed that He had a being before He was born of Mary; that He was created before all other creatures, and was more perfect than any of them, but that He was no 'more than a mere creature; that thus He had a beginning, and that there was a time when He was not ; that He had not the same substance with the Eternal Father and Creator of all things. This heresy was condemned at the General Council of Nice, A.D. 325.

(*a*) THE DOCETÆ :

This word comes from the Greek δοκέω (I appear), and is

Heresies against the Human Nature. applied to a sect of heretics who, so early as the first century, tried to explain the Incarnation by maintaining that our Lord's human nature and form were only *apparent* ; hence, that His acts and sufferings were only apparent. This theory arose from the Gnostic notion that matter was the source of evil, and that consequently the visible creation was the work of an evil principle. The MANICHÆANS, who flourished in the third century, held a similar doctrine, consequent on their maintaining two supreme principles, the one good, the other evil.

(*b*) THE APOLLINARIANS:

These also erred concerning the humanity of our Lord.

They accepted the teaching of Apollinarius, Bishop of Laodicea, who denied the human nature of Christ; and held that the *Word* took the place of the human soul; that therefore Christ had a body but not a human soul. This teaching was condemned as heretical in the Council of Alexandria, A.D. 360.

(c) THE MONOTHELITES :

In the seventh century we have the Monothelites (from the Greek, meaning *one will*), who acknowledged our Lord to have a real body and soul, but held that He had only one will, a Divine will.   The heresy was condemned in A.D. 680.

(a) THE NESTORIANS :

Nestorius, patriarch of Constantinople in the early part of the fifth century, taught that the Blessed **Heresies against the Union of the Natures.** Virgin was the mother of the man Christ, but that she could in no sense be called the "Mother of God."   He was therefore accused of maintaining the two-fold Personality of Christ instead of His two-fold nature in one and the same Person, and was condemned at the Council of Ephesus, A.D. 431.

(b) THE EUTYCHIANS :

In the fifth century also, Eutyches of Constantinople, the originator of the Eutychian heresy, while defending the unity of our Lord's Person against the Nestorians, fell into the opposite error by denying the two natures; hence, the Eutychians are spoken of as *Monophysites*, from Greek words meaning one nature.   They asserted that Christ had only a Divine nature; that at the moment of the Incarnation the human nature was changed into the Divine.   This heresy was condemned at Chalcedon, A.D. 451.

Any one of these heresies would render fruitless the work of Redemption, which rests on the great **The evil of these heresies.** fact taught us by faith, that God the Son became Man to save us; and this dogma entirely concerns the Person of Jesus Christ   Now God the Son, the Second Person of the Blessed Trinity, from the time of His Incarnation possesses both a Divine and a human nature—that is, He is both God and Man, yet this God-Man is but One Person, Jesus Christ; and all the actions produced and all the properties possessed by either nature may truly, justly, and rightly be attributed to Him. All possessed an infinite dignity, and all were infinitely agreeable to His Heavenly Father.   •

If, therefore, we were to admit that in Jesus Christ there were two distinct Persons, we should have to admit that the Person who suffered and died for us was only Man, that the satisfaction He offered was not of infinite value, and that, consequently, it was insufficient for our Redemption.

On the other hand, if we were to deny the reality of the human nature, or, with the Monophysites, affirm that at the time of the Incarnation the human nature was changed into the Divine, we should be forced to admit that our Lord, being God and not Man, could not have died for us; for it was as Man, that is, according to His human nature, that He suffered.

CHAPTER XVI

THE FOURTH ARTICLE OF THE CREED

"Suffered under Pontius Pilate, was crucified, dead, and buried."

THE great work which Jesus Christ came on earth to
Why Christ came upon earth. accomplish was that of man's Redemption, or that of reconciling man with an offended God. But to do this He had to satisfy the Divine Justice for our sins, and to apply to each one of us the merits of His atonement in order that we might thus regain the right of inheritance to the Kingdom of Heaven:

"For you are bought with a great price" (1 Cor. vi. 20)
And again: "He is the propitiation for our sins: and
not for ours only, but also for those of the whole world"
(1 John ii. 2).

Now His sufferings and His precious Blood, being the
sufferings and the Blood of the Son of God,
were of infinite value, and, though a single act
or a single drop of His Blood possessed in itself
sufficient merit to redeem fallen man, yet for love of us
He, of His own free choice, poured out His Blood to the
very last drop: "He was offered because it was His own
will" (Isa. liii. 7). "Therefore doth the Father love Me;
because I lay down My life, that I may take it again. No
man taketh it away from Me: but I lay it down of Myself,
and I have power to lay it down: and I have power to take
it up again" (John x. 17, 18). This sacrifice of His life He,
both as Priest and Victim, offered on the altar of the Cross
to His Heavenly Father for the salvation of all mankind.

Christ's every action infinite.

In order that we might be the more sensible of His
boundless love for us, and of the punishment
which our sins had merited, and also that we
might learn to bear our own crosses and trials
with greater patience and resignation, our Saviour freely
chose to undergo a series of cruel sufferings, and to end
them by dying a painful and ignominious death. He
endured so terrible an agony in the Garden of Gethsemani
that His sweat became as drops of blood trickling down
upon the ground. He was betrayed by Judas, one of His
trusted Apostles, was abandoned by His disciples, and
even denied by Peter. He was accused before the
High Priests Annas and Caiphas, before Herod, and
before the Roman Governor of Judea, Pontius Pilate,
by whom He was condemned to death. He was put in
comparison with Barabbas, a malefactor and notorious
murderer, and was rejected for him. Stripped and

Chief sufferings of Christ.

fastened by the wrists to a low pillar, He was cruelly scourged thereat. A crown of thorns was then platted and pressed violently upon His sacred head; a purple garment was thrown about His shoulders; a reed was put in His hand for a sceptre, and He was derided as a mock king. At length, after enduring these and other torments, He was condemned to be crucified. The Cross was laid upon His shoulders; and, tottering under the cruel burden, and more than once falling, He struggled on His painful journey till He came at last to the top of Calvary. Again He was stripped of His clothes, stretched upon the Cross, and nailed by His hands and feet to the hard wood. The Cross, with its precious burden, was then raised and dropped with a thud into the hole prepared to receive it, thus sending a thrill of the most agonising pain through His sacred frame; and there, on that first Good Friday, the Saviour of mankind hung suspended for three hours, bleeding and dying in fearful agony between two malefactors, until, spent with suffering for the love of sinful man, He bowed His head and died. At that moment His blessed soul separated from His body, though the Divinity remained united both with the soul and with the body. "Surely He hath borne our infirmities, and carried our sorrows. . . . But He was wounded for our iniquities, He was bruised for our sins : the chastisement of our peace was upon Him, and by His bruises we are healed" (Isa. liii. 4, 5). With reason might we exclaim with the Royal Psalmist: "With the Lord there is mercy; and with Him plentiful redemption" (Ps. cxxix. 7).

Thus, "at a great price" indeed, Christ won for us Justification and eternal life, together with all **Fruits of the Passion.** that is necessary to obtain it. It is for us to correspond with the graces that have been so dearly gained, and that are so liberally offered to us. The just who died before Christ were saved through His future merits; while those who have gained heaven since the time of His coming upon earth have saved their souls through the same merits.

On the Cross our Saviour merited for us the adoption of sons and the consequent right of inheritance to the kingdom of heaven ; yet all will not be saved: " Being consummated, He became, *to all that obey Him*, the cause of eternal salvation " (Heb. v. 9); that is, to all who believe in Him and make a right use of the graces He offers. In order, then, that the merits of His Passion and Death may be applied to us, certain conditions are required on our part: we must believe with sincerity, heartily repent of our sins, keep the Commandments, practise good works, and use all the means of grace so freely held out to us all.

The Sufferings and Death of Christ afford us the most striking proof of His love for us, and we cannot The Sign of meditate on them or think of them too often. the Cross. It is for this reason that the Church, in all her prayers and ceremonies, makes such frequent use of the saving Sign of the Cross. Tertullian, speaking for the very early Christians, says: " Whenever we move, at our coming in and going out, when we sit down to table, when we retire to rest, we imprint on our foreheads the Sign of the Cross." It is a sign which marks out those who use it as followers of the Crucified Redeemer ; it is the standard of the Son of God, under which they who fight are assured of victory over the enemies of their salvation; it is a sign of which the devil has a special dread, since it is by the Cross that he was overcome; and hence it has special efficacy in all temptations, difficulties and dangers. It was in this sign, " *In hoc signo vinces*," that victory was miraculously granted to Constantine over the pagan Emperor Maxentius.

The Catechism tells us that the Sign of the Cross reminds us of the Blessed Trinity, and that God the Son died for us

on the Cross.   In the words, "In the name of the Father,
Of what the   and of the Son, and of the Holy Ghost," with
Sign reminds   which the Sign of the Cross is so often accom-
us.   panied, the phrase "In the name," not "In
the names," especially expresses our faith in the *Unity* of
God, *i.e.*, in the mystery that the Three Persons, although
distinct, have one and the same nature and one and the
same Divinity; while our faith in the Blessed Trinity is
shown by our naming in order the three Divine Persons.
The sign itself recalls to us the Cross on which the Saviour
of mankind poured out the last drop of His Blood.   Hence,
when we begin and end our prayers with the Sign of the
Cross, it is a striking proof that, what we pray for, we hope
to obtain through the merits of Christ's Passion and Death.

To encourage the use of this sacred symbol of our faith,
the Church has granted 50 days' indulgence for making the
Sign of the Cross and accompanying it with the usual
words; and an indulgence of 100 days when we at the
same time use holy water.

CHAPTER XVII

THE FIFTH ARTICLE OF THE CREED

" He descended into hell ; the third day He rose again from the dead."

AT the very moment of Christ's death on the Cross His
            blessed soul went down into that part of hell
Limbo.   called Limbo—not the abode of torment prepared for the devil and the lost souls, but that place of
rest where the souls of the just who died before Christ
were detained, and where they awaited the time of their
Redemption.   It is thought that now Limbo is the abode
or state of those infants who have died without Baptism.

The reason for Christ's descent into Limbo was, we are
told, to announce the happy tidings of Redemption to the

holy souls detained there, and of their approaching admission into heaven, when, on the day of His Ascension, He should lead them thither in triumph with Him : " Coming, He preached to those spirits that were in prison" (1 Pet. iii. 19). His very presence would change Limbo into a Paradise of delight, as we gather from His words to the good thief as He was hanging on the Cross : "Amen, I say to thee, this day thou shalt.be with Me in paradise" (Luke xxiii. 43).

It is also considered most probable that our Saviour visited Purgatory at this time, to console and enlighten the souls who suffered there, and to tell them of their expected Redemption : "I will penetrate to all the lower parts of the earth, and will behold all that sleep, and will enlighten all that hope in the Lord" (Ecclus. xxiv. 45).

Visit to Purgatory.

Although for part of three days our Saviour's soul remained separated from His body, yet the Divinity, as we remarked before, was never for a moment separated from either. Had our Lord raised Himself to life again immediately after being taken down from the Cross, He might have given His enemies room for denying the reality of His death, but to remove all possibility of doubt on this point, and to fulfil the signs and prophecies relating to His Resurrection, He chose to remain in the tomb from three o'clock on Good Friday afternoon till the early morning of Easter day: "An evil and adulterous generation seeketh a sign ; and a sign shall not be given it, but the sign of Jonas the prophet" (Matt. xii. 39). "The Son of Man shall be betrayed into the hands of men : and they shall kill Him, and the third day He shall rise again" (Matt. xvii. 21, 22).

Why Christ remained in the tomb.

On the third day after His death, therefore, Christ, by His own Divine power, reunited His soul to His body

and rose again immortal and impassible—that is, never
again to undergo death, and no longer capable
The Resurrec-
tion. of pain or suffering: "I lay down My life,
that I may take it again. . . . And I have
power to lay it down, and I have power to take it up
again" (John. x. 17, 18). Others have been raised from
the dead by the power of God, but not by their own
power; whereas Christ raised Himself to life again by His
own power, thus proving that He was God. Moreover,
Christ, being once risen, is no longer subject to death
as are those who are miraculously raised to life. And
Christ, in raising Himself from the dead, became the cause
and principle of the resurrection of all men, according to
the words of St. Paul: "As in Adam all die, so also in
Christ all shall be made alive" (1 Cor. xv. 22).

Our Redeemer after His death still retained in His
body the marks of His sufferings, as we gather
Christ still
retains the
marks of His
wounds. from His words to St. Thomas: "Put in thy
finger hither, and see My hands, and bring
hither thy hand, and put it into My side; and
be not faithless but believing" (John xx. 27). And there
the marks will ever remain to show that He rose again
in the self-same body in which He had suffered and died
for us, and as tokens of His victory and triumph over sin
and the devil. They ever plead to His eternal Father for
mercy on our behalf; they remain for the consolation of
the just, whom they serve to remind of the price paid for
their Redemption; and for the confusion of the wicked, by
reminding them of the justice of their condemnation.

The Resurrection is one of the fundamental articles of
our Faith. Indeed it was the particular sign
Importance of
the Resurrec-
tion. chosen by our Lord Himself in proof of His
Divine mission: "As Jonas was in the whale's
belly three days and three nights, so shall the Son of Man
be in the heart of the earth three days and three nights".

(Matt. xii. 40).   And in St. John: "Destroy this temple, and in three days I will raise it up. . . .   But He spoke of the temple of His body" (John ii. 19 and 21).   On the fact of the Resurrection, moreover, rests our belief in Christianity, for St. Paul assures us: "If Christ be not risen again, then is our preaching vain, and your faith is also vain. . . .   But now Christ is risen from the dead, the first-fruits of them that sleep" (1 Cor. xv. 14 and 20).

The Jews, remembering the words of our Lord, that after three days He would rise again, placed, with Pilate's authority, a guard of soldiers before the sepulchre, and set a seal on the great stone that had been rolled to the entrance, in order, as they thought, to prevent the disciples from carrying away the body secretly.   But their precautions served only to confirm the truth of the Resurrection; "for an Angel of the Lord descended from heaven: and coming, rolled back the stone, and sat upon it: and his countenance was as lightning, and his raiment as snow" (Matt. xxviii. 2, 3).   The guards, we are told, were terror-stricken at what they saw, and became as dead men; but recovering from their first alarm, they hastened into the city and told the chief priests what they had seen.   But the priests, after taking counsel with the ancients, bribed them to say that, while they were asleep, the disciples came by night and stole the body away.   They gave them a great sum of money to spread the story in the city, and promised to save them from the anger of Pilate if word of this reached his ears.   And they did as they were commanded (Matt. xxviii.).

Fruitless precautions of the Jews.

The only proof, then, that the Jews can urge against the Resurrection is that of *sleeping* witnesses, who were bribed to contradict the truth of what they had already spread throughout the city.

Impossible for the Apostles to steal the body.

Now could anything be more trivial than to bring in as

witnesses of a fact men who own that it was done while they were asleep? If they were asleep, how could they see the disciples come and take the body away? How could the disciples pass them, and break the seal, and roll away the stone—which we are told was very great—without disturbing the soldiers? Why were the guards not punished for neglecting their duty? The timid disciples who, when our Lord was arrested in the Garden of Gethsemani, left Him and fled, were not the men to embark on such a bold and hopeless venture.

But in proof of the Resurrection, we have the testimony of the guards before they were bribed to be silent, and that of the disciples to whom our Lord on many occasions appeared before the Ascension. Ten different manifestations of our Saviour are mentioned in Scripture. On the day of His Resurrection He showed Himself alive five times :

Proofs of the Resurrection.

1. To Mary Magdalene, in the garden near the sepulchre.

2. To the devout women on their returning from the sepulchre.

3. To St. Peter.

4. To the two disciples on the way to Emmaus.

5. To the assembled Apostles, except Thomas.

Between the day of His Resurrection and that of His Ascension, He appeared other five times :

1. After eight days, to the eleven, Thomas being present.

2. To seven Apostles by the Sea of Galilee (John xxi. 2).

3. On a mountain in Galilee to the great body of His disciples.

4. To St. James the Less, mentioned by St. Paul (1 Cor. xv. 7).

5. On the day of His Ascension, in Jerusalem, and at Mount Olivet, when He was taken from them. Later

we have the Apostles proclaiming the Resurrection of Christ even before the very Council that had put Him to death; and this they did at the expense of imprisonment and persecution. They preached the fact to an incredulous world, and convinced the world of its truth. And it must be borne in mind that the Apostles themselves were not disposed easily to believe in such a miracle. Hence we have St. Thomas exclaiming: "Unless I shall see in His hands the print of the nails, and put my finger into the place of the nails, and put my hand into His side, I will not believe" (John xx. 25), and our Saviour condescending to the weakness of His disciple by appearing again and inviting him, as we have seen above, to gratify his wish.

Well, then, might St. Paul declare the fact of the Resurrection* to be the ground of our faith,

The *Promise* fulfilled. and that the *promise* of the Messias made of old was fulfilled in the risen Christ: "God raised Him up from the dead the third day; who was seen for many days by those who went up together with Him from Galilee to Jerusalem; who, to this present time, are witnesses of Him to the people. And we declare to you that *the promise which was made to our fathers, this same hath God fulfilled to our children, raising up Jesus again*" (Acts xiii. 30-33); and St. Peter proclaimed: "God raised Him up from the dead, and gave Him glory, that your faith and hope might be in God" (1 Pet. i. 21).

* The fact of the Resurrection, this "Feast of Feasts," falling on a Sunday caused the Church to honour this day in a special manner, by substituting it as the day of rest instead of the Sabbath (Saturday). The Feast can fall on any date from March 22 to April 25, as it is always the Sunday after the first full moon following the Vernal Equinox.

CHAPTER XVIII

THE SIXTH ARTICLE OF THE CREED

" He ascended into heaven : sitteth at the right hand of God the Father Almighty."

IN the forty days' interval from the Resurrection to the Ascension we have seen that our Lord appeared

From the Resurrection to the Ascension. on various occasions to His Apostles, whom He instructed in all the mysteries of His kingdom : "To whom He showed Himself alive after His passion, by many proofs, for forty days appearing to them, and speaking of the kingdom of God" (Acts i. 3). It was still necessary that He should instil into them a further light; for, as we are told, "He opened their understanding that they might understand the Scriptures" (Luke xxiv. 45); He then fulfilled the promise of spiritual supremacy already made to St. Peter (Matt. xvi. 19) by charging him with the care of His whole flock, that is, of His whole Church, thus making him the infallible teacher and supreme head of His Church on earth : " Feed My lambs : feed My sheep " (John xxi. 15. 17); He gave His Apostles and their successors in the ministry, the Bishops and priests of His Church, the power of *binding* and *loosing* : " Whose sins you shall forgive, they are forgiven them ; and whose sins you shall retain, they are retained " (John xx. 23) ; and He also gave them the great commission to carry His Gospel to the uttermost ends of the earth : "Going therefore, teach ye all nations : baptising them in the name of the Father, and of the Son, and of the Holy Ghost, teaching them to observe all things whatsoever I have commanded you : and behold I am with you all days, even to the consummation of the world " (Matt. xxviii. 19, 20).

On the fortieth day after His Resurrection He led His
disciples towards Bethania as far as the Mount
The Ascension. of Olives. There, with hands uplifted, He
gave them His parting blessing ; and as He blessed them,
He raised Himself up before their eyes from the earth
towards heaven ; and as He ascended a cloud took Him
out of their sight. He was not borne up, but, as God-
Man, went up, body and soul, of His own Divine power
to heaven, where, as God, He has been from all eternity.
Nor did He ascend alone, but He took with Him also the
souls of the just who had been detained in Limbo : " Thou
hast ascended on high, Thou hast led captivity captive ;
Thou hast received gifts in men " (Ps. lxvii. 19).

In various parts of Scripture many reasons are assigned
for Christ's Ascension into heaven ; for example—

1. *As Man, He went to take possession of the glory
which He had merited by His life and death :*
Why Christ Ascended. " Ought not Christ to have suffered, and so to
enter into His glory ?" (Luke xxiv. 26). And
St. Paul says : " He humbled Himself, becoming obedient
unto death, even to the death of the Cross. Wherefore
God hath exalted Him, and hath given Him a name which
is above every other name " (Phil. ii. 8, 9).

2. *To be our Mediator with His Eternal Father :*
" Christ, at the right hand of God, maketh intercession
for us " (Rom. viii. 34). And St. John reminds us : " If
any man sin, we have an advocate with the Father, Jesus
Christ the Just " (1 John ii. i).

3. *To draw our hearts after Him, and to prepare a
place for us :* " In My Father's house there are many
mansions. . . . I go to prepare a place for you. And if I
shall go, and prepare a place for you, I will come again
and take you to Myself, that where I am you also may
be " (John xiv. 2, 3).

4. *To send the Holy Ghost upon His Church :* " It is

expedient for you that I go ; for if I go not, the Paraclete will not come to you : but if I go, I will send Him to you " (John xvi. 7).

When we speak of our Saviour *sitting at the right hand of God,* we do not mean that God, who is a pure spirit, has hands, but we use the words merely in a figurative sense, to imply that Christ, as God, is equal in all things to the Father, and as Man is exalted above all the Angels and Saints : " He hath raised Him up from the dead, and set Him at His right hand in the heavenly places, above all principality, and power, and virtue, and dominion, and every name that is named " (Eph. i. 20, 21).

Sitteth at the right hand of God.

CHAPTER XIX

THE SEVENTH ARTICLE OF THE CREED

" From thence He shall come to judge the living and the dead."

As the disciples stood gazing upwards after our Saviour at the time of His Ascension, behold two men, or rather Angels, in white garments, stood beside them and said : " Ye men of Galilee, why stand you looking up to heaven ? This Jesus who is taken up from you into heaven shall so come as you have seen Him going into heaven " (Acts i. 11).

At the last day Jesus Christ will come again from heaven with great power and glory to demand of all mankind a strict account of the manner in which they have spent their lives, and will judge all the nations of the earth : " When the Son of Man shall come in His majesty, and all the Angels with Him, then shall He sit upon the seat of His majesty. And all the nations shall be gathered together before Him, and He shall separate them one from another, as

The Last Day.

the shepherd separateth the sheep from the goats. And
He shall set the sheep on His right hand, but the goats
on the left. Then shall the King say to them that shall
be on His right hand: Come, ye blessed of my Father,
possess ye the kingdom prepared for you from the foundation of the world. . . . Then shall He say to them also
that shall be on His left hand: Depart from Me, ye cursed,
into everlasting fire which was prepared for the devil and
his angels. . . . And these shall go into everlasting
punishment: but the just, into life everlasting " (Matt.
xxv. 31-46).

When the day of judgment is to be we cannot tell:
igns before   " Of that day and hour no one knoweth, no
.e General   not the Angels of heaven, but the Father
ndgment.   alone " (Matt. xxiv. 36). Yet we have been
forewarned of many signs that shall come to pass on the
earth and in the heavens before the end of the world,
that the faithful may not be led astray nor taken off their
guard: " The Gospel of the kingdom shall be preached in
the whole world, for a testimony to all nations, and then
shall the consummation come " (Matt. xxiv. 14). There
shall be " wars and rumours of wars; nation shall rise
against nation; and there shall be pestilences, and famines,
and earthquakes in places. Now all these are the begin-
nings of sorrows " (Matt. xxiv). False prophets shall
appear, and men calling themselves the Christ shall seduce
many: " There shall arise false Christs, and false prophets,
and they shall show great signs and wonders, insomuch as
to deceive (if possible) even the elect " (Matt. xxiv. 24).
The judgment shall not take place before the coming
of Antichrist, the man of sin: " Let no man deceive
you by any means; for unless there come a revolt first,
and the man of sin be revealed, the son of perdition,
be not terrified, as if the day of the Lord were at hand "
(2 Thess. ii. 2. 3). After these things " there shall be

5

signs in the sun, and in the moon, and in the stars ; and upon the earth distress of nations, by reason of the confusion of the roaring of the sea and of the waves ; men withering away for fear and expectation of what shall come upon the whole world. For the powers of heaven shall be moved ; and then they shall see the Son of Man coming in a cloud with great power and majesty " (Luke xxi. 25-27).

Then will come the *General Judgment,* when, before the whole world, we must give an exact account of our every thought, word, deed, and omission : " The Lord will bring to light the hidden things of darkness, and will make manifest the counsels of the hearts " (1 Cor. iv. 5). If of every idle word we must render an account, how much more of blasphemy : " I say unto you that every idle word that men shall speak, they shall render an account for it in the day of judgment " (Matt. xii. 36). And St. John : " They were judged every one according to their works " (Apoc. xx. 13). At the day of judgment the wicked moreover shall be condemned for neglecting to perform good works : " I was hungry, and you gave Me not to eat : I was thirsty, and you gave Me not to drink. I was a stranger, and you took Me not in : naked, and you clothed Me not : sick and in prison, and you did not visit Me. . . . Amen I say to you, as long as you did it not to one of these little ones, neither did you do it to Me " (Matt. xxv. 42-45).

The General Judgment.

Many reasons are assigned by the Fathers why, in addition to the particular judgment, a general judgment is also necessary

In the first place, the virtuous are often persecuted in this life, and the wicked often prosper ; therefore God's wisdom and justice, in His dealings with each individual, will then be more clearly vindicated and acknowledged by all men : " The heavens shall declare His justice ; for God is judge " (Ps. xlix. 6).

Reasons for a General Judgment.

Secondly, our bodies, having shared in our virtuous or' guilty life, will then become sharers of our glory or condemnation.

Thirdly, as the good or evil which a man does in this life does not end with his death—for example, take an author of good or bad literature—but the results of his influence and example may extend to all time, the last judgment will clearly show forth the complete reward or punishment meted out to everyone.

Fourthly, our Lord, who on earth was dishonoured, unjustly condemned, and put to an ignominious death on the Cross, will then be glorified before the whole world.

When we say that Christ will come to judge "*the living*" and "*the dead*," it is supposed that he living and those who are living on earth when He comes e dead. to judge the world will probably die, and rise at once like the rest of mankind. By "*the dead*" we mean all who shall have lived and died on earth from the creation of Adam to the end of the world. After the General Judgment, purgatory will cease to be; heaven and hell alone will remain.

Although many of the Fathers assert that the whole world will be the scene of judgment, yet it is he Scene of commonly believed that the Valley of Josaphat idgment. marks the place where the Judge will sit—the valley lying east of Jerusalem between the Temple and Olivet, near the scenes of our Lord's humiliations: "I will gather together all nations into the valley of Josaphat . . . for there will I sit to judge" (Joel iii. 2-12). And St. Matthew, describing the awful summons, tells us, "He shall send His Angels with a trumpet and a great voice; and they shall gather together His elect from the four winds, from the farthest parts of the heavens to the utmost bounds of them" (xxiv. 31).

' Every one moreover will be judged at death as well as
at the last day: "It is appointed unto men
The Particular   once to die, and after this the judgment"
Judgment.
(Heb. ix. 27). This is the "*Particular Judgment*" to be undergone by all the children of Adam the
very moment the soul leaves the body: "It is easy before
God in the day of death to reward every one according to
his ways" (Ecclus. xi. 28).

CHAPTER XX

ON DEVOTION TO THE SACRED HUMANITY OF JESUS CHRIST

THE Seventh Article is the last Article of the Creed
which refers, in a special manner, to the Second Person
of the Blessed Trinity; and therefore it may be well
at this point briefly to summarise a few facts in reference
to the Incarnation, in order that we may clearly understand both the Catholic standpoint in regard to the
homage and adoration which we pay to the Sacred
Humanity of Christ, and, when we come to speak of the
Holy Eucharist, devotion to the Blessed Sacrament of the
Altar.

The Catholic Church, as we have seen, believes and
teaches that in Jesus Christ there are two
The Word was   natures, the nature of God and the nature of
made Flesh.
Man, and that these two natures, though distinct from each other, are inseparably united together—by
the Hypostatic Union—in the single Person of God the
Son made Man for us.

As both these natures are truly His own, all that He
does, all that He possesses, whether as God or Man, must
be attributed to the Person of the Word made Flesh; for
it is God the Son who acts, it is God the Son who possesses:

just as everything which a man does or suffers, whether in mind or body, is rightly attributed to the personality of that man.   Therefore we say with the strictest truth that our Lord is God and that He is Man ; that " in Him a God is Man, and a Man is God ; in Him a God suffers, a God dies for men "; and consequently that " His words, His sufferings, His Blood, are the words and sufferings and Blood of the Son of God." *   All these things, then, are Divine : ". For in Him dwelleth all the fulness of the Godhead corporeally " (Col. ii. 9).

Christ's infinite atonement. The dignity of His Person being *infinite*, whatever He offered for us possessed an infinite value, and therefore Christ offered an infinite atonement to the infinite majesty of God offended by sin.

His Infinite dignity. Since then all things belonging to Jesus Christ, such as His sacred Flesh and Blood, are, by reason of His Divine personality, Divine and of infinite dignity, they are deserving of supreme homage and adoration.

Homage and gratitude due to Christ. Christ, therefore, having become our Mediator and our Intercessor, interposing Himself between us and an offended God, for the purpose of reconciling us to Him, has merited both our *homage* and our *gratitude;* and we are bound to offer Him our worship on account of the dignity of His Person, as well as our gratitude on account of the inestimable benefits He has conferred upon us.

Supreme worship due to Christ. To His Sacred Person we owe the highest worship we can pay to the Godhead—the worship of *latria*, or of supreme adoration, as He is really and truly God, the Second Person of the Adorable Trinity.   Such worship, we learn from Scripture, was con-

* Father Schouppe.

stantly paid to Him in His human nature. When the
Eternal Father introduced His Only-begotten Son into
the world, He said: "Let all the Angels of God adore
Him" (Heb. i. 6). The Wise Men of the East recog-
nised in the Divine Infant their Saviour and their God,
and, "entering into the house, they found the Child with
Mary, His mother, and falling down they adored Him"
(Matt. ii. 11). And on a certain occasion when our
Lord appeared to His Apostles in Galilee after His
Resurrection, we are told that they, "seeing Him,
adored" (Matt. xxviii. 17). This supreme homage and
adoration, then, which is founded, as we have seen, on the
Hypostatic Union, must be given to all that belongs to
Him, because in Him all is Divine, all is adorable. Not
only must we adore His Divinity, but His Humanity also,
since in Him they are inseparably united. We adore His
Sacred Body, His Precious Blood, His Sacred Heart, His
wounded Hands and Feet, because they belong to God
the Son and are inseparably united to His Divine nature.

One way of displaying our gratitude to our Blessed
Lord is by selecting some part of His Sacred
Humanity, and honouring it with a special
devotion, to thank Him for the benefits which
it represents. For example, in worshipping the Precious
Blood we honour it as the price paid for our redemption,
since it was to merit our salvation that our Saviour
poured out the last drop of His Blood. In adoring the
Sacred Wounds we honour them not only as the channels
through which His Precious Blood was poured out for us,
but, at the same time, as His Divine members wounded for
our sake. They ever plead with His Eternal Father for
our pardon and forgiveness, and ask for our love in return
for the great love He has shown us by dying for us.

In worshipping the Sacred Heart we also render Him a
most pleasing honour; for in this devotion we especially

The Precious Blood and Sacred Wounds.

show our gratitude to His wounded Heart pierced for love
of us, and make some slight return for the love
The Sacred Heart. He has so generously lavished upon us. As the
heart is the symbol of love and is regarded as
the seat of the affections, so may we regard the Sacred
Heart of our Lord as the symbol of God's undying affection
for mankind. Christ Himself has even chosen it as the
model for our imitation: "Learn of Me, because I am
meek, and humble of heart" (Matt. xi. 29).

CHAPTER XXI

THE EIGHTH ARTICLE OF THE CREED

" I believe in the Holy Ghost."

As in the first Article of the Creed we declare our belief
in God the Father, the *Creator ;* and in the next six Articles
in God the Son and the work of *Redemption ;* so in the
eighth Article we declare our belief in God the Holy Ghost,
to whom especially is ascribed the work of *Sanctification.*

Though distinct in Person, the Holy Ghost is the same
Lord and God as the Father and the Son, each
Procession of the Holy Ghost. existing from all eternity in a manner proper
to Himself. God the Father is begotten of no
one; God the Son is begotten of the Father and takes
His origin from Him: "born of the Father from all
eternity;" and God the Holy Ghost originates not by
generation but by *procession,* not from the Father alone,
nor from the Father through the Son, but eternally proceeds from the Father and the Son as from a single
principle: "There are *Three* who give testimony in
heaven, the Father, the Word, and the Holy Ghost; and
these Three are *One*" (1 John v. 7). The Divinity of the
Holy Ghost is also shown in St. Peter's words to Ananias:
" Why hath Satan tempted thy heart, that thou shouldst

lie to the *Holy Ghost ?*   Thou hast not lied to men, but to *God* " (Acts v. 3, 4).

Now in order to consider the Father as begetting the Son, the Son as begotten of the Father, and the Holy Ghost as proceeding from the Father and the Son, we naturally conceive the Father as existing before the Son, and the Father and the Son as existing before the Holy Ghost, yet this priority exists only in thought, not in reality, not in priority of being, since all the Three Divine Persons are co-eternal : " In the Trinity there is nothing which precedes, nothing which comes after, nothing which is greater or less ; the Three Persons are eternal and equal in all things."

Throughout the Scriptures we find Divine perfections constantly attributed to the Holy Ghost ; for example, *Omniscience :* " The Spirit searcheth all things ; yea, the deep things of God " (I Cor. ii. 10) ; *Omnipotence :* " The Holy Ghost shall come upon thee, and the power of the Most High shall overshadow thee " (Luke i. 35) ; *Omnipresence :* " Whither shall I go from Thy Spirit ? or whither shall I flee from Thy face?" (Ps. cxxxviii. 7) ; *Justification :* " You are sanctified, you are justified in the Spirit of our God" (1 Cor. vi. 11).

His Divine Attributes.

We find the Third Person of the Blessed Trinity variously spoken of as the Holy Ghost, the Holy Spirit, the Paraclete or Comforter, the Sanctifier, the Gift of the Most High, the Giver of Life, the Spirit of Truth, and the Spirit of Love.

Names applied to Him.

On more than one occasion He has made Himself known by His visible presence. At the time of our Lord's baptism, the Holy Ghost appeared in the form of a dove and rested upon Him ; and, on the day of Pentecost, in the form of tongues of fire. He moreover still comes down in an invisible manner when He takes up His abode in our souls with His sanctifying grace :

His appearance in the world.

"Know you not that you are the temple of God, and that the Spirit of God dwelleth in you? But if any man violate the temple of God, him shall God destroy" (1 Cor. iii. 16, 17).

In the descent of the Holy Ghost on Whit-Sunday was fulfilled that promise of our Lord to His Apostles, "I will ask the Father, and He shall give you another Paraclete, that He may abide with you for ever, the Spirit of Truth . . . and He shall be in you" (John xiv. 16, 17). Now the tenth day after Christ's Ascension, or the fiftieth after the Pasch or Easter, found the disciples assembled together expecting the fulfilment of this promise. Suddenly there came a sound from heaven as of a mighty wind, which filled the whole house in which they were sitting, and there appeared to them cloven tongues as it were of fire, resting upon each of them; "and they were all filled with the Holy Ghost, and they began to speak with divers tongues, according as the Holy Ghost gave them to speak" (Acts ii. 4).

"Parted tongues" "of fire." This *visible form* which the Holy Ghost assumed was expressive of the effects produced in the souls of the Apostles; the "*parted tongues*" denoted the gift of tongues or of languages,* and the universality of their preaching; while their being "*of fire*" denoted the fire of charity, the zeal with which He inspired them, and the efficacy of their words.

The "sound," the "mighty wind." The *sound* and *the mighty wind* were symbols of the Divinity. It was thus also that formerly, on Mount Sinai, thunder and lightning, the

---

* Some interpreters have explained this gift in the sense that, while the Apostles continued to speak the same language as before, every stranger to whom they preached heard them or understood them as if they spoke his own tongue. But the common opinion is that the Apostles received by infusion the knowledge of languages of which before they were ignorant, in such a way as to understand them and to speak them when the interests of their ministry required it.

dark cloud and the smoking mountain, marked the
majesty of God.   Moreover, as Jesus Christ, our Pasch, in
order that He might perfectly correspond to the figure, was
offered on the day of the great Jewish Passover, so fifty
days after, that He might accomplish the figure of the
Old Law given on Mount Sinai, He sent down the Holy
Ghost on His Apostles on the day of the Jewish Pentecost,* to inspire them to publish the New Law.

One of the principal effects of the descent of the Holy
Ghost on the Apostles was " to confirm their
faith."   Whereas, hitherto, they had been weak
and timid, and had hidden themselves for fear of
the Jews, they now no longer shrank from danger, but fear-
lessly went forth to preach the Crucified One.   Before, they
had been dull, and had with difficulty been able to grasp
the doctrines which our Lord preached to them, but now
all doubt and ignorance being dispelled from their minds,
they became infallible teachers : " The Paraclete, the Holy
Ghost, whom the Father will send in My name, He will
teach you all things, and bring all things to your mind,
whatsoever I shall have said to you " (John xiv. 26).

To confirm the
faith of the
Apostles.

Another effect was " to sanctify them."   The Holy
Ghost descended in the form of fiery tongues.
Now as fire gives light and warmth, raises,
purifies, and changes into itself whatever it
embraces, so did the Holy Spirit of God work in the souls of
the Apostles, and continues to work in the souls of those
who worthily receive Him : He animates and fills the soul
with the true fire of love, cleanses it from sin, and makes it
holy and pleasing to God : "You are washed, you are sanctified, you are justified in the Spirit of our God" (1 Cor. vi. 11).

To sanctify
them.

A further effect was " to enable the Apostles
to found the Church."   It is by virtue of the
Holy Ghost that they are to preach and teach:

To enable them
to found the
Church.

* The Feast to commemorate the giving of the Law on Mount
Sinai.

"The Paraclete, the Holy Ghost, whom the Father will send in My name, He will teach you all things" (John xiv. 26); as well as to guide and rule: "Take heed to yourselves, and to all the flock over which the Holy Ghost hath placed you bishops, to rule the Church of God, which He hath purchased with His own blood" (Acts xx. 28).

The effect of their preaching was instantaneous. St. Peter, Effect of the on the very day of Pentecost, converted three Apostles' thousand, and, in another sermon soon after-preaching. wards, as many as five thousand. A like success also attended the preaching of the other Apostles: "They going forth, preached everywhere; the Lord co-operating with them, and confirming the word with signs that followed" (Mark xvi. 20). And again: "The Lord added daily to their society such as should be saved" (Acts ii. 47).

Thus we see established the Catholic Church, that visible society of men, joined together in one body and one spirit in Christ, which may be traced throughout the ages down to our own days, and which will continue, in virtue of our Lord's promise, to the end of time.

CHAPTER XXII

THE NINTH ARTICLE OF THE CREED

" The Holy Catholic Church ; the Communion of Saints "

THE Catholic Church, as a visible society upon earth, is The Catholic the collective body of Christians who, professing Church. the same Faith, and partaking of the same Sacraments, are in submission to the Pope, the successor of St. Peter, whom Christ appointed to be the Head of His Church, and whom He commissioned to feed the *whole* flock. It is composed, then, of all baptised persons who believe—at least implicitly—and profess the doctrines

of Christ, and at the same time are in communion with His
visible representative.

The stability of the foundation of the Church, laid by
Jesus Christ Himself, was clearly set forth in
His words to the Apostle Simon when, in giving
him a name expressive of his future office, He
said : "Thou art Peter,* and upon this rock I will
build My Church, and the gates of hell shall not prevail
against it " (Matt. xvi. 18). That foundation was to be so
firm that the forces of hell were to be powerless against
it ; for if they overturned the foundation, they would
overturn also the Church that rested upon it. By these
words Christ established that religious society, the Church,
the Kingdom of God upon earth, of which Peter was to be
the Head.

Church founded on a rock.

Now a Kingdom or State is necessarily composed of two
orders of citizens, those who are to command,
and those who are to obey. So too in God's
Kingdom upon earth, we have those who are
to command and teach, and those who are to obey
and be taught. The first constitute the teaching and
governing Church, and are composed of the Bishops and
priests ; the ordinary people, the laity, are the taught
and governed.

Rulers and ruled.

The authority of the Pastors of the Church as teachers
may be gathered from the words of our Lord,
who Himself was sent to teach and to preach :
"The Spirit of the Lord is upon Me : wherefore
He hath anointed Me, to preach the Gospel to the poor He
hath sent Me " (Luke iv. 18). How perfectly He fulfilled
that mission we again gather from His own Divine lips :
" All things whatsoever I have heard from My Father, I
have made known to you " (John xv. 15). And now, with
full commission to teach the same things, He sent His

The Pastors' commission to teach.

* Petra, in Greek and in Latin, means *a rock.*

Apostles * : " As the Father hath sent Me, I also send you "
(John xx. 21). And further : " All power is given to Me
in heaven and in earth. Going therefore, teach ye all
nations; baptising them in the name of the Father, and
of the Son, and of the Holy Ghost; teaching them to
observe all things whatsoever I have commanded you "
(Matt. xxviii. 18-20). " He that heareth you heareth
Me ; and he that despiseth you despiseth Me ; and he that
despiseth Me despiseth Him that sent Me " (Luke x. 16).
And again : " He that believeth, and is baptised, shall be
saved ; but he that believeth not shall be condemned "
(Mark xvi. 16). In the above words we see enforced the
strict obligation of our hearing and receiving the teaching
of the Church ; while to show that the mission of the
Apostles was not to end with them, but was to be continued by their successors to the end of time, our Lord
added : " And behold I am with you all days even to the
consummation of the world " (Matt. xxviii. 20). " I will
ask the Father, and He shall give you another Paraclete,
that He may abide with you for ever : the Spirit of Truth
. . . He shall abide with you, and shall be in you " (John
xiv. 16, 17).

The Pastors of the Church have therefore the right to
rule and govern, to make laws and precepts,
Their commis-
sion to rule. and power to enforce their laws : " Take heed
to yourselves, and to all the flock over which
the Holy Ghost hath placed you bishops, to rule the Church
of God " (Acts xx. 28). Note also our Lord's promise to
St. Peter : " Whatsoever thou shalt bind upon earth,
it shall be bound also in heaven ; and whatsoever thou
shalt loose upon earth, it shall be loosed also in heaven "
(Matt. xvi. 19). And this authority on the part of the
Pastors of the Church necessitates a corresponding obedience and submission on the part of the faithful : " Obey

* Apostle means *sent*.

your prelates, and be subject to them; for they watch, as being to render an account of your souls" (Heb. xiii. 17). And in St. Luke: "He that heareth you heareth Me; and he that despiseth you despiseth Me" (x. 16).

CHAPTER XXIII

THE NINTH ARTICLE OF THE CREED (*continued*)

THE POPE THE HEAD OF THE CHURCH.

Since Christ at His Ascension was to leave His Apostles and, though still the invisible Ruler of His Church, could no longer remain as its visible Ruler, it was necessary that the Church, being a visible community or body, should have a visible Head if it was to continue to preserve unity of Faith and Government. Hence, before His departure, Christ established, in His place, a visible Head or Vicar to govern in His name. It was to this office that He appointed St. Peter and his successors. This is especially clear from Scripture, and from the fact that St. Peter, immediately after the Ascension, began to exercise his high office, and was acknowledged by the Apostles, and the Church generally, as the supreme Pastor.

Need of a visible Head.

In regard to Peter's appointment we must bear in mind the following facts especially, viz., that Christ built His Church upon Peter as upon a *rock* or foundation-stone; that He gave to him, but not to the other Apostles, the *power of the keys;* that He prayed for him that his faith might never fail, and bade him confirm his brethren; and that He made him the supreme Pastor, and commissioned him alone to feed the *whole* flock.

Facts regarding Peter's appointment.

1. Christ gave to Simon the surname Peter, that is *a rock*, and declared that He made him the foundation.

stone of His Church: "I say to thee that thou art Peter;
and upon this rock I will build My Church, and
the gates of hell shall not prevail against it"
(Matt. xvi. 18).' Peter is here declared to be
the *rock* upon which the Church is to be
built, Christ Himself being both its principal foundation and founder. By building His Church upon a rock
He thereby secured it against all storms and floods,
that is, against the powers of darkness, against whatever
Satan can do, either of himself or by his agents. By
this promise we are fully assured that neither idolatry,
nor heresy, nor error shall at any time prevail over the
Church of Christ. Here, then, Christ promises to Peter that
he and his successors shall be to the end of time, as long
as the Church shall last, its supreme pastors and princes.

"Upon this Rock I will build My Church."

2. Christ gave to St. Peter the power of the keys,
which power is symbolical of supreme authority
and dominion. Besides the power of *binding*
and *loosing*, which was conferred on all the
Apostles, Christ promised to Peter alone the keys of the
Kingdom. This again is equivalent to making him
supreme ruler and Head of the Church upon earth: " I
will give to thee the keys of the kingdom of heaven: and
whatsoever thou shalt bind on earth, it shall be bound
also in heaven: and whatsoever thou shalt loose upon
earth, it shall be loosed also in heaven " (Matt. xvi. 19).
Now the keys of a city, or of its gates, are presented or given
to the person to whom is entrusted the supreme power, and
are ever regarded as the symbol of authority.   All the
Apostles, then, and their successors, the Bishops and priests of
the Church, partake of the power of binding and loosing, but
with a due subordination to the one head invested with
the supreme power. The power of the keys, moreover,
confers the right to make rules and laws for the government of the Church.

The power of the keys.

3. Christ prayed that Peter's faith might never fail,
When Satan wished to tempt the Apostles in
order that he might make them fall from their
faith in Christ, and get them into his power,
Christ said to Peter : " Simon, Simon, behold Satan hath
desired to have you, that he may sift you as wheat : but I
have prayed for thee, that thy faith fail not : and thou, being
once converted, confirm thy brethren " (Luke xxii. 31, 32).
Such a prayer could not fail to be heard. And the
faith of Peter, established by the coming of the Holy
Ghost, has never failed, nor can it fail, built as it is on a
rock, which is Christ Himself, and guided by the Spirit of
Truth which Christ promised. When Christ bade Peter
confirm his brethren, He meant the other Apostles and
Bishops, over whom He made and constituted him and his
successors the chief Head.   By a wonderful dispensation
of Providence, the see of Rome, Peter's see, is the only one
of the sees, founded by the Apostles, that has kept the
Faith, and that has come down to our own days in the
unbroken succession of its Bishops.*

Christ's prayer for Peter.

4. Christ commissioned Peter alone to feed His whole
flock, both His lambs and His sheep, both laity
and clergy, in order that there might be *one* fold
and *one* shepherd, that is, one Church and one
Chief Pastor. In thrice putting the question to Peter,
"Simon, son of John, lovest thou Me more than these ?"
(John xxi. 15-17), our Lord drew from him a threefold profession of love to correspond to his triple denial. After the
first and second protestation of love, our Lord bade him,
" Feed My lambs " ; and after the third, " Feed My sheep."
Now to feed, in the language of Scripture, means to guide,
rule, and govern ; and from the very first ages, the
Catholic Church has always acknowledged the supreme
power of the successors of St. Peter, in spiritual matters,

" Feed My lambs"; "Feed My sheep."

* Bishop means *overseer.*

over all Christian Churches. Our Lord had already promised the spiritual supremacy to St. Peter (Matt. xvi. 19), and in this commission He fulfilled that promise by charging him with the care of His whole flock, that is, of His whole Church.

The Evangelists, in giving us the names of the Apostles, always begin with Peter's name first, although Andrew, his brother, was called to the Apostleship before him. St. Matthew expressly styles him "the first": "Now the names of the twelve Apostles are these: The first, Simon who is called Peter" (Matt. x. 2). When the disciples were assembled together after the Ascension, we have Peter, in virtue of his supremacy, standing up and addressing them on the necessity of choosing another Apostle to fill the place of Judas. It was Peter who, in the name of all the Apostles, rebuked Ananias and Saphira for their deception: " Ananias, why hath Satan tempted thy heart that thou shouldst lie to the Holy Ghost ?" (Acts v. 3). In the case of the conversion of Cornelius we find that it was to Peter that God first announced that the time was come to preach the Gospel to the Gentiles as well as to the Jews. And again, in the first Council at Jerusalem, and whenever anything important is to be decided, we find Peter rising first and acting as Head of the rest. Nor was his supremacy ever called in question.

Peter's supremacy shown from facts.

And as the office of Peter was not to expire with him, we find his successors invariably exercising the same supreme authority from his time down to the present day. If the Church was to subsist in unity throughout all time, it was necessary that this supremacy and the Rock on which the Church was built should also continue. If a visible Head were needed in the Church's infancy when her members were few and our Lord's words were still fresh in the minds of His disciples,

Peter's office continued in the Papacy.

6

how much more is it needed now when we find her spread over all nations differing in language, laws, and customs, and when heresies have arisen and multiplied, if she is still to remain the *one body* in Jesus Christ!

Now the Bishop of Rome, the Pope, has ever been regarded as the lawful successor of St. Peter, and the visible Head of the Universal Church, the true Church of Jesus Christ—a fact proved by history and tradition. A General Council has never yet been held which was not presided over either by the Pope or by his delegates; nor has a decision of a Council ever been universally received unless it has received the Pope's confirmation. "*Ubi Petrus, ibi Ecclesia*"—where Peter is, there also is the Church—is an ancient axiom, in which Peter stands for the successor of St. Peter, the Pope the Bishop of Rome.

CHAPTER XXIV

THE NINTH ARTICLE OF THE CREED (*continued*)

The Government of the Church.

In order to maintain unity and union in His Church, Christ, as we have seen, appointed St. Peter to
The excellence of the power given to Peter. be His visible representative on earth. It is true that He gave His Apostles collectively the power of binding and loosing, and of governing the Church: " Amen I say to you, whatsoever you shall bind upon earth, shall be bound also in heaven ; and whatsoever you shall loose upon earth, shall be loosed also in heaven " (Matt. xviii. 18); but what He promised and gave to the Apostles collectively, He first promised and gave to St. Peter in particular Moreover the power conferred on Peter excelled that granted to the other Apostles, inasmuch as to him, who was the Head and Pastor of the whole Church was granted jurisdiction over the other Apostles.

Thus Peter received full and independent power, while that of the Apostles was subordinate to his.

Now when Christ conferred on His Apostles His own power, and sent them into the whole world to preach, to baptise, and, under the supremacy of Peter, to govern all who were baptised, He evidently bestowed upon them a threefold office, the *teaching*, the *priestly*, and the *pastoral* office.

The Apostles receive a three-fold office.

The *Teaching Office* embraces the power of proclaiming the doctrine which Christ came on earth to preach, as well as the deciding of religious controversies, and the condemning of heresies: " All things whatsoever I have heard of My Father, I have made known to you " (John xv. 15); "Going therefore, teach ye all nations . . . teaching them to observe all things whatsoever I have commanded you " (Matt. xxviii. 19, 20).

The *Priestly Office* consists in the power to offer Sacrifice, to bless, to administer the Sacraments, and to perform the other services of the Church.

The *Pastoral Office* consists in the power to rule and govern the Church, to make laws, and to maintain the discipline of the Church even, if necessary, by the infliction of punishments.

According as they had been commanded by their Divine Master, the Apostles went forth into the whole world preaching and baptising ; and all such as believed and were baptised they gathered into congregations. Thus in many places arose communities of Christians, who professed the same Faith, partook of the same Sacraments, and who, united with one another, formed one great Christian community under one visible Head, St. Peter.

Communities of Christians.

These communities the Apostles ruled in all spiritual matters. They made laws and regulations; they threatened, they judged, they punished ; and even cut off from the community of the faithful those who persisted in leading evil lives: "Some have made shipwreck concerning their faith . . . whom I have delivered to Satan, that they may learn not to blaspheme" (1 Tim. i. 19, 20); but, on their repenting, they were received back again: "What I forgave . . . for your sakes have I done it in the Person of Jesus Christ" (2 Cor. ii. 10).

And as the work of Jesus Christ on earth was to endure, the threefold office, which was common to all the Apostles, was to pass from them to their successors, and to continue through them, without interruption, to the end of time: "Behold I am with you all days, even to the consummation of the world" (Matt. xxviii. 20); an assertion which cannot have referred to the Apostles only, since they were not destined to live beyond the ordinary span of human life.

Christ's work to endure.

Then, as the Church was to last for all time, and as St. Peter was to have his successors in the Roman Pontiffs, so the Apostles also had to have their successors in the Episcopacy as well as in the Priesthood. Hence they chose Elders from among the faithful, and these they ordained Bishops to rule the newly founded Christian communities, charging them, in like manner, to ordain and appoint others: "For this cause I left thee in Crete, that thou shouldst set in order the things that are wanting, and shouldst ordain priests* in every city, as I also appointed thee" (Tit. i. 5).

Successors of the Apostles.

Those Bishops, therefore, who are rightly consecrated, and who are in communion with the Head of the Church, the Pope, are the true successors of the Apostles. No one separated from its Head can be a member of the Church; and no power has been conferred on the Apostles and their successors except when they are in union with him on whom

* Presbyter meant either Priest or Bishop.

Christ conferred full and supreme power over the whole Church: " *Ubi Petrus, ibi Ecclesia.*"

The Bishops, then, by Divine appointment, have power
The Bishops. to govern the Church, but only with, and under, its supreme Head, the Pope: " Take heed to yourselves, and to the whole flock, over which the Holy Ghost hath placed you bishops, to rule the Church of God, which He hath purchased with His own blood " (Acts xx. 28). A Bishop rules the diocese or bishopric assigned to him by the Pope, and he exercises his office in the particular congregations or parishes of his diocese through the Priests or Pastors sent to them. And the Priest is allowed to perform the duties of his Priesthood only when he is expressly authorised to do so by his lawful Bishop.

The Priests receive their ordination and mission from
The Priests. God only through a lawfully consecrated Bishop: " We are ambassadors for Christ, God as it were exhorting by us " (2 Cor. v. 20); and what Christ said to His disciples, when He sent them forth in His name, is also said to them : " He that heareth you heareth Me ; and he that despiseth you despiseth Me " (Luke x. 16).

Then only can good order be maintained in the Church
Obedience to when the faithful continue in ready obedience
Authority. to the Priests, the Priests to the Bishops, the Bishops to Christ's representative on earth, the Pope: "Some indeed He gave to be apostles, and some prophets, and others evangelists, and others pastors and teachers, for the perfection of the saints, for the work of the ministry, unto the edification of the body of Christ " (Eph. iv. 11, 12).

CHAPTER XXV

THE NINTH ARTICLE OF THE CREED (*continued*)

The Endowments of the Church.

From what has been said above we may conclude that the Church possesses three distinct *Endowments,* which are absolutely inseparable from her; viz., Indefectibility in Existing, Authority in Ruling, and Infallibility in Teaching.

By Indefectibility in Existing we mean that the Church of Christ, which all are commanded to hear and obey, is

Indefectibility in Existing.

destined to endure and be perpetuated in the world, unshaken by the downfall of nations and institutions, and to continue thus stead-fast and firm even to the end of time: " Upon this rock I will build My Church, and the gates of hell shall not prevail against it" (Matt. xvi. 18); and " Behold I am with you all days, even to the consummation of the world " (Matt. xxviii. 20). Christ, by building His Church upon a rock, has thereby, like a wise builder, secured it against all storms and floods, that is, against all the powers of darkness and whatever Satan can do either by himself or his agents. By His Divine promise we are assured that the adverse powers of the devil will never be able to prevail against His one visible and lasting Church, " the house of the Lord prepared on the top of mountains, and exalted above the hills, that house into which all the nations shall flow " (Isa. ii. 2).

The Church has also received from Jesus Christ all the

Authority in Ruling.

power necessary for her perfect government. She teaches and commands in the name of God, and to her doctrines and commands in the spiritual order all, both great and small, prince and peasant, must humbly submit; for her authority in teaching is in-

fallible, and her power in what pertains to her government
is sovereign; and since both are inherent in her very constitution, she is, in the exercise of these two prerogatives,
absolutely independent of all temporal power: " As the
Father hath sent Me, I also send you" (John xx. 21). · "He
that heareth you heareth Me, and he that despiseth you
despiseth Me" (Luke x. 16). " If he will not hear the
Church, let him be to ˙ thee as the heathen and the
publican" (Matt. xviii. 17). Could anything be more
clear, or more forcibly point out man's duty in submitting
to the judgment of the Church? " Obey your prelates,"
says St. Paul, " and be subject to them; for they watch, as
being to render an account of your souls " (Heb. xiii. 17).
In spiritual matters, then, that is, in all such as regard
faith and morals, religion and conscience, we are in duty
bound to obey our pastors.

Since man is composed of a body and a soul, the world
is governed by two powers essentially distinct,
The Spiritual
and the Tem-   the temporal power which has reference to the
poral Authority. civil order, and the spiritual power which
regulates whatever concerns religion. The spiritual power
belongs to the Pastors of the Church, the temporal power
to those who are at the head of our civil communities. This
distinction of authority our Lord Himself clearly recognised
when He said: " Render therefore to Cæsar the things
that are Cæsar's, and to God the things that are God's "
(Matt. xxii. 21).

But the authority of the Church differs from the civil
authority. The power of the state is deter-
The two powers mined by the people according to the time,
distinct.   place, and customs of a country, and rests on
natural right, and on the natural order established by God;
whereas the power of the Church is supernatural in its
origin, coming as it does immediately from God. It is,
therefore, independent of the people, and is, moreover, by

Divine right, independent, in its own particular sphere, of the temporal power.

Since, then, the power of the Church comes direct from God, it follows that it is of a higher order than that of any human authority. But, though essentially distinct, the two powers are not opposed to each other. On the contrary, it is intended that they should help each other in the good government of the people. And this good government will be the more readily brought about when, on the one hand, the Church enjoins submission to the temporal power and causes " to be rendered to Cæsar the things that are Cæsar's," and when, on the other hand, the temporal power commands " to be rendered to God the things that are God's."

But mutually helpful.

As the Church, moreover, is appointed to guide men to heaven, it follows that she must be guarded against error in her teaching. Eternal life is promised to those who hear and obey the Pastors of the Church, while eternal damnation is denounced against those who refuse to believe. Now if the *Teaching Church* erred—and we are bound to obey her— the *Hearing Church* would thus be bound by Christ to believe what is false, and Christ would have to reward error and punish truth. Then would the Church have failed in her mission, and have injured alike the interests of God and of man ; the power of hell, the spirit of lies, would have prevailed against her. But this is contrary to the expressed declaration of Christ : " I am with you all days, even to the consummation of the world" (Matt. xxviii. 20). " And I will ask the Father, and He shall give you another Paraclete, the Spirit of Truth, that He may be with you for ever " (John xiv. 16, 17). Hence, the very nature of the Church and of her Divine Founder requires that she be guarded against the very possibility of teaching what is not true : " The gates of hell shall not prevail against it "

Infallibility in Teaching.

(Matt. xvi. 18).   Well, therefore, might St. Paul, speaking
of the Church, apply to her the glorious title, "The Church
of the living God, the pillar and ground of truth"
(1 Tim. iii. 15).   How important, then, it is for us to
know the exact meaning of the term *infallibility*, and
where this *Infallible Teaching Body* resides!

By reason of Christ's promise to be with His Church
Infallibility.   for all time, and the constant indwelling of the
Spirit of Truth, her infallibility consists in the
impossibility of her faith, her teaching, or her decisions,
in regard to faith or morals, not being in conformity with
the Divine word, whether according to Scripture or Tradition.   All the faithful, then, are obliged to believe as
revealed whatever she believes, to profess whatever she
teaches, and to submit to all her decisions as soon as they
become known.

If individual teachers have fallen into error, it is because
The Teaching   they taught differently from the whole Teach-
Authority of   ing Body of the Church ; whereas Infallibility
the Church.   is promised not to Bishops singly; but to all
collectively when united with the Pope, so that the Bishops,
with the Pope, constitute the Teaching Authority of the
Church.   If, then, differences arise in matters of Faith, we
must adhere to the decisions of the Church, and all are
strictly bound to submit to such decisions when the Pope,
in his office of Supreme Pastor and Teacher, defines a
doctrine concerning faith or morals to be held by the
universal Church ; *i.e.*, when he speaks *ex cathedra*.   "And
some indeed He gave to be apostles, and some prophets,
and others evangelists, and others pastors and teachers,
. . . that we may not now be children, tossed to and fro,
and carried about with every wind of doctrine, in the
wickedness of men, in craftiness, by which they lie in wait
to deceive" (Eph. iv. 11-14).

Yet we do not mean to assert that the Pope is infallible

The Pope. as a private person ; for example, when he is speaking to one or several ; or, as a Bishop, he is preaching to a congregation ; or when he is writing as a theologian.   In all such cases he might make a mistake ; and, since he has free-will, it is in his power to go wrong and commit sin like any other man ; but we mean that, when he addresses the Universal Church as her supreme Pastor and Teacher, and requires certain doctrines to be accepted under pain of excommunication from the fold of the Church, he is then acting under the guidance of the Holy Spirit, and cannot therefore go wrong.   " When I say that the Pope is infallible," the Catechism tells us, " I mean that the Pope cannot err when, as Shepherd and Teacher of all Christians, he defines a doctrine, concerning faith or morals, to be held by the whole Church."

The Church teaches no new doctrine. When the Church pronounces on a disputed point of doctrine, and decides what is to be believed, her decision is not a fresh Divine revelation, *i.e.*, she does not teach anything new, but only unfolds the word of God entrusted to her in Scripture and Tradition.   She does but manifest more or less fully and authoritatively a truth transmitted as revealed by God : " Keep the good thing deposited in trust to thee by the Holy Ghost who dwelleth in us " (2 Tim. i. 14). " If any one preach to you a Gospel, besides that which you have received, let him be anathema " (Gal. i. 9).   To show how impossible it is for the Church to err, or to have at any time erred, in matters of Faith, we have only to turn to our Lord's promise : " When He, the Spirit of Truth shall come, He will teach you all truth ; for He shall not speak of Himself, but what things soever He shall hear, He shall speak ; and the things that are to come He shall show you " (John xvi. 13).

CHAPTER XXVI

THE NINTH ARTICLE OF THE CREED (*continued*)

THE FOUR MARKS OF THE CHURCH.

"I believe in ONE, HOLY, CATHOLIC, AND APOSTOLIC Church"
(*Nicene Creed*).

To impress on our minds the vital importance of our belief in the truths of Religion our Lord said : " He that believeth, and is baptised, shall be saved ; but he that believeth not shall be condemned " (Mark xvi. 16) ; and to show us that the means of arriving at such faith are within the reach of all, and that the Church which He came on earth to establish is plainly to be recognised by unmistakable signs, He spoke of it as a *light* set upon a candlestick for all men to see, and as a *city* which cannot be hid owing to its being built upon a mountain (Matt. v. 14, 15).

To be seen by all. Were the Church not a visible and lasting institution, with the clearest marks to distinguish her, our Lord could not and would not have commanded all men, under pain of eternal damnation, to hear and obey her: "If he will not hear the Church, let him be to thee as the heathen and the publican " (Matt. xviii. 17). But to show us that our salvation or condemnation rests with ourselves, He says in another place : " This is the judgment : because *the light* is come into the world, and men have loved the darkness better than the light " (John iii. 19).

Only one true Church. Seeing, then, that Christ has established a Church that can never fail, that He has commanded us to listen to her as we would listen to Himself, and that He commands us to believe under pain of eternal damnation, this one true Church must possess marks sufficiently plain to be recognised by all who seek her in real earnest.   We say this *one true Church*, because our Lord came on earth to establish not a number of Churches, but only one Church : " Upon this rock I will build My Church " (Matt. xvi. 18); and "There shall be *one* fold and *one* Shepherd " (John x. 16); while St. Paul, writing to the Romans, reminds them : " We, being many, are *one* body in Christ " (Rom. xii. 5).

Now the *marks* by which we are to know the one true Church are her four essential properties, which **The Marks of the Church.** must unmistakably manifest themselves to the whole world, and which we find clearly enumerated in the Nicene Creed: "I believe in *One, Holy, Catholic,* and *Apostolic* Church." Hence, according to the words of the Catechism, "the Church of Christ has four marks by which we may know her : she is ONE—she is HOLY—she is CATHOLIC—she is APOSTOLIC."

As the Church is the Kingdom of God upon earth, she must be *One*, for " a kingdom divided against itself shall be brought to desolation " (Luke xi. 17).

She must be *Holy*, having an all-holy Founder, and being designed to lead men to holiness: " A glorious Church, not having spot or wrinkle, nor any such thing, but that it should be holy and without blemish " (Eph. v. 27).

She must be *Catholic*, because she has been established to teach all nations, and to carry on our Lord's work to the end of time : " Going therefore, teach ye all nations, . . . and behold I am with you all days, even to the consummation of the world " (Matt. xxviii. 19, 20).

She must be *Apostolic*, for her doctrines and traditions must be those of the Apostles, and her Pastors must have come down from the Apostles in an unbroken succession. Now, if the distinctive marks are found united in the Roman Catholic Church and in her alone, then that Church must be the true Church of Jesus Christ.   Let us now consider more fully the application of each of these four marks in order.

We have seen that the true Church of Christ must be ONE, in that Christ founded but one Church;
The Church is ONE. but the Church, Catholic and Roman, is One because all her members are united in one Faith ; they have all the same Sacrifice and Sacraments ; and they are all united under one Head : " One Lord, one Faith, one Baptism " (Eph. iv. 5). And this her unity, made up as she is of men of every land, causes her to stand out before the world, undivided in herself, as a strongly marked individual being. " He that holdeth not this unity of the Church," writes St. Cyprian, " doth he think that he holdeth the Faith ?"

The Church, then, is *one* in her DOCTRINE, which is the same throughout the world, and moreover does not vary from century to century. She is *one* in COMMUNION, since all her members have the same means of salvation, and
One in Doctrine, in Communion, in Government. participate in the same Sacrifice* and Sacraments. And she is *one* in GOVERNMENT, since all her members acknowledge and obey one supreme Ruler—the Pope, the Vicar of Christ upon earth. She is indeed the *one fold* guided by the *one Shepherd*.

Though the members of the Catholic Church are spread throughout the nations, and differ in language,
Her members in unity. laws, and customs, yet they are closely united by the ties of Religion. They hold the great principle of unity, the infallible decisions of the Church, preserved as she is from error by the promises of Christ Himself: " I am with you all days, even to the consummation of the world " (Matt. xxviii. 20); and He prayed His Eternal Father : " Holy Father, I pray Thee

---

* Though externals, *i.e.*, the rites, may differ, the Mass, whether it be said according to the Dominican, the Carthusian, the Greek, the Armenian, the Coptic, or other rite, is one and the same *Sacrifice*.

for those who believe in Me, that they all may be *one*, as Thou, Father, in Me, and I in Thee, that they also may be one in Us ; that the world may believe that Thou hast sent Me " (John xvii. 21, 22).

But the Rule of Private Judgment contains within itself the very principle of division. Hardly does a new sect arise but it is straightway torn asunder by many divisions, because every one of its members has a right to interpret and believe the Scriptures as he wishes. If, for example, we look at the Reformers of the sixteenth century, we find that their principle of the Bible and each man's interpretation of it soon split them into endless divisions and subdivisions. They destroyed the very principle of unity, and have become as " children tossed to and fro, and carried about with every wind of doctrine " (Eph. iv. 14). If they were justified in casting off the authority of Rome, we naturally ask ourselves what claim they can have to the obedience of others.

Result of Private Judgment.

In striking contrast with the various sects, we see in the Catholic Church one perfect society, wherein reigns, as we have seen, complete Unity of Faith, Unity of Worship, and Unity of Government. In the Catholic Church there exists no difference in dogma: everywhere and in every age the same truths of Revelation are taught and handed down by her; and to-day her belief agrees, in every point, with Apostolic Tradition. Her teaching has developed, but her belief has not changed ; it has never suffered the slightest alteration. She has, it is true, sometimes made use of new terms, but this is only the better to express her ancient doctrines and to confound innovators. Any addition in words to her ancient symbols has only been made to render more clear to the faithful what she believed before.

No difference in the Church's dogma.

We have seen also that the true Church of Christ must be HOLY, coming as she does direct from God, and teaching

the revealed Truth of God.   But the Catholic Church
fulfils this mark also, inasmuch as she offers
The Church to all the means of becoming holy, particu-
is Holy. larly the Holy Mass, the Sacraments,
and the Commandments of the Church which pre-
scribe duties that must necessarily lead to holiness;
every article of her Faith tends to the holiness of her
children; and in all ages she has produced innumerable
Saints, whose holiness has been attested by miracles and
extraordinary manifestations of virtue.   The fact that
abuses have at times arisen in some of her members is no
argument against the sanctity of the Church as a whole;
otherwise Christ would not have compared His Church to
a field in which wheat and cockle grow together, or to a
net that contains good and bad fishes (Matt. xiii. 25, 47).
And Noe's Ark, which was a figure of the Church, contained both clean and unclean animals.

But while the Catholic Church is one in doctrine,
and while she is holy, and while thousands
A mark wanting of her children have arrived at holiness, on
in the *sects*. the other hand we find the different sects
rejecting many articles of Faith and means of sanctification, and, instead of being in perfect agreement in
their teaching, often falling into inconsistencies and
perverting the truth by teaching contradictory doctrines.
Their founders were not distinguished for the holiness
of their lives, nor can they point to any one of their
members the sanctity of whose life bears the hall-mark of
miracles.

The true Church of Christ must also be CATHOLIC or UNI-
VERSAL; but the Roman Catholic Church is
The Church is Catholic *in point of time*, having continually
CATHOLIC. existed from the time of Christ.   Even her
enemies cannot show any other beginning for her.   She is
Catholic in *point of place*: she is spread among the nations,

and produces everywhere the same fruits of virtue and good works; and she is constantly spreading in accordance with our Lord's commission: "Go ye into the whole world, and preach the Gospel to every creature" (Mark xvi. 15). "The Gospel of the kingdom shall be preached to every creature" (Matt. xxiv. 14). And she is Catholic in that *she teaches all revealed Truth*; she is the one Ark of Salvation for all: "Teach them to observe all things whatsoever I have commanded you" (Matt. xxviii. 20). "The Paraclete, the Holy Ghost, whom the Father will send in My name, He will teach you all things, and bring all things to your mind whatsoever I shall have said to you" (John xiv. 26).

Yet how seldom does a sect extend over a single nation, much less over the whole world! A sect, moreover, either bears the name of the place to which it is confined, as the Church of England, the Church of Scotland, the Calvinistic Church of Wales; or the name of its founder who established it centuries after the time of the Apostles, such as the Lutherans, the Zwinglians, the Wesleyans. But to this day the Roman Catholic Church is acknowledged throughout the world, even by her enemies, as *the Catholic Church*.

The *sects* are not Catholic.

The true Church of Christ must be APOSTOLIC in the unbroken succession of her Pastors from the Apostles; in her Doctrine and in her Mission; nor can any Religion be the true Religion except the one which was founded by Christ on His Apostles, with Peter as their Head, and which has received her Faith, her Orders, and her Mission from them by uninterrupted succession.

The Church is APOSTOLIC.

No Church, then, can be heir to the promises which Christ made to His Apostles unless it can point to a descent from Apostolic times.

In her Succession.

But which of the Churches, except the Catholic Church, can trace her origin back to the Apostles? She alone can point to an unbroken descent, and can give the name and reign of every Pope from St. Peter to the present reigning Pontiff.

Moreover, the Catholic Church is Apostolic in her teaching, which is grounded on the Doctrines and *In her Doctrine.* Traditions of the Apostles from whom she has received her Faith, her Orders, and her Mission ; and each generation, from the Apostles, has received and handed down *all truth* taught by Jesus Christ. What she believes now she has always believed : she has never taught other truths than those transmitted to her by the Apostles, either by writing or by word of mouth ; there is no dogma in her teaching which is not as old as Christianity itself ; nor a single article whose origin can be explained without going back to the Apostles.

Mission also is essential to the true Church: " As the Father hath *sent* Me, I also *send* you " (John *In her Mission.* xx. 21). " Go ye into the whole world, and preach the Gospel to every creature " (Mark xvi. 15). Christ thus gave His Apostles a *mission*, that is, He sent them to exercise their spiritual office, to teach the doctrines entrusted to them, and to enforce His commands in spite of the opposition of the world.

To show that all true preachers must be *sent* and have their mission from God, we have St. Paul *Mission neces-* writing to the Romans: " How shall they hear *sary.* without a preacher, and how shall they preach *unless they be sent ?*" (Rom. x. 14, 15). Here is an evident confutation of the claims of all new teachers who have usurped to themselves the ministry without any lawful mission derived by succession from the Apostles, to whom Christ spoke the words quoted above : " As the Father hath sent Me, I also send you." And this power of mission, given to the Apostles to be exercised throughout the world and for all time, was, from its very nature, to be handed on to their successors in the ministry.

Now the Catholic Church, as we have seen, can trace
Apostolicity wanting in the sects. the succession of her Pastors, without interruption, from the Apostles; and she alone is the depository of their doctrines and traditions, as well as of their mission or Divine authority. She has at all times jealously guarded and maintained unbroken the succession of her Pastors, seeing that they are lawfully ordained, and that thus their orders and mission come down, without interruption, from the Apostles themselves. Whoever denies that the Catholic Church is Apostolic, both in her orders and her mission, is driven to the blasphemous conclusion that the promises of Christ have not been fulfilled, and that there has been a time when the gates of hell have prevailed against His Church. But the various *sects* that have arisen have all come into the world too late to claim the title "Apostolic"; and in every case it can be shown not only who was their author, but when and where they came into being.

The Catholic Church alone, then, can prove her claim
The Catholic Church is the one true Church. to the titles ONE, HOLY, CATHOLIC, and APOSTOLIC. She has ever been visible from the first preaching of the Gospel till now. She has all the *Endowments* of the true Church, and all the *Marks* which distinguish the Church of God from all heretical and schismatical sects; she is then the one true Church of Jesus Christ. From her we are to receive our Faith, and it behoves all men to hearken to her voice and obey her commands; for has not Christ promised that He will ever be with her in her teaching, and that the Holy Ghost shall guide her into all truth?

CHAPTER XXVII

THE NINTH ARTICLE OF THE CREED (continued)

THE CHURCH THE ARK OF SALVATION FOR ALL.

SEEING, then, that God has marked out the path by which
He would lead men to heaven, He must neces-
Faith admits of sarily make our salvation dependent on the
no indifference.
fulfilment of the conditions which He Himself
has laid down. And if, as we have already pointed out, the
Catholic Church is the one true Church established by Christ
for this great end, and if she has received from Him her
doctrine, her means of grace, and her authority, it is
incumbent on every man, under pain of eternal damnation,
to enter her fold, to believe all that she proposes for our
belief, to make use of the means of grace which she holds
out to us, and humbly to submit to her authority. No
one can afford to treat with indifference so important a
matter; for our Lord Himself utters this terrible threat
against the unbeliever : " He that believeth not shall be
condemned " (Mark xvi. 16).

We may consider the Church as one whole, as a person
composed of *body* and *soul*; a body, which is
Body and Soul the exterior visible society of the faithful; a
of the Church.
soul, which is no other than the interior gifts
of the Holy Spirit—viz., faith, hope, and charity.

Now one may belong to the body of the Church without
belonging to the soul, just as one may belong to the soul
without belonging to the body. The just man who
professes the Catholic Faith belongs to the body and to
the soul of the Church; whereas one who has the Faith,
without being in a state of grace, belongs, for the time
being, only to the body of the Church. Adult non-
Catholics who have been rightly baptised, and who are

in good faith and in a state of grace, belong to the soul of the Church.

All baptised persons, then, who are in error through no

Who belong to
the *soul* of the
Church? fault of their own, but who in all sincerity seek after the truth, and try, according to the best of their knowledge, to do God's will; and even those who, though not baptised, are invincibly ignorant of the true Church, but who have an implicit desire of submitting to her, are united to the soul of the Church, although they are separated from the body. They even share in many of her graces, but are deprived of countless blessings and consolations of our Holy Religion, such as the Holy Sacrifice of the Mass, the Sacrament of Penance, and that great consolation of the dying, the beautiful Sacrament of Extreme Unction.

If, however, a man, outside the body of the Church, has the

The culpably
ignorant. opportunity of knowing her, but through indifference and neglect will not take the trouble to procure this knowledge, his ignorance becomes culpable, and he is responsible to God for his neglect. He thus remains outside the Church through his own fault, and becomes as the branch cut off from the trunk, which can produce no fruit : "If he will not hear the Church, let him be to thee as the heathen and the publican " (Matt. xviii. 17).

When, however, among Christian societies, we are seeking

Exterior con-
stitution of the
Church. for the true Church, we must especially consider it in its exterior visible constitution; *i.e.*, we must look for a society composed of all those who, professing the same Faith and participating in the same Sacraments, pay obedience to their lawful Pastors, and especially to a visible Head.

When, therefore, we sincerely use the words,

The one Ark
of Salvation. "*I believe in the Holy Catholic Church,*" we profess that Jesus Christ has established a visible Church, infallible in her teaching, ruling with Divine authority, speaking in the name of her heavenly Founder, and destined to endure for all time: "He that heareth you, heareth Me" (Luke x. 16). Then must we believe and obey her, for she is in very truth the One Ark of Salvation for all, and there can be no salvation for such as, through their own fault, are not within her fold.

CHAPTER XXVIII

THE NINTH ARTICLE OF THE CREED (concluded)

"The Communion of Saints."

By the Communion of Saints is meant the union which exists among all the members of the Church who are on Earth, in Heaven, and in Purgatory; for, with the faithful who compose the Church on Earth, are also spiritually united the Saints in Heaven and the Holy Souls in Purgatory. Thus, we have the *Church Militant* on Earth, the *Church Triumphant* in Heaven, and the *Church Suffering* in Purgatory.

The Church threefold.

Yet, since all share in the "Communion of Saints," these three Churches are, properly speaking, but one Church existing in different states, but united as members of one body, whose Head is Jesus Christ, and participating in one another's prayers and spiritual goods: "For as in one body we have many members . . . so we, being many, are one body in Jesus Christ, and every one members one of another" (Rom. xii. 4, 5); and "He is the Head of the body, the Church" (Col. i. 18).

Yet united in Christ.

By reason of this union, all the spiritual goods that exist in the Church, and all the good works practised within her, are useful to each one of her members. Every one of our bodily mem.

All benefited by this union.

bers has its own function to perform, and this it exercises not merely for its own benefit, but for the benefit of the body as a whole. The eye, for example, does not see for itself, but for the whole body; and so it is with the different members of the Church.

From the words "I believe in the Communion of Saints" we gather that all the members of **Saints of the Church.** this great Communion are styled "Saints," because they either are so in reality, or, having been sanctified by the waters of Baptism, they are called upon to become Saints by leading a virtuous life and striving daily to increase in virtue : " This is the will of God, your sanctification" (1 Thess. iv. 3).

Such sinners as are not cut off from the Church forfeit most of the blessings which come from our **How sinners benefit.** participating in the Communion of Saints ; yet, in virtue of their external union with the Church—by Faith and Hope—they still possess a right to the Sacraments as a means of pardon, and receive many graces and blessings which tend to lead them to a change of life.

"The Faithful on Earth," the Catechism tells us, "are in communion with each other by professing the same Faith, obeying the same authority, and assisting each other with their prayers and good works." **The Church Militant.** Having the same Faith and the same Holy Sacrifice of the Mass, and being united under one Head, they share, on account of this union, in the prayers and good works of the whole Church Militant: " If one member suffer anything, all the members suffer with it ; or if one member glory, all the members rejoice with it. Now you are the body of Christ, and members of member " (1 Cor. xii. 26, 27).

Nor does death dissolve all union between the living and the dead any more than it dissolves their union with

Christ their Head.   Hence we honour the Saints in Heaven
as the glorified members of the Church; we
unite with them in blessing and praising God;
we ask them to intercede for us and obtain
for us blessings and favours ; we partake of the merits
which they acquired while they lived on earth; and are
assisted by their intercession with God on our behalf.
Moreover, by turning away from our sins and imitating
their virtues, we promote their accidental glory in heaven:
"There shall be joy before the Angels of God upon one
sinner doing penance" (Luke xv. 10).

The Church Triumphant.

We are in communion with the Church Suffering by praying for the souls in Purgatory; by helping them
by means of almsdeeds and other good works
and penances ; by trying to gain Indulgences in
their behalf; but especially by offering the Holy Mass for
them.   In this way we perform an act of charity most
pleasing to God in obtaining for them an abatement
of their temporal punishment ; and they, in turn, pray
for us.   Even though they are unable to help themselves, it is a pious belief that their prayers avail us ;
and when at length they reach the harbour of their rest,
can we suppose that they will fail to remember those who
were the means of shortening the time of their sufferings?
"It is a holy and wholesome thought to pray for the dead
that they may be loosed from sins" (2 Mach. xii. 46).

The Church Suffering.

PURGATORY.

As many outside the Church call in question the very
existence of Purgatory, it has been thought well to give
here, at some length, the teaching of the Church in regard
to this subject.

Purgatory is the place or state of suffering in the next
world prepared by Almighty God for the expiation of

unrepented venial sins; and in which those souls also
are detained for a time who have not fully
What is Purgatory?   paid the debt of temporal punishment due to
those sins the guilt and eternal punishment of
which have been forgiven in this world.   The Catholic
Church, then, teaches us—

(1) That there is a Purgatory.

(2) That souls suffer there.

(3) That they are assisted by the prayers and good
works of the living, and especially by the Holy Mass,
which, as a propitiatory Sacrifice, has the power of satisfying the Divine Justice for the living and the dead.

There are many proofs for the existence of Purgatory.
We have the constant teaching of the Church; and Holy
Scripture tells us that God will render to every man
according to his works; that nothing defiled shall enter
heaven; and that some will be saved "*yet so as by fire*"
(1 Cor. iii. 15).   The fire of which St. Paul here speaks is,
according to many of the Fathers and Catholic divines,
the fire of Purgatory.   We may enumerate the chief proofs
as follows:

1. FROM THE OLD TESTAMENT.

It is written that Judas Machabeus sent money to
Jerusalem for sacrifice to be offered for the soldiers who
had fallen on the field of battle, that they
First Proof.   might be delivered from their sins: for, adds the
Sacred Text, "*it is a holy and wholesome thought to pray
for the dead*" (2 Mach. xii. 46).

Now the Jews did not pray for those souls who were
already in Abraham's bosom, since they had no sins to
expiate; nor did they pray for those who were in hell,
since for such their prayers would be of no avail.   They
must, then, have believed that, between Heaven and
Hell, was a middle state.   This state or this place is
what we call Purgatory.

2. FROM THE NEW TESTAMENT.

Our Saviour, in the Gospel, tells us that *blasphemy against the Holy Spirit shall be forgiven neither in this world, nor in the world to come* (Matt. xii. 32).

Second Proof.

There are then some sins which are forgiven in the next world. Now this is not in Heaven, where nothing defiled can enter; nor is it in Hell, whence there is no redemption; it is therefore in a place which is neither Heaven nor Hell. It is in the place that we name Purgatory.

3. THE TRADITION OF THE CATHOLIC CHURCH.

From the time of the Apostles the Church has never ceased to pray and to offer the Holy Sacrifice of the Mass for her departed children. Tertullian (b. A.D. 150), St. Justin, St. Augustine and all the other Fathers of the Church bear witness to this custom; and they tell us moreover that the teaching comes down from the Apostles, and therefore from Jesus Christ.

Third Proof.

4. THE TRADITION OF ANCIENT SECTS SEPARATED FROM THE CATHOLIC CHURCH.

These sects are very numerous, and are spread throughout the East; they are the Nestorians, the Armenians, the Greeks, and many others. They have all preserved, and still preserve, the custom of praying for the dead. They did not borrow the custom from the Church after their separation; they hold it, therefore, from the Apostles and from Christ. To the existence, then, of Purgatory, and to the belief that the prayers of the living can benefit the dead, witness is borne in every age of the Church's history.

Fourth Proof.

CHAPTER XXIX

THE TENTH ARTICLE OF THE CREED

"The Forgiveness of Sins."

" BLESSED be the God and Father of our Lord Jesus
Christ . . . in whom we have redemption through His
Blood, the *remission of sins*, according to the riches of His
grace " (Eph. i. 3, 7).

In the Tenth Article of the Creed we profess our belief

Forgiveness
to be found in
the Church.

in the forgiveness of sins, viz., that Christ left
to the Pastors of His Church, the Bishops, and
the Priests commissioned by them, the power
to forgive sins; for to them only did He say : "Whose sins
you shall forgive, they are forgiven them ; and whose sins
you shall retain, they are retained " (John xx. 23).   There
is, then, in the Church of God forgiveness of sins for those
who properly apply for it ; that is, for those who truly
repent, and worthily receive the Sacraments instituted by
Christ for the remission of sins.

" All power," said our Lord to His disciples, " is given

Christ's promise
to His
Apostles.

to Me in heaven and in earth;" and this
spiritual power He communicated to His
Apostles and their successors in the ministry, as
to His vicars : " As the Father hath sent Me, I also send
you : Receive ye the Holy Ghost : whose sins you shall
forgive, they are forgiven them ; and whose sins you shall
retain, they are retained " (John xx. 21-23).   These words
clearly express the power given to the Apostles and their
successors of forgiving sins in His name.   In exercising
this power they act as His ministers and instruments,
even though they be sinners themselves.

To prove that, " as Man," He possessed the power
to forgive sins on earth, our Lord even condescended to

work a miracle; and as the power of working miracles

Christ's power
proved by a
miracle.

and of forgiving sins is proper to God, He proved, by appealing to the miracle, that He had the power of remitting sins. Now falsehood cannot be confirmed by a miracle, as God would then be bearing testimony to what was not true. To the man, then, sick of the palsy He said: "Son, be of good heart, thy sins are forgiven thee." And when the Scribes said within themselves: "This man blasphemeth," Jesus, in answer to their thoughts, continued: "Why do you think evil in your hearts? Whether is it easier, to say, Thy sins are forgiven thee: or to say, Arise, and walk? But that you may know that the Son of Man hath power on earth to forgive sins,—then said He to the man sick of the palsy—Arise, take up thy bed, and go into thy house. And he arose, and went into his house" (Matt. ix. 2-7). Now it was this same power of forgiving sins that Christ gave to His Apostles after His Resurrection.

The chief means by which this power is exercised, and

Chief means of
forgiveness.

the channels through which the grace of forgiveness flows into our souls, are the Sacraments of Baptism and Penance. Baptism remits *original sin*, together with all actual sins that one may have committed before receiving Baptism; while Penance remits all sins committed *after Baptism,* and hence is of no avail in the case of one who has not been baptised.

Sin, we are told, is an offence against God, by any

What is sin?

thought, word, deed, or omission, against the law of God; and we are further told that there are two kinds of sin, *original* sin and *actual* sin.

Now *original sin* is that guilt or stain of sin in which we

Original Sin.

are conceived and born into the world, and is a result of Adam's sin when he ate the forbidden fruit: "As by one man sin entered into this world, and by sin death, so death passed upon all men, *in whom all have sinned* " (Rom. v. 12). This sin of Adam, who was the origin and head of all mankind, would have excluded both him and us eternally from heaven, had not the Son of God purchased our redemption ; and it is by *Baptism* that the merits of this Redemption are applied to our souls for the remission of *original sin :* " Unless a man be born again of water and the Holy Ghost, he cannot enter into the kingdom of God " (John iii. 5).

All men sinned in Adam, their first parent, and so his sin and its consequent evils are handed down to all his posterity in their very conception. This sin, which is called *original sin,* because we contract it from our origin and head, consists, according to most theologians, in two things, first that the soul is turned away from God, its true end, secondly that it is conceived devoid of sanctifying grace. The first of these two states constitutes the guilt of sin, the second its stain. Had Adam not sinned, we should all have been created in a state of sanctifying grace and pleasing to God.

Original sin is removed from the soul by Baptism, the regenerating waters of which wash away the **Removed by Baptism.** stain contracted in our birth. No shadow of sin remains after this spiritual cleansing, but we are still liable to the consequences of original sin, concupiscence and all the miseries of life—sickness, pain, sorrow, and death.

By original sin, then, man, both with regard to his body and with regard to his soul, fell from the state **Baneful effects of original sin.** of integrity, of justice, and of holiness in which he was created. As a consequence of the fall he lost many gifts which enlightened his understanding with light from on high, strengthened his will against evil, assured to him the mastery over his lower nature, and rendered him exempt from all the ills of life. Thus, *ignorance,* which left the understanding in darkness ; *weak-*

ness, which left the will incapable of doing anything towards salvation without the help of grace; *concupiscence,* which makes itself felt in the cravings of the lower appetites for sensual indulgence; the infirmities of the body, pain, and death: these are some of the consequences of original sin which remain even after its guilt has been forgiven.

Every descendant of Adam has, by generation, contracted the guilt of original sin, with one admirable exception. Mary, the Immaculate Virgin-Mother of God, was, through the merits of her Divine Son, alone of all the children of men conceived without the least guilt or stain of original sin.

CHAPTER XXX

THE TENTH ARTICLE OF THE CREED (*continued*)

THE IMMACULATE CONCEPTION.

OUR Blessed Lady's glorious privilege of being preserved from original sin through the special grace of God and the future merits of her Divine Son, is called the Immaculate Conception, the feast of which we celebrate on the 8th December. The feast itself is very ancient, dating as far back as the twelfth century; and great indulgences have been granted by different Pontiffs to those who worthily celebrate it.

The Immaculate Conception of the glorious Virgin Mary, Mother of God, although only solemnly defined and proclaimed as an article of Faith by Pius IX., on the 8th December, 1854, has ever been the belief of the Church, and no one can now call it in question without at the same time making shipwreck of his Faith.

An Article of Faith.

Although the Immaculate Conception was always *im.*

plicitly contained in the Church's teaching of the absolute purity and sinlessness of Mary, yet, before the *explicit* definition that it was so contained, there was *at one period* a contrary opinion among certain theologians and doctors. This, however, was held as an opinion, not as a doctrine of the Church, and was quite dead before the definition of Trent or of Pius IX.

It may be remarked, in regard to the proclamation of this doctrine, that the Church did not then acquire a new revelation which was wanting to her in the beginning. When it is said that our Saviour grew in grace and in wisdom, we do not mean that He was wiser at any period of His life than He was at the moment of His conception, but that He chose to manifest increasing signs of wisdom as He increased in years; in like manner the Church, which possesses, from her very origin, the wisdom of God, manifests it only according to the order of Providence and the needs of her children.

Another prerogative of Mary is her Assumption into heaven. It is a general belief in the Church

Another prerogative of Mary.

that the Blessed Virgin, immediately after her death, was raised to life again and taken up body and soul into heaven, there to remain in everlasting bliss. So far, however, the Assumption of our Blessed Lady has not been defined as an article of Faith, yet it is a truth that no Catholic would call in question.

So, too, before the dogma of the Immaculate Conception

Belief of the Universal Church.

was proclaimed, it was the teaching of the Church throughout the ages that Mary, in the first moment of her conception, was preserved from original sin. This pious belief was founded on the teaching of the Fathers and of theologians, as well as on the conduct of the Church; for, if the Church had not regarded the Immaculate Conception as an assured fact, she would never have established a feast in honour of our

Lady's Conception, which she did long before the definition of the dogma.

In explaining this doctrine, the Fathers take their
stand on the words of the Angel Gabriel to the
Blessed Virgin : " Hail, *full of grace*, the Lord
is with thee ; blessed art thou among women "
(Luke i. 28), and on the consideration that she, who was
destined to conceive in her womb the Incarnate Word, the
Holy of Holies, must be herself eminently holy, and consequently ought to be preserved, not only from every actual
sin, but also from the least stain of original sin. Gabriel's
words would have fallen short of the truth had Mary, for
a single instant of her existence, been deprived of grace.

Hail, *full of grace*.

The Fathers, moreover, assert that, when God, immediately after man's fall, cursed the serpent and
said : " I will put enmities between thee and the
woman, and between thy seed and *her seed;* she
shall crush thy head " (Gen. iii. 15), it was of Mary that
He spoke, who, by *her seed*, that is to say, her Son, was to
crush the head and demolish the empire of the devil. It
was not fitting, they say, that she who, by becoming the
mother of God, crushed the serpent's head, should have
been even for a moment infected by the serpent's breath,
or a slave of him whose kingdom she had come to destroy
through her Divine Son. The enmity between her and
the serpent is her triumph over sin, her glorious Immaculate Conception. " We cannot think," says St. Bernardin
of Siena, " that the Son of God would have willed to be
born of the Blessed Virgin, or to have clothed Himself
with her flesh, if she had been stained with original sin."

She shall crush thy head..

That God should preserve Mary from original sin was
also befitting the honour of the three Persons
of the Blessed Trinity ; of the Father, whose
cherished daughter she was ; of the Son, whose
mother she was, since He condescended to take

Mary in rela-
tion to the
Three Divine
Persons.

His flesh and blood from her; and of the Holy Spirit, who, in the Mystery of the Incarnation, took Mary to be His spouse, on whom, on account of her exalted dignity, He showered His choicest graces: "Thou art all fair, my love, and there is no spot in thee" (Cant. iv. 7).

If, furthermore, God was able—as He certainly was—to preserve Mary from original sin, and to form her in a state of holiness as He had formed Eve and the Angels, and if her close relationship with the three Divine Persons made it eminently fitting that He should do so, we may justly conclude that He actually did thus form her. This has ever been the Tradition of the Church and the belief of the Fathers; so that, when the saintly Pius IX. declared and solemnly defined, as a dogma revealed by God, that the Blessed Virgin was conceived without the least guilt or stain of original sin, he was but giving the public seal of the Church to what had been the general and constant belief of the universal Church.

CHAPTER XXXI

THE TENTH ARTICLE OF THE CREED (continued)

ACTUAL SIN : THE GRAVITY OF MORTAL SIN.

ONE thing, and only one thing, can separate man from the love of God : viz., sin, which is an offence

Sin. committed by a rational creature against God, his Creator. It is a voluntary act of disobedience against the Divine law; or, as the Catechism defines it, any thought, word, deed, or omission against the law of God.

Sin is a *voluntary* transgression of the law of God, and must not be confused with temptation, which is

Temptation. not an evil. "Blessed is the man that endureth temptation; for when he hath been proved, he shall receive the crown of life" (James i. 12). There are *three* degrees in temptation, the *suggestion, pleasure in the thought*, and *consent*. It is the free acceptance of the will that properly constitutes sin. *First*, then, the devil, or our own frail nature, tempts us by a suggestion of evil thoughts in our *imagination*. To have such thoughts or imaginations may be no sin. On the contrary, if our will remains displeased with them, and resists them, such resistance is meritorious. *Secondly*, these representations may be followed by a delight or delectation in the senses, or in the body only, but if the impression made is against the will, which in no way consents to it, there is again no sin. *Thirdly*, when the will, thus enlightened as to the wickedness of the object, and free to resist, fully consents to what is proposed, sin at once enters the soul.

We have seen that there are two kinds of sin, original sin and actual sin ; and as we have already treated of original sin, we come now to the all-important subject of actual sin.

Actual sin is the sin we commit through our own will,

Actual sin. by our own act, and is thus distinguished from *original* sin, which is the sin in which we were conceived. And as actual sins may vary in the degree of their guilt, they are divided into mortal sins and venial sins.

Mortal sin is a grievous offence against God. It brings

Mortal sin and venial sin. death into the soul by causing us to lose the friendship of God, and by destroying sanctifying grace which is the supernatural life of the soul. Venial sin is committed whenever we transgress the law of God in a slight matter, or in a grave matter when, at the time, either our understanding does not wholly grasp the evil presented to it, or there is wanting full consent of the will.

This difference between light and grievous offences is clearly indicated in St. Matthew by the use of the words *mote* and *beam:* " Why seest thou the mote that is in thy

8

brother's eye; and seest not the beam that is in thy own eye?" (Matt. vii. 3). And again in Proverbs: "A just man shall fall seven times, and shall rise again; but the wicked shall fall down into evil" (xxiv. 16).

Now mortal sin is committed when, by thought, word,
Mortal sin. deed, or omission, we wilfully violate the law of God in any matter deemed at the time important. It deprives the soul of sanctifying grace, closes heaven against it, and renders it deserving of eternal death and everlasting damnation: "I know thy works, that thou hast the name of being alive, and thou art dead" (Apoc. iii. 1). Hence, of all evils mortal sin is the greatest, and this for the following reasons:

1. It is a grievous offence against God—an outrageous
Its malice. insult offered to infinite Majesty. The more exalted in dignity the person offended is above him who offers the insult, the greater the offence; and who are we—miserable creatures—that we should dare to rise up against the infinite majesty of our Creator? It is a revolt against God, an act of wilful disobedience to His holy will: "Thou hast said: I will not serve" (Jer. ii. 20).

2. It is an act of base ingratitude to the best of Fathers, to whom we owe all the good we have or can hope for: "I have brought up children, and exalted them, but they have despised Me" (Isa. i. 2).

3. It is treating with disdain the graces and merits purchased for us by the sufferings and death of our Saviour: "They are fallen away . . . crucifying again to themselves the Son of God, and making Him a mockery" (Heb. vi. 6).

The malice of mortal sin is brought home to our minds
from many considerations:
How seen. 1. In the sight of an all-holy God sin must ever be hateful and abhorrent: "To God the wicked and his wickedness are hateful alike" (Wisd. xiv. 9).

2. It has ever brought in its train the most terrible punishments. One single sin of pride caused the rebel angels to be hurled down from heaven to the lowest depths of hell. One sin of disobedience deprived Adam of original justice, drove him out of Paradise, brought suffering and death upon the whole human race, and closed the gates of heaven to us. It was sin that caused God to shower upon the earth the destroying waters of the Deluge, and brought down fire and brimstone upon Sodom and Gomorrha. On one occasion, for the sins of fornication and idolatry, as many as 24,000 Israelites were slain, as we gather from the twenty-fifth chapter of the Book of Numbers. Indeed the Scriptures give countless instances of the awful severity with which God visited sin, to show how heinous it was in His sight.

3. Yet nothing shows the malice of sin so much as the Passion and bitter death that our Divine Redeemer underwent to satisfy the Divine Justice offended by man's base ingratitude.

In its consequences, too, mortal sin is a most lamentable evil:

Effects of mortal sin.
1. By depriving us of sanctifying grace it destroys the supernatural life of the soul, and separates us from the love and friendship of God.

2. By destroying sanctifying grace in the soul it robs us—as long as the soul remains in this state—of the merit of past and present good works: "All his justices which he hath done shall not be remembered" (Ezech. xviii. 24).

3. Man was made to the image and likeness of his Creator, but mortal sin defaces that image and renders what before was pleasing in the sight of God now hateful and abominable.

4. It brings remorse of conscience, draws down upon us the judgments of God, and condemns us to endless misery.

And yet God, who is infinitely good, cannot punish sin more than it deserves.

Since, then, mortal sin is the greatest of all evils, it is of the utmost importance to know, as clearly as possible, what is its nature. To constitute a mortal sin *three* conditions are required :

What constitutes a mortal sin.

1. *Gravity of matter;* that is, the evil we do, or the duty we leave undone, must actually be, or appear to us to be, a matter of grave importance.

2. *Full advertence of the mind;* that is, we must have a clear and perfect knowledge of the malice of our act, or a belief at least that what we are about to do is a grievous wrong. *Wilful* ignorance does not excuse us from understanding the gravity of an act.

3. *Free and full consent of the will;* that is, realising that what we are about to do is grievously wrong, we nevertheless deliberately resolve to do it. Temptation, as we have shown, is not a sin. If we reject the temptation to do evil without yielding the slightest consent, there is no sin; and if our consent is but partial or imperfect, the sin can only be venial.

If a single one of these three conditions were wanting, there would be either no sin at all, or venial sin at the most.

CHAPTER XXXII

THE TENTH ARTICLE OF THE CREED (*continued*)

VENIAL SIN.

VENIAL sin is that sin which does not kill the soul, yet displeases God, and so often leads to mortal sin. It cools the fervour of Charity, and is deserving of temporal punishment either in this world or hereafter in Purgatory. It is called venial from the

Venial sin.

Latin word *venia*, pardon ; and this because it is more easily pardoned than mortal sin. Its pardon may be obtained not only by the Sacrament of Penance, but also by a sincere act of sorrow, by prayer and the worthy reception of the Sacraments of the living, and by other good works and penances.

Venial sin, as we have seen, is an offence against God in a slight matter, or in a grave matter when either full knowledge or full consent is wanting. Thus every actual sin in which any of the three conditions necessary to constitute a mortal sin is absent, remains only a venial sin ; that is, the sin is venial when the matter is not grave ; when full advertence of the mind is wanting ; and when there is not full consent of the will. It is no sin at all if there be no advertence or no consent. Yet, even in a small matter, a person might be guilty of a mortal sin if in his mind he believed it to be grave, and deliberately committed the offence. But any number of venial sins cannot constitute a mortal sin, and consequently cannot destroy sanctifying grace in the soul.

What constitutes a venial sin.

But although venial sin does not deprive us of the friendship of God, yet it is, after mortal sin, the greatest of evils, and may never be committed to obtain any good however great.

Venial sin a great evil.

A great danger arising from the commission of frequent venial sin is that it may lead us by degrees to the commission of grievous sin, particularly when it has become a habit with us: "He that contemneth small things shall fall by little and little" (Ecclus. xix. 1). And St. James: "Behold how small a fire kindleth a great wood" (iii. 5). Venial sin, too, renders us less pleasing to God ; while tepidity in a Christian life, and in the service of God, is oftentimes more dangerous than absolute wickedness : "Because thou art lukewarm, and neither cold nor hot, I will begin to vomit thee out of My

The dangers of venial sin.

mouth" (Apoc. iii. 16). It also weakens the soul and
cools the fervour of charity. If mortal sin kills the soul
by depriving it of the grace and friendship of God, venial
sin, in some measure, wounds it by diminishing the power
of grace and the ardour of Divine love. For just as small
ailments or a bruise do not kill the body, but injure its
strength and impair its vitality, so venial sin enfeebles
the soul and hinders many graces which God would otherwise give it. That it argues a weakness of our love of God
we gather from the words, " He that hath My commands
and keepeth them, he it is that loveth Me" (John xiv. 21).
No sinful affection can be referred to God.

From the foregoing, then, we learn with what care we
Especially when should try to avoid even venial sins, especially
deliberate or such as are deliberate or habitual, both on
habitual. account of the evil they are in themselves, and
of their terrible consequences : "Every idle word that men
shall speak, they shall render an account for it in the day
of judgment" (Matt. xii. 36). And, as no one would
venture to say that for an idle word God would condemn
a soul to hell for all eternity, there must be a place of
temporal punishment hereafter for the expiation of these
lesser faults. There is, then, Purgatory to be faced as a
consequence of venial sin : ",Amen, I say to thee, thou shalt
not go out from thence, till thou pay the last farthing"
(Matt. v. 26).

CHAPTER XXXIII

THE ELEVENTH ARTICLE OF THE CREED

" The Resurrection of the Body."

As death is the separation of the soul from the body, so the
Resurrection is their reunion. At death man's
Death. soul quits its mortal abode, the body, and
appears before the judgment-seat of God, but his body

returns to the earth whence it came: "The dust shall return into the earth from whence it was, and the spirit to God who gave it" (Eccles. xii. 7). "It is appointed unto men once to die, and after this the judgment" (Heb. ix. 27).

Before the general judgment all mankind must die : death is no respecter of persons, and is decreed against all the children of Adam: "As by one man sin entered into the world, and by sin death, so death passed upon all men" (Rom. v. 12).

The body will remain in the earth till the last day, when God will send His Angel to call the dead to life ; and in an instant man's soul will be reunited to his body from which it had been separated by death: "For the trumpet shall sound, and the dead shall rise again incorruptible" (1 Cor. xv. 52). "The hour cometh wherein all that are in the graves shall hear the voice of the Son of God. And they that have done good things shall come forth unto the resurrection of life ; but they that have done evil unto the resurrection of judgment" (John v. 28, 29). Then all, both good and bad, shall live for ever, the good in everlasting happiness, the wicked in everlasting misery.

The Resurrection of the body.

Every soul will be united again to the same body which it had in this life, in order that, as the body was its partner in doing good or evil, it also may share its reward or punishment: "We must all appear before the judgment-seat of Christ, that every one may receive the proper things of the body, according as he hath done, whether it be good or evil" (2 Cor. v. 10). Since man, then, has to be judged, and rewarded or punished according to his works, God's justice, to be complete, demands that he should rise again ; for man is not a soul separated from a body, nor a body separated from a soul, but the union of soul and body. Moreover,

Why our bodies shall rise again.

by our resurrection from the dead, Christ's victory over death is complete : " When this mortal hath put on immortality, then shall come to pass the saying that is written : Death is swallowed up in victory. O death, where is thy victory ?   O death, where is thy sting ?" (1 Cor. xv. 54, 55).

God is able to raise the dead to life. Since God can do all things, He can as easily raise our bodies from the dust as He was able, in the beginning, to make Adam's body out of the slime of the earth.   And if He was able to give us life when we had it not, He can just as easily restore it after He has once taken it from us.   To show this, St. Paul gives us the example of a grain of wheat, which must corrupt and die, as it were, in the ground ; and then, being quite changed, it comes up with a blade, a stalk, and an ear, quite different from what it was when sown ; yet it becomes wheat again : so God can raise our bodies from the dust as He pleases.   St. Paul also tells us that, as there are many different bodies, some terrestrial, some celestial, some more, some less glorious, differing in beauty and other qualities, and that, as the sun is brighter than the moon, and one star brighter than another, so shall it be with the risen bodies of men at the general resurrection (1 Cor. xv.).

Importance of this doctrine. " If there be no resurrection of the dead," says St. Paul, " then Christ is not risen again.   And if Christ be not risen again, then is our preaching vain, and your faith is also vain " (1 Cor. xv. 13, 14). Hence, our very hope of salvation rests on the doctrine of the Resurrection, as on a solid foundation.   But " I know that my Redeemer liveth, and in the last day I shall rise out of the earth ; and I shall be clothed again with my skin, and in my flesh I shall see my God ; whom I myself shall see, and my eyes shall behold, and not another : this, my hope, is laid up in my bosom " (Job xix. 25-27).

When we rise again in the perfect state of man—body and soul united—there will be a great diffei-

Qualities of a glorified body. ence between the good and the bad; for the bodies of the just, as we gather from St. Paul's first Epistle to the Corinthians (xv.), will then possess four principal qualities or endowments:

1. *Impassibility*, which will render them incapable of suffering or pain. And St. John, in the Apocalypse, tells us: "God will wipe away all tears from their eyes; and death shall be no more, nor mourning, nor crying, nor sorrow shall be any more; for the former things are passed away" (xxi. 4).

2. *Brightness*, which will render them glorious as the sun. Yet all will not have an equal brightness, but a brightness according to the merits of the blessed: "One is the glory of the sun, another the glory of the moon, and another the glory of the stars" (1 Cor. xv. 41).

3. *Agility*, which will deliver the body from the weight which bears it down to the earth, and will enable it, as quick as thought, to pass from one part of creation to another: "It is sown in weakness, it shall rise in power" (1 Cor. xv. 43).

4. *Subtility*, by which the body will share the spiritual existence of the soul, and which will render it capable, like the Body of our Saviour after His Resurrection, of passing through all material substances: "It is sown a natural body, it shall rise a spiritual body" (1 Cor. xv. 44). "Our Lord Jesus Christ will reform the body of our lowness, that it may be made like to the body of His glory" (Phil. iii. 21).

The very reverse of these gifts or endowments will be the lot of the reprobate, as a punishment of their self-indulgence and wickedness.

The thought of the resurrection of the body should be an incentive to us never to abuse our body by sin, but to

yield our members " to serve justice unto sanctification "
What the (Rom. vi. 19). It should enable us, too, to
Resurrection suffer pain, and even death itself, with perfect
teaches. resignation to the will of God : " For I know
that my Redeemer liveth, and in the last day I shall rise
out of the earth" (Job xix. 25). And, lastly, it should
prove a fruitful source of consolation on the death of
those whom we love : " We will not have you ignorant,
brethren, concerning them that are asleep, that you may
not be sorrowful, even as others who have no hope"
(1 Thess. iv. 12).

CHAPTER XXXIV

THE TWELFTH ARTICLE OF THE CREED

" And Life Everlasting. Amen."

THE words " *Life Everlasting* " mean that after this life ·
there is another that will last for all eternity ;
Life Ever- that after the General Judgment man will die
lasting. no more, but will continue for ever either in a
state of perfect happiness with God, or of misery with
the devil. We were all created for the enjoyment of
perfect happiness, and were placed in the world to know,
love, and serve God, that thereby we might attain to that
great end of our creation. Thus two eternities await us,
one of which will surely be our lot, an eternity of happiness
if we remain faithful to God, or an eternity of misery if
we wilfully despise Him.

When we speak of heaven, or of the eternal life of
the Blessed, we mean not only that the Saints
Heaven. will live for ever, but that their happiness will
be unalloyed and without end ; that the joy of heaven,
once gained, can never be lost : " The just shall go into
everlasting life " (Matt. xxv. 46).

The happiness of heaven consists in the Beatific Vision, that is, in seeing, loving, and enjoying God for all eternity. The just will then see God as He is, and be united with Him in bonds of the most perfect charity: "We now see through a glass in an obscure manner; but then face to face" (1 Cor. xiii. 12). With the Beatific Vision is conjoined the possession of all good things. The wants and ills of this life shall pass away, to be replaced by eternal joy and glory in the company of the Angels and the Saints: "For the Lamb shall rule them, and shall lead them to the fountains of the waters of life, and God shall wipe away all tears from their eyes" (Apoc. vii. 17). The unceasing delight of the Saints exceeds all that can be described or imagined; for "eye hath not seen, nor ear heard, neither hath it entered into the heart of man, what things God hath prepared for them that love Him" (1 Cor. ii. 9). What we do know is that they possess and enjoy all that can be desired, and that their state of blessedness, made perfect by the union of all good things, shall last for ever.

Yet all will not be equally happy, nor will reward be according to success, but according to patience under trials and sufferings, and diligence in God's service: "Every man shall receive his own reward according to his own labour" (1 Cor. iii. 8): "He who soweth sparingly shall also reap sparingly; and he who soweth in blessings shall also reap blessings" (2 Cor. ix. 6). And again, in the words of St. Paul: "There is one glory of the sun, another glory of the moon, and another glory of the stars; for star differeth from star in glory. So also is the resurrection of the dead" (1 Cor. xv. 41, 42). Thus, not only will those who have acquired great merit reap a greater reward of honour and glory, but their glory will differ according to the special virtues and merits of each: "He will render to

every man according to his works " (Matt. xvi. 27). Yet
amid this inequality all will be perfectly content and
happy, rejoicing in one another's happiness, and blessing
the justice of God.

There are, however, *three classes* of the Saints to whom
a special glory is promised, and whose crowns
will be marked with a distinctive brightness:

Special glory
assigned.

1. *The Doctors* of the Church, learned in
the law of God and true wisdom, and leading men to
the knowledge and love of God: "They that instruct
many to justice shall shine as stars for all eternity"
(Dan. xii. 3).

2. *The Martyrs*, who have overcome the world and
laid down their life rather than deny their faith even in
appearance. And just as our Saviour still bears in His
glorified Body the marks of His Sacred Wounds, so too
will they ever retain the traces of their sufferings in their
own glorified wounds.

3. *The Virgins*, who by their self-denial have overcome the temptations of the flesh: "They sing, as it were,
a new canticle before the throne, and follow the Lamb
whithersoever He goeth" (Apoc. xiv. 3, 4).

Since, then, the good are destined to live for ever in
the glory and happiness of heaven; and since
Christ has given to all, without exception, the
power to be made the sons of God (John i. 12),
with what care should we work out our salvation! With
St. Paul we should learn to regard the sufferings of this
present time as not worthy to be compared with the
glory to come that shall be revealed in us (Rom. viii. 18).
"Before man is life and death; that which he shall choose ·
shall be given him" (Ecclus. xv. 18).

Salvation
offered to all.

If God's justice thus induces Him to reward with
unspeakable glory and happiness the fidelity of the just,
it also requires Him to visit with a corresponding

severity all those who refuse to serve Him, and who
trample underfoot the graces He so generously
holds out to them. The happy state and
abode of the just we call Heaven; the miserable
eternity of the lost we call Hell, the state and place
in which Divine justice punishes, and will punish for all
eternity, all those who die in unrepented mortal sin.
It is of Faith that there is a Hell; that its duration is
eternal; and that the wicked will there be tormented
for ever in company with the devil and the lost angels.
Our Lord Himself has told us this in the terrible doom
that He will pass on the reprobate immediately after
the Last Judgment: "Depart from Me, ye cursed, into
everlasting fire, which was prepared for the devil and his
angels" (Matt. xxv. 41).

Eternity of Hell.

In this place of punishment the wicked will experience
various kinds of torment (Luke xvi. 28); but
Faith tells us of two in particular, the pain of
loss and the pain of sense. The pain of loss will
arise from their regret at having irreparably lost God,
their only good; and the thought of the many graces they
have abused will fill them with internal torture and despair.
This is the greatest pain that a being endowed with reason
can possibly suffer. The fact that they are separated from
God and all that is good will afflict the lost with incon-
ceivable grief; and this their misery will be unceasing and
eternal: "It is better for thee to enter lame into life everlasting, than, having two feet, to be cast into the hell of
unquenchable fire; where *their worm dieth not*, and the fire
'is not extinguished" (Mark ix. 44, 45). This *worm*, or
fruitless repentance of the wicked, is the gnawing of
conscience ever reproving them for their base folly: "I
have lost God; I have lost Him through my own fault;
I have lost Him for a mere trifle; I have lost Him
irrevocably!"

The pain of loss.

The second pain of the damned is the pain of sense,
or the suffering caused by the fire of Hell,
The pain of sense. which burns, but without consuming, and
which shall never be extinguished; that fire in
which the lost are always dying, yet never die: " And
the rich man also died, and was buried in hell.   And lift-
ing up his eyes when he was in torments, he saw Abraham
afar off, and Lazarus in his bosom; and he cried and said:
Father Abraham, have mercy on me, and send Lazarus, that
he may dip the tip of his finger in water to cool my tongue,
for I am tormented in this flame " (Luke xvi. 22-24).

These two pains—the pain of loss and the pain of sense
—correspond with the malice of sin, which is a despising
of God, our Creator, and an irregular love of the creature.
" He that committeth sin," says St. John, " is of the
devil" (1 John iii. 8).

But as all the just will not be equally happy, so neither
will the pains of the lost be of equal intensity.
Punishment in proportion to sin. Each will suffer in proportion to his sins and
to his abuse of the graces offered to Him:
" Unto whomsoever much is given, of him much shall be
required " (Luke xii. 48); and " God will render to every
man according to his works" (Matt. xvi. 27).

All ought often to dwell on the sufferings of Hell with
a view to escaping them, since the thought of
The thought of Hell. the everlasting pains of the damned is sufficient to deter men from sin: " In all thy
works remember thy last end, and thou shalt never
sin " (Ecclus. vii. 40).   " Enter ye in at the narrow gate;
for wide is the gate and broad is the way that leadeth to
destruction, and many there are who go in thereat.   How
narrow is the gate and straight is the way which leadeth
to life; and few there are who find it !" (Matt. vii. 13, 14).
It is the diligent servant who shall enter into the joy of
his Lord; but the unprofitable servant shall be cast into

the exterior darkness, where there " shall be weeping and gnashing of teeth " (Matt. xxv.).

The Creed is brought to a close by the word "*Amen*," a Hebrew word meaning " *so be it*," by which
Amen. we renew our expression of belief in the twelve Articles of the Creed, as well as our express resolve to live up to our belief, and to remain steadfast in it until death.

PART II

HOPE

" Blessed be the man that trusteth in the Lord, and the Lord shall be his confidence " (JER. xvii. 7).

CHAPTER XXXV

THE THEOLOGICAL VIRTUE OF HOPE

WE are told that, to save our souls, we must worship God by *Faith, Hope,* and *Charity.* We have treated **Necessity of** of Faith under the Articles of the Creed, and **Hope.** we come now to the second of the Theological Virtues, the virtue of Hope, which St. Paul calls the anchor of the soul, secure and firm (Heb. vi. 19); and St. Augustine " the walls of the Spiritual House of the soul." Faith alone, the Catechism teaches us, will not save us without good works; we must also have *Hope* and Charity.

Like Faith, Hope is a virtue which cannot be attained by our own efforts: it is a gift of God infused into our souls at Baptism, and, like Faith, is absolutely necessary for salvation : " We are saved by Hope" (Rom. viii. 24).

The Theological Virtue of Hope, then, is a supernatural **Hope defined.** gift of God, by which we firmly trust that God will give us, through the merits of Jesus Christ, eternal life, and all the graces and helps necessary to obtain it, if we do what He requires of us. It is thus a desire and expectation of salvation, together with an assured confidence of obtaining it through the infinite goodness, power, and mercy of God, if, on our part, we make a right use of the helps He holds out to us.

128

Our Hope, then, rests on a sure foundation, grounded as
it is, first, on God's infinite goodness, on His
almighty power, and on His fidelity to His
promises; and secondly, on the infinite merits
of our Saviour. Even the greatest and most abandoned
sinner need never despair, but can always hope for pardon,
if only he will repent, and turn away from his sins: "If
the wicked do penance for all his sins which he hath committed, and keep all My Commandments, and do judgment and justice, living he shall live, and shall not die"
(Ezech. xviii. 21); and this, not because the sinner
deserves any favour, but because God is good. It is by
the virtue of Hope that we pay direct homage to God's
infinite goodness, power, and fidelity to His promises.

Grounds or motives of Hope.

Two great qualities must ever stand out in this most
necessary virtue, complete distrust in ourselves,
and perfect confidence in God: "Without
Me you can do nothing" (John xv. 5). And
what blessings may he not hope for who thus places his
entire confidence in God? "Because he hath hoped in
Me, I will deliver him. . . . He shall cry to Me, and I will
hear him" (Ps. xc. 14, 15).

Qualities of Hope.

Hope is called a Theological Virtue, too, because, like
Faith, it has God not only for its motive, but
also for its immediate object. The object of
our Hope is God Himself, whom we look forward to
possess for all eternity, seeing that He has promised us
all the means for arriving at the possession of Him.

Object of Hope.

But when we have really set our hearts on the attaining
of some object, we must necessarily desire the
means by which alone we may attain it. These
means we call the secondary objects of our
desire. And as we cannot come to the possession of God
without making use of the graces which He holds out to us,
these graces and helps become the *secondary object* of Hope,

Primary and secondary object.

God Himself being its great *primary object*. In a word, then, the grace of God in this world and Himself in the next form the complete object of the Christian's Hope.

Even temporal goods, such as health and prosperity, we may hope for and pray for from God, in so far The hope of as they may help us, or at least not hinder us, temporal goods. in the way of salvation. But to set our hearts on the things of this world without any reference to God, merely with a view to our own personal gratification, might become sinful according as our desires were more or less inordinate ; for to do these things, expressly excluding all reference to God, is wrong: "Be not solicitous, there-fore, saying : What shall we eat, or what shall we drink, or wherewith shall we be clothed ? . . . Your Father knoweth that you have need of all these things. Seek ye, there-fore, first the kingdom of God and His justice, and all these things shall be added unto you " (Matt. vi. 31-33).

Since to hope is to expect with confidence that God will give us eternal life, Hope cannot exist after The Subject death. The Blessed in Heaven are already in of Hope. possession of what formerly they hoped for ; and even with the souls in Purgatory the great goal of their lives on earth is secure: "We are saved by hope. But hope that is seen is not hope: for what a man seeth, why does he hope for ?" (Rom. viii. 24). Nor can it exist in the lost souls, for their sentence also is irrevocably fixed: "Depart from Me, ye cursed, into *everlasting* fire" (Matt. xxv. 41). Moreover, as Hope is based on Faith, it cannot exist without Faith ; so that, even in this world, the man who is without Faith is necessarily without Hope: "You were at that time without Christ . . . and strangers to the testaments, having no hope of the promise, and without God in this world " (Eph. ii. 12). Faith, Hope, and Charity, as we have already seen, are infused into our Faith and Hope may still remain if the mortal sin be not directly subversive of these virtues, as apostasy and despair.

Although Hope is a gift of God, we are bound to
nourish it by the constant practice of it. We
are commanded to worship God by Faith, *Hope*,
and Charity, and consequently we are under
the obligation of practising this virtue sufficiently often
to keep up the habit of it. It is nourished by faith and
prayer, and is strengthened by repeated acts. We are
bound, furthermore, on particular occasions to make acts
of this virtue ; for example,

Acts of Hope necessary.

1. When we come to understand what God is and His
promises to us.

2. When we are tempted against it by despair and the
only way to put the temptation to flight is by making an
act of Hope; for it is by making the contrary acts that
we more effectively resist temptations of this kind.

3. When we are in danger of death. In this terrible
moment we should unite ourselves to God by Hope by
recalling to our minds the infinite merits of Jesus Christ,
who died for the salvation of all.

But this obligation is sufficiently fulfilled by all Catholics
who say their usual prayers, hear Holy Mass, or receive
the Sacraments in a spirit of faith and hope.

The sins directly opposed to Hope are *Despair* and
Presumption. Despair is a distrust of obtaining either salvation or the necessary graces and
helps to that end. It is a most pernicious evil, since it
deadens all our spiritual endeavours, fills the soul with
sadness, causes us to abandon prayer, and leaves us exposed
to every vice.

Despair.

We sin by despair whenever, on account of the difficulties
we meet with, we give up hope of arriving at eternal
happiness; whenever we regard our sins either as too
numerous or too great for pardon ; or our passions as too
strong to be overcome ; and, in a lesser degree, by what is
called diffidence in God when, by a want of confidence in
the goodness of God, we give up hope of obtaining what
we ask for in prayer because it is deferred.

The sure remedies against despair are prayer, making acts of Hope, reflecting on the merits of our Saviour, on the goodness, power and promises of God, on His care for the least of His creatures, and on His extreme readiness to pardon even the greatest sinners, as we gather from the Parables of the Prodigal Son and the Lost Sheep.

Remedies against Despair.

The second sin opposed to Hope is Presumption, which is a rash expectation of salvation and the graces necessary to lead us to it, without taking the means thereto; for example, without faithfully keeping the Commandments of God or of the Church. It is nothing less than making the Divine Goodness an excuse and an encouragement to sin.

Presumption.

Those sin by presumption who, relying on the mercy of God, continue in their sins with the intention of repenting before it is too late; or who make their salvation depend upon their own strength and not upon God; or who rashly expose themselves to the proximate occasions of sin in the expectation that God will come to their rescue.

The remedies against presumption are chiefly prayer and humility. We should remember what the Saints have done to gain heaven, and ever bear in mind the words of our Saviour: "The kingdom of heaven suffereth violence, and the violent bear it away" (Matt. xi. 12).

Its remedies.

Hope, then, or true confidence in God, requires that we should not be excessively uneasy about our salvation—which may mean despair, as was the case with Cain: "My iniquity is greater than that I may deserve pardon" (Gen. iv. 13); and that we should not throw off all sense of fear and anxiety in regard to it—which may mean presumption: "With fear and trembling work out your salvation" (Phil. ii. 12).

CHAPTER XXXVI

THE MEANING OF GRACE

By the virtue of Hope we expect with confidence that God will give us eternal life and all the means necessary to obtain it if, on our part, we faithfully observe His holy Law. Now, as we cannot, without the help of God's grace, do any good work towards our salvation, and as God's grace is obtained chiefly by Prayer and the Holy Sacraments, we propose to treat next of Grace and Prayer, inasmuch as they relate to Hope and are the great means by which our hopes are realised.

"Without Faith," says St. Paul, "it is impossible to please God" (Heb. xi. 6); yet Faith alone is *Necessity of good works.* not sufficient, and will not avail without good works: "What shall it profit . . . if a man say he hath Faith, but hath not works? Shall Faith be able to save him? . . . By works a man is justified, and not by Faith only. . . . For as the body without the spirit is dead, so also Faith without works is dead" (James ii. 14, 24, 26). Therefore it is not enough to have Faith, we must practise it by doing good works.

But of ourselves, that is by our own natural strength, we can do nothing that will secure our eternal *Necessity of Grace.* salvation. God's grace is absolutely necessary: "For without Me you can do nothing" (John xv. 5). And here by Grace we mean those supernatural helps given to us by God, through the merits of our Saviour, for our eternal salvation. Nor will Grace work alone without our co-operation; for, as St. Augustine says, "He who made us without our concurrence will not save us without our concurrence."

To see God as He is in Himself belongs to God alone,

and no man, by his nature, can lay claim to a destiny so
sublime; eternal salvation, the vision of God
Grace is supernatural. face to face, as well as the means which lead to
it, is a good which belongs entirely to the super-
natural order.   Thus it is that the supernatural order
comprises two things, *a supernatural end*, and *the means*
of attaining that end.   The supernatural end consists in
the Beatific Vision of God in heaven ; and the means by
which this supernatural end is to be attained must also
be supernatural : this supernatural means is *Grace*.

Man, merely by his natural gifts, may perform many
acts of natural virtue which entitle him to a
The state of grace. certain degree of peace and joy, but not to the
bliss of heaven.   The morally good actions
which he performs may proceed from his own good will,
yet, of themselves, they can neither merit nor obtain grace
or salvation, but they can prepare him for the reception of
grace : " No man can come to Me, unless it be given him
by My Father " (John vi. 66).   If it were otherwise, it
would not have been necessary for our Saviour to come
down from heaven to merit for us grace and salvation by
His bitter Passion and Death : " Not that we are sufficient
to think anything of ourselves, as of ourselves ; but our
sufficiency is from God " (2 Cor. iii. 5).   But to raise us
above the mere state of nature, to enable us to become
holy, children of God and heirs to the kingdom of heaven,
a higher principle than that of nature is necessary ; and
this higher principle is what we mean by *Grace*.

When God created man, He was in no sense bound to
grant him the happiness of being made with a
How Adam's loss is restored. right to the direct vision of God, and, in a
sense, to share in His own Divine nature : " By
whom He hath given us very great and precious promises :
that by these you may be made partakers of the Divine
nature " (2 Pet. i. 4).   Yet this right was freely conferred

upon Adam, until, by his disobedience, he lost his rights as a child of God. After his fall, his *natural* gifts and powers were left to him, it is true, though impaired ; but his *supernatural* gifts were taken away. And as Adam stood for the whole human race, all mankind became involved in his sin, and fell with him ; yet " God so loved the world as to give His Only begotten Son, that whosoever believeth in Him may not perish, but may have life everlasting " (John iii. 16). God the Son, then, in becoming man and dying for our salvation, restored to man the gifts which he had lost, by purchasing for him the right to grace and everlasting glory and happiness.

We see then that by Grace is understood all those
Grace defined. *supernatural* gifts and helps which God in His goodness has bestowed upon us to enable us, by doing His will, to attain the state of adoption of sons and the right to an eternal reward. Grace, in general, may be defined as a supernatural and gratuitous gift of God,'bestowed upon us for our sanctification and salvation.

Grace comes to us from God, and from God alone ; but, since the fall of Adam, it has been given to man only in view of the merits of Jesus Christ, who offered Himself to God the Father as a Victim of propitiation for the whole human race. It is the fruit of the Passion of Christ flowing to us from His Sacred Wounds as from an in-exhaustible source. Without it we can do nothing in the order of salvation ; it is the essential condition of our union with God, and by it we are reinstated in the supernatural order : " For by grace you are saved through faith, and this not of yourselves ; for it is the gift of God " (Eph. ii. 8).

But the graces which God gives us to raise us to this
External and supernatural union with Him are partly within
Internal Graces. and partly without us, and, consequently, may be divided into *external* and *internal* graces.

External graces include all those visible and sensible means and helps to salvation which exist outside ourselves, as sermons, instructions, spiritual books, missions, Catholic education, and the like. We are bound to attend to these graces, and profit by them, and we shall have to render an account of them hereafter, since they generally become—by our making a proper use of them—the occasions on which God bestows upon us His inward graces.

Internal graces include those spiritual gifts which God bestows inwardly on our souls, as Faith, Hope, Charity, inspirations, and good thoughts.

Although all graces are, of their very nature, gratuitous, having been freely bestowed upon us by God without any deserts on our part, yet there are certain internal graces which we speak of as "graces gratuitously bestowed," falling as they do under no special class. These graces, such as the working of miracles and the gift of tongues, are given more for the profit of others than for the benefit of him who possesses them. St. Philip Neri and the Curé d'Ars had special graces or special insight bestowed upon them to help souls particularly in the confessional. This internal grace was given not so much for their own sanctification as for those who came to them for spiritual consolation.

Graces gratuitously bestowed.

St. Paul, in order to curb the vanity of such as seemed to be somewhat puffed up with these "gratuitously bestowed graces," and likewise to comfort those who had received no such extraordinary favours, clearly points out that it is the same Holy Spirit who distributes these graces according as they are conducive to the welfare of the Church and the glory of God: "To one indeed, by the Spirit, is given the word of wisdom; and to another the word of knowledge, according to the same Spirit; to another faith; to another the grace of healing; to another the working of miracles; to another prophecy; to another the discerning of spirits; to another diverse kinds of tongues; to another interpretation of speeches. But all these things one and the same Spirit worketh, dividing to every one according as He will " (1 Cor. xii. 8-11).

Again, to show that the gift of miracles and of prophecy is bestowed on men not for their own good, but for the advantage of others, and that even the wicked may possess these graces, we have the words of our Lord : " Many will say to Me in that day : Lord, Lord, have we not prophesied in Thy name, and cast out devils in Thy name, and done many miracles in Thy name ? And then will I profess unto them, I never knew you : depart from Me, you that work iniquity " (Matt. vii. 22, 23).

It remains for us next to treat of grace under the two headings of *Actual Grace* and *Habitual Grace*, for Sacramental Grace explains itself. As the name implies, it is the special grace separately signified and conveyed to the soul by each of the Sacrament'

CHAPTER XXXVII

ACTUAL GRACE

God renders the soul pleasing in His sight by *acting* upon it from time to time and by permanently *abiding* within it, that is by *Actual Grace,* and by *Habitual* or *Sanctifying Grace.*

Actual Grace, which may be termed the action of the Holy Ghost on the soul, is a passing Divine Meaning of influence, a supernatural help given to us by Actual Grace. God at a particular moment to avoid an evil or to do some good, and thus to work out our salvation. It works in the soul by enlightening the understanding to see what is good and what is evil ; it helps us to overcome temptation by inclining the will to choose the good and

to avoid the evil ; and it gives a supernatural dignity
to our actions: "Give me understanding, and I will
search Thy law, and I will keep it with my whole heart"
(Ps. cxviii. 34).

From the words of St. Paul we gather how necessary
this grace is before we can begin, or continue,
Necessity of Actual Grace. or fulfil even the least work in the way of
salvation : " It is God who worketh in you both
to will and to accomplish according to His good will"
(Phil. ii. 13). Without Actual Grace the sinner cannot
rise from his sins, nor can the just man persevere in virtue;
for, since our salvation is a good of a supernatural order,
it can be secured only by means of a supernatural help, viz.,
the grace of God. Works performed without grace may,
as we have already seen, be good *natural* actions, but they
cannot be meritorious except through the merits of Christ,
and grace is the only means by which His merits can be
applied to our souls : " No man can come to Me unless it
be given him by My Father " (John vi. 66).

God offers grace to the soul whenever He suggests a
good thought, or shows it the truth, or points
Co-operation with Grace necessary. out some duty to be fulfilled, or some good to
be done ; yet co-operation with this proffered
grace is necessary : " Behold," He says, " I stand at the
gate and knock ; if any man shall hear My voice, and open
to Me the door, I will come in to him, and will sup with
him, and he with Me " (Apoc. iii. 20). Yet, although it
would be wrong to resist the proffered grace, God still
leaves us free to accept or reject it : " To-day if you shall
hear His voice, harden not your hearts" (Ps. xciv. 8).
And again : " Jerusalem, Jerusalem . . . how often would
I have gathered together thy children, as a hen gathereth
her chickens under her wings, and thou wouldst not"
(Matt. xxiii. 37). If we will the suggested good, and
accept what God wishes of us, He will give us further grace

to enable us to carry our good resolution into effect. We ought always, then, to ask God that we may be ever faithful to the graces which, in His goodness, He is constantly · offering us.

But with those who correspond, God's grace is all-powerful: "I can do all things in Him who strengtheneth me" (Phil. iv. 13). Strengthened with grace, the just man overcomes every temptation and will brave persecution, and even death itself, rather than offend God; while the most abandoned sinner, with the same supernatural help, may cast off the chains of sin which fetter him and be restored to the friendship of God. Although from the sinner God withholds His special graces, yet He always leaves him the grace of prayer that, by a proper use of this grace, he may obtain further graces and save his soul. They who perish, perish by their own fault, because they refuse to listen to the voice of God calling them to salvation.

Grace is all-powerful.

God, then, gives all men sufficient grace to work out their salvation: "To every man is given grace according to the measure of the gift of Christ" (Eph. iv. 7). It is, moreover, His will that all men be saved; and if man will but do his part, nothing will be wanting on the part of God: "Who will have all men to be saved, and to come to the knowledge of the truth" (1 Tim. ii. 4). Even the most hardened sinners receive graces which, if corresponded with, will bring them back to God: "As I live, saith the Lord God, I desire not the death of the wicked, but that the wicked turn from his ways and live" (Ezech. xxxiii. 11). And our Lord Himself tells us in St. Matthew: "The Son of Man is come to save that which was lost" (xviii. 11).

Distribution of Grace.

Although God wills the salvation of all men, yet He does not give an equal amount of grace to all, but distributes to every one according as He wills, giving more

to some and less to others; and of the graces each one
has received he must render a strict account: "Unto
whomsoever much is given, of him much shall be
required" (Luke xii. 48). All men, then, have it in
their power to receive supernatural help from God which
will enable them, by carefully corresponding with it, to
attain eternal life.

CHAPTER XXXVIII

SANCTIFYING OR HABITUAL GRACE

SANCTIFYING or Habitual Grace is a supernatural gift of
God which the Holy Ghost freely communi-
cates to our souls, and by which we are made
children of God, pleasing in His sight, and
heirs to the kingdom of heaven. It is an *abiding*
influence dwelling in our souls and rendering us just and
holy before God.

Sanctifying Grace defined.

It is through Sanctifying Grace that we are born again
children of God, and that our souls receive
supernatural life: "Behold what manner of
charity the Father hath bestowed upon us,
that we should be called, and should be the sons of God"
(1 John iii. 1). Sanctifying Grace is to the soul what
life is to the body. Hence, when we say that mortal sin
kills the soul, we mean that it takes away from the soul
Sanctifying Grace, which is its supernatural life.

The life of the soul.

Not only is Sanctifying Grace the gift of the Holy
Spirit, but there is given to us the Spirit Himself, who resides in our soul as in His own
temple, who sanctifies it, and makes it partaker of His Divine love: "The Charity of
God is poured out into our hearts by the Holy Ghost
who is given to us" (Rom. v. 5). With Sanctifying

The soul becomes the temple of the Holy Ghost.

Grace, then, God Himself comes into our hearts according to those words of our Lord: "If any one love Me, My Father will love him, and We will come to him, and will make Our abode with him" (John xiv. 23).

Other graces accompany Sanctifying Grace. Sanctifying Grace is always united with Charity; yet it brings along with it other graces besides Charity. With it are infused into the soul the other Theological Virtues as well as the Cardinal and other moral virtues, and the gifts of the Holy Ghost.

We sometimes speak of Sanctifying Grace as the "Grace of Justification," because by it man is sanctified, and passes from the state of sin to the state of justice or righteousness. It may be acquired by Baptism, by Penance, or by an act of perfect charity; and once possessed, it can be driven away only by mortal sin. It is preserved by fidelity to the law of God; it is increased by prayer and good works, and by the worthy reception of the Sacraments.

To conclude, we may briefly sum up the effects of Sanctifying Grace as follows:

Effects of Sanctifying Grace. 1. It cleanses the soul from the guilt of mortal sin, and remits the eternal punishment due to mortal sin: "You are washed, you are sanctified, you are justified in the Name of our Lord Jesus Christ, and in the Spirit of God" (1 Cor. vi. 11).

2. It makes the soul beautiful and holy, and pleasing in the sight of God.

3. It makes us the temples of the Holy Ghost, friends and sons of God, and heirs to the kingdom of heaven, with a title to eternal happiness.

4. It renders our good works meritorious by giving them a special value.

CHAPTER XXXIX

MERIT

Good works proceeding from grace are meritorious—

Merit and meritorious works.
i.e., are worthy of a reward in the sight of God. Merit, then, is the fruit of Grace, since it is by Grace that we are able to perform meritorious works, to which God will assign their just reward in heaven. It is by our union with Jesus Christ that our actions, of themselves without value or merit, become, as it were, gold, silver, or precious stones: " He that planteth and He that watereth are One; and every man shall receive his own reward according to his labour " (1 Cor. iii. 8).

What consti- tutes a good work.
The just man, or man in the state of grace, is like a branch of the vine united to the parent stem. Such a branch, on account of the sap which it draws from the vine itself, bears abundant fruit. In like manner the works of the just man derive their intrinsic value from the infinite merits of Jesus Christ, whose living member he is through Sanctifying Grace: " I am the vine; you are the branches; he that abideth in Me, and I in him, the same heareth much fruit : for without Me you can do nothing " (John xv. 5). The fruits, then, which the just man produces by the help of grace are good or *meritorious* works: " Every good tree yieldeth good fruit " (Matt. vii. 17).

Briefly, then, a meritorious work is a good work per- formed in the state of grace, with the intention of serving and honouring God thereby, and is worthy of an eternal reward. Such works merit an increase of Sanctifying Grace, eternal life, and an increase of glory for eternity.

In our good works, God especially regards our good

intentions by which, even from the smallest actions, we may reap a great reward: " Whosoever shall give to drink to one of these little ones a cup of cold water only in the name of a disciple: Amen, I say to you, he shall not lose his reward " (Matt. x. 42).   Nor is it a matter of indifference to the Christian whether he perform good works or not; for "every tree that yieldeth not good fruit shall be cut down and cast into the fire " (Matt. iii. 10).

Necessity of a good intention.

A man in mortal sin can do good, but without thereby meriting an eternal reward: " As the branch cannot bear fruit of itself, unless it abide in the vine, so neither can you, unless you abide in Me " (John xv. 4).   Yet he can merit in this sense, that he may make himself a suitable object for God's mercy; and his good works may obtain from the Divine mercy the grace of conversion: " Redeem thou thy sins with alms, and thy iniquities with works of mercy to the poor: perhaps He will forgive thy offences " (Dan. iv. 24).

Can the sinner merit?

In order to merit, then, the following conditions are required:

1. We must be in the state of grace, since merit is the fruit of grace: " You cannot bear fruit unless you abide in Me."

Conditions for merit.

2. The action must be done with a good intention; that is, with a view to the honour and glory of God.   If, then, each morning, we offer the good works of the day with a holy intention, how meritorious they will prove when performed in the state of grace!

3. The act done must be a free act, and not one done under compulsion, but with a liberty of choice that excludes all necessity.

4. What is done must be done only during the present life, for at death man's state for eternity is fixed, and he can merit no longer: " As the tree falls, so shall it lie."   " I

must work the works of Him that sent Me, whilst it is day : the night cometh when no man can work " (John ix. 4).

5. We can merit only when God has promised a reward ; yet to all our actions, if they are not sinful and the other conditions are present, He has attached merit.

Seeing, then, that without grace we can do no good work of ourselves towards our salvation, we come to the all-important question, How are we to obtain God's grace ? The ordinary means is Prayer, the duty of which will form the subject of our next chapter.

CHAPTER XL

PRAYER

PRAYER is laid down as one of the most essential parts of
Why we pray. our religious worship. But, one may ask, does not God know our needs even before we express them ? That is quite true ; but when we disclose our wants to God in prayer it is certainly not in order to make known to Him something that He does not know already ; it is, like suppliants, to beg His assistance, and to acknowledge our dependence on Him ; to offer Him the submission of our will ; and to acknowledge our confidence in Him, and His sovereign dominion over us as over all things else.

Would anyone say that a child does wrong in asking a favour of its father, and exposing its wants to him, wants that the father is already aware of ? Or that the father is wanting in duty and goodness to his child in requiring that the child should make known to him its desires ? Is it, then, contrary to His goodness that God, who is master alike of His gifts and His actions, should have left man, in creating him, under the necessity of having recourse to Him by prayer, and should have engaged Himself to grant, on our asking, the helps that we stand in need of for the fulfilment of His designs and our own eternal destiny? Furthermore, God alone can satisfy the needs of our mind and heart, and thus it is that prayer has ever been in use among all peoples.

Now prayer is founded on Hope, and is its outward expression: we employ prayer as a means of obtaining what we hope for. To keep the Commandments we need the assistance of God's grace, and this grace cannot be obtained without prayer—the means God Himself has appointed: "For every one that asketh, receiveth; and he that seeketh, findeth" (Matt. vii. 8). And although grace is a purely gratuitous gift freely bestowed upon us by God, it is nevertheless His wish that we should ask it of Him: "We ought always to pray, and not to faint" (Luke xviii. 1).

Prayer founded on Hope.

The Catechism defines prayer as "the raising up of the mind and heart to God." It is the communion of the soul with God. By it we pay Him our homage, by adoring, praising, and thanking Him, and we beg of Him all that is necessary both for soul and body. It is, as Teresa of the Child Jesus beautifully styles it, an uplifting of the heart; a glance towards heaven; a cry of gratitude and love uttered equally in sorrow and in joy.

Meaning of Prayer.

It is chiefly through prayer that we receive all kinds of graces except those which can be obtained only by the Sacraments, which are the channels by which these special graces are conveyed to those who receive them validly and lawfully. Even the sinner, by his prayers, penances, and good works, can move the Divine mercy to give him graces to break away from his sins, and to return to God by sincere repentance.

Prayer and the Sacraments.

Besides the homage which we pay to God in prayer by adoration, praise, and thanksgiving, we also, as we have

10

seen, beg of Him to bestow upon us His favours, particularly the forgiveness of our sins, the grace
to lead a good life, and that crowning grace of
all, the grace of final perseverance.

*Homage and
petition.*

Without the special assistance of God the sinner cannot
break the bonds of his sins, neither can the just
man hope to continue in the state of grace.
The most saintly would fall did not God succour
them with a special help. This special assistance is what
is meant by the grace of perseverance: it is on this that
our eternal salvation depends: " He that shall persevere
unto the end, he shall be saved " (Matt. x. 22). In the
Prophet Ezechiel we read : " If the just man shall turn
away from his justice, and shall commit iniquity, he shall
die in his sins ; and his justices which he hath done shall
not be remembered " (iii. 20). Without perseverance the
works of such a man would be as seeds which flourish in
the beginning, but which afterwards wither and die without producing fruit. Final perseverance, or perseverance
until death, is a grace apart, and one for which we must
pray to God. It cannot be merited, but prayer and submission to the law of God will surely obtain it.

*Prayer neces-
sary for per-
severance.*

Since God commands us to pray, prayer becomes a
necessity *by precept :* " Watch ye and pray that
ye enter not into temptation " (Matt. xxvi. 41).
It is also necessary *as a means,* because without
it, as we have seen, it is impossible to keep the Commandments, and, in general, to obtain the graces necessary for
salvation : " You have not, because you ask not "
(James iv. 2). " Ask and ye shall receive" (John xvi. 24).
Moreover, it is necessary that we pray often : " We ought
always to pray, and not to faint " (Luke xviii. 1); which
some interpreters take to mean daily, or, at any rate, frequently ; and that we should always walk in the presence
of God by a spirit of prayer, love, and sorrow for sin,

*Necessary by
precept and as
a means.*

As each one has a soul to save, he is bound to take the necessary means to this end, and therefore to pray.

Besides the obligation of praying frequently, there are certain times and seasons when prayer becomes a special duty; for example, the Sundays and Holydays of Obligation; when we are exposed to strong temptation which can only be overcome by prayer; in times of affliction and great public calamity; in preparing for the Sacraments; and when we are in danger of death.

When to pray.

A Christian ought not to fail to say his morning and night prayers, and grace before and after meals. Are there any who could not find time to offer in the morning the works and sufferings of the day to God, and to recite the Our Father, the Hail Mary, the Apostles' Creed, and even a short Act of Faith, Hope, and Charity; and in the evening to add the "I Confess" and an Act of Contrition?

Nor are we to pray for ourselves only, but also for all others—for the living and for the souls of the faithful departed; and not only for those near and dear to us, but even for our enemies: "Pray for them that persecute you and calumniate you" (Matt. v. 44). We should pray for the Church and for the Pope, and for the spread of our holy Faith; we should pray, too, for our rulers, for our spiritual and temporal superiors; and for the conversion of sinners: "I desire that supplications, prayers, intercessions, and thanksgivings be made for all men, for kings, and for all who are in high station, that we may lead a quiet and a peaceful life, in all piety and chastity" (1 Tim. ii. 1, 2).

For whom we must pray.

Prayer, if accompanied with the proper dispositions, is a certain means of obtaining grace; and the proper dispositions are, *attention, humility, confidence, resignation,* and *perseverance.*

When we pray, we should place ourselves in spirit in
the presence of God, and continue to remember
Prayer with attention. that we are speaking to God, in spite of the
distractions which may intrude themselves upon
us: "Before prayer prepare thy soul, and be not as a man
that tempteth God" (Ecclus. xviii. 23). If our distractions are wilful, we not only do not pray well, but we
offend God: "This people honoureth Me with their lips,
but their heart is far from Me" (Matt. xv. 8). Yet
involuntary distractions do not take away from the value
of our prayers: nay, when we struggle against them, they
even increase our merit.

"To whom shall I have respect, but to him that is poor
and little, and of a contrite spirit?" (Is. lxvi. 2).
With humility. When, then, we direct our prayers to God, we
should cast ourselves entirely on the Divine mercy, and
sincerely acknowledge our own weakness and nothingness:
"The prayer of him that humbleth himself shall pierce
the clouds, and it will not depart till the Most High
behold" (Ecclus. xxxv. 21). "God resisteth the proud,
and giveth grace to the humble" (James iv. 6).

To a humble diffidence in ourselves we should join a
firm trust that God will hear our prayer: "Let
**With confi-
dence.** him ask in faith, nothing wavering; for he that
wavereth is like a wave of the sea that is moved
and carried about by the wind" (James i. 6). He, then,
that has not a lively faith and firm hope, but prays with a
certain feeling of distrust in God's power and goodness,
need not imagine that he will receive what he so faintly
asks for: "All things whatsoever you shall ask in prayer,
believing, you shall receive" (Matt. xxi. 22). Whatever,
therefore, we ask that is necessary for salvation, if only we
ask it with confidence, humility, and perseverance, we may
be assured God will grant when it is best for us.

We pray with resignation when we submit our will to

the will of God, that is, when we leave it to Him to grant what we ask, how and when it shall please Him best: "Father, not my will but Thine be done" (Luke xxii. 42). In this spirit of submission, having always in view the greater honour and glory of God, we may ask also for temporal goods, such as health and success. When God, however, does not grant our petitions, it is that He may bestow upon us something more useful and profitable for our salvation, in comparison with which all else is but of little moment.

With resignation.

Even when God seems not to hear our prayers we must nevertheless persevere; and, far from desisting, we should continue to pray with the greater fervour: "Know ye not that the Lord will hear your prayers, if you continue with perseverance?" (Judith iv. 11). God sometimes defers the granting of our petition to make us more humble or to try our faith.

With perseverance.

There are two kinds of Prayer, *Vocal Prayer* and *Mental Prayer.* Vocal Prayer (*Vox*, the voice) is that which comes from the heart and is expressed in words. We pray vocally, for example, when with devotion we say the Our Father, or piously join in the public prayers of the Church. But besides this kind of prayer there is an Interior or Mental Prayer (*Mens*, the mind), made in the heart without a set form of words, and generally called Meditation. Strictly speaking, mental prayer means prayer of the mind only; nevertheless, in practice, prayers and ejaculations from the heart, especially in one's own words, even though uttered with the lips and again and again repeated, do not make the prayer cease to be mental in the practical sense of the term.

Two kinds of Prayer.

Meditation consists in piously reflecting on the Divine Perfections, on the life and Passion of our Blessed Lord, or on some other of the great truths of Religion, that we may know them better and,

Mental Prayer.

by dwelling on them, excite in our hearts pious sentiments and draw from them practical resolutions for our
conduct.

Thus, in Meditation, the three powers of the soul are
brought into action; the *Memory*, in calling these great
truths to our mind; the *Understanding*, by reflecting on
them in such a way as to stir up within us pious affections
and to derive therefrom practical conclusions; and the
Will, by making resolutions, and praying for grace faithfully to carry them into effect.

For those who aspire to advance in piety and to arrive
at perfection, Meditation is a necessary practice. It
is forgetfulness of the truths of Religion that fills the
earth with crime and sends countless souls to perdition:
" With desolation is all the land made desolate, because
there is none that considereth in his heart " (Jerem. xii. 11).
Whereas he who thinks often and seriously on death, on
the judgments of God, and on eternity, will not sin : " In
all thy works remember thy last end, and thou shalt never
sin " (Ecclus. vii. 40).

Although we pray whenever we raise up the mind
and heart to God, the Church is especially the
House of God, the place of prayer, where everything is arranged to raise our minds to the
contemplation of heavenly things : " It is written : My
house is the house of prayer "(Luke xix. 46). Prayer, too,
said in common, and particularly if said in the church, is
especially efficacious, as we gather from the words of our
Lord : " Where two or three are gathered together in My
name, there am I in the midst of them " (Matt. xviii. 20).

The Place of
Prayer.

CHAPTER XL

THE LORD'S PRAYER

" Your Father, " said our Lord to His disciples, " knoweth what you stand in need of before you ask Him :

The " Our Father." you therefore shall pray in this manner " (Matt. vi.) ; and He taught them the " Our Father." This, then, is the most excellent of all prayers, first because Christ Himself taught it to us, and secondly because it includes the various duties of praise and submission which we owe to God, and mentions all the good which we need for ourselves both for this world and the next. Its shortness and simplicity make it possible for all to learn it, and so all ought to use it because our Lord deigned to compose it for us, and He Himself bade us recite it. The Prayer itself contains a *Preface* and *seven Petitions*.

The Preface, which is composed of the words " *Our Father* who art in heaven," teaches us to go

Our Father. to God with a childlike reverence, love and confidence, as to a loving father ; and we say *Our* Father, and not *My* Father, to remind us that we are all brethren and should pray for one another as members of the same family. The importance of this Christian duty is particularly emphasised by St. James in the words, " Pray for one another that you may be saved " (v. 16). Another reason for calling God " Our Father " is that *by creation* He has given us our life and all that we possess, and *by adoption* through Jesus Christ He sees in us the brethren of His Divine Son, and consequently His own children and heirs to His heavenly kingdom.

The words, " who art in heaven," do not mean that God is in heaven only, but they remind us that,

Who art in Heaven. when we pray, He would have us withdraw our minds from the things of earth and fix them on those of heaven. We tell our Father, too, that He is in heaven to remind Him that He is happy, rich, and all-powerful, while we, His children, are on earth, exiled, poor and suffering, and exposed to countless dangers.

After the Preface comes the *first Petition*, " Hallowed be Thy name." Now, the word " hallow " means to make holy, or to honour what is holy ; and it is in the latter sense that we use it here.

Hallowed be Thy Name.

In this petition, then, we pray that God's name may be praised, and never be profaned or blasphemed ; and that God Himself may be known, loved, and glorified by all men. We pray, in a word, for the advancement of God's honour and glory, which should be the ultimate end of all our actions—even the most ordinary, for by them all we can glorify God, if only we perform them with a view to pleasing Him : " Whether you eat or drink, or whatsoever else you do, do all for the glory of God " (1 Cor. x. 31).

In the *second Petition*, " Thy Kingdom come," we pray, (1) that the Kingdom of God, the Church, may extend more and more and spread throughout the whole world ; (2) that God may come and reign in our hearts by His grace in this world ; that He may lead us in the path of virtue and make us true members of His Spiritual Kingdom : " The Kingdom of God is within you " (Luke xvii. 21); and (3) that after this life we may be found worthy to reign with Him in His heavenly kingdom.

Thy Kingdom come.

In the *third Petition*, " Thy will be done on earth as it is in heaven," we pray that both we and all men may receive grace to do God's holy will in all things, and obey His commands as faithfully and cheerfully here on earth as the blessed do in heaven. What a happiness if men had no other wish but, with our Lord, to do the holy will of God in all things ! " My food," said our Lord, " is to do the will of Him that sent Me " (John iv. 34). In this petition,

Thy will be done.

then, we pray that the Divine will may be the rule of all our actions.

In the *fourth Petition*, "Give us this day our daily bread," we pray that God may supply our daily wants both for soul and body, and thereby we acknowledge our total dependence upon Him. As to *the body* we ask for what is necessary, such as food and clothing, and the means whereby we may obtain them. As to our *spiritual wants*, we pray for what is necessary for the life of the soul; for the Word of God: "Not in bread alone doth man live, but in every word that proceedeth from the mouth of God" (Deut. viii. 3); for grace, that daily spiritual food, deprived of which the soul languishes and dies; but especially ought we to pray for the grace of the Holy Eucharist, the true Bread of Eternal Life in which is received Christ Himself, the very Author of grace.* The words "*this day*" teach us moreover not to be too anxious about the future, though they do not forbid us a wise forethought: "Be not solicitous for to-morrow" (Matt. vi. 34). He who supplies our wants to-day will also supply them to-morrow. Here again, in this petition, we are taught to pray not for ourselves only, but also for all others: "Give *us* (not give *me*) this day our daily bread."

The *fifth Petition*, "Forgive us our trespasses as we forgive them that trespass against us," teaches us to pray daily for the pardon of our sins and the grace of a true repentance. Yet our prayer is that God will forgive us our sins as we forgive others the injuries they have done to us. We see, then, that our forgiving others is made a necessary condition of our obtaining pardon of God. Thus man's judgment is put into his own hands, so that none can complain, seeing that every one is the author of his own sentence: "For if you

---

* Pius X., in his decree on the daily reception of the Blessed Sacrament, spoke of this as a petition for *daily* Communion.

forgive men their offences, your Heavenly Father will also
forgive you your offences" (Matt. vi. 14). "Forgive thy
neighbour if he hath hurt thee; and then shall thy sins
be forgiven to thee when thou prayest" (Ecclus. xxviii. 2).
Therefore, as often as we say the "Our Father," we pass
judgment upon ourselves.

We are taught in the *sixth Petition*, "Lead us not into
temptation," to pray either to be delivered
from temptations, or so to gain the victory
over them as not to fall into sin. Those who,
in time of temptation, pray with confidence to God for
deliverance are sure of being heard, according to the words
of St. Paul: "God is faithful, who will not suffer you to
be tempted above that which you are able; but will make
also with temptation issue that you may be able to bear
it" (1 Cor. x. 13). In this petition, then, we do not mean
to imply that God Himself tempts us, but that, for our
greater merit, He allows us to be tempted; for even the
most violent temptations are occasions of merit and
triumph to those who, relying on God's help, manfully resist
them. Temptation itself is not a sin, but to yield to it,
or to expose ourselves heedlessly and needlessly to it, is
always sinful: "Watch ye and pray that ye enter not into
temptation" (Matt. xxvi. 41).

Lead us not into temptation.

The *seventh* and *last Petition*, "Deliver us from evil,"
teaches us that, after praying for pardon for
past sins, we are to beg to be delivered from
further sin, and from all such evils, spiritual
and temporal, as are the consequences of sin, especially the
punishment which sin merits in the next life; and that
God may preserve us from whatever He sees will be an
evil to us whether of soul or body.

Deliver us from evil.

After praising God and praying for all our spiritual
and temporal wants we confirm our prayer by
adding "Amen"—*i.e.*, "So be it"; by which we
express our confidence in God and an earnest desire of

Amen.

being heard.   We should pronounce it fervently and with great faith, as it is a repetition of the whole prayer, and, as it were, a last effort made to move the Divine compassion.

The Lord's Prayer is intended to be said at least every day, as may be gathered from the words, "Give us *this day* our *daily bread*." If we were to continue daily to carry out the lessons taught us in the "Our Father," we should always lead a good life, and be in proper dispositions for receiving daily that supersubstantial Bread, the Body of Christ, which is the best and most excellent support of the life of the soul.

CHAPTER XLII

VENERATION AND INVOCATION OF THE SAINTS

AFTER being taught to honour God and to pray to Him in the Lord's Prayer, we are next taught to honour the Saints and implore their intercession, because by doing so we honour God Himself in those whom He has glorified.   The Catholic Church not only teaches that it is permitted, but that it is good and useful, to invoke the Angels and Saints to assist us by their prayers in obtaining graces and favours from God through His Son, Jesus Christ, our only Redeemer and Mediator.   It is in this sense that we speak of praying to the Saints: "We should ask the Angels and Saints to pray for us because they are our friends and brethren, and because their prayers have great power with God."

Prayer to the Saints.

The honour or worship which we pay to Mary and to the Angels and Saints is then not only permitted, but is a most consoling devotion.   We find a most tender mother in her who is the Mother of God, faithful guardians in those who are the servants of God, and friends in those who themselves are the friends of God. We thus invoke them with confidence, our Blessed Lady especially, not indeed to obtain directly from them what we ask, but to ask them to intercede with God for us that through their prayers He may grant our petitions.

"There shall be joy before the Angels of God upon one sinner doing penance" (Luke xv. 10). From these words it is plain that the Angels in heaven take an interest in our welfare, and rejoice at our repentance; and consequently that they have a knowledge of our actions. And what is here said of the Angels is equally true of the Saints, as we may argue from the words of our Lord Himself: "For they are equal to the Angels, and are the children of God" (Luke xx. 36); and again: "They shall be as the Angels of God in heaven" (Matt. xxii. 30).

The Blessed in Heaven pray for us. — That the Blessed Spirits pray for us is also clearly stated in many parts of the Sacred Scriptures. We have the Angel Raphael saying to Tobias : "When thou didst pray with tears, and didst bury the dead . . . I offered thy prayer to the Lord : for I am the Angel Raphael, one of the seven who stand before the Lord" (Tob. xii. 12, 15). And in the Prophet Zacharias we read: "And the Angel of the Lord answered and said : O Lord of hosts, how long wilt Thou not have mercy on Jerusalem, and on the cities of Juda, with which Thou hast been angry?" (Zach. i. 12).

We pray for one another. — Prayer for one another, too, has at all times been the practice of the faithful, and it is often through the prayers of our friends, even while they are on earth, that God bestows His graces and favours upon us. St. Paul is but carrying out the same practice when, in commending himself to those to whom he is writing, he so earnestly asks their prayers : "I beseech you, brethren, through our Lord Jesus Christ, that you

help me in your prayers for me to God " (Rom. xv. 30);
words moreover which clearly show that, when we address
ourselves to the Saints, it is not a mark of distrust in Jesus
Christ since it is through His merits alone that we expect
grace and salvation from God.   Again, in one of his Epistles
to the Corinthians, he writes : " God hath delivered, and
doth deliver us out of so great dangers ; in whom we trust
that He will yet also deliver us, *you helping withal in prayer
for us* " (2 Cor. i. 10, 11).   St. James, too, exhorting the
faithful thus mutually to assist one another, bids them
" Pray for one another that you may be saved ; for the continual prayer of a just man availeth much" (James v. 16).

If, then, as these words show, it was in the power
of the Saints, when they were living on
earth, to obtain favours for us from God, how

Death does not
sever the
Communion of
Saints.

much more powerful will their intercession be
now that they are in heaven !   For death
does not dissolve the communion between them and us.
St. Paul, in asking the prayers of the Corinthians, did not
suppose that this was derogatory to Christ's mediation,
nor to the hope that he had in God.   And can it be
derogatory to God if we solicit the aid of the Saints in
heaven, when we are recommended to seek that of sinners
on earth ?   Or is it to be supposed, asks St. Jerome, that
the intercession of our fellow-men beneath is more available with God than the prayers of those who enjoy the
Beatific Vision above ?

It is not, then, derogatory to God's honour thus to
honour the Saints and invoke them.   " There

Jesus Christ
the one
Mediator.

is," says St. Paul, " one God, and one Mediator
of God and men, the man Jesus Christ, who
gave Himself a redemption for all " (1 Tim. ii. 5, 6).   If
we take all these words together, we can easily understand
in what sense the Apostle calls our Saviour the one only
Mediator.   He is the only Mediator who at the same time

is our Redeemer; the only Mediator who could mediate between God, the Person offended by sin, and men the offenders; the only Mediator who reconciled God to man-kind by His Incarnation and Death, by the infinite price of His Blood, by His own merits, independently of the merits of any other. As, then, there is but *one God* who created all, so there is but *one Mediator* who redeemed all. But yet the name of mediator is not so appropriated to Christ but that, in an inferior and different sense, it may be applied to the Angels and Saints in Heaven, and even to men on earth who pray to God for the salvation of others. In this sense we may call them mediators, inter-cessors, or advocates; and we may ask them to pray, intercede, and medi..te for us not only without injury, but with honour done to Christ, since we acknowledge that all they pray and ask for is only begged and hoped for through Christ our Redeemer, and by His merits. We pray to God that He may help us by His omnipotence, but we pray to the Saints that they may help us by inter-ceding with Him for us. Even in addressing ourselves to our Blessed Lady, the Queen of Angels and Saints, our petition is, "Pray for us, O Holy Mother of God, *that we may be made worthy of the promises of Christ."* "O most pure Virgin and Queen of Angels, obtain for us purity of soul and body, *through Jesus Christ our Lord."*

We see, then, that the honour which we pay to the Angels and Saints differs essentially from the **Different grades of worship.** worship we give to God. To God we pay supreme adoration; that is, we adore and worship Him absolutely as our Creator and the Sovereign Lord of all things. This worship, which can be given to God alone, is the worship of *Latria* (adoration). We are strictly bound to adore Him as our Sovereign Lord, and to acknowledge our entire dependence on Him both in the order of nature and of grace. This worship is very different from, and infinitely superior to, the honour or homage known as *Dulia*, or *Hyperdulia* (superior honour or homage). The worship of *Dulia* is that which the Church gives to the Angels and Saints, while *Hyperdulia* is the special worship we pay to the Blessed Virgin, who, on account of her pre-eminent dignity as Mother of God, is raised in honour above all the Angels and Saints. Yet the honour given directly to the Saints is indirectly given to God Himself, who is the author of every grace and of every good gift.

From times the most ancient the Church has approved and cherished the veneration of the Saints, implored their intercession, raised stately churches in their honour, and celebrated their festivals.

CHAPTER XLIII

THE HAIL MARY '

In the last chapter we spoke of the honour due to the Angels and Saints as the special friends of God ; but we have to honour in a particular manner, and invoke above all the Angels and Saints, Mary, the Immaculate Mother of God ; because, on account of her exalted dignity as Mother of God, she surpasses even the Angels in grace and glory, and because, for this very reason, her intercession with God is most powerful. After the "Lord's Prayer," then, it has long been the custom of the faithful to recite the "*Angelical Salutation*," or "*Hail Mary*." After the Lord's Prayer, moreover, the Hail Mary, on account of its origin, is the most excellent of all prayers, composed, as it is, for the most part, of words directly inspired by the Holy Ghost.

The Prayer itself is divided into two parts, the first of which is a *Prayer of Praise :* "Hail [Mary], full of grace, the Lord is with thee ; blessed art thou amongst women, and blessed is the fruit of thy womb [Jesus]" ; while the second part is a

Mary to be honoured above Angels and Saints.

The "Hail Mary."

Prayer of Intercession: "Holy Mary, Mother of God, pray for us sinners, now, and at the hour of our death. Amen." The first part consists of the salutation addressed to our

Its division.

Lady by the Angel Gabriel at the time of the Annunciation : " Hail, full of grace, the Lord is with thee; blessed art thou amongst women ; " and of the words of her cousin, St. Elizabeth : " Blessed art thou amongst women, and blessed is the fruit of thy womb." The words [Mary] and [Jesus] of the first part, together with the Prayer of Intercession, have been added by the Church.

" Hail, full of grace " means that Mary possesses every

Hail, full of grace.

grace that befits her exalted position as Mother of God; that she possesses the greatest share of Divine grace granted to any creature. Why then should so many non-Catholics be offended at the salutation given by Catholics to the Blessed Mother of God, who would not have been raised to this unparalleled dignity had not her soul been first prepared for it by the most sublime graces?

"The Lord is with thee"; first of all by the graces

The Lord is with thee.

conferred upon her from the time of her Immaculate Conception, and by her straightway becoming the Mother of God after she had given her consent to the Incarnation with the words, " Behold the handmaid of the Lord "; for at that same moment was conceived in her the Saviour and Redeemer of the world.

" Blessed art thou amongst women." These words were

Blessed art thou amongst women.

addressed to Mary because she was chosen from among all women to be the Mother of God; because she alone, in becoming a mother, did not cease to be a pure virgin; and because Mary, unlike the first woman, who brought a curse upon mankind, was destined to bring salvation.

And blessed is the Fruit of thy womb." Blessed indeed

Blessed is the Fruit of thy womb.

is Jesus on account of His Divine nature, and because He is the source of grace and salvation to all. And blessed is Mary, too, on account of her Son, with whom she is inseparably linked.

The Catholic Church makes such frequent use of the words of the " Hail Mary " as well to honour Jesus Christ and His Virgin Mother, as because they were the first glad tidings of Christ's Incarnation and man's redemption. They are the very abridgment and sum of the whole Gospel. As the Catechism tells us : " We should frequently say the Hail Mary to put us in mind of the Incarnation of the Son of God, and to honour our Blessed Lady, the Mother of God."

Mary, then, is to be honoured with a special devotion

Reasons for honouring Mary.

above the Angels and Saints ; (1) because she is above all other creatures in sanctity, and because, as Mother of God, she surpasses them all in dignity ; (2) because our Lord Himself honoured her and loved her on earth ; and can we imagine that He honours and loves her less now that she is with Him in heaven ? and (3) because He Himself gave her, as He was hanging on the Cross, to be the mother of all mankind ; while, at the same time, she adopted us as her children : " Woman, behold thy son "; and to St. John, who represented all the human race : " Behold thy mother " (John xix. 26, 27).   •

Since, then, Mary has been given to us by Christ Himself to be our Mother, let us, therefore, with the greatest assurance of being heard, implore her help in all our needs; but especially let us ask her to obtain for us that inestimable grace, the grace of a happy death. This simple petition forms the second part of the " Hail Mary ": " Holy Mary, Mother of God, pray for us sinners, now, and at the hour of our death. Amen."

11

CHAPTER XLIV

DEVOTIONS IN HONOUR OF OUR BLESSED LADY

MANY practices of devotion are recommended by the Church

Devotions in honour of Mary.

in honour of the Blessed Virgin; for example, to celebrate her festivals by hearing Mass and approaching the Sacraments on them; to recite the Litany in her honour, and to wear her scapular.   But the devotions most widely in use are those of the *Angelus* and the *Rosary*.

One of the most familiar sounds in a Catholic country is

Meaning of the Angelus.

that of the Angelus Bell, a sound that still falls upon the ear even in many parts of Protestant England.   The bell is rung in the morning, at noon, and in the evening, to call on the faithful to pause for a moment to contemplate the great mystery of the Incarnation.   The Angelus itself, so named from the first word with which the devotion begins in Latin, is simple, and, like the Rosary, can readily be learnt even by the most illiterate.   It brings to our mind the mystery of the Incarnation, how it was announced to Mary, her consent to become the Mother of God, and how the great mystery was brought about.   The whole prayer is thus occupied with the mystery of our Lord's becoming Man for us, and runs thus:

The Angel of the Lord declared unto Mary.   And

The Angelus.

she conceived by the Holy Ghost.   Hail, Mary, etc.

Behold the handmaid of the Lord.   Be it done unto me according to thy word.   Hail, Mary, etc.

And the Word was made flesh.   And dwelt amongst us. Hail, Mary, etc.

Pray for us, O holy Mother of God.   That we may be made worthy of the promises of Christ.

Let us pray.

Pour forth, we beseech Thee, O Lord, Thy grace into our hearts, that we, to whom the Incarnation of Christ Thy Son was made known by the message of an Angel, may by His Passion and Cross be brought to the glory of His Resurrection, through the same Christ our Lord.   Amen.

We see in the Angelus, then, a prayer of gratitude to God for the great blessings bestowed upon mankind through the mystery of the Incarnation, and a means of honouring Mary and recommending ourselves to her care and protection.

The Rosary, too, is a most useful and simple form of prayer, mental as well as vocal, and hence the practice of saying it has spread throughout the world, chiefly through the exertions of the Order of Preachers—the Dominicans.   It has been enriched by successive Pontiffs with many and great Indulgences, and has given rise to a Festival in honour of Our Lady of the Rosary, which is kept on the 7th October.

The Rosary.

The devotion is called the Rosary because it is, as it were, a *chaplet* woven, not of material flowers, but of prayers and meditations wherein are wreathed together, as into a bunch of fragrant roses, the chief mysteries of our holy religion.

Meaning of Rosary.

Like the Angelus, the Rosary is particularly connected with the Incarnation of our Divine Saviour. It is divided into *three parts*, each part consisting of five Mysteries, and so we have the five Joyful, the five Sorrowful, and the five Glorious Mysteries. Each Mystery of the Rosary is composed of one Pater, ten Aves, and one Gloria ; yet the devotion itself does not consist merely in the repetition of these prayers, but in our repeating them whilst thinking of those Mysteries of our Lord's Life and Passion which have been chosen for

Division of the Rosary.

our contemplation.   Indeed dwelling on these Mysteries
to the best of our ability whilst we are saying the prescribed prayers constitutes an essential part of the devotion.

The *five Joyful* Mysteries of the Rosary are the
Annunciation, the Visitation, the Birth of our Saviour,
the Presentation, and the Finding of the Child Jesus in
the Temple.

The *five Sorrowful* are the Prayer and Sweat of Blood
of our Saviour in the Garden, the Scourging at the
Pillar, the Crowning with Thorns, the Carrying of the
Cross, and the Crucifixion.

The *five Glorious* are the Resurrection, the Ascension,
the Descent of the Holy Ghost, the Assumption, and the
Coronation of our Lady.

Thus the Rosary, taken as a whole, is a mental and vocal
prayer, founded, in honour of our Lady, on the Incarnation,
Life, Death and Triumph of our Saviour.

If we are asked why for every " Our Father " we repeat
the " Hail Mary " so often, we might answer that, while
the " Our Father " makes no direct reference to the great
Mysteries of our Redemption and its Author, we cannot
dwell on the words of the " Hail Mary " without calling
to our minds the sublime Mystery of the Incarnation, and
without constantly thinking of Jesus, to whose Holy
Name it is easy to attach a brief reflection as we go
through the different mysteries.

If then we honour Mary, if in all our necessities we
ask her to assist us, if we earnestly strive to imitate her
virtues, particularly her purity, humility, charity and
humble submission to the will of God, we shall indeed love
and glorify in a special manner her Divine Son.

PART III

CHARITY

"If I speak with the tongues of men and of angels, and have not charity, I am become as sounding brass, or a tinkling cymbal" (1 Cor. xiii. 1).

CHAPTER XLV

NECESSITY AND NATURE OF CHARITY

THE most excellent of the Theological Virtues is Charity, since it is by Charity that we approach nearest to God, and become His true image: "And now there remain Faith, Hope, and Charity, these three; but the greatest of these is Charity" (1 Cor. xiii. 13). It is the third great means by which we are to worship God: Faith alone, the Catechism tells us, will not save us without good works; we must also have Hope and Charity.

The excellence of Charity.

Charity is a supernatural gift of God by which we love God above all things for His own sake, and our neighbour as ourselves for God's sake. It is a virtue bestowed upon us without any merit on our part, by the pure mercy of God, through the merits of Jesus Christ, and infused into our souls at Baptism: "The Charity of God is poured out into our hearts by the Holy Ghost, who is given to us" (Rom. v. 5). By that Sacrament there is given to us not only the gift of the Holy Spirit,

What is Charity?

but the Holy Spirit Himself, who resides in our soul as in His own temple, who sanctifies it, and makes it a partaker of His Divine love.

By Faith our union with God is only begun.   It is the virtue of Charity which constitutes the roof of the spiritual house of the soul, that sacred edifice whose foundation, as we have seen, is Faith, and whose walls are Hope. "If I have all Faith," says St. Paul, "so that I could remove mountains, and have not Charity, I am nothing" (1 Cor. xiii. 2).   Faith, then, without good works, and especially without Charity towards God and our neighbour, cannot avail to life eternal.

Necessity of Charity.

From our definition of Charity we see that it has a twofold object, God being its principal, and our neighbour its secondary, object. These two branches of Charity, the love of God for Himself, and of our neighbour for God, are inseparable : love of the one cannot exist without love of the other. Nay, by one and the same Charity we love both God and our neighbour: "If any man say, I love God, and hateth his brother, he is a liar" (1 John iv. 20).   Yet these are not two virtues, but the one single virtue of Charity with a double object; on the one hand God in Himself, and on the other, God still, in His children, who are our neighbours.

Twofold object of Charity.

For our Charity to be real our love of God must be *sovereign*, that is, we must love God above all things, and with our whole heart, so that we are willing to suffer any loss rather than separate ourselves from Him by mortal sin.   God being supremely worthy of our love, it is just that we should thus love Him above every created good, and refer all our affections to Him.

Charity must be sovereign.

Our Charity, too, should be *active*, that is, we should *do* what we know to be pleasing to Him : " For this is the charity of God, that we keep His commandments" (1 John

Charity must be active,

v. 3). "He that hath My commands and keepeth them, he it is that loveth Me" (John xiv. 21). It is by love that we are moved to do the will of the Beloved, and to avoid all that is displeasing to Him ; *i.e.*, with reference to God, to embrace good and to reject evil. It is a lively faith working by Charity that gives us the victory over the greatest temptations, and over all the enemies of our salvation. It is the love of God and the promises of eternal happiness in the next world that, with the Divine assistance, make the yoke of Christ sweet and His burden light.

We should love God as He loves us. Now God loves

Generous and constant.

us with a *generous* love : with a bountiful hand He has given us all that is necessary both for soul and body. He loves us, too, with a *constant* love ; for from all eternity He has loved us, and He does not cease to love us, and to wait for our repentance, even when we have offended Him by sin. And we ought to love God with a *sacred* love, since it is in view of His greater glory and our eternal salvation that He loves each one of us.

There are many arid strong reasons why we are bound

Grounds or motives of our Charity.

to love God. We must love Him, (1) because, by reason of His own infinite perfection, He is most worthy of our love ; (2) on account of His goodness. Not only is He infinitely good in Himself, but He is infinitely good also to us ; He has loved us first, and has bestowed innumerable blessings upon us both for soul and body; (3) we must love Him on account of His promises. He has promised us eternal happiness as the reward of our fidelity : He is our last end, and we must love Him therefore as the very end of our being ; and (4) because He has commanded us to love Him : "Thou shalt love the Lord thy God with thy whole heart, and with thy whole soul, and with thy whole mind, and with thy whole strength" (Mark xii. 30).

Now our love of God may be either *perfect* or *imperfect*, the essential difference lying in the motive from which our love proceeds.   Perfect *love of God*, which is a love of *benevolence* or friendship, consists in

Perfect love of God.

loving God for His own sake, that is, in loving Him above all things, because He is infinitely good and lovable in Himself; and because, beyond all other beings, He is worthy of our love: "He that abideth in Charity, abideth in God, and God in him" (1 John iv. 16).

Our love of God, then, is *perfect* :—(1) when, in loving Him for His own sake, we so centre our affections in Him that we never allow ourselves any thought or desire contrary to Charity.

(2) Also when, even in desiring to possess God, our object is His glory rather than our own advantage ; for the possession of God is the consummation of Charity.   Hence St. Paul's desire " to be dissolved and to be with Christ ' (Philip. i. 23) was an act of Charity, an act of perfect love of God.

(3) And when we love Him on account of His Infinite Goodness, even inasmuch as it is of advantage to us in helping us to do His will and to gain our last end ; for it is not so much the favours and gifts bestowed on us that we love, as the Divine Goodness in itself, the source of all good and of every gift.   But to love God *only* as a means of obtaining eternal life, or of escaping hell, is not to love Him with the love of perfect Charity. Such love is rather the love of *Hope*.

Charity, too, is not a mere matter of feeling, but a love of *preference*.   It is in the will, which

Charity a love of preference.

deliberately chooses God before all things, and is determined to sacrifice all rather than offend Him mortally. Even though for our parents and friends we

may experience a greater *feeling* of affection than we do for
God, yet the possession of such a sentiment is not a sign that
our love for God is imperfect.   So long as we are prepared
to give them up, should He require the sacrifice, we show
by our very willingness to submit to His will that we do
prefer Him to them.   In Charity our heart is so fixed on
God that, for His sake, we will .not allow ourselves any
thought, affection, or desire contrary to His Divine love.

But our love of God may be *imperfect*.   We may
love Him for what He has done for us, or
may do for us ; because He has created us,
preserved us, redeemed us, sanctified us, and
bestowed upon us countless blessings both spiritual and temporal ; because in Him is our happiness, and without Him
we must be eternally miserable.   This is an interested love
by which we love God less for Himself than for His gifts,
or the advantages we expect from Him.   If then we love
God on account of the benefits He has conferred upon us,
our love is not the love *of charity*, but the love *of gratitude ;*
and if we love Him merely as a means of arriving at eternal
happiness, our love is, as we have seen, the love *of hope*
rather than the love *of charity.*

Though such love really springs from, and is, a love of self,
yet when it relates to the goods which are eternal, it is holy
and agreeable to God, but less perfect than the love *of
charity*.   From the love of gratitude, too, charity easily
springs forth.   Moreover, for perfect love, it is not necessary to exclude imperfect love of God ; nor does imperfect
love of God destroy charity if there is really present love
of God for His own sake.

A short summary of the above facts may be found
serviceable.

Charity is a virtue, or supernatural habit, infused by
God into our souls, by which we love God for His own
sake, and our neighbour as ourselves for God's sake.

The *object* of Charity is God and our neighbour—God for His own sake, and our neighbour for God's sake.

The *motive* of Charity is God Himself, who is infinitely amiable, and who, on account of His infinite perfections, is most worthy of all our love.

Yet all love of God is not the love of Charity: it may be *perfect* or *imperfect* according to the motive from which our love proceeds.

Perfect love of God, which is a love of *benevolence*, is the love of, and has the nature of, *Charity* : by it we love God *for His own sake.*

Imperfect love of God is the love of *gratitude* or of *hope.* This is an interested love : we love God for what He has done for us, or for what He will do for us.

Charity is not a mere matter of feeling, not a tender emotion, *commonly* spoken of as love, but it is a love of *preference.* It is in the will, which deliberately prefers God before all things, and is resolved to sacrifice all rather than offend Him mortally.

Charity is destroyed by mortal sin, for by mortal **How Charity** sin the love of God is banished from our **is weakened** hearts ; and it is weakened and its growth **or destroyed.** impeded by venial sin, since it is impossible to refer any sinful affection to God. It is most perfect when it seeks all that can be most pleasing to God, and His holy will in all things.

Charity is called the mother and queen of virtues, because **Charity the** whoever possesses Charity, which is the love of **queen of** God and our neighbour, possesses to some **virtues.** extent all the other virtues, and because she dominates all the other virtues, " Love is the fulfilling of the Law " (Rom. xiii. 10).

The love of God is increased and perfected in us by prayer : " Ask, and you shall receive " (John xvi. 24); by frequently and worthily approaching the Holy Sacraments; by often meditating on the Divine Perfections, on How the love the Life and Passion of our Blessed Lord, and of God is on the great love of God for us; by fidelity increased. to every duty; by acts of penance and charity done in a state of grace; and by referring our every thought, word, and action to God, thus faithfully adhering to the motto, " *Ad Majorem Dei Gloriam,* to the greater glory of God."

The precept of the love of God, as that of Faith and What Acts of Hope, obliges us to make acts of Charity when Charity are we have attained the use of reason; whenever we necessary. are under a temptation which cannot be conquered except by an act of Charity; from time to time during our lives; and particularly at the approach of death. Yet to do this does not require any set form of words, or even words at all, nor even the express intention of fulfilling the precept: we perform acts of Charity by giving alms, by hearing Mass, or doing any good work for the love of God. Whoever devoutly recites the Lord's Prayer, in pronouncing with sincerity the words " Hallowed be Thy name," " Thy will be done on earth as it is in heaven," makes an act of the love of God.

CHAPTER XLVI

LOVE OF OUR NEIGHBOUR

THE second object of Charity is our neighbour, that is, all persons without exception—even our enemies—for God's sake. This love of our neighbour, moreover, is inseparable from the love of God: " He that loveth not his brother whom he seeth, how can he love God Second object whom he seeth not ?" (1 John iv. 20). This, of Charity. then, is God's express wish and command, *that he who loveth God love also his neighbour;* and Christ

Himself prescribes even what the measure of our love is to be : "Thou shalt love thy neighbour as thyself" (Mark xii. 31). "The love of our neighbour," says St. Paul, "worketh no evil. Love, therefore, is the fulfilling of the law" (Rom. xiii. 10).

Now this love of our neighbour God both wishes and commands :

Why we must love our neighbour. 1. Because, like ourselves, all men are children of God, whom He has created to His own image and likeness : "Have we not all one Father ? Hath not God created us ? Why then doth every one of us despise his brother ?" (Mal. ii. 10).

2. Because we are all children of Adam, brothers of Jesus Christ, and members of His mystical body.

3. Because we have all been redeemed with the precious Blood of Jesus Christ and called to the same heavenly inheritance.

4. Because Jesus Christ Himself not only commands it, but in His Life and Death has shown us how to do it : "This is My commandment, that you love one another as I have loved you" (John xv. 12). He even gives it as the distinguishing mark of His true followers : "By this shall all men know that you are My disciples, if you have love one for another" (John xiii. 35).

One of the great aims of Religion is to uproot that self-love which took possession of the heart of man **Aim of Religion.** as a consequence of original sin, and to plant in its stead a universal Charity which shall make of all men a single brotherhood : "If we love one another, God abideth in us, and His charity is perfected in us" (1 John iv. 12).

Our love for our neighbour must be as the love of God is for us. It must be *universal,* which means that **Love must be universal.** it must exclude no one, be he friend or enemy : "For if you love them that love you, what re-

ward shall you have? Do not even the publicans this?"
(Matt. v. 46). "He will have *all men* to be saved, because
He gave Himself a redemption for all" (1 Tim. ii. 4, 6).

We must love our neighbour with a *generous* and *disin-*
terested love, which consists in doing to others
what we would reasonably wish them to do to
us, and in never doing to them what we would
not wish them to do to us: "All things whatsoever you
would that men should do to you, do you also to them"
(Matt. vii. 12). And this for God's sake, and not for
the applause of men or for any temporal gain: "My little
children, let us not love in word nor in tongue, but in deed
and in truth" (1 John iii. 18).

It must be
generous.

Our love for our neighbour should be a *sacred* love; that
is, it should come from a sincere desire to
promote his real happiness in this life, and with
a view to his eternal salvation; and, like the
love of Christ, it should be *constant* : "Having loved His
own who were in the world, He loved them unto the end"
(John xiii. 1).

It should be
sacred and
constant.

· Nor is it enough merely to abstain from revenging ourselves on those who have injured us. God commands us to love our enemies, that is, to wish
them well, to pray for them, and to be ready
to assist them in their needs: "Love your enemies; do
good to them that hate you; and pray for them that persecute and calumniate you" (Matt. v. 44). We must
therefore not only lay aside all thoughts of revenge with
regard to our enemies; but we must forgive them from our
hearts; we must even return good for evil. Yet this love
of our enemies does not compel us to give up our just rights.
This we are not bound to do; and at all times we may
claim them if we take the proper means.

We must love
our enemies.

, To love our neighbour for God's sake is the most solid
foundation we can give to our love. Moreover, since

God is always infinitely worthy of our love, our neighbour must always be due for his share of it also; it
must therefore never fail whatever may be his wrongs
in our regard. If he does not merit our love, God does;
then we must love him to please and to obey God: " But
if you will not forgive, neither will your Father, who is in
heaven, forgive you your sins" (Mark xi. 26). Charity,
then, complete and perfect is " To love the Lord thy God,
with thy whole heart, and with thy whole soul, and with
thy whole mind, and with thy whole strength: and to
love thy neighbour as thyself" (Mark xii. 30, 31).

CHAPTER XLVII

THE COMMANDMENTS: CONSCIENCE

JUST as the Apostles' Creed is the abridgment of what, as
Christians, we are to believe, so is the *Decalogue*

Aim of the Com-
mandments.

(Greek, *ten words*), or the Ten Commandments,
the abridgment of our duties towards God,
ourselves, and our neighbour. The one aim of the Commandments is to help us to carry out the great commandment of love of God and of our neighbour, to
which all the others refer; for " Love," says St. Paul, " is
the fulfilling of the law " (Rom. xiii. 10). And our Lord
Himself tells us, " He that hath My Commandments and
keepeth them, he it is that loveth Me" (John xiv. 21).
Now, as Charity must be the motive which influences
all our actions, according to the words of St. John, " Let
us not love in word, nor in tongue, but in deed, and in
truth " (1 John iii. 18), the Commandments come in to
regulate it.

Hence, in the Decalogue we find both *positive* and
negative precepts; the former commanding us what to
do in order to practise charity towards God and our

neighbour; the latter forbidding us to do whatever may
lessen or destroy in us this same virtue.   Then
indeed ought we to love and faithfully observe
the Commandments, seeing that they are the
great proofs of God's love for us; for it is in the careful
observance of them that He has willed that we shall find true
rest and peace for the soul.   We are made for God, and our
hearts will have neither peace nor repose unless all our affections be referred to Him.   The motives, then, which should
induce us cheerfully to keep the Commandments are the
will of God and our own happiness.   Indeed our happiness
absolutely depends on our fidelity in observing them:
"If thou wilt enter into life, keep the Commandments"
(Matt. xix. 17).

Motives for keeping the Commandments.

The Commandments are no obstacle to our liberty;
they serve but to check our wandering from
the path of true liberty and happiness.   And
since God requires us to keep them under pain of
everlasting condemnation, it follows that, since
they are *obligatory*, it must be *possible* to keep them; for
God could not punish us for not doing what is impossible.
Without the help of God's grace it would be impossible to
observe them, but His grace makes it not only possible, but
comparatively easy if we do what is required of us: "For
My yoke is sweet and My burden light" (Matt. xi. 30).   And
this grace He never refuses to those who ask it of Him, and
who adopt the proper means to keep them: "God is faithful,
who will not suffer you to be tempted above that which
you are able; but will make also with temptation issue
that you may be able to bear it" (1 Cor. x. 13).

The Command- ments do not hinder true liberty.

The Ten Commandments, in the form in which we now
have them, were given by God to, Moses on
Mount Sinai; but before they were thus for-
mally given, man was not left in the dark as to
what was right and what was wrong.   From the beginning

The Light of Nature.

God imprinted upon the heart of man a sense of right and wrong, called the *light of nature,* and gave him a con- science ; and it was by disregarding this light of nature and this voice of conscience that man became wicked. Yet, though the moral law might have been discovered by the light of nature, God revealed it to Adam, who handed it down to his descendants. But as it became obscured by the corruption and wickedness of mankind, God again and again renewed it : " God having spoken on divers occasions and in many ways, in times past, to the fathers by the prophets, last of all in these days hath spoken to us by His Son " (Heb. i. 1, 2).

Now a law, in general, is a precept, just and abiding, given for promulgation to any society by one

The Moral Law.

who has a right to govern it. By the *Moral Law,* then, is meant the law of right and wrong, or that law given by God which governs the free actions of man. It may be divided, according to the way in which it has become known to us—*i.e.,* according as it emanates *necessarily* or *freely* from the Creator, into *natural* law and *positive* or *revealed* law. *Natural law* differs from *positive law* inasmuch as it is given not to particular men, but to all men ; for God has created all men for the same end, and given them the same nature ; and consequently all men are bound by its precepts, since the same things are right or wrong for all.

There is, therefore, only *one Natural Law,* but there are *two Positive Divine Laws,* the *Mosaic Law* which was revealed by God to Moses, and the *Evangelical Law* which was given by Jesus Christ.

By *natural law,* then, is meant the moral order which must be observed by man that he may arrive at his

Natural Law.

natural destination ; and this order consists in the whole of man's natural duties towards God, himself, and his neighbour. This law is graven on man's rational nature and was communicated to him simultaneously with his creation.

Natural law admits of no change or dispensation ; for, being founded on human nature, it is, like it, invariable. It is, however, capable of being perfected ; indeed it required the positive Divine laws to render it perfect. The natural law is in itself imperfect since it regards only the natural destinies of man ; but as man, by grace, has been raised to a supernatural end or destiny, it is necessary that a higher law, relating to the higher end, should be joined to the natural law. This second law, which does not abolish, but rather perfects the natural law, has therefore been given to man in the form of the Mosaic Law and the Evangelical Law.

Natural Law capable of being perfected.

The moral part of the *Mosaic Law* is only the clear and definite expression of the natural law, the general rules of which are contained in the *Decalogue.*

The Mosaic Law.

The *Evangelical Law* is composed, (1) of *dogmatic truths* which must be believed ; (2) of *precepts* which are binding on all ; and (3) of *counsels* some of which are addressed to all men, others all men are not called upon to follow. The *precepts* relate to the morals of the faithful and to the Divine worship ; the *counsels* relate to perfection, and some concern only those whom God has called to a state of life specially couse-crated to His service—*e.g.*, voluntary poverty and perpetual chastity. The Church, whose mission it is to interpret the Divine Law, cannot abrogate or annul it in any point. She possesses this power only in regard to her own laws, which are called Ecclesiastical Laws, or those laws which emanate from the Sovereign Pontiff and the Bishops for the government of the Church.*

The Evangelical Law.

* See Father Schouppe's "Abridged Course of Religious Instruction," Part III, chapter i.

12

Now it is by the *voice of Conscience* that the interior application of laws to particular actions is made;

Conscience.

and *Conscience* is an act of judgment passing sentence on the lawfulness or unlawfulness of an act which is to be done or to be avoided in the particular circumstances in which we find ourselves placed.

Conscience is not the *light of nature*, but the eye which measures and takes in the light. Nor is it the

A rule of conduct.

law, for law is an external rule apart from our acts and does not alter; but it is a practical judgment; it is our application of the law to our own particular case. We are never allowed to act contrary to the dictate of conscience when we can prudently judge it to be right, for then it is to be regarded as a rule of conduct; and when we act thus, our action becomes good or bad according to the idea we have of its goodness or malice.

But now comes the distinction between a *right* or *true* conscience, and an *erroneous* or *false* conscience.

A right and a false conscience.

A *right* conscience is one whose judgment is in real conformity with the law of God; it is an *erroneous* conscience when it is only in apparent conformity, that is, when it represents to us an action as good which is really bad, or *vice versa*.

These errors of conscience may be *vincible* or *invincible*. They are *vincible* when he who acts neglects to take the proper means of discovering the truth, despite certain suspicions which arise as to the goodness or badness of his act, and as to his obligation to examine whether the act is really good or bad: such errors are due to culpable ignorance. They are *invincible* when there is no manner of suspicion in his mind regarding the nature of his act either during its performance or on consideration of its cause.

Therefore, (1) a *right* conscience must be followed at all times, either by doing what it commands, or by avoiding what it condemns. (2) An *invincibly erroneous* conscience ought to be obeyed. So long as a man's conscience really declares certain things to be right, and he has no suspicion that his conscience is an erroneous one, he ought to follow it. (3) A *vincibly erroneous* conscience, in so far as our error is voluntary, does not excuse us from sin. We must not, then, act according to the voice of such a conscience; we must rectify it by removing, as far as possible, the error upon which our judgment is based; and to this end we must apply ordinary common diligence.

Conscience may be *certain*, *doubtful*, or *scrupulous*, according to the motive on which it is grounded.

A *certain* conscience is one which is supported by motives so strong that there is no reasonable **A certain conscience.** doubt as to the goodness or badness of the contemplated act; that is, in obeying it, we feel morally certain that we are right. Now, moral certainty is that kind of certainty which a prudent man would act upon in a matter of importance, and which excludes all doubt capable of making us suspend our judgment.

A *doubtful* conscience is one which finds itself so balanced between the goodness or malice of an **A doubtful conscience.** action that it cannot prudently decide either that the action contemplated is good or that it is bad. Such a conscience must be rectified by examination and by seeking prudent direction on the doubtful points. If the latter is not available, it must be remembered that, if we have carefully considered whether there is some law which binds us to do or not to do a certain act, and we are still in doubt whether there is, then we are not bound to do it or omit it as the case may be.

A *scrupulous* conscience, which is really a diseased conscience, is one which, through a groundless **A scrupulous conscience.** fear, regards as forbidden what is really permitted; *i.e.*, for some frivolous reason it apprehends sin where there is none, or judges that a harmless act is sinful. He who is subject to scruples must not act against his conscience, but he can, and must, act against his scruples by submitting entirely to the advice of his director. This is the only true remedy for healing such a spiritual malady.*

CHAPTER XLVIII

DIVISION OF THE COMMANDMENTS

WHAT THE FIRST COMMANDMENT ENJOINS.

THE Moral Law, which in its very nature is eternal, and
The Decalogue which, as we have seen, God in the beginning
confirmed by impressed on human nature, was afterwards
Christ. more clearly promulgated in the Decalogue, through Moses, to the people of Israel at Mount Sinai. It was finally ratified by our Lord Himself, who perfected it, and entrusted it to His Church to be laid down for the observance of all the faithful.

Christians, then, are bound to keep the Commandments
of the Old Law, because Christ came not to
Why binding destroy but to fulfil the Law (Matt. v. 17) by
on Christians.
• explaining the full meaning of the Command-
ments, and by teaching men to keep them not only in the letter, but in the spirit; and because they contain the Moral Law which is binding on all men since it is grounded on human nature, and written by God in all hearts (Rom. ii. 15).

The Decalogue, then, is as old as the world. In giving it to Moses, God only caused to be committed to writing a Law already existing, inasmuch as owing to human passions, it is liable to be neglected or changed; and when the Son of God came upon earth, He recalled men, both by word and

* See Gousset's "Théologie Morale," vol. i., p. 25 *sqq.*

example, to the perfect observance of the Decalogue: "If thou wilt enter into life," He said, "keep the Commandments" (Matt. xix. 17).

The Ten Commandments in order are expressed as follows:

The Ten Commandments. 1. I am the Lord thy God, who brought thee out of the land of Egypt, and out of the house of bondage. Thou shalt not have strange gods before Me. Thou shalt not make to thyself any graven thing nor the likeness of anything that is in heaven above, or in the earth beneath, nor of those things that are in the waters under the earth. Thou shalt not adore them nor serve them.

2. Thou shalt not take the name of the Lord thy God in vain.

3. Remember that thou keep holy the Sabbath day.

4. Honour thy father and thy mother.

5. Thou shalt not kill.

6. Thou shalt not commit adultery.

7. Thou shalt not steal.

8. Thou shalt not bear false witness against thy neighbour.

9. Thou shalt not covet thy neighbour's wife.

10. Thou shalt not covet thy neighbour's goods.

The two Tables. The Ten Commandments were originally written on two tables of stone and were afterwards kept in the Ark of the Covenant. The first table comprised, in the first three Commandments, the duties we owe to God, while the second table comprised, in the last seven Commandments, our duties towards ourselves and our neighbours. It will be seen that the Commandments, in every case, forbid by name the greatest sin of each kind, leaving the lesser sins implied, together with the acts and circumstances that lead up to them.

Bearing in mind the words of St. Paul, "Love is the

fulfilling of the Law" (Rom. xiii. 10), and considering the commands and prohibitions of the Decalogue as merely the development of the great law of Charity—"Thou shalt love the Lord thy God with thy whole heart. . . . and thy neighbour as thyself" (Mark xii. 30, 31)—we shall be in a position to understand more clearly the explanation of each particular Commandment.

A more perfect summary of the First Commandment could not be found than in the words of our Lord when He was tempted by Satan in the desert: "It is written: The Lord thy God shalt thou adore, and Him only shalt thou serve" (Matt. iv. 10). This Commandment, then, sets before us God as our sovereign Lord, and requires us to pay due honour and adoration to Him, while at the same time it forbids us to acknowledge any other god than the one true God.

The First Commandment.

As the Catechism has it: "We are commanded to worship the one, true, and living God by Faith, Hope, Charity, and Religion." Indeed, these virtues are implied in the very precept of worship, for we cannot worship God without knowing and loving Him, and we cannot love Him without Faith and Hope. Then, by virtue of the First Commandment, we must know God, we must believe in Him, hope in Him, and love Him, and we must render Him that supreme worship which is His due: in a word, we must "glorify Him as God" (Rom. i. 21).

We must worship God by Faith, Hope, Charity and Religion.

We must know God. Now the light of reason, as well as the light of Faith, clearly reveals to us the existence of God, the Maker and Preserver of all things. This is shown to us from the world and from the creatures in the world, as the Creator may be discovered from the creatures: " For the invisible things of Him, from the creation of the world, are clearly seen, being understood from the things that

We are bound to know God.

are made ; His eternal power also and Divinity "
(Rom. i. 20).

By Faith we pay homage to God's supreme truth by
firmly believing all that He has revealed to
We must believe in God. His Church, and this on the authority of His
Divine word; that is, because He, the very
truth, has revealed it.

By Hope we pay homage to His goodness, power, and
fidelity to His promises, by expecting with
We must hope in Him. confidence that He will give us eternal happiness and all the means necessary to obtain it,
through the merits of Jesus Christ. Not only is He
infinitely good and faithful to His promises, but He
is willing and desirous to help us, and being infinitely
powerful, He *can* help us.

By Charity we pay homage to God's infinite perfections,
which make Him infinitely worthy of all our
We must love Him. love. By this virtue we love God above all
things for His own sake and our neighbour
as ourselves for God's sake. We worship Him by Charity
when, for His sake, we would rather lose all things, even
life itself, than act against His will: "If you love Me,
keep My Commandments" (John xiv. 15).

By the virtue of Religion we offer to God that supreme
homage and adoration which is His due; we
*We must wor-
ship Him by
Religion.* acknowledge His absolute dominion over us and
our entire dependence upon Him, and render
Him a worship worthy of Him. Now such worship,
to be perfect, must be *interior* and *exterior, direct* and
indirect.

We honour God with *interior* worship when we make
acts of Faith, Hope, and Charity, and in our
*Interior
worship.* minds and hearts perform acts of reverence,
adoration, and thanksgiving, and of obedience
and humble resignation to His holy will.

Yet this interior worship is not enough ; for man, who is composed of soul and body, owes to God the homage of his whole being; hence we must pay Him also *exterior* and public worship. Such worship increases our interior worship, strengthens our faith, and is necessary for preserving and spreading our holy religion. God has ever commanded it, and our Lord Himself has told us : "Where two or three are gathered together in My name, there am I in the midst of them " (Matt. xviii. 20). Now this exterior worship comprises all those outward acts by which we acknowledge our faith in God and honour Him, such as making the sign of the cross, genuflecting, or praying in common. We worship Him publicly by attending the services of the Church, and especially by being present at the Holy Sacrifice of the Mass, in which is offered to Him a complete acknowledgment of His dominion over us and our dependence upon Him.

Exterior worship.

As the worship of God is enjoined by the First Commandment, so too is the obligation of honouring Him in His Saints, since it is for His sake that we honour those whom He Himself honours and loves. Duty, moreover, binds us to honour and reverence everything belonging to Him.

God honoured in His Saints.

When we honour God in Himself, our worship is *direct ;* it is *indirect* when we honour Him in His Saints ; for the honour given directly to the Saints refers indirectly to God, the Author of all sanctity. And by honouring the Saints we not only honour God, but we are incited to imitate the virtues they practised with such fidelity on earth.

Direct and indirect worship.

As we have already (Chapter XLII.) treated of veneration and invocation of the Saints, we shall here confine ourselves to explaining the honour paid by Catholics to Relics, Crucifixes, Images, and Holy Pictures, which, we shall see, is a relative honour, in so far as they relate to Christ and His Saints, and are memorials of them.

Besides honouring the Saints directly in themselves, we also honour them indirectly in their relics and images; yet we honour these relics and images, not for their own sakes, nor for any intrinsic value they possess, but because they relate to God and to the friends of God. When we pray before an image of our Lord or of His Saints, we pray to our Lord and to the Saints whom these images represent, and to whom the honour is referred. Such images serve but to bring to our minds the mysteries of our Religion, the history of our Redemption, and the holy lives of the Saints. So, too, with the Crucifix: when we look upon it, are we not reminded of the sufferings our Saviour endured upon the Cross for our salvation?

Relics and images.

It has ever been the practice of the universal Church to honour the relics of the Saints. The bodies of the Saints were once the temples of the Holy Ghost, and one day they will rise again, to share the glory of their souls. Not only does the Church sanction such honours being given, but she even requires relics of the Saints to be inserted in all altars where the Holy Mass is offered. God, moreover, has often been pleased to work wonderful miracles through the Relics of the Saints, as we gather both from the Holy Scriptures and from the history of the Church: "When the body had touched the bones of Eliseus, the man came to life, and stood upon his feet" (4 Kings xiii. 21). And in the Acts we read: "They brought out the sick into the streets . . . that when Peter came, his shadow, at the least, might overshadow any of them, and they might be delivered from their infirmities" (v. 15). Of St. Paul it is written: "There were brought from his body to the sick handkerchiefs and aprons, and the diseases departed from them"

The Church has always honoured the relics of the Saints.

(Acts xix. 12). What wonder, then, if God works miracles by the relics of Saints and Martyrs to testify to the sanctity of His servants, and to encourage us both to give them a reasonable honour and to imitate their lives!

CHAPTER XLIX

WHAT THE FIRST COMMANDMENT FORBIDS

As the First Commandment enjoins the practice of the virtues of Faith, Hope, Charity, and Religion, it naturally follows that it forbids whatever is opposed to these virtues. Now as Faith, Hope, and Charity have already been treated of at length, we shall content ourselves here with merely naming the chief sins against them, and with explaining more fully the meaning of the sins that are committed against the virtue of Religion.

We can sin against Faith by refusing to believe what the Church teaches; by wilful doubt in matters of Faith; by denying any article of Faith; by culpable ignorance of the doctrines of the Church; and by exposing ourselves to the danger of losing our Faith through the neglect of our spiritual duties, reading irreligious books, attending non-Catholic schools when Catholic schools are within our reach, and taking part in the services or prayers of a false religion.

Sins against Faith.

We may sin against Hope by defect and by excess; by defect when we fall into *Despair*; and by excess when we give way to *Presumption*. Now we sin by *Despair* when we regard our sins as being too great for pardon, or our passions as too strong to be overcome; also when, considering the joys of Heaven beyond our reach, we abandon ourselves to the pleasures of sense and to the enjoyment of the goods of this world, without doing anything towards our eternal salvation;

Sins against Hope.

while in a lesser degree, we sin by distrust when we are wanting in confidence in God.

We sin by *Presumption* when we flatter ourselves that we shall obtain eternal salvation without taking the necessary means to attain it; for example, when we do not faithfully keep the Commandments of God and the Church; or when we rashly expose ourselves to the danger of sin, expecting God to extricate us. We also sin by presumption when we continue to sin either relying on the ease with which we imagine we can obtain pardon, or supposing that God will pardon many sins just as readily as He will forgive a single offence.

Every mortal sin is directly opposed to Charity. We sin against Charity by indifference to God and Sins against to things divine; by hatred of God and going Charity. against Him and His Church; and by neglecting to make acts of the love of God. Indeed all sins offend God and thus weaken or destroy Charity within us; " He that hath My commandments and keepeth them, he it is that loveth Me " (John xiv. 21).

The sins opposed to Religion may be brought under *three* principal heads, *Idolatry*, *Superstition*, and *Irreligion*. Sins against —IDOLATRY, which means the worship of idols Religion— or images, is the giving to any creature whatso-Idolatry. ever the adoration or supreme honour due to God alone, viz., the absolute worship of *latria*.

The First Commandment, as we are told in the Catechism, does not forbid the making of images, but the making of idols; that is, *it forbids us to make images to be adored or honoured as gods*. The Church, which is the guardian of truth, enjoins the faithful to show relative honour to relics, crucifixes, images, and holy pictures, as they relate to Christ and His Saints and are memorials of them, but she forbids us to pay them absolute honour, since, being without faculties or sense, " they can neither see, nor hear, nor help us." To give *divine* worship, then, to the Saints and Angels, or to holy things, instead of that inferior honour and worship which is their due, would be a great sin against the First Commandment, and nothing less than idolatry.

But those non-Catholics who regard respect paid to holy things as in itself idolatry are strangely inconsistent, since, in many parts of the Old Testament, we find the making of images enjoined by Almighty God Himself: " Thou shalt make also two Cherubim of beaten gold, on the two sides of the Oracle "(Exod. xxv. 18). Again, " He graved Cherubim on the walls. . . . He made also in the house of the Holy of Holies two Cherubim of image-work ; and he overlaid them with gold " (2 Paralip. iii. 7, 10). Would God have allowed such things to be made and placed in such an honourable position if they were so dangerous as to be inseparable from idolatry ?

Superstition. SUPERSTITION, like idolatry, is a sin against Religion by way of excess, and consists in turning away from God, and from the means of help which He has ordained, to seek the aid of the devil in order to obtain something which we desire to possess, or in attributing to things a power which they do not possess either by nature or by the prayers of the Church. In either case there is a withdrawing from God's Providence. To put our confidence, then, in fortune-tellers, to trust to charms and spells and dreams, or to such things as have no natural connection with what is sought, is to be guilty of superstitious practices, and is condemned by the Church.

The devil, being a pure spirit, can know and do many things that are beyond the power of man. His long experience of the ways of men and his knowledge of the laws of nature give him an advantage over our weaker powers that enables him to foresee much that must remain hidden from us. Yet we must never have recourse to him with the object of discovering future or hidden things by means of his help. His hatred of God must for ever make him God's enemy, and therefore ours also.

Superstitious practices may be brought under two main headings : (1) *Divination,* which consists in having recourse to the devil for the purpose of getting to know hidden things or things to come. Since this is paying homage to the power and knowledge of the evil one, it is always a sin against the First Commandment. (2) *Vain Observation,* which consists in looking to natural events and chance and accident for results which can depend on God only; and also in making use for great ends of frivolous means which naturally have not the virtue of producing the effects expected of them, and which have not been instituted by God or by the Church for those ends.

Division of Superstition.

It is not, however, a vain or superstitious practice, but on the contrary a praiseworthy one, to carry about one's person an Agnus Dei, a Scapular, a relic or an image of our Lady or of a Saint, when piously done with a simple intention of showing our trust in the invocation of the Saints, and realising that these things possess only such efficacy as God has given them through the prayers and blessings of the Church.

Divination.

The principal ways in which recourse may be had to the devil are by *Magic, Witchcraft, Necromancy,* and *Fortune-telling.*

Magic.

Magic is a so-called art by which men profess to do things contrary to the laws of nature. It consists in having recourse to the devil with the object of working wonders by his assistance.

Witchcraft.

Witchcraft is dealing with the devil either directly or through some one who has entered into a compact with him, and that generally with the intention of injuring others.

Necromancy consists in holding pretended communica-
tions with the souls of the dead.   The devils
Necromancy.   often pretend to be the souls of the dead, and it
is generally by their intervention that responses are given.
Spiritualism, séances, table-turning, planchette, etc., are
only modern forms of necromancy.

Fortune-telling is a pretended foretelling of the future.
It is a sin when done in earnest, as it implies
Fortune-telling.   some compact with the evil one : " Let there
not be found among you any one that consulteth fortune-
tellers " (Deut. xviii. 11).

Since it is superstition to attach great importance to
things that are not entitled to any, or to but
*Vain
Observation.*   little, or to assign to things a virtue which God
has not given them, we may class under *Vain
Observation* such sins as are committed through *Charms and
Spells*, *Omens*, *Dreams* and *Astrology*.

Charms are things done, used, or worn, and Spells are
words or sentences used, to produce effects
Charms and
Spells.   which they have no natural tendency to bring
about ; for example, placing a horse-shoe over
the door for good luck.

Omens are casual events or occurrences which are thought
to portend good or evil ; for example, certain
Omens.   days are considered to be lucky or unlucky ;
while spilling the salt on the table is thought to forebode
misfortune to the person who spills it.

To consider dreams as foreboding the future is usually
superstition, since ordinary dreams do not come
Dreams.   from God as manifesting His will : " Neither let
there be found among you any one that observeth dreams
and omens " (Deut. xviii. 10).

Astrology is the pretended science of foretelling future
events by the situation and different aspects of
Astrology.   the heavenly bodies, which are supposed to have
an influence on human affairs.

IRRELIGION includes those sins against Religion which arise by way of defect, such as the want of due reverence for God, or of due respect to persons, places, or things consecrated to God. It therefore includes *Impiety*, which is the sin of those who outrage or blaspheme God or His Church ; and *Sacrilege*, which is the profanation of what is holy, and which may be personal, local, or real, according as it is directed against a person, a place, or a thing consecrated to Divine worship.

Irreligion.

It is *Personal Sacrilege* to violate or to treat with great irreverence persons of either sex consecrated to God by Holy Orders or by vow. It would, for instance, be a sacrilege to strike them maliciously, and a sin of impurity committed by or with such persons would also be a sacrilege : " Touch ye not My anointed ; and do no evil to My prophets " (Ps. civ. 15). And again : " With all thy soul fear the Lord, and reverence His priests " (Ecclus. vii. 31).

Sacrilege of holy persons.

Local Sacrilege consists in any violation, profanation. or desecration of places consecrated to God, such as a church or a .cemetery. Any sin committed in a church is a sacrilege, but not necessarily a mortal sin of sacrilege. Theft, for example, would probably not constitute a mortal sin of sacrilege unless the matter stolen were grave and belonged to, or were under the care of the Church. To put. such places to a profane use would be the crime of sacrilege · " Make not the house of My Father a house of traffic " (John ii. 16).

Sacrilege of holy places.

Real Sacrilege is the violation of things that are consecrated to God's service, or that relate to Him in a special manner, as a consecrated chalice or the sacred vessels. To steal such things or to employ them in profane uses, to exercise a holy office without ordination, or to administer or receive the Sacraments unworthily, would be a sacrilege.

Sacrilege of holy things.

Related to real sacrilege of holy things is the sin of

Simony.

Simony, so called from the sin of Simon Magus, who offered money to the Apostles to induce them to give him the sacred power which they possessed. It is the buying or selling of spiritual things, sacred offices and the like, for money: "May thy money perish with thee, because thou hast esteemed the gift of God to be purchased with money" (Acts viii. 20).

CHAPTER L

THE SECOND COMMANDMENT

" Thou shalt not take the name of the Lord thy God in vain."

THE First Commandment, as we have seen, bids us adore

The Second Commandment follows from the First.

God as God and reverence Him. Not to take His name in vain would seem to be implied in this same duty. Yet, to impress upon us how all-important is this obligation, God has given us another distinct commandment requiring us to worship Him *in our words*, and a special threat is denounced against all those who shall dare to violate it: "The Lord will not hold him guiltless that shall take the name of the Lord his God in vain" (Exod. xx. 7).

But if we love God and worship Him, we shall naturally

What this Commandment enjoins.

speak of Him with respect and reverence. The Second Commandment, therefore, enjoins the duty of praising God, of invoking His name with love and respect, and of doing all in our power to promote its honour; an injunction concisely summed up in the words of the Catechism: "By the Second Commandment we are commanded to speak with reverence of God and all holy persons and things, and to keep our lawful oaths and vows."

This Commandment, therefore, is directed against sins of word, but particularly against those words which immediately offend God, as distinguished from those which offend Him through being directed against our neighbour.   It forbids all such words as are contrary to the respect we owe to the holy name of God, namely, false, rash, unjust, and unnecessary oaths, as also blaspheming, cursing, and profane words, and the violation of our lawful oaths and vows.

What the Second Commandment forbids.

We have seen that we are bound to speak with reverence not only of God, but of all holy persons and things; that is, of the Angels and Saints, of Religion and its ministers ; and this because they relate to God.   Now the sin most directly opposed to this reverence is Blasphemy, which consists in speaking, or voluntarily thinking, contemptuously of God or His Saints.   To be guilty of blasphemy, then, it is not necessary that our words or thoughts be aimed directly against God, for there is a blasphemy which aims at God indirectly, since it is aimed at His Saints, His Church, and whatever has immediate reference to Religion.   Thus to cast insults at the Angels and Saints, and particularly at our Lady, the Queen of Angels and of Saints, to turn to ridicule the sacred truths of Religion, the Holy Mass, the Sacraments, or the Sacred Scriptures, and to attribute to creatures what belongs to God alone, are all sins of blasphemy.   " He that blasphemeth the name of the Lord, dying let him die " (Lev. xxiv. 16).   While blasphemy is the worst sin by which we take God's name in vain, cursing and profane words are lesser sins of a like nature.

Blasphemy.

By cursing we mean calling upon God to inflict some evil on our neighbour, or ourselves, or on any of God's creatures.   Because cursing denotes a creature's calling upon the Creator to work its evil will, it dishonours God, and thus offends against the Second Com-

Cursing.

mandment, besides being opposed to the love which Christ requires of all His followers ; for when we deliberately call down ill upon our neighbour we are going directly against the second great Precept of Charity : "Thou shalt love thy neighbour as thyself."

If a curse is but a thoughtless expression, and no irreverence whatever is meant, it would be at the most a venial sin, or it might be no sin at all, particularly in the case of one sincerely trying to master a habit of using bad language. But even in its most innocent form, the practice of using bad language is blameworthy, and should be carefully avoided. The offence would be more serious through any scandal that might be given to others ; but the gravity of the sin depends as a rule on whether the harm imprecated is grievous or trivial, and deliberate or unintentional. It might indeed prove a check on a man given to cursing were he to reflect that the evil which he invokes upon others is more likely to fall in some way on his own head.

The sinfulness of cursing.

Profanity, or using *Profane Words*, by which is understood the speaking of what is sacred without due reverence, is also forbidden by this Commandment as being contrary to the respect which we owe to God and to what belongs to Him, or as tending to lessen it. To quote the sacred Scriptures irreverently, or habitually to employ such expletives as "hell," "devil," "damn," etc., so often introduced into ordinary conversation, is so far profane, and unbecoming the lips of a sincere Christian. Profane words are more or less serious according as they are, or are not, spoken out of deliberate contempt of what is sacred : "Let no evil speech proceed from your mouth, but that which is good to the edification of faith, that it may afford grace to the hearers" (Eph. iv. 29).

Profane words.

CHAPTER LI

THE SECOND COMMANDMENT (*continued*).

ON KEEPING OUR LAWFUL OATHS AND VOWS.

BESIDES the sins of Blasphemy, Cursing, and Profanity, the Second Commandment, as we pointed out above, forbids all false, rash, unjust, and unnecessary Oaths, while, at the same time, it enjoin the keeping of our lawful Oaths and Vows. We must see, then, what is meant by an Oath, and what by a Vow.

Now to swear, or to take an oath, is to call God to witness the truth of what we say, or our sincerity in what we promise. Thus an oath is an act of religion by which we honour God, when we make it with *truth*, with *judgment*, and with *justice*; for to call upon God to witness is to acknowledge that God is the very truth, and knows all things. It is the greatest pledge we can give of the truth and sincerity of our words.

An Oath.

In the ordinary affairs of life an oath is not necessary; we must therefore content ourselves with simply affirming or denying. Only when God's honour, or our own, or our neighbour's good requires it is an oath lawful, and even then the three conditions of truth, judgment, and justice must be present: "Thou shalt swear, as the Lord liveth, in *truth*, in *judgment*, and in *justice*" (Jer. iv. 2). The matter of the oath, then, must be true; it must be taken with mature deliberation; and it must involve no sin. If our oath is wanting in truth, we are guilty of *perjury* or *false swearing*; if it is wanting in judgment, we are guilty of *rash swearing*; if it is wanting in justice, we are guilty of an *unjust* oath. An oath that involved a sin, *i.e.*, if it were taken to con-

When an Oath is lawful.

firm a sin, would be deficient in justice ; for example, it would be an unjust oath if I were to swear to the truth of what I said in detracting my neighbour. If I were to strengthen a calumny by an oath, my oath would be wanting both in truth and in justice. An oath to break the Seventh Commandment, or to sin against any virtue, would thus come in the class of unjust oaths.

Unnecessary Oaths arise from swearing lightly, *i.e.*, without reflection, or for trivial reasons. They are disrespectful to God, and often expose us to the danger of perjury. Moreover, as the quality of judgment is wanting in them, they are generally rash, and may be unjust. Yet, unless they are combined with grave irreverence towards God, or with scandal or perjury, rash and unnecessary oaths are only venial sins.

Unnecessary Oaths.

Promises made on oath are binding unless the thing promised is bad in itself or forbidden. But an oath to do a wicked action must not be fulfilled. To take an oath to do anything unlawful is a sin in itself: a second sin would result from its fulfilment, for we are never obliged to offend God. When Herod promised on oath to give the daughter of Herodias whatsoever she should ask, he sinned by taking a rash oath, and exposed himself to the sin of an unjust oath as well, since he knew not what injustice her request might lead him into. Yet he committed a second and more grievous sin by keeping an oath which led him to the unjust beheading of St. John the Baptist.

Promises made on oath.

The Second Commandment may be broken, too, by neglecting to keep our vows : " When thou hast made a vow to the Lord thy God, thou shalt not delay to pay it, because the Lord thy God will require it " (Deut. xxiii. 21).

Vows.

Now a vow is a free and deliberate promise made to God either to do something good which one was not bound

to do, and this with the intention that the promise shall
be binding under pain of sin; or to undertake a second
A Vow more   obligation of religion to do something which
than a mere   one was already bound to do. Thus, if I take a
resolution.   vow to pay a just debt, I am bound to pay the
debt both from the virtue of justice and from the virtue of
religion. If I do not pay, I commit two sins. A vow,
then, must be a free act; but, once made, it is strictly binding. It differs from a good resolution, which is but a firm
intention to do a thing without binding ourselves under
pain of sin to do it.

A vow may be *solemn*, or it may be *simple*; it is *solemn*
when made in certain Religious Orders ap-
Solemn and   proved by the Church, and accepted by the
simple Vows.   Church as perpetual; or in any other way in
which the Church has approved the taking of solemn
vows; for example, vows of poverty, chastity, and obedience taken in some Religious Orders, or a vow of chastity
taken on entering Holy Orders. The vow is *simple* when
one of the conditions required in a solemn vow is wanting.

Vows are pleasing to God because they are voluntary
offerings made to Him; and there is more merit in doing
good works by vow than without a vow, since by a vow we
make a sacrifice of the will to God. In many parts of the
Scriptures we find Almighty God pleased to accept the
vows of His faithful servants: "And Jacob made a vow,
saying: If God shall be with me, and shall keep me in the
way by which I walk . . . and I shall return prosper-
ously to my father's house, the Lord shall be my God"
(Gen. xxviii. 20, 21). "And Anna made a vow, saying:
O Lord of hosts . . . if Thou wilt give to Thy servant
a man-child, I will give him to the Lord all the days of his
life" (1 Kings i. 11).

In making a vow we should be guided by discretion and
prudence, and should seek the advice of a confessor; but

a vow once made must be kept, unless it be impossible or unlawful to do so: "If thou hast vowed any thing to God, defer not to pay it; for an unfaithful and foolish promise displeaseth Him. . . . And it is much better not to vow, than after a vow not to perform the things promised" (Eccles. v. 3, 4). By virtue of the power which Christ gave to His Church of binding and loosing, she can, for a just reason, dispense from a vow, or commute the good work vowed for some other good work. If one who is subject to the will of another were to make a vow, such a vow could be annulled; or if a person, after taking a vow, found that circumstances arose which made the keeping of his vow very difficult or unadvisable, he might be dispensed from it or have it commuted, that is, changed for some other good work, by proper authority; but no power can dispense when, by doing so, the rights of another would be interfered with.

Vows to be observed.

With regard to the making of vows it would be well to bear in mind this simple rule: To make a vow is of counsel, but to comply with it is of precept. We should moreover remember that the strict observance of the Second Commandment, by obliging us to show our respect for God, helps us to preserve His love within us; for love soon ceases to exist where respect is set at naught.

CHAPTER LII

THE THIRD COMMANDMENT

" Remember that thou keep holy the Sabbath-day."

MAN is composed of soul and body; and as both soul and body come from God, so must each, in its own way, pay honour to its Creator. Now just as the First Commandment obliges us to worship God by an *interior* worship, the worship of our minds and

Necessity of exterior worship.

hearts, the Second to give Him the worship of our tongues, so does the Third Commandment enjoin us by a positive precept to dedicate a particular portion of our time to *exterior* and public worship of Him, and thus to give Him the worship of our exterior actions. The sanctification then of a certain part of our time serves not only as a public profession of our Faith, and to benefit our spiritual life, but must be accomplished to fulfil the direct command of God.

We ought to employ all our time in the service of God, and strive to sanctify all our actions by directing them to His greater honour and glory ; but, lest our worldly occupations and the supplying of our temporal wants should occupy our attention so much as to make us forget God, He Himself has appointed one day in the week to be in a special manner and immediately dedicated to rendering Him our homage. This He did for three great ends : (1) that order and unity might be given to the worship we owe Him ; (2) that the obligation of worshipping Him might be constantly recalled to our minds ; and (3) that our *interior* worship might be preserved, which, without *exterior* worship, would become neglected and forgotten.

A definite time appointed for exterior worship.

In the Old Law this day was the *seventh* day of the week, the Sabbath-day (the day of *rest*), and was set apart in memory of God's resting on that day after the six days of Creation : " Six days shalt thou labour, and shalt do all thy works. But on the seventh day is the Sabbath of thy God : thou shalt do no work in it. . . . For in six days the Lord made heaven and earth . . . and rested on the seventh day : therefore the Lord blessed the seventh day and sanctified it " (Exod. xx. 9-11). Another reason why the Jews were commanded to observe the Sabbath-day with particular strictness was the benefit God conferred upon

Establishment of the Sabbath-day.

them by delivering them from the Egyptian bondage.
He required that His people should prove their gratitude
on that day in particular for the *rest* which He had granted
to them: "Remember that thou didst serve in Egypt, and
the Lord thy God brought thee out from thence with a
strong hand, and a stretched out arm.   Therefore hath He
commanded thee that thou shouldst observe the Sabbath-
day" (Deut. v. 15).   The Law of the Sabbath, then, we
see extends as far back as the creation of man.

Among Christians the day of rest has been transferred
from the seventh day to the first day of the
week—called the Lord's Day—to show that
the Jewish ceremonies were abolished, and to
honour the great mysteries of our Religion; for it was on
a Sunday that our Lord in His human nature rose again
from the dead, that He appeared to the Apostles and gave
them power to forgive sins and to teach all nations, and
that He sent down the Holy Ghost upon His Church,—all
which things are calculated in a special manner to excite
our piety, since they betoken a new and more excellent
spiritual deliverance and creation.

The Christian Sunday.

Now the Third Commandment ordains that we should
sanctify the Lord's Day, and forbids us to
profane it: " Keep you My Sabbath. . . .
He that shall profane it shall be put to death:
he that shall do any work in it, his soul shall perish out of
the midst of his people " (Exod. xxxi. 14).   God in a
particular manner insists on the observance of this Commandment, which begins with the word " *Remember,*"
because men are apt to forget or to transgress a precept
that seems to interfere with those worldly concerns and
profits, which they love more than God and their own souls.

What the Third Commandment ordains.

Two things, therefore, are required of us; that we spend
the day in such works as may sanctify it, and that we perform no unnecessary servile works.   Merely to rest from

servile works, and spend the day in idleness, is not enough :
" Remember that thou keep *holy* the Sabbath-day " (Exod
xx. 8).

To hear Mass devoutly, to approach the Sacraments, to
attend the evening service, to hear the Word
of God preached, to read some spiritual book,
to visit the sick, to comfort the afflicted, are
all works which especially help to sanctify the Lord's
Day ; but of all these works, only one, the assisting at
Holy Mass, is enjoined by positive precept, and is obligatory under pain of mortal sin ; and this obligation extends
to all who have come to the use of reason, and who are
not prevented from attending by some grave reason.

The obligation of hearing Mass.

But those persons are dispensed from the obligation of
hearing Mass who are either physically or morally unable
to do so ; for example, the sick and those in charge of the
sick, as well as those in charge of children too young to
accompany them to church.   Inclemency of the weather
might in some cases prove a sufficient excuse ; and those
also would be dispensed who, on account of distance, could
not get to church without grave inconvenience.   Yet, if a
person for some sufficient reason is unable to attend Mass,
he should not fail, when possible, to say suitable prayers at
home, and unite in spirit and intention with those who are
actually present in person.   What is said of the sanctification of the Sunday applies generally to Holydays of
Obligation.

Of all devotions to hear Mass is the most excellent, and
the one most calculated to honour God and to procure our
eternal salvation.

Now to hear Mass it is necessary to be present where
Mass is being celebrated, and in such a way as to form
part of the congregation, and so to attend with the mind
as to join in the act of Divine worship.   We are obliged,
moreover, to hear an entire Mass ; so that wilfully and

without cause to absent one's self during any part of the
Mass is wrong; and to be absent during a considerable
portion of the Mass, for example, from the beginning till
after the Offertory, or during an essential part of it, such
as the Consecration, would be a mortal sin.

Besides hearing Mass we should assist as far as possible
at the other public services of the Church; for, as the
Catechism has it, "We are commanded to rest from servile
The other
devotions of
the Church. works that we may have time and opportunity
for prayer, going to the Sacraments, hearing
instructions, and reading good books."   Therefore, although the Church does not command, she earnestly
exhorts all her children to assist at the other Divine offices,
the neglect of which would indeed be blameworthy, particularly if it arose from sloth or indifference, or gave bad
example to others; but the strict observance of the Sunday does not exclude lawful and proper recreation.

This observance of the Sunday is a public profession of
Value of public
prayer. our faith, and is greatly calculated to increase
our faith, when we behold the glorious spec-
tacle of almost the whole world united in one
and the same act of supplication.   "How much more
effectual then than the prayers of the *individual*, or of
the *family*, or of the *nation* must be the prayer of the
Church, that great assemblage of souls, of families, and of
nations, the entire Christian world on its knees at the feet
of the great Creator bearing our prayers with authority
right up to the throne of God!"   If we remember that
public prayers offered in the name of the Church, and by
the ministers of the Church, are more powerful than our
private devotions, shall we allow some trifling inconvenience to hinder us from uniting our voices with the rest
of the faithful and with the whole Church?

Now the Third Commandment forbids whatever is calculated to prevent us from sanctifying the day consecrated

to the service of God; hence it is that we are bidden to abstain from servile works on Sundays and Holydays of Obligation.

We distinguish three kinds of works; *liberal*, in which

Liberal, common, and servile works.

the mind is employed more than the body, and which tend directly to the cultivation of the mind, such as reading, writing, studying, and teaching; *common*, in which both mind and body may be equally employed, and which are done equally by all classes of persons, such as fishing,* shooting, and hunting, when accompanied with no great toil; and *servile* (Lat., *servus*, a slave, a servant), in which the body is occupied more than the mind, such as manual labour, sewing, and all such works as are generally done by servants, mechanics, or tradesmen, and which more directly administer to the needs of the body. The prohibition of the last class of works extends, too, to all public business transactions, and to law proceedings, as the latter are generally attended with noise and contention. And be it remembered that those who cause others to perform servile works are as guilty as those who themselves do the works. Liberal and common works are allowed even for the sake of gain.

Such ordinary works as relate to our daily necessities

Household work.

and the cares of the household are allowed so long as they do not expose us to the danger of missing Mass unnecessarily; but only such of these should be done on a Sunday as cannot conveniently be done beforehand or put off till another day.

Occasions, however, may arise which may free us from

When servile work is permitted.

the obligation of resting from servile works: (1) *a dispensation*, for weighty reasons, may be given by the Bishop or the parish priest;

* Fishing with the rod and line, for example, is not unlawful, but going out to sea and plying the trade in an ordinary way is forbidden. But in all the above cases one must never expose oneself to the danger of missing Mass.

(2) *urgent necessity*, for example fire or flood, the gathering in of the crops when they would be likely to suffer from bad weather; (3) *piety*, that is, when the service of God or the interests of Religion require such works as the adorning of the altar or the church; and (4) *our neighbour's good*, since charity allows us to work for the sick or the poor when their necessities are pressing.

CHAPTER LIII

THE FOURTH COMMANDMENT

I. *"Honour thy father and thy mother."*

THE first three Commandments were written on the First Table of the Law, and have reference to God, while the Fourth Commandment is the first of those inscribed on the Second Table, or of those which concern ourselves and our neighbour. It has for its object the duties of children towards their parents, and, by implication, the duties of parents towards their children. It is concerned, too, with the mutual duties of superiors and inferiors.

Duties implied in the Fourth Commandment.

This Commandment, as St. Paul observes (Eph. vi. 2), is the first Commandment with a *promise:* "Honour thy father and thy mother, that thou mayest be long-lived upon the land which the Lord thy God will give thee" (Exod. xx. 12). Though the promise is of a temporal nature, it should bring to our minds the eternal reward that awaits all our virtuous actions, and especially the virtue of obedience, a virtue so much loved by our Lord, and one which seems to sum up the whole of His life on earth: "He was obedient unto death, even to the death of the Cross" (Phil. ii. 8). He Himself tells us: "I came down from heaven, not to do My own will, but the will of Him that sent Me" (John vi. 38).

Obedience.

The Divine Spirit Himself shows that nothing is more excellent and amiable in Christians than ready obedience to
parents and superiors; for the Evangelists, guided by the
Holy Ghost, relate nothing of our Saviour from His twelfth
to His thirtieth year, except that He was subject to our
Blessed Lady and St. Joseph: "He went down with
them and came to Nazareth, and was subject to them"
(Luke ii. 51).

The word "honour," used in this Commandment,
embraces three things: love, respect, and
obedience; hence it is that, by the Fourth
Commandment, we are commanded to love,
reverence, and obey our parents in all that is not contrary
to the law of God or of the Church, and to show our love
in a practical way by assisting them in their wants both
spiritual and temporal. And we must understand that
under the name of "Parents" are included our grand-
parents, who also have a like claim to our love and
respect.

What "honour" embraces.

Now the love which we owe our parents is a real internal
affection, which must show itself in our words
and actions, and in our whole conduct towards
them. It is a love that will lead us to be ready to
help them in their every necessity; that will show itself in
our bearing with them even in their faults and weaknesses;
and that will be a constant love which will never desert
them in life, and will move us to pray for them after their
death: "He that honoureth his mother is as one that
layeth up a treasure: he that honoureth his father shall
have joy in his own children, and in the day of his prayer
he shall be heard" (Ecclus. iii. 5, 6).

Love.

We must respect and reverence our parents seeing
that they take the place of God in our
regard; and an affront offered to them will
be taken as offered to God Himself: "He that feareth

Reverence.

the Lord honoureth his parents" (Ecclus. iii. 8). We must, moreover, humbly and readily defer to their advice; we must speak to them and act towards them with becoming respect and submission; in a word, we must honour them in our whole general conduct towards them, and this although they may be poorer and more uneducated than we ourselves chance to be: "Honour thy father in work and word, and all patience, that a blessing may come upon thee from him" (Ecclus. iii. 9, 10).

As the Catechism tells us, "We are bound to obey our parents in all that is not sin," that is, in all that is not in itself bad or unjust. Our obedience too must be prompt and cheerful. We should do in a pleasant manner whatever they command, and obey them as we would obey God Himself: "Children, obey your parents in all things, for this is pleasing to the Lord" (Coloss. iii. 20).

Obey.

We are also commanded to assist our parents in their wants; and the assistance we owe them extends to their spiritual as well as to their bodily needs. Therefore besides succouring them in their poverty, in sickness, and in their old age, we are bound to attend to their spiritual wants: we must pray for them particularly when they are ill; we must see that they receive the Sacraments of the Church; and when they are dead, we must continue our prayers for them, and secure for them the prayers of others. "Son, support the old age of thy father, and grieve him not in his life; and if his understanding fail, have patience with him, . . for the relieving of the father shall not be forgotten" (Ecclus. iii. 14, 15).

Assist them in their wants.

It might not be out of place here to say a word on the respect and reverence which young people owe to their elders,—a duty so often overlooked. That it is a duty on the part of youth to respect the persons of those older than themselves has always been

Respect due to our Elders.

recognised by the noblest of mankind ; hence too, considering their greater experience, due attention should be paid
to their good advice. The fulfilment of this duty is
not only ennobling in youth, and a solace to age, but
most pleasing to God : " Rise up before the hoary head,
and honour the person of the aged man ; and fear the
. Lord thy God " (Levit. xix. 32).

What is
forbidden. As the Fourth Commandment commands us
to love, reverence, and obey our parents, it
naturally follows that it forbids whatever tends
to destroy or weaken the honour which we owe them.

We sin against the love that is due to our parents whenever we entertain feelings of dislike or hatred
Sins against
filial *love*. for them, or use injurious language towards
them : " He that curseth his father and mother,
his lamp shall be put out in the midst of darkness " (Próv.
xx. 20). To wish them evil, or to do them an evil ; to
grieve them by giving them unnecessary trouble or anxiety ;
to make them angry ; not to bear with their failings ; to
refuse to assist them in their needs ; to neglect to pray
for them : all these things are sins against the Fourth
Commandment as being contrary to that filial love which
it so strictly enjoins.

We sin against the respect we owe our parents whenever
in our heart we despise them, or slight them ;
Against respect
or *reverence*. whenever we speak to them harshly, or treat
them insolently ; whenever we speak ill of them
or, through pride or vanity, are ashamed of them ; and
whenever we scoff at their advice. To threaten them, to
raise a hand against them, or to strike them would be
grievously sinful : " He that striketh his father or mother
shall be put to death " (Exod. xxi. 15).

Against
obedience. We sin against that dutiful obedience
which God requires of us when we refuse to
do the commands of our parents, or grumble
at their bidding ; when we disregard their warnings,

neglect to listen to their advice, or offer resistance to their corrections; and when we either dispute their commands, or show opposition or stubbornness, or do their bidding with a murmur. This duty of obedience is greatly modified by circumstances when the children are of age, and are removed from the protection of their parents; but children are never released from the duty of love and reverence.

II. Duties of Parents towards their Children.

The Fourth Commandment, besides requiring children to pay due honour to their parents, requires also of the parents the proper fulfilment of the many duties they themselves owe to their offspring. And these duties extend not only to the bodies of their children, but, as parents hold the place of God in their families, to their souls also. Indeed the great thought of parents should be to bring up their children for God, and with a view to their eternal life.

The Fourth Commandment in regard to parents.

Parents, then, must love their children; they must provide for their bodily wants, and do all in their power to preserve them in life and in health. As soon as possible they must see that they are baptised. It is their duty, too, to instruct and correct them, to watch over them and set them a good example, to secure them a good Catholic education, to warn them and guard them against bad companions, and, as far as they can, secure for them a suitable establishment in life. Nor must they unduly oppose a religious vocation in their children, seeing that, before belonging to them, their children belong to God: "And you, fathers, bring up your children in the discipline and correction of the Lord" (Eph. vi. 4). "The rod and reproof give wisdom; but the child that is left to his own will bringeth his mother to shame" (Prov. xxix. 15).

What parents are required to do.

III. Duties of Inferiors towards Superiors.

Besides our Parents, there are others also who have a
Our Superiors. claim to our respect and obedience, such as
our Bishops and Pastors, our Guardians and
Teachers, the Civil Authorities, and our Lawful Superiors.
In proportion as these hold the place of our parents and
may be considered as so far representing them, our love,
respect, and obedience must be in proportion to the love,
respect, and obedience which children owe to their parents.

"Obey your prelates, and be subject to them ; for they
watch as being to render an account of your
Duties we owe to our Pastors. souls, that they may do this with joy, and not
with grief " (Heb. xiii. 17). It is of them our
Lord has said : " He that heareth you heareth Me, and he
that despiseth you despiseth Me " (Luke x. 16). We
must then obey our Bishops and Pastors since God has
placed them over us, and will demand of them an account
of our souls, if perchance by their neglect we have remained
in our sins. We must follow their commands and instructions with a ready obedience, that we may please God, and
be a subject of joy and comfort to them in their heavy
and responsible tasks. We should never fail in our love
for them, nor in our outward actions be ever wanting in
the reverence and respect that is their due. If by speaking
ill of them we were to lower their character in the eyes of
others, we should be guilty of a grave sin against justice
and religion, and be the cause of serious scandal.

That our Pastors may have no earthly cares to draw
them from their spiritual duties, it is right and
Duty of sup-porting our Pastors. just that the faithful provide for the temporal
support of those through whom they receive
spiritual blessings, and whose lives are spent in work and
prayer for their spiritual good : " Let him who is in-

14

structed in the word communicate to him who instructeth him, in all good things " (Gal. vi. 6).   By *communication* is here meant the assisting of others in their wants ; and this we should do in regard to our Pastors, not only in return for what we have received, but that we may be made partakers of their good works and merits.

To Guardians and Teachers, and to all charged with the education and instruction of youth, there is owing, on the part of the ward or the pupil, a duty similar to that of children towards their parents, at any rate as far as reverence and obedience go ; for to them parental authority has been delegated for the time being, and they must be regarded as the immediate representatives and assistants of our parents.

Duties to our Guardians and Teachers.

To those, too, who are placed in authority over us in our respective countries we owe respect and submission.   It is our strict duty to obey them according to the laws, so long as these are not contrary to the law of God and the rights of the Church. It is moreover forbidden to belong to any Secret Society that plots against the Church or the State, or to any Society that, by reason of its secrecy, is condemned by the Church.   To guard us against the evil of resisting authority we have the earnest exhortation of St. Paul : " Let every soul be subject to the higher powers ; for there is no power but from God ; and those that are, are ordained of God. Therefore, he that resisteth the power resisteth the ordinance of God, and they that resist purchase to themselves damnation " (Rom. xiii. 1, 2).   From these words of St. Paul we see that all men, even Bishops and Priests, must be subject and obedient to temporal rulers in regard to the laws of the civil government, honouring them and obeying them and their laws, as this is the will of God, seeing that the power by which they act is from God. And since to resist them is to resist God, every Christian is

Duties to our Temporal Rulers.

bound to obey them even for conscience' sake. St. Paul does not say there is no *prince* but from God, but only that there is no *power* but from God, meaning no lawful form of government, and speaking of true and just laws. St. Peter, too, bids us " be subject to every human creature for God's sake; whether it be to the king as excelling, or to governors, as sent by Him for the punishment of evil-doers, and for the praise of the good" (1 Pet. ii. 13, 14). It might even become our duty, if danger threatened our rulers, to sacrifice not only our property but life itself in defending them against their enemies.

Servants, too, owe respect, submission, and fidelity to their masters and mistresses in all that is not contrary to the law or to the will of God. It is wrong then in servants to murmur at their commands, to show any reluctance in obeying them, or to censure their conduct. They should regard their masters as holding the place of God, and their commands as those of God Himself: "Exhort servants to be obedient to their masters, in all things pleasing, not contradicting; not defrauding, but in all things showing good fidelity, that they may adorn the doctrine of our Saviour in all things" (Tit. ii. 9, 10). This good fidelity consists in preserving and using with care what belongs to their masters; in not doing them any injustice, or allowing injustice to be done to them. Failure in this fidelity, at least in regard to things committed to their care, would be a sin as much against the Seventh Commandment as against the Fourth. Servants, therefore, ought to display in their whole conduct a strict love of justice.

Duties of Servants to their Masters.

Nor does our duty of obedience to superiors cease even if they chance to be wicked, provided that they do not require us to do anything bad or unlawful: " Be subject to your masters with all fear, not only to the good and gentle, but also to the froward " (1 Pet. ii. 18).

IV. Duties of Superiors towards Inferiors.

But if Parents have obligations in regard to their children, so have all other Superiors in regard to their inferiors; and these obligations vary in proportion to the share which Superiors possess of the position and authority of the Parents.

The duties of Ecclesiastical Superiors naturally regard **Ecclesiastical Superiors.** what concerns the spiritual welfare of those under their charge. It is for them to teach, preach, and exhort, to administer the Sacraments; to reprove when reproof is necessary; to prevent or remove scandals; to comfort the afflicted; to visit the sick and the dying, even though they endanger their own lives; and to be ready at all times, night or day, to attend to the urgent spiritual needs of their flocks, and constantly to pray for them.

The duties of Guardians and Teachers towards those **Guardians and Teachers.** under their charge differ but little from those of Parents towards their children since, till their wards are of age, they hold the place of Parents in their regard. The conscientious Teacher will work assiduously for the advancement of his pupils in virtue and knowledge; he will keep a jealous watch over their conduct; he will see that, as far as in him lies, they attend to their religious duties; he will keep out of their reach books that might prove dangerous to faith or morals; and will, by his own good example, encourage them to grow up in piety and a credit to their religion.

All those who are set over others in temporal things are **Temporal Rulers.** bound, as far as lies in their power, to see to the temporal welfare of their subjects, so that they may be best able to work out their eternal salvation. The duties of their office they must carry out with justice and wisdom; they must bear in mind that, according to the words of St. Paul, they are God's ministers for *good*, and that the power which they wield is from God, to whom they must one day render an account.

Masters and Mistresses are bound to treat their servants with kindness, and to see that they have proper nourishment. They must pay them just wages, for "the labourer is worthy of his hire"; they must guard them against evil and the dangerous occasions of sin; avoid giving them scandal; and see that they have time and opportunity for practising their religious duties. God will exact the same justice from them that they mete out to others : "Masters, do to your servants that which is just and equal, knowing that you also have a Master in heaven" (Col. iv. 1).

Masters and Mistresses.

CHAPTER LIV
THE FIFTH COMMANDMENT
" Thou shalt not kill."

⟨ THE Fifth Commandment, "Thou shalt not kill," contains a twofold prohibition; it forbids the murder of the body, and the spiritual murder of the soul brought about by our leading others into sin. ⟩

Murder of two kinds.

It forbids, then, all wilful murder, or the unjust taking of our neighbour's life, as well as every thought, word, or deed that may tend to this, such as anger, hatred, revenge, fighting, quarrelling, and injurious words; it forbids the taking of our own life, and whatever may tend to shorten or endanger it without necessity. It also forbids the murder of our neighbour's soul by scandal and bad example. "You have heard that it was said to them of old : Thou shalt not kill: and whosoever shall kill shall be in danger of the judgment. But I say to you that whosoever is *angry* with his brother is in danger of the judgment" (Matt. v. 21, 22).

Murder, one of the four sins crying to Heaven for vengeance, consists in the unlawful putting to death of a human being with premeditated malice. And parents, nurses, and others who, through malice or grave negligence, bring about the death of a child, or wilfully produce abortion, which is the untimely birth of a child, are guilty of the horrible crime of murder; and they also are more or less guilty, according to the amount of negligence or imprudence displayed, who endanger the life of a child either before or after its birth. "Whosoever shall shed man's blood, his blood shall be shed; for man was made to the image of God" (Gen. ix. 6).

What constitutes murder.

Yet the putting to death of another is not always a sin. Soldiers, for example, fighting in a just war, do not sin by taking life. Those too may lawfully take another's life who are acting as executioners of a legal sentence of death, or who cannot save their own lives in any other way when attacked by an unjust aggressor. In the last-mentioned case, however, viz., that of self-defence, we are never allowed to exceed the limits of a just defence; that is, if we are able to escape the danger which threatens in any other way, we are not justified in taking the life of our assailant. He must first have made an assault on our life, or have given unmistakable signs that he has it in his mind to do so; then we may lawfully defend ourselves, even if we take his life in so doing.

Homicide sometimes justifiable.

Moreover, what would be right in our own self-defence would be right if done in defence of our neighbour.

To kill another by-accident would not break this Commandment, for then the action would not be wilful. But one would be guilty of mortal sin who through grave negligence caused the death of another, or even ran the risk of causing his death; for example, by rolling a heavy stone down a frequented path without taking care to find out whether the path was absolutely clear.

Accidental killing.

Suicide. Suicide, or self-murder, is also forbidden by the Fifth Commandment, which simply asserts, "Thou shalt not kill." It does not lay it down, "Thou shalt not kill' thy neighbour." No one, then, is allowed to take his own life. To do so would be to usurp the rights of God, since we are not the masters of our own life: it belongs to Him alone. He, then, who wilfully puts an end to his own life commits a crime against the Divine Majesty by usurping the dominion of God; he commits a crime against his own soul by meriting eternal damnation; and a crime against human society of which he is a member, and towards which he has obligations to fulfil.

Endangering our life. Nor are we allowed to expose our life or health to danger except when a higher duty requires it, or to obtain some great good. It would be right and good to expose ourselves to extreme danger to save the life of another, or through charity to visit or nurse the sick; and a soldier, in time of war, might, in the absolute certainty of losing his own life, perform an act that would injure the enemy, or secure an advantage for his comrades.

Duelling. The Fifth Commandment also forbids the fighting of a duel, which may be defined as a premeditated combat between two persons for the purpose of deciding, with deadly weapons, some private difference or quarrel. In the eyes of God duelling is a double crime: it includes the desire of killing or wounding another, and the unlawful risking of our own life.

Anger. Besides forbidding murder this Commandment forbids everything that leads or tends to it,—such as *Anger*, which is a passing feeling of resentment against those by whom we believe we have been injured: it includes, too, some desire of seeing the offender punished. Yet anger is not always a sin. There is a *just* as well as an *unjust* anger, as we gather from the words of St. Paul, "Be angry and sin not" (Eph. iv. 26).

Now anger is just when it is not inordinate; that is, when there is a just cause for it, and the feeling is moderate and subject to reason, and when the desire for the punishment of the offender is in proportion to the offence, and does not arise from a spirit of revenge. A father might justly and with reason be wroth with his son, or a teacher with his pupil, on account of some wrong committed, and might be compelled of necessity to exact adequate punishment; yet, even in such a case, we should keep our anger within just bounds.

Hatred. But *Hatred* is a settled feeling of dislike for another; it grieves at his prosperity and rejoices at his adversity; it wishes evil as it is evil; it is the very opposite of fraternal charity: " Whosoever hateth his brother," says the Beloved Disciple, " is a murderer " (I John iii. 15).

Revenge. *Revenge,* which is a result of anger and hatred, is a rendering of evil for evil; it is the deliberate infliction of injury, or even the desire of so doing, in return for an injury received.

Fighting and Quarrelling. *Fighting,* too, and *quarrelling,* as well as injurious words and the like, are sins against this Commandment, because they tend to the more terrible crime of murder, and are often its forerunners : " The works of the flesh are manifest, which are . . . enmities, contentions, wraths, quarrels, dissensions . . . of the which I foretell you that they who do such things shall not obtain the kingdom of God " (Gal. v. 19-21).

SPIRITUAL MURDER.

All that we have said thus far of sins forbidden by the Fifth Commandment has been in reference to what is directed against the life of the body; we now come to speak of the different ways in which we may destroy or injure the spiritual life of our neighbour's soul—namely, sins of *Scandal.*

Scandal, which literally means a *"stumbling-block,"* includes whatever may be to our neighbour the occasion of his spiritual downfall ; and con-
Scandal.
sists, therefore, in every word, deed, or omission, whether really or only apparently bad, which is the occasion of sin to another.

Scandal is *direct* when a person does or says what is in itself evil *with the intention* of causing another to sin—*e.g.*, when one incites another to
Direct and
Indirect
Scandal.
adultery, theft, perjury, etc. If one induces another to commit sin simply to cause him to sin for sin's sake or to make him lose his soul, the scandal becomes *Diabolical Scandal.* Scandal is *indirect* when, without in-tending to be the cause of another's sin, one does or says that which, it is foreseen, will be to that other the occa-sion of sin. Thus, for scandal, it is not necessary that we actually cause our neighbour to commit sin ; it is enough that we knowingly put him in the danger of sin. A person would be guilty of indirect scandal, for example, if, without any thought of inducing others to follow his example, but foreseeing that they may do so, he were to do or say before them something wrong in itself, or having the appearance of wrong, and of a nature to cause them to fall into sin : " Destroy not him for whom Christ died " (Rom. xiv. 15).

There is also what is termed the *Scandal of the Weak,* which proceeds from the weakness or ignorance of him who takes the scandal. Through frailty or ignor-
Scandal of the
Weak.
ance he is misled merely by the *appearance of evil ;* as, for example, when a person breaks the law of fasting or abstinence *without leave,* from seeing another break it who has leave to do so.

Then comes *Pharisaical Scandal,* or that pretended

scandal which would discover evil where no evil, but
rather good actions, exist. It is scandal taken
where no scandal is given, and receives its name
from those Pharisees who pretended to be
scandalised at the actions and discourses of our Lord as
an excuse for their refusal to hear Him. Its only cause
is the malice of him who takes the scandal; nor is it
necessary to avoid doing good because the ill-disposed
choose to be scandalised at our conduct.

Pharisaical
Scandal.

Now real scandal is a terrible evil ; an evil condemned
by our Lord in no unmistakable terms : " He that shall
scandalise one of these little ones that believe in Me, it
were better for him that a mill-stone were hanged about
his neck, and that he were drowned in the depths of
the sea. Woe to the world because of scandals "
(Matt. xviii. 6, 7). How careful, then, should we be to
avoid giving the least scandal !

Although the Fifth Commandment directly expresses a
prohibition, "Thou shalt not kill," yet it includes certain positive obligations regarding
the preservation and protection of the life of
soul and body, both in regard to ourselves and our neighbour. We are bound, as far as we can, to live in peace
and concord with our neighbour ; we are under the obligation of promoting our own life and health, and of seeking,
according to our condition in life, the spiritual as well as
the corporal welfare of others : " Let your light so shine
before men that they may see your good works, and glorify
your Father who is in heaven " (Matt. v. 16).

Positive
obligations.

CHAPTER LV

THE SIXTH AND THE NINTH COMMANDMENTS

" Thou shalt not commit adultery" ; " Thou shalt not covet thy neighbour's wife."

BOTH the Sixth and the Ninth Commandments have reference to the same object, and both have a like design : they forbid whatever is contrary to holy purity, and enjoin chastity, decency, and modesty in all our thoughts, looks, words, and actions.

The aim of these Commandments.

The Sixth Commandment forbids adultery, or sins of impurity with another's wife or husband, and all other *external* acts of impurity, such as unchaste touches, looks, jests, words, or actions of any kind ; in a word, it forbids whatever violates modesty, whether in regard to ourselves or others. And although every deliberate seeking for impure pleasure, and every deliberate consent to it, however slight it may be, is a mortal sin, yet the guilt arising from adultery is far greater than from an act of impurity between two un- married persons, for in the former case there is added a grave breach of justice. Some sins of impurity, then, are more grievous than others, and may vary according to the persons with whom the sin is committed, and according as the sin is more unnatural and abominable.

The Sixth Commandment.

The Ninth Commandment forbids all *interior* sins of thought and desire contrary to chastity ; for as it is a sin against purity intentionally to look at immodest objects for an unlawful purpose, it is also a sin wilfully to represent such objects to the mind. We sin, then, against the Ninth Commandment whenever we consent to impure thoughts, and desire their accomplishment ; whenever we take pleasure in them even

The Ninth Commandment.

without desiring their accomplishment; and whenever we are conscious of such thoughts and wilfully neglect to put them away.

We can never be secure against the recurrence of temptations to impurity. We shall have to fight

Temptation no sin.

against evil thoughts and desires and our own corrupt inclinations and passions all the days of our life: "The life of man upon earth is a warfare" (Job vii. 1). Yet it is not a sin to be tempted. Sin consists in wilfully causing the temptation, or in entertaining it, or taking pleasure in it, or consenting to it. If we knowingly and deliberately take pleasure in the impression felt, the sin is mortal; if our consent is only imperfect or partial, the sin is venial; if the will entirely refuses consent, there is no sin. Then must we shun the causes of these temptations, and take warning from the words of Holy Writ: "He that loveth the danger shall perish in it" (Ecclus. iii. 27).

Every direct sin, then, contrary to holy purity, whether of thought, look, word, or action, is mortal if it receives full consent: "For know ye this, and understand," says St. Paul, "that no fornicator, nor unclean, nor covetous person . . . hath any inheritance in the kingdom of Christ" (Eph. v. 5). And, again, he says: "Know you not that you are the temple of God? But if any man violate the temple of God, him shall God destroy" (1 Cor. iii. 16, 17).

Sins against the virtue of purity are to be avoided chiefly by flying from the occasions, and avoiding such

What we must avoid.

temptations as may lead to them. Now the principal things that we must shun, as leading to impurity, are bad company; too free intercourse with persons of the opposite sex; indecent plays and dances; immodest songs, books, and pictures; and the sins of gluttony, drunkenness, idleness, and the neglect of prayer.

" If thy eye scandalise thee," says our Lord, "pluck it out, and cast it from thee" (Matt. xviii. 9).   In these words does He, with great earnestness, command us to shun and renounce all persons and things, however near and dear they may be to us, sooner than remain in the occasions of sin.

Since these Commandments forbid whatever is contrary to holy purity, it follows that they enjoin a becoming decency and modesty in all our thoughts, looks, words and actions; and that, on our part, we are bound most carefully to preserve the innocence of our souls, and to avoid defiling our bodies, which are to be considered not as our own, but as redeemed by our Saviour, and consecrated to Him, and as one day to rise again and to be glorified together with Him in heaven.

What we are commanded.

To keep the flesh and its inordinate passions in due subjection we must pray fervently, and especially have recourse to our Lady, St. Joseph, our Angel Guardian, and our Patron Saint, ever keeping before our minds the words of our Lord: " Watch ye and pray that ye enter not into temptation," (Matt. xxvi. 41).   We should frequent the Sacraments and, like St. Paul, constantly practise mortification and self-denial: " I chastise my body, and bring it into subjection " (1 Cor. ix. 27). And again he says: "If you live according to the flesh, you shall die ; but if, by the Spirit, you mortify the deeds of the flesh, you shall live " (Rom. viii. 13).   Lastly, we should practise humility, and place our confidence in God, who will not allow us to be tempted above our strength: "I can do all things in Him who strengtheneth me " (Philip. iv. 13).

Practices recommended.

Of all the virtues, Purity is among the most lovable: it brings a delightful peace into the soul ; it renders man like to the Angels, and makes him most pleasing in the sight of God.

CHAPTER LVI

THE SEVENTH AND THE TENTH COMMANDMENTS

" Thou shalt not steal" ; *" Thou shalt not covet thy neighbour's goods."*

THE Seventh and the Tenth Commandments forbid all injustice towards our neighbour with regard to his property or temporal goods. They not only require us to act honestly towards him by forbidding us all acts of injustice, but they command us to be so far contented with what is our own as not to be envious of what belongs to him.

The Seventh Commandment forbids the *outward* act of stealing; that is, it forbids us to injure our
What these Commandments forbid. neighbour in his property by theft, by cheating, by usury, by wilfully damaging his possessions, or by any other unjust act. The Tenth forbids the *inward* desire to steal ; that is, it forbids us to desire to appropriate unjustly what belongs to another; and, in general, it forbids every irregular attachment to riches, either in pursuing them too ardently, or in possessing them too closely and fondly. These inward desires are both bad in themselves and often lead to the outward act of stealing.

In condemning theft, the Seventh Commandment forbids us at the same time to cause any injury to our neighbour's property, and bids us *restore* what we possess unjustly, and repair the wrongs we have done.

Now stealing is the unjust taking away or withholding
Stealing. what belongs to another against his will, when he has a right not to be deprived of it. And there are three principal ways in which we can do this; namely, by larceny or theft, by rapine or robbery, and by fraud.

Larceny or theft consists in taking what belongs to
Larceny.   another secretly and without the latter per-
ceiving it; for example, a servant is guilty of
larceny who does less work than he ought, and yet exacts
full and entire pay for the work expected of him; so too
with tailors and dressmakers if they keep back for their
own benefit some of the material entrusted to them; and
servants also would be guilty of this sin were they to take
from their masters in order to make up for the smallness
of their wages.

A person is guilty of *rapine* or robbery who takes what
Rapine.   belongs to another either openly or by violence.
A judge would commit this sin if, through
bribery, he were to pass an unjust sentence; as also a
master if he should refuse to pay his servants their hire;
indeed, this is one of the sins crying to Heaven for vengeance: "The cry of them hath entered into the ears of
the Lord" (James v. 4).

The third kind of theft is called *fraud*, and includes all
Fraud.   manner of cheating in buying or selling; in
passing off false coin; in using false weights
and measures; or in supplying goods inferior to what has
been agreed upon. It also embraces usury, or the exact-
ing for the loan of money of more interest than the
general practice and the laws of the country allow, where
no special risk is incurred: "As you would that men
should do to you, do you also to them in like manner"
(Luke vi. 31).

Thus we see that there are various ways in which we
Many things   may break the Seventh Commandment. Not
constitute   only to steal, but to assist in stealing; know-
stealing.   ingly to buy or to receive stolen property; wilfully and maliciously to destroy or damage what belongs
to another; to originate an unjust lawsuit; not to return
the things we have found or borrowed; to neglect or to

refuse to pay our debts: these and the like are all sins against this Commandment. Moreover, if what is stolen be something dedicated to the Divine service, in addition to the sin of theft there will be added the greater crime of sacrilege. "Neither thieves nor covetous persons . . . nor extortioners shall possess the kingdom of God" (1 Cor. vi. 10).

Not all sins of theft, however, are mòrtal sins, but the guilt depends to a great extent on the value of the thing stolen, or the amount of injury inflicted on another. The taking of a small sum, even of a few shillings, would, as a rule, not constitute a mortal sin; but to take such a sum from a poor person would be a very grave matter if the thief knew that it would cause him a serious injury; for the loss in this case, though trifling in itself, results in grave wrong.

On what the guilt depends.

We may sin grievously through small thefts and frauds committed so frequently that the owner suffers a considerable loss; or even when we have the intention of repeating them and of thereby reaching a considerable sum, because each of these petty thefts is committed with a gravely bad intention.

When any of the above or other acts of injustice have been committed, it is not enough to repent in order to obtain pardon; *restitution* also is necessary; that is, we must restore the ill-gotten goods and, as far as in us lies, repair the injury we have done. Without restitution we cannot hope for pardon from God. We must, therefore, give back what has been taken away, or its value, and we must repair the damage done. If we cannot do this at once, we must sincerely have the intention of doing so should it ever be in our power; and if we are able to make partial restitution, we must do so as soon as possible. And this obligation of restitution, which can be cancelled only by the consent of the person wronged,

Restitution necessary.

rests not only on him who did the act of injustice, but on all who have taken a guilty part in it : on the receiver of the stolen goods; on those who took part in the theft; and on those who, being obliged in justice to prevent the theft or the loss, did not do so.

Restitution is to be made as soon as possible to the owner, or, if he be dead, to his heirs ; but if this cannot be, the sum must be given to the poor or devoted to religious purposes : " What doth it profit a man if he gain the whole world, and suffer the loss of his own soul ?" (Matt. xvi. 26).

To whom Restitution must be made.

True charity, which is the love of God, and of our neighbour for God's sake, is the best preventative against sins of the Seventh and the Tenth Commandments ; for we are told by St. Paul : " Charity is patient, is kind ; charity envieth not, dealeth not perversely, is not puffed up " (1 Cor. xiii. 4). From a careful consideration of the last two chapters, we clearly see that Religion forbids not only guilty actions, but even the deliberate thought and desire to commit them. •

CHAPTER LVII

THE EIGHTH COMMANDMENT

" Thou shalt not bear false witness against thy neighbour."

¹ THE great design of the Eighth Commandment is to direct us in our duties in regard to truth, and our neighbour's honour or reputation. ²Other Commandments instruct us in what we owe to our neighbour in *thought* and *deed*, the Eighth Commandment regulates our *words* in his regard. ³ The sins, then, which it directly forbids are those of False Testimony, Rash Judgment, and Lies ; together with Calumny, Detraction, and Tale-bearing, and all such words as injure our neighbour's character.

Design of the Eighth Commandment.

15

⁴ False Testimony is here taken in the sense of a deposi-

False Testimony. tion made upon oath, but contrary to truth, in a court of justice. As it is a more solemn breach of truth, it is always a grievous sin; and as it involves the violation of an oath, it includes the sin of perjury, and therefore also breaks the Second Commandment. ⁷Moreover, should it be the cause of injury to another, it would also be a sin of injustice which would require not only repentance, but restitution also for the wrong done.

⁸ Perjury admits of no lightness of matter; and even if false testimony were given in favour of one unjustly accused, nevertheless the sin would be grievous, on account of the insult offered to God in calling upon Him to bear witness to what we know to be false. ⁹ In giving evidence, then, in a court of justice, the simple truth must be told just as we know it.

¹⁰We injure our neighbour by *False Suspicion* when,

Rash Judgment. without sufficient reason or a just cause, we surmise evil of him; ¹¹and by *Rash Judgment* when, without sufficient reason or a just cause, we believe the evil to be true. We must not, therefore, think or believe evil of our neighbour without sufficient foundation.¹²Yet to entertain a bad opinion of another would not be a sin if we had clear grounds for what we thought. A liar has only himself to blame if his words àre doubted even when he is speaking the truth. But, as appearances so often deceive, proofs of another's guilt must be well founded.

¹³To constitute a sin of rash judgment, then, the matter must be something prejudicial to our neighbour's character, and there must be no reasonable foundation for forming such a judgment; for example, it would not be rash judgment to doubt the word of a liar; or to suspect that a person had been drinking when his breath clearly be-

trayed him. But whenever we find that our suspicions are rash and unjust, we must not dwell on them, but reject them as soon as possible.

The guilt of the sin of rash judgment will naturally be in proportion to the wrong we do to our neighbour's character, and to the motives on which our judgment is founded. It is directly opposed to charity, which "thinketh no evil, rejoiceth not in iniquity, but believeth all things, hopeth all things" (1 Cor. xiii.). Where our neighbour's conduct will bear a favourable interpretation, we should never condemn; and we should always judge his indifferent actions in the most favourable sense: "Judge not, that you may not be judged" (Matt. vii. 1).

The suspicions of parents, masters, mistresses, and other superiors, which arise from motives of prudence, and from anxiety to guide those under their charge in the way of righteousness, are not unjust, seeing that they are acting in the cause of duty.

Lies. We now come to the subject of *Lies*, or those words—and sometimes actions—whereby we induce others to believe as true what we know at the time to be false. To say, then, what we believe not to be true, or to promise what we never intend to carry out, is a lie; in a word, a lie is a deliberate speaking against our own mind. So that, if a person were to aver that he was going to do something and had no intention of doing it, he would still have told a lie, even though he afterwards performed the act.

Three kinds of Lies. There are *three kinds* of lies : there is the *Jocose Lie*, or the lie told in jest; the *Officious Lie*, which is a lie told to save ourselves or others some inconvenience—to ward off some evil or to procure some advantage for ourselves or our neighbour; and the *Malicious Lie*, which is told with the express purpose of injuring another. This last is a mortal sin whenever it causes

a serious injury to our neighbour's goods or honour; it is
venial, if the wrong caused be but trivial.   The jocose lie
and the officious lie, though wrong, never exceed a venial
sin when they do no grave injury to anyone, or cause no
grave scandal.

Every lie is essentially opposed to God, who is truth
itself; and it is opposed, too, to the end for which speech
was given us—viz., to communicate our thoughts, not to
be at variance with them.   The spoken word, then, should
answer to the inward word and thought.   But, generally,
when words contrary to the truth are said in jest, there is
no lie if the untruth is quite evident.

Hypocrisy also is a kind of lie, and consists in trying to
win the esteem of others by assuming the cloak of a virtue
which we do not possess, or by pretending to be better than
we are.   *Dissimulation*, too, which means hiding under a
false appearance, since it tends directly to deceive, is a lie
in action, no less to be condemned than the lie in word.

Calumny or *Slander* is the sin of him who speaks evil of

Calumny.
his neighbour when he knows it to be false; who
imputes to his neighbour a wrong of which he
knows him to be innocent; or who exaggerates a real fault.
Calumny is a double sin: it sins not only against truth, but
against justice also, since it robs our neighbour of his honour
and reputation, which are goods that a man can call his
own, and to which he has a just right, so long as he has
not publicly forfeited them.   Hence, to obtain pardon for
this sin, it is not only necessary to confess it with sorrow,
but we are bound to make restitution by retracting the
calumny, and repairing the wrong in whatever way we can.

Now, while calumny consists in wilfully laying to the

Detraction.
charge of our neighbour a fault of which he is
innocent, *Detraction* is the injury done to his
honour and reputation by unjustly revealing his hidden
faults and defects: it consists, then, in making known his
real but secret faults without necessity.

There are several ways in which we may become guilty of this sin—(1) by our words, when we make known, without a just cause, the vices or secret faults of our neighbour to those who do not know them; (2) by our silence, when we refrain from praising, when we ought to praise, his good actions; and (3) by signs, when, on hearing another praised, we mark our disapproval by showing impatience, by smiling maliciously, or by testifying in any other way that we do not approve of what is said. However careful we are about speaking the truth in such cases, we nevertheless sin by unnecessarily and unjustly revealing faults that have not been made public before. Where no evident compensating good then is to be gained, we do wrong in speaking of the faults of others : we should do to others as we would be done by.

Those who have injured another by speaking ill of him, even by making known his real faults, are bound to make him satisfaction by restoring his good name as far as they can. Where the sin, then, has been one of detraction, they cannot indeed contradict what they have said, because they have said what is true, but they must do all in their power, by speaking well of the person, to restore the good name that their detracting tongue has injured or taken away. When the injury caused is serious, the sin is mortal; but the guilt will naturally vary according to the loss and the injury inflicted, and according to the number of persons who have heard the detraction. The intention, too, in divulging our neighbour's faults must be taken into account. But even if with a harmless intention I say what I foresee may do my neighbour's character a grave injury, I commit a mortal sin.

When we may make known another's faults. There are at times circumstances when Christian charity requires us to make known our neighbour's faults to those whose duty it is to correct them. In such cases not only are we allowed, but we are even bound, to reveal them. It would be our duty, too, to make them known if, by doing so, we could hinder him from perverting others, or from doing some greater evil.   But in this, our sole object must be charity, for if self-interest or the desire of praise were our object in exposing the faults of our companions to our superiors, we should be acting wrongly.

Backbiting. We have next to deal with those forms of detraction called *Backbiting* and *Tale-bearing*, and any words by which the character of our neighbour is unjustly injured.   By backbiting we understand the very common, but by no means trivial, sin of taking a pleasure in speaking of a person's known faults in his absence.   To do it before his face would be contumely.

Tale-bearing. To carry tales backward and forward, too, is wrong; for besides sowing the seeds of discord and disunion, it destroys brotherly love and charity. When we repeat to a person the unfavourable things that another has said of him, we become guilty of this detestable sin ; and there is no more certain way of destroying the peace and harmony of families and friends than that of tale-bearing : " The whisperer and the double-tongued is accursed ; for he hath troubled many that were at peace " (Ecclus. xxviii. 15).   " The tale-bearer shall defile his own soul, and shall be hated by all " (Ecclus. xxi. 31).

Of those who listen to Detraction. And if it is wrong to take away our neighbour's character by calumny, detraction, and the like, it is also wrong to take pleasure in listening to the evil which is asserted of him.   It is wrong to encourage the detractor by paying attention to him or by questioning him ; we should rather shun his company. If we cannot do that, we should try, if possible, to make excuses for our neighbour, or in some way to show our disapproval of what is said.   If we have authority over the detractor, we should impose silence upon him : " Hedge in

thy ears with thorns, and hear not a wicked tongue"
(Ecclus. xxviii. 28). "He that keepeth his mouth keepeth
his soul; but he that hath no guard on his speech, shall
meet with evils" (Prov. xiii. 3).

Before bringing this section to a close, let us once more

Concluding
words on the
Decalogue.

cast our thoughts over the commands contained
in the Decalogue. ✓We find that the first three,
in establishing our duties towards God, are
directed towards freeing the world from idolatry, and preserving it from irreligion, which is the source of all temporal evils. The Fourth Commandment would establish
the duties of superiors and inferiors on the basis of mutual
charity : it is the foundation of the family and of society.
The Fifth and the rest of the Commandments are calculated to preserve what belongs to us—our life, our virtue,
our fortune, and our reputation—against the passions of
the wicked. How earnestly, then, should we thank God
for the inestimable blessings He has conferred upon us by
giving us the Commandments, since, without them, the
whole fabric of human society must necessarily crumble
to dust! "This is the charity of God, that we keep His
commandments; and His commandments are not heavy"
(1 John v. 3).

PART III

"He that heareth you heareth Me; and he that despiseth you despiseth Me" (Luke x. 16).

CHAPTER LVIII

THE NATURE OF THE COMMANDMENTS OF THE CHURCH

The right of the Church to give commands is derived
The Church's right to make laws. from Jesus Christ Himself, who directed her to guide and govern the faithful in His name. By the Commandments of the Church, then, we mean those laws and regulations made by the Pastors of the Church, in virtue of the authority given to her by her Divine Founder to rule and govern : " I will give to thee the keys of the kingdom of heaven. And whatsoever thou shalt bind upon earth, it shall be bound also in heaven ; and whatsoever thou shalt loose upon earth, it shall be loosed also in heaven " (Matt. xvi. 19). This metaphor of the keys clearly expresses the supreme power and prerogative given to Peter, the Prince of the Apostles and Head of the Church.

All the Apostles, however, and their successors partake
The power of binding and loosing. of the power of binding and loosing, but, as we have seen under the Ninth Article of the Creed, with a due subordination to the one head invested with the supreme power : " Amen I say to you,

232

whatsoever *you* shall bind upon earth, shall be bound also in heaven; and whatsoever *you* shall loose upon earth, shall be loosed also in heaven" (Matt. xviii. 18). "And behold I am with you all days, even to the consummation of the world" (Matt. xxviii. 20). And St. Paul, speaking to those ministers of God who are Bishops (*i.e., overseers*) placed by Divine institution to govern the Church, or the churches under them, charges them: "Take heed to yourselves, and to the whole flock over which the Holy Ghost hath placed you bishops, *to rule* the Church of God which He hath purchased with His own Blood" (Acts xx. 28).

These laws of the Church are of strict obligation, **Binding power of the Church's laws.** and bind under pain of sin: "He that heareth you heareth Me; and he that despiseth you despiseth Me" (Luke x. 16). "If he will not hear the Church, let him be to thee as the heathen and the publican" (Matt. xviii. 17)—passages which clearly show that it is the bounden duty of every man, in things spiritual, to submit to the judgment of the Church. Nor can there be a plainer condemnation of those who make particular creeds, and will not submit the articles of their belief to the judgment of the authority appointed by Christ. We must, then, pay a ready obedience to the Bishops and Pastors whom God has placed over us, and cheerfully follow their commands and instructions. "Obey your prelates, and be subject to them. For they watch as being to render an account of your souls" (Heb. xiii. 17). And again, addressing the Romans, St. Paul shows how all-important it is for each one to submit to lawfully constituted authority: "Let every soul be subject to the higher powers; for there is no power but from God: and those that are, are ordained of God. Therefore, he that resisteth the power, resisteth the ordinance of God; and

they that resist, purchase to themselves damnation"
(Rom. xiii. 1, 2).

The Commandments of the Church, then, cannot be
The Church can dispense from her laws. broken wilfully without incurring the guilt of
mortal sin if the matter is grievous; and they
must be observed by the faithful as strictly as
the Ten Commandments. Yet, unlike the latter, they
admit of dispensation in cases where it is impossible to
observe them, or where they cannot be carried out without
grave inconvenience. Since her discipline may vary, the
Church, for weighty reasons, can dispense from her own
laws, but never from the laws of God. The doctrine of
the Church is, of necessity, always the same, because it
comes from God; but her laws and regulations she made
herself, and adapts to times, places, and circumstances.

The Commandments of the Church, besides exercising
End of these Commandments. us in that obedience and submission which we
owe to the Church, our Mother, have, as their
end, the putting in practice of certain duties
commanded by God Himself, and of certain injunctions
given by our Lord and His Apostles. They thus help us
to carry out the Commandments of God by assigning the
time and manner of fulfilling duties which, if left to ourselves, would in all likelihood fall into neglect.

Among the many ordinances of the Church there are
Chief Commandments of the Church. six which in a special manner regard the whole
body of the faithful, and which, in the
Catechism, are spoken of as the *chief* Commandments of the Church; they are:

1. To keep the Sundays and Holydays of Obligation
holy by hearing Mass and resting from servile works.

2. To keep the days of fasting and abstinence appointed
by the Church.

3. To go to Confession at least once a year.

4. To receive the Blessed Sacrament at least once a year,
and that at Easter or thereabouts.

5. To contribute to the support of our Pastors.

6. Not to marry within certain degrees of kindred, nor to solemnise marriage at the forbidden times.

CHAPTER LIX

THE FIRST COMMANDMENT OF THE CHURCH

" To keep the Sundays and Holydays of Obligation holy by hearing Mass and resting from servile works."

THE First Commandment of the Church obliges us, in addition to keeping the Sundays holy, to set apart special days, and to sanctify them by hearing Mass and resting from servile work. The Festivals which we in England are required to sanctify in the same manner as the Sundays are the eight Holydays of Obligation instituted in honour of our Lord, of His Blessed Mother, and of the Saints. Given in chronological order, they are: Christmas-day, the Circumcision, the Epiphany, the Ascension, Corpus Christi, Saints Peter and Paul, the Assumption of our Lady, and All Saints. These solemnities of the Catholic Church, besides calling to our minds the mysteries of our Redemption, give a special joy to each season of the year; they serve to commemorate God's special benefits to us, and to stir up within us a grateful acknowledgment of His goodness and mercy.

Holydays of Obligation.

Besides these Feasts of Obligation, there are other feasts which were formerly Days of Obligation, but from which the duty of hearing Mass and abstaining from servile work has been removed; for example, the Feasts of the Apostles. Such days are now spoken of as *Days of Devotion.* As on these days, and on all Sundays and Holydays of Obligation, the parish Priest fulfils the special duty of offering the Holy Sacrifice for the intentions and welfare of his flock, the faithful are

Days of Devotion.

specially recommended to hear Mass, to approach · the
Sacraments, and to perform special acts of devotion,
although the obligation of observing them as a Sunday
no longer exists.

But we are strictly bound to hear Mass and to abstain
from servile work on the Holydays of Obligation
Binding force of Holydays. named above, inasmuch as these duties are laid
upon us by an authority ordained by Jesus Christ.
Hence to disobey those commands, or any of the commands of the Church, is the same as disregarding the precepts of God Himself, since we owe the self-same obedience
to the Church as we owe to God ; for " he that despiseth
you despiseth Me ". (Luke x. 16).

As the duty of assisting devoutly at Mass and of resting
from servile work has already been spoken of in
To hear a whole Mass necessary. the explanation of the Third Commandment of
the Decalogue, we need only repeat here that,
to fulfil perfectly the obligation of hearing Mass, we must
be present during the whole Mass ; that wilfully and without sufficient reason to be absent during any part of it is
wrong ; and that to miss an essential part would constitute
a mortal sin.

If we are dispensed from the obligation of hearing Mass
on account of some weighty reason, we should try, as far
as possible, to set aside a special time for recollection, and,
during that time .especially, to unite ourselves in spirit
with the Priest who is celebrating Mass, and with the
faithful who are able to be present in church.

CHAPTER LX

SECOND COMMANDMENT OF THE CHURCH

*" To keep the Days of Fasting and Abstinence appointed by the
Church."*

How often, both in the Old and in the New Testament, do
we find passages strictly enjoining fasting and abstinence !

And in determining what every Christian must do in this matter of abstaining from food, the Church is but **Abstinence enjoined in Scripture.** pointing out the way in which we are to satisfy this most important duty of self-mortification. By requiring us on certain days to refrain from taking the usual number of meals, or by restricting us in regard to what we may eat, she is but prescribing the times and manner in which we may, in part, comply with an obligation as old as the human race. " The days will come when the bridegroom shall be taken away from them : and then they shall fast in those days" (Mark ii. 20).

The first and only prohibition given by God to Adam in **Importance of self-mortification.** Paradise was one of *abstinence :* " Of every tree of paradise thou shalt eat. But of the tree of knowledge of good and evil thou shalt not eat. For in what day soever thou shalt eat of it, thou shalt die the death " (Gen. ii. 16, 17). Again we find a like precept of abstinence given to Noe after the flood : " Flesh with blood you shall not eat " (Gen. ix. 4). Yet to eat flesh with blood was a matter of indifference in itself, like the eating of the forbidden fruit; but it was prescribed by God as a test of man's obedience. This command relative to abstention from blood the Apostles required to be observed by the first Christians, in order that offence might not be given to the Jews. But after the lapse of a certain time, the Church thought proper to remove this particular discipline. Innumerable other passages from Scripture might be cited to show the importance attached by the Jews to the laws of abstinence ; but we will merely direct attention to the heroic sacrifice of the aged Eleazar, who, even to save his life, refused to eat swine's flesh, because it was forbidden by the law; and to that of the seven Machabees, who, together with their mother, were most cruelly tortured to death for refusing to violate the same precept. In the New Testament, too, we find the Apostles commanding the newly converted Christians, in the name and by the authority of the Holy Ghost, "to abstain from things sacrificed to idols, and from blood, and from things strangled" (Acts xv. 29).

With regard to the necessity of *fasting*, too, the proofs from Scripture are equally strong and conclusive.

Fasting enjoined. In the Old Testament we read in the Book of Joel : "Be converted to Me with all your heart in *fasting*, and in weeping, and in mourning" (Joel ii. 12). And in the New Testament, not only in St. Mark, but in St. Matthew as well, we find our Lord answering the disciples of John : "Can the children of the bridegroom mourn as long as the bridegroom is with them? But the days will come when the bridegroom shall be taken away from them, and then they shall *fast*" (Matt. ix. 15). Of the Apostles we read : "When they had ordained to them priests in every church, and had prayed with *fasting*, they commended them to the Lord" (Acts xiv. 22).

Fasting and abstinence, then, have always held an important position in the Church of God. We must therefore not only try to gain a clear knowledge of what these terms mean, but we must learn the times fixed by the Church when we are obliged, under pain of mortal sin, to put in practice so strict a duty.

Fasting Days, to use the words of the Catechism, are

Fasting and Abstinence Days. days on which we are allowed to take but *one meal*, and are forbidden to eat flesh-meat without special leave; whereas *Days of Abstinence* are days on which we are forbidden to eat flesh-meat, but are allowed the usual number of meals. On Fasting Days we are restricted both as to the quantity and the kind of food we may eat, but on Days of Abstinence we are restricted only as to the kind.

Those who object to the Catholic practice of fasting and abstinence often, in favour of their contention, advance

those much-abused words of our Saviour : " Not that
which goeth into the mouth defileth a man "
Objections (Matt. xv. 11). It is on this plea that
raised against so many disregard the Fasting Days and
them. Days of Abstinence prescribed by the Church. But they
evidently misapply the text. It is not the meat which
defiles the soul, but the sin of disobedience to the command and will of God : this it is that draws down punishment. Thus, when God laid His easy command upon
Adam, it was to give him an opportunity of showing his
ready obedience, and at the same time to assert His own
dominion over him ; and when Adam took the forbidden
fruit, it was not the apple which entered into his mouth,
but his disobedience to the command of God, that defiled
him. The same is to be said of the Jew who, in the time
of the Old Law, should have eaten swine's flesh ; or the
Christian convert who, in the days of the Apostles, contrary to their ordinance, should have eaten blood ; or of any
of the faithful who should, at the present time, transgress
the ordinance of God's Church by breaking the fasts. In
all these cases the soul would be defiled, not indeed by that
which goeth into the mouth, but by the disobedience of the
heart in wilfully transgressing the ordinance of God, or of
His Church. So with flesh-meat eaten on a Friday : it is as
good and wholesome on that day as on any other day of the
week ; but the act of eating it is at fault, because that is
forbidden by an authority constituted by our Lord Himself :
" He that despiseth you despiseth Me " (Luke x. 16).

Now the Church commands us to fast and abstain that
we may, in this way, mortify the flesh and
Why we are satisfy God for our sins : " Do penance, for the
bound to fast. kingdom of God is at hand " (Matt. iv. 17).
Fasting and abstinence serve to appease the anger of God
and ward off His judgments from us, as we see in the case
of the people of Ninive. After they had fasted and done

penance for their sins, "God had mercy with regard to the evil which He had said that He would do to them, and He did it not" (Jonas iii. 10). Fasting, moreover, besides satisfying the debt of temporal punishment due to our past sins, strengthens us against future temptations by humbling our pride, moderating our sensual desires, and curbing our evil inclinations generally : "I humbled my soul with fasting" (Ps. xxxiv. 13). It tends, moreover, to raise the mind, and disposes us the better for meditation and prayer ; it was practised by our Lord Himself and the Apostles, and has been the practice of the Saints of all times. Of our Lord we read that He *fasted* forty days and forty nights (Matt. iv. 2). And of the Apostles : "When they had ordained to them priests in every church, and had prayed with *fasting*, they commended them to the Lord" (Acts xiv. 22).

CHAPTER LXI

ON FASTING AND ABSTINENCE

I. ON FASTING.

WE must now learn the times and seasons set apart by the Church for fasting and abstinence, and the laws which she has laid down regarding them.

Those are bound to fast who have arrived at the age of twenty-one unless they are excused by physical or moral impossibility, or by dispensation. Thus the following are excused: those who make their living by hard manual work ; those who work hard for the sick out of charity ; the sick, the convalescent, and the delicate ; very poor people who cannot be sure of one full meal ; and those who have reached their sixtieth year. In case of doubt we should consult our Pastor or Confessor, who will grant a dispensation for any serious reason. If we cannot fast,

Those who are bound to fast.

we are still bound to abstain, unless we are dispensed from the second law also, or unless there is some serious urgent reason for eating meat.

On Days of Fasting we are restricted to *one full meal*, and that must not be taken much before mid-

Chief point in fasting.

day; we are also forbidden, outside Lent, to eat flesh-meat, but *by universal law* we are allowed to take it during Lent on all days except Fridays and Saturdays, Ash Wednesday and Ember Wednesday; and whenever flesh-meat is allowed, fish is now permitted at the same meal. Taking but one full meal constitutes the chief point in fasting; but the Church allows an evening collation of not more than eight ounces, and in the morning it is customary in this country to take a small quantity of bread, which must not exceed two ounces.

As regards the kind of food which may be taken at the

Collation.

evening collation, flesh-meat is never allowed, but such food as bread, fruit, vegetables, or a little fish is permitted. As to the use of milk, butter, cheese, etc., the indult published by each Bishop for his own diocese at the beginning of Lent should be consulted.

Milk, butter, cheese, eggs, dripping, and lard are now allowed on all days *at the principal meal*, even on Ash Wednesday and Good Friday, but their use at the collation is settled by custom and the indults of the Bishops; and then such as are allowed may be taken in small quantities only, as part of the collation, and by way of condiment.

To take a drink out of meal-time on a fast-day would not break one's fast; but the drink must not consist of milk, or soup, or any other such nourishing liquid.

The times and seasons set apart by the Church for fulfilling the obligation of fasting are:

Times of fasting.

(1) The *Forty Days of Lent*, that is, every day from Ash Wednesday to Easter, except the

Sundays. This fast was established to remind us of our

16

Lord's fast of forty days in the desert; in remembrance of His Passion and Death; and as a preparation for the solemn and glorious feast of Easter.

(2) The *Four Vigils*, or Eves of the four great feasts of Christmas-day, Pentecost, the Assumption of our Lady, and All Saints. Vigil, which means a *watching*, indicates the preparation we ought to make, by prayer and fasting, for worthily celebrating the approaching festival.

(3) The *Ember-days*, that is, the Wednesdays, Fridays, and Saturdays of four fixed weeks in the year; viz., the first whole week in Lent, Whit-week, the week the Wednesday of which follows the feast of the Exaltation of the Cross (14th September), and the third week in Advent.* The Ember-days were instituted to consecrate to God the four seasons of the year; to ask His blessing on the fruits of the earth, and to thank Him for blessings received; and, as it is at these times that ordinations regularly take place, to ask Him to grant good and holy Pastors to the Church.

II. On Abstinence.

By Days of Abstinence we mean those days on which the Church forbids us to eat flesh-meat, but allows us to take the usual number of meals.

The present discipline of the Church requires us to abstain:

When we must abstain. (1) *During Lent*, on all Fridays and Saturdays, and on Ash Wednesday and Ember Wednesday.

(2) *Outside Lent*, on all fast-days and all Fridays. But the law of fasting, or of abstinence, or of both, ceases when a fast or an abstinence day falls on any Sunday in

---

* Advent embraces the four Sundays immediately preceding Christmas-day, and thus contains at least three full weeks.

the year, or when, outside Lent, it falls on a Holyday of Obligation; hence, if a feast with a Vigil falls on a Monday, the fasting and abstinence for the Vigil cease and are no longer to be anticipated on the Saturday. Furthermore, the fasting and abstinence of Lent cease from mid-day on Holy Saturday.

The Church has appointed the Friday as a day of abstinence in memory of our Lord's Passion and Death, and has always considered this day especially fitting for the practice of mortification and penance, and for meditation on the great mystery of our Redemption.

The law of abstinence is binding on all who have reached the age of seven years and have come to the use of reason, unless they are excused by a just cause, such as ill-health, poverty, or the nature of their duties. Those who cannot, without grave inconvenience, manage to abstain from flesh-meat, ought, if possible, to consult their Pastor or Confessor, who will assign some other good work instead. They are guilty of a mortal sin who, without sufficient reason, break, or wilfully cause others to break, the law of abstinence.

Who must abstain.

III. Dispensations and Commutations.

The following dispensations and commutations at present hold in this country. Flesh-meat is allowed in the British Isles on all fast-days outside Lent which chance to follow a Friday or other day of abstinence, and, in England and Wales, Bishops have the power to dispense on the 26th December when this falls on a Friday.

Wednesday has been substituted for Saturday as an abstinence day in Lent; hence the days to be observed as abstinence days in Lent are all Wednesdays and Fridays and Ember Saturday.

[N.B.—As each Bishop has power, in his own particular diocese, to modify the Dispensations of Lent, care should be taken to consult the list of such relaxations, which will be found at the entrance to every Church, or published in the Diocesan Calendar.]

CHAPTER LXII

THE THIRD COMMANDMENT OF THE CHURCH

" To go to Confession at least once a year."

Obligation of confession.

"WHOSE sins you shall forgive, they are forgiven them ; and whose sins you shall retain, they are retained " (John xx. 23). These words clearly express the power of forgiving sins which Christ, as God, gave to His Apostles and to their successors, the Bishops and Priests of His Church, who, although sinners themselves, have power to forgive sins in the name of Him who gave them that power. And, as the words distinctly assert, there is bestowed upon the Ministers of God the power not only of forgiving, but also of retaining; not only of absolving and loosing, but also of binding and of refusing or deferring absolution, according to the dispositions that are found in sinners when they accuse themselves of their sins. Hence, it necessarily follows that there is on the sinner's part an obligation to declare and confess his sins to the ministers of God, who are appointed the spiritual judges and physicians of their souls.

At least once a year.

It was at the fourth Council of Lateran, A.D. 1215, that the law was made requiring all the faithful, after coming to the use of reason, to confess their sins *at least* once a year to a Priest approved by his Bishop to hear confessions. In the early days of the Church, the faithful were in the habit of confessing with sufficient frequency, and were in need of no express command requiring them to go to confession, but in course of time the laxity of so many Christians in carrying out the obligation rendered a distinct command necessary.

To ensure our complying, then, with the Divine precept of confession, the Church requires us to approach the sacred tribunal of Penance, and make a *good* confession, *at least* once a year, thus merely fixing the period beyond which we must not go in fulfilling the general command of God. Yet this is by no means all that she wishes of us. The very words *at least* clearly imply her wish that we should not rest content merely with an annual confession.

The implied wish of the Church.

Yearly confession, moreover, is a practice with which we should by no means be satisfied. There are many reasons why we should confess our sins more frequently; and there may be occasions which even make more frequent confession an obligation: .

Frequent confession necessary.

.1. If we have had the misfortune of falling into mortal sin, God requires us to return to Him by confession or perfect contrition without great delay: "Delay not to be converted to the Lord, and defer not from day to day ; for His wrath shall come on a sudden, and in the time of vengeance He will destroy thee " (Ecclus. v. 8, 9). A man in mortal sin is not only at enmity with God, but is in danger of dying in that state, and must therefore confess his sins without undue delay.

2. It is of obligation to confess when we are in danger of death, if we are conscious of mortal sin.

3. So long as a man is in mortal sin he is incapable of doing any works which merit heaven. He should therefore go to confession in order that he may not lose the merit of his good works.

4. Frequent confession, besides being a remedy for sins, committed, is a preventative against relapses into sin, and

enables the habitual sinner to conquer his predominant passion.

The precept of confession is binding on all who have **For all above the age of seven.** come to the use of reason; and as the age of seven is generally given as the time about which children begin to understand the gravity of mortal sin, it may be said to become binding at that age, and they should then be carefully instructed and prepared for this all-important duty.

The Church has not determined the precise time of the year when we are bound to go to confession, **Time for yearly confession.** but, as she obliges us to receive Holy Communion once a year, and that at Easter or thereabouts, she would seem clearly to point to the same period as a fitting time for the annual confession by way of preparation for the Paschal obligation.

CHAPTER LXIII

THE FOURTH COMMANDMENT OF THE CHURCH

" To receive the Blessed Sacrament at least once a year, and that at Easter or thereabouts."

" EXCEPT you eat the flesh of the Son of Man, and drink **To Communicate is a Divine command.** His blood, you shall not have life in you " (John vi. 54). The Fathers of the Church see in these words a Divine precept, bidding us receive both the Body and Blood of Jesus Christ in order that we may secure eternal life: " He that eateth this bread shall live for ever " (John vi. 59).

The Fourth Commandment of the Church, in obliging **At least once a year.** the faithful to communicate *at least* once a year—just as in the case of making an annual confession—merely prescribes the time that must not be exceeded in carrying out the Divine command. The same Lateran Council (A.D. 1215) which established the law of yearly confession, for similar reasons and motives, and to stimulate the devotion of her children, also enforced the precept obliging the faithful to communicate at least once a year; and, though in regard to the annual confession no specific time of the year was named, she fixed the time of the annual communion for Easter or thereabouts. By *universal law* the time for fulfilling the Paschal precept of *worthily* receiving Holy Communion is from Palm Sunday until Low Sunday; but if circumstances require it, Bishops may anticipate the time so as to begin on the fourth Sunday of Lent or extend it up to and including Trinity Sunday.* To neglect this obligation without necessity or a just cause would then be a grievous sin; and it would have to be fulfilled as soon as possible afterwards. The faithful, moreover, are exhorted to make their Easter Communion in their own parish; but if they make it elsewhere, they ought to give information of the fact to their own parish Priest.

Several reasons might be assigned why the Church chose
Why at Easter. Easter as the most fitting time for carrying out this devotion. Easter-day itself is the greatest feast of the Church; and it was within the Easter period that our Lord instituted the Holy Eucharist and gave Himself in Holy Communion to His disciples, and that He died and rose again from the dead.

But to Communicate merely at Easter is not sufficient, either for our necessities or for our devotion.
The wish of the Church. Here, too, the words " *at least* " at Easter imply that the Church by no means intends her precept to express her full wish and desire. On the contrary, she would have us approach the Holy Table frequently, because to all frequent Communion is beneficial, while to many it is an absolute necessity if they are to lead a virtuous life; for just as the body, if deprived of its natural food,

* Many Bishops have power further to modify this law.

languishes and dies, so too the soul, when deprived of its spiritual food which is the Bread of Life.

How earnestly did the saintly Pope, Pius X., urge the faithful to go frequently to Holy Communion!

How often to Communicate. Nay, his longing desire was that all who could should imitate the practice of the early Christians by approaching the Sacred Banquet daily. If we cannot do this, we are urged to go weekly, or monthly, or at least on the principal Feasts of the Church. It is our bounden duty, too, to Communicate on the near approach of death.

In the Catechism we are told that Christians are bound to receive the Blessed Sacrament as soon as

At what age to Communicate. they are *capable* of being instructed in this sacred mystery. So that, as soon as a child is old enough to understand the nature of this great Sacrament, and the dispositions necessary to receive it with fruit, it should be prepared without delay for receiving the Body and Blood of Christ. "He that eateth My flesh, and drinketh My blood, hath everlasting life; and I will raise him up at the last day" (John vi. 55).

CHAPTER LXIV

THE FIFTH COMMANDMENT OF THE CHURCH

"To contribute to the support of our Pastors."

"THE Lord ordained that they who preach the Gospel should live by the Gospel" (1 Cor. ix. 14).

The duty of supporting our Pastors. By the Fifth Commandment of the Church we are commanded to contribute to the support of our Pastors—a duty we find distinctly expressed in the words we have quoted from St. Paul, and which has already been treated of at some length under the Fourth Commandment of God. We have yet to speak of the duty we are under of contributing to the proper upkeep of Religion, for, as the Catechism has it: "It is a duty to contribute to the support of Religion according to our means, so that God may be duly honoured and worshipped, and the kingdom of His Church extended."

The antiquity of the practice of supporting God's Priests by tithes is shown in the Sacred Scriptures as early as the Book of Genesis, where Abraham, on his return from rescuing Lot, meets Melchisedech, the king of Salem and priest of the most High God, to whom Abraham presents the tithes of all the spoils which he had taken. And in many parts of the Old Testament we find that the people were commanded by God Himself to pay tithes of the produce of the land for the support of the Priests and the maintenance of Religion: "I have given to the sons of Levi all the tithes of Israel for a possession for the ministry wherewith they serve Me in the tabernacle of the covenant" (Num. xviii. 21).

A duty commanded by God.

Nor is the obligation of supporting the Priests of the New Law, and of contributing to the support of Religion, less binding now, seeing that they are forbidden to take part in worldly business for their own support: "Labour as a good soldier of Christ Jesus. No man being a soldier to God entangleth himself with secular business; that he may please Him to whom he hath engaged himself" (2 Tim. ii. 3, 4). And again: "If we have sown unto you spiritual things, is it a great matter if we reap your carnal things?" (1 Cor. ix. 11). Nothing can be more according to the will of God than that Religion should be generously supported, so that due honour and worship may be paid to Him, and that the Gospel may be preached throughout the world. Every one, therefore, should give according to his means—the rich man in proportion to his abundance, and the poor

Binding upon all.

man what little he can afford.   God accepts our offerings
in proportion as they are according to our abilities.   The
widow's mite was most acceptable to Him and meritorious
to herself, because, though small in itself, it was accepted
by God as great considering her extreme poverty.

CHAPTER LXV

THE SIXTH COMMANDMENT OF THE CHURCH

" Not to marry within certain degrees of kindred, nor to solemnise
marriage at the forbidden times."

THE Sixth Commandment of the Church contains a two-
fold prohibition : it forbids marriage between relations
within certain degrees of kindred, and forbids the solemnisation of marriage at certain stated time.

In the first place, then, by the command of the Church,
marriage within certain degrees of kindred is
forbidden.   She even declares that marriage
between blood relations within the third degree
is not only unlawful, but is null and void in the
sight of God.   Now brothers and sisters are blood relations
in the *first degree* from the common stock ; their children,
or first cousins, are related in the *second degree ;* and the
children of these, or second cousins, are related in the
third degree.   If the two parties are unequally removed
from the common stock, they are considered relations
according to the degree of the one who is farthest
removed.   This is what we mean by the relationship of
consanguinity.

Marriage is also forbidden between those who are related by *affinity* to the second degree : that is,
the marriage of a widower with the relations
of his deceased wife, up to the second degree, would be

Marriage within the third degree forbidden.

Affinity.

null and void, as would be the marriage of a widow with the relations of her deceased husband to the same degree. Yet this impediment of affinity exists only between the husband and his wife's relations, and between the wife and her husband's relations; but not among the relations themselves. A husband's brother, therefore, might lawfully marry the sister or any of the relations of the wife. Thus we see that the relations by blood to the husband are related to the wife by affinity; and that the relations by blood to the wife are related by affinity to the husband.

A spiritual relationship or affinity arises between the person who baptises and the baptised, and also Spiritual Relationship. between the godfather or godmother and the baptised, so that neither the person who baptises nor the godparents may marry with the baptised; but no spiritual relationship is contracted between the two godparents themselves. The same spiritual relationship, but not the same impediment of marriage, will arise also in regard to the person confirmed and those who are sponsors in Confirmation.

The impediments of consanguinity, affinity, and spiritual relationship contracted in Baptism are called Diriment impediments. *diriment* impediments, and render the contract null and void; so that even second cousins could not marry without a dispensation. Yet the Church, for special reasons, often grants a dispensation for parties to marry who are within the forbidden degrees of kindred. But only the Church can grant such dispensation.

We must now speak of the *times* in which it is forbidden to solemnise marriage. They are from Forbidden times. the first Sunday of Advent till after Christmasday, and from Ash Wednesday till after Easter Sunday. These times, it will be noticed, include the seasons of Advent and Lent, the first of which is devoted by the Church to special preparation for our Saviour's

Nativity, and the second to the consideration of His Passion and Death. Yet to solemnise marriage within the forbidden times does not render the marriage null but only unlawful.

The Church does not forbid parties to marry within these times; but she forbids them to *solemnise* their marriage, that is, she forbids them to celebrate it with the usual pomp, festivity, and rejoicing, and does not,

Marriage nevertheless permitted. unless the Bishop judges it advisable in a particular case, allow the Priest to say the nuptial Mass or to give the nuptial blessing.

If for any special reason the parties marry within the times stated, the marriage should be celebrated in as quiet and private a manner as possible, out of regard to the wishes of the Church and the solemn mysteries she is then commemorating, and unless for a just cause the nuptial blessing has then been given, it should be applied for later on, except in the case of a mixed marriage, or of a widow on her remarriage.

PART IV

THE SACRAMENTS

"You shall draw waters with joy out of the Saviour's fountains" (ISA. xii. 3).

CHAPTER LXVI

THE SACRAMENTS IN GENERAL

The word Sacrament means something *sacred* or *holy*,
A Sacrament. and is applied with special appropriateness to those *seven sacred channels* through which flow to us the graces which Jesus Christ has merited for us by His Passion and Death. The Sacraments are indeed holy, both in themselves and in their effects, and they never fail to produce holiness in those who receive them in proper dispositions. Jesus Christ Himself, while He was upon earth, instituted them as channels to bring His grace to the soul; for God alone has the power to institute them.

In the words of the Catechism a Sacrament is
Essentials of "an outward sign of inward grace, ordained a Sacrament. by Jesus Christ, by which grace is given to our souls." Three things, then, are necessary to constitute a Sacrament: namely, an outward or sensible sign, a corresponding inward or invisible grace, and institution by Jesus Christ.

The *outward sign* is so called because it makes known to us the invisible grace that is being produced in the soul. Thus in Baptism, the water poured

253

on the head of the child is an outward sign of the grace that is being wrought in the soul, namely, the interior cleansing of the soul from original sin. And we speak of it as a *sensible* sign because it strikes one or other of our senses; for example, in Baptism, we both see the water poured by the Priest, and we hear the words which he pronounces.

The outward sign. This outward sign, or external part of the Sacrament, is divided into *matter* and *form*. The *matter* of the Sacrament is the outward sensible thing used in its administration, together with the application of it to the recipient; the *form* consists of the words pronounced by the minister when he is applying the matter. To take Baptism again, the *matter* of the Sacrament is the water together with the pouring of it on the head of the child; and the words, "I baptise thee in the name of the Father, and of the Son, and of the Holy Ghost," constitute the *form*. For just as water for cleansing must be distinctly applied for that purpose, so, in Baptism, the end of the Sacrament is distinctly shown by the Priest pouring the water and using the words at the same time.

The inward grace. The outward signs of the Sacraments not only signify grace, but, at the very moment of their being applied, they actually impart the grace they signify, unless we on our part put some obstacle in the way. When, in Baptism, we see the Priest pouring the water, and hear the words that he pronounces at the same time, we know that the soul of the child is at that very moment really cleansed from original sin: "He that believeth and is baptised, shall be saved" (Mark xvi. 16), said our Lord; and in regard to the Sacrament of Penance: "Whose sins you shall forgive, *they are forgiven them*" (John xx. 23).

All the Sacraments have been instituted by Jesus Christ; for none but God could have instituted them, since only He could give to sensible things, or to outward

The institution by Christ. signs, the power of giving grace and sanctifica-tion. Between the outward ceremony and its inward spiritual effect there can be no natural
, connection, and hence it could not produce any effect on the soul, still less a spiritual effect, except in virtue of our Lord's institution, who ordained the Sacraments for the purpose of conveying His merits to our souls.

It is of faith that Christ instituted *seven*, and only

Seven Sacra-ments. seven, Sacraments ; and the Church, "The pillar and ground of truth" (1 Tim. iii. 15), has in every age proclaimed this truth. The Fathers of the Church speak of it ; and even many of the sects who broke away from the Church in the early cen-turies, as well as some others who separated from her in more recent times, for example the Greek Church, still teach the doctrine of the Seven Sacraments. Given in the order of the Catechism, the Sacraments are Baptism, Confirmation, Holy Eucharist, Penance, Extreme Unction, Holy Order, and Matrimony ; and they supply wants in man's spiritual life, which form a wonderful parallel to the needs of his bodily life.

As in the natural order man is born, so in the

Baptism. spiritual order he is born to the life of grace by Baptism.

For a time he is a weak and helpless infant, and must

Confirmation. needs grow strong. In like manner, after being spiritually born, he is weak and feeble in grace ; but by Confirmation he becomes a strong and perfect Christian, ready to fight as a true soldier of Jesus Christ.

As in the natural life he must be nourished by whole-

Holy Eucharist. some food if he is to maintain and increase his strength, so in the spiritual order, the life
- of grace which he received in Baptism, and which was strengthened in Confirmation, requires that food and

nourishment so abundantly supplied in the Sacrament of the Holy Eucharist.

If he falls sick, he must be supplied with such medicine as will restore him to health ; so in the spiritual life a remedy is provided in the Sacrament of Penance for the ills of his soul brought on by sin, an infallible remedy that will restore him to the state of grace.

Penance.

When at length his last hour draws nigh and he has to die, it is then that his body requires special comfort and assistance. His soul, too, stands in urgent need of help and strength to battle against despair and the last dreadful assaults of the Devil. This spiritual consolation and support is given by the Sacrament of Extreme Unction.

Extreme Unction.

And just as human society requires rulers to preserve it in order, so too are there rulers in the spiritual society of the Church, provided for it by the Sacrament of Holy Order.

Holy Order.

Furthermore, the Church has to spread and increase in the world ; and one generation must needs succeed another. Now, as the good of society depends to a vast extent on the way in which parents bring up their children, in the Sacrament of Matrimony the union of husband and wife is blessed and sanctified that they may people the Church with a succession of good Christians.

Matrimony.

Yet, although all the Sacraments are necessary for the Church as a whole, they are not all necessary for each of her separate members ; and they differ from each other not only in point of necessity, but also in point of dignity. Of all the Sacraments, Baptism is the most necessary, seeing that, without it, we cannot get to heaven: " Unless a man be born again of water and the Holy Ghost, he cannot enter into the kingdom of God " (John iii. 5); but the Holy

Sacraments differ in dignity and importance.

Eucharist is the most excellent, containing as it does Jesus Christ Himself, the source of all grace.

The Sacraments admit of several classifications. (1) They *Sacraments of the living* and *Sacraments of the dead.* may be divided into Sacraments of the. *living* and Sacraments of the *dead.* The Sacraments of the *living* are five, namely, Confirmation, Holy Eucharist, Extreme Unction, Holy Order, and Matrimony; and are so called because, in order to receive them worthily, the soul must possess spiritual life, that is, it must be in the state of grace. The other two Sacraments, Baptism and Penance, are called Sacraments of the *dead* because, when they are received, the soul is either spiritually dead through being in mortal sin, or need not be in the state of grace. They are instituted to give sanctifying grace to those who are without it; they raise the soul from the death of sin to the life of grace. These two Sacraments impart what is called *first grace,* while the Sacraments of the living, presupposing a state of grace, give *second grace;* that is, they increase sanctifying grace in those who already possess it.

There may be circumstances in which the Sacraments of the *living* confer first grace, that is, when, like the Sacrament of Penance, they restore spiritual life to the soul. For example, if a person in mortal sin, yet believing himself to be in the state of grace, were to receive a Sacrament of the living with such attrition as is necessary for receiving sacramental absolution, it is the generally received opinion that he would obtain the pardon and remission of his hidden sin. Extreme Unction certainly forgives mortal sin in these circumstances.

(2) They may be divided into those which give *a character* and those which do not. The three *Sacraments which imprint a character.* Sacraments of Baptism, Confirmation, and Holy Order, imprint an indelible mark or seal on the soul, and can be received but once. The remaining four Sacraments do not imprint such a character, and may

17

be received frequently. The spiritual character imprinted on the soul distinguishes those so marked as the children, soldiers, or ministers of God, and will add to their greater glory or condemnation in the next world.

(3) A still further principle of division would be into Sacraments of *free choice* and those which are for all. The Sacraments of free choice are Holy Order and Matrimony, which are to be received by such as are called to the clerical or to the married state. The other five Sacraments are instituted for all who are old enough and sufficiently instructed to receive them.

Sacraments of free choice.

In order to produce their effects the Sacraments require a *subject* to receive them. They are instituted for man and for man only; yet all men are not able to receive all the Sacraments. A woman cannot receive the Sacrament of Holy Order; a child, before coming to the use of reason, cannot validly receive the Sacrament of Penance, Extreme Unction, or Matrimony; one in health may not receive Extreme Unction; and before we can participate in the other Sacraments, Baptism is necessary. Of all the Sacraments, the Sacrament of the Holy Eucharist alone exists in itself, apart, that is, from its being received; so that what before consecration was but bread and wine, after consecration is truly the Body and Blood of Jesus Christ; and the Blessed Sacrament continues as long as the species remain. But the other Sacraments exist only during the application of the matter and form to the recipient; for example, the Sacrament of Baptism exists only during the pouring of the water and the pronouncing of the words.

Subject of the Sacraments.

Although, as far as the Sacraments themselves are concerned, they infallibly produce their effect, yet, as far as the recipient of them is concerned, certain dispositions are required before they can be *validly* (or really) and *lawfully* (or fruitfully) received.

Dispositions required in the subject.

To receive a Sacrament *validly* or really there is need, in the case of adults, of an *intention* or wish expressed or implied to receive it.   And, although children are baptised before they are capable of having any wish in the matter, their desire is supplied by the Church.   The subject, moreover, must be *fit*; that is, he must be one capable of receiving the Sacrament. Thus, if a grown-up person were to be forcibly baptised, or if one already baptised were to be rebaptised, the baptism in either case would be null and void, as the wish would be wanting in the one case and fitness in the other.

Valid reception.

If, in addition to intention and fitness, the subject also possesses the necessary dispositions for gaining the grace of the Sacrament, then, besides receiving the Sacrament validly, he also receives it *lawfully*, or with fruit to his soul.   Thus, if a baptised person were to receive a Sacrament of the living in a state of mortal sin, he would receive the Sacrament validly, but not lawfully; but if he were in a state of grace at the time, he would receive it both validly and lawfully: that is, he would receive the grace for which the Sacrament was instituted.   He, however, who deliberately receives a Sacrament unworthily commits a very grievous sin—a sacrilege

Lawful reception.

The Sacraments always give grace to those who receive them in proper dispositions; and, as we have seen above, Baptism, Confirmation, and Holy Order imprint an indelible mark or seal on the soul, wherefore the Sacrament conferring it may not be repeated.   And besides introducing or increasing sanctifying grace in the soul, each Sacrament confers a special grace peculiar to itself.   This is what we mean by *Sacramental* grace, namely, a right, founded on sanctifying grace, to receive actual graces corresponding to the end for which the Sacrament was instituted.

Effects of the Sacraments.

In order to receive the grace of a Sacrament certain
dispositions are essential; yet it is not the
Certain dispositions necessary. dispositions that produce the grace, they
merely remove the obstacles that would prevent its being received into the soul; just as the window
does not produce the light that is in the room, but merely
removes the obstacle that would prevent the light from
entering. Nor do the Sacraments produce grace either by
the merits of him who administers or of him who receives
them, but in virtue of their institution by Jesus Christ,
who ordained them to convey the merits of His Precious
Blood to our souls.

If an adult were to receive Baptism unworthily, or Confirmation, or Holy Order—Sacraments which can be received
but once—he would receive the Sacrament validly; yet
the grace of the Sacrament would not flow in upon the soul,
but would remain, as it were, in abeyance till the obstruction
was removed by an act of perfect contrition or a good
confession. The same is most probably the case in regard
to Matrimony and Extreme Unction.

We have next to deal with the Minister of the Sacraments,
or the person who has the power of conferring
The Minister of the Sacraments. them. The Minister represents the Person of
Jesus Christ, and if he has the intention of doing
what the Church does, and can and does use the matter and
form instituted by Christ, he administers the Sacrament
validly. Each Sacrament has its proper Minister, who may
be a Bishop, or a Priest, or, in some cases, a lay person;
for even men and women are able to administer Baptism
validly in all cases, and lawfully in case of necessity.

Nor is holiness, or even faith, necessary in the Minister
for the valid administration of the Sacraments;
Holiness in the Minister not necessary. yet, if he were in the state of mortal sin, he
would commit a sacrilege by treating a function
so sacred with disrespect. St. Augustine, speaking on this
subject, tells us that those who were baptised by Judas were

baptised by Christ; and that even if a murderer were to baptise, so long as the Baptism was of Christ, it would be Christ
Himself who baptised, for in every case the Minister stands
for the Person of Christ.   The Sacraments are the channels
of grace to our souls, and may be compared to the channels
through which water is conveyed to a city.   Whether
these are of clay, of iron, or of silver, they are in every
case equally capable of performing what is required of
them.   And whether a seal be made of gold, or silver, or
some baser metal, it is equally capable of imprinting the
royal image upon wax.   The physician, even when in ill-
health himself, may nevertheless be able to heal his patients.

Certain ceremonies are also employed in the solemn
administration of the Sacraments, and this use
Ceremonies.
of ceremonies is as ancient as Christianity itself.
They serve to increase our devotion and reverence, they
make us understand better the effects and mysteries
of the Sacraments, and they are the outward expressions
of the inward dispositions that are necessary in the
recipient.   Although not essential for the valid administration of the Sacraments, they could not be omitted
without sin except in case of necessity.   A Sacrament
would produce all its effects without them.

CHAPTER LXVII

SACRAMENTALS

SACRAMENTALS are certain pious practices and things which
bear an outward resemblance to the Sacraments,
Definition.
and which have been instituted by the Church
for producing certain salutary effects.

The great difference between Sacramentals and the
Sacraments is that the Sacraments were *insti-*
Sacramentals
differ from   *tuted by Jesus Christ* as the channels by which
sacraments.   grace flows into the soul.   Their action is infallible; and their salutary effects, which are independent

of the good or bad dispositions of the Minister, can be hindered only by the unworthy dispositions of him who receives them. Whereas the Sacramentals were *instituted by the Church*, and receive their efficacy from the prayers and blessings of the Church and the pious intentions of those who make use of them. They are more effectual than the ordinary good works we perform, since they partake more of the acts of the universal Church than of the individual Christian.

There are many Sacramentals, and theologians generally group them under six distinct heads; viz. :
Kinds of Sacramentals. *Orans* (praying), *tinctus* (anointings), *edens* (eating), *confessus* (confessing), *dans* (giving), and *benedicens* (blessing).

1. *Orans* (praying) refers particularly to public prayer, and especially to those prayers prescribed by the Church and instituted in her name ; as, for example, the Rogations ; and prayers said in a consecrated church.

2. *Tinctus* (anointings) includes anointings in which blessed oil is used—as in the blessing of bells, and the consecration of churches and of altars ; and also the use of Holy Water.

3. *Edens* (eating) refers to the eating of blessed bread and of other foods blessed by the Church.

4. *Confessus* (confessing) includes all external expressions of sorrow for our sins in the services of the Church, as the receiving of ashes on Ash Wednesday ; the public acknowledgment of our sins during the Confiteor at Mass and in the Divine Office ; and the humble striking of our breast in token of our heart-felt sorrow for having offended God.

5. *Dans* (giving) signifies almsgiving, and other works of mercy, when prescribed and recommended by the Church, either during the penitential seasons of Advent and Lent, or when, in some special case, she invokes our charity.

6. *Benedicens* (blessing) comprehends the various bless-

ings given by the Pope, Bishops, and Priests, whether in
the case of persons or things; hence, under this heading,
would come the blessing of the *Agnus Dei*, and other
objects of devotion, as well as of altars, chalices, and bells.

Sacramentals are capable of producing certain effects,
not of themselves, but by reason of the prayers
The effects of and blessings of the Church and our own pious
Sacramentals.
intentions. The *four* chief effects of Sacramentals are these :

1. *The remission of venial sin,* which is blotted out from
the soul, not by the direct power of the Sacramentals, but
through the sorrow for sin and love of God which they
excite in the soul.

2. *The remission of the temporal punishment due to sin,*
This may be brought about in two ways—(1) by means of
any indulgence which may be attached to the Sacramental
used ; or (2) by means of the satisfaction resulting from
the performance of penitential works, and from the turning
away of the heart from sin.

3. *The subduing or the putting to flight of evil spirits.*
Such an effect is not confined to exorcisms, but may be
produced by other Sacramentals also, especially by the
use of Holy Water.

4. *They secure temporal blessings,* either *directly* as the
result of our prayers, or *indirectly* by rendering ineffectual
the wiles of the devil against us.

CHAPTER LXVIII

BAPTISM

THE word *Baptism* is derived-from the Greek, and signifies
immersion, or *washing* generally.   As a Sacra-
Meaning and
definition of   ment Baptism is the *first* of all the Sacraments
Baptism.   because in the order of time it is the first
received, and because, without it, no one can receive any

of the others ; and the *most necessary* because, without it,' no one can enter heaven: "Unless a man be born again of water and the Holy Ghost, he cannot enter into the king- dom of God " (John iii. 5). In the words of the Catechism we define Baptism as a Sacrament which cleanses us from original sin, makes us Christians, children of God, and members of the Church. If it is received in proper dispositions by an adult, it also takes away the actual sins he may have committed before being baptised, and remits all punishment due to them. Such a one must have sorrow—at the least attrition—for his actual sins.

We distinguish *three kinds* of Baptism—Baptism of

The different kinds of Baptism.

water, Baptism of *blood*, and Baptism of *desire*. Of these Baptism of water alone is the Sacrament instituted by Jesus Christ as the door of the spiritual life. Baptism of blood is so called because it consists in martyrdom, where the shedding of one's blood for Christ's sake takes the place of the Sacra- ment. Baptism of desire is the wish, whether explicit or implicit, to receive the Baptism of water, accompanied with perfect charity. Baptism of blood and Baptism of desire, however, are not Sacraments, but receive the name of Bap- tism because they purify the soul from sin, and supply the place of the Sacrament in those who are unable to receive it.

We cannot state with certainty the exact time when

When instituted.

the Sacrament of Baptism was instituted, but' St. Thomas, following St. Gregory Nazianzen and St. Augustine, is of opinion that its insti- tution took place at the time of our Lord's baptism by St. John. We there see the *matter* represented by the water which was consecrated, and to which was given its regenerating power by coming in contact with the sacred humanity of Christ; the *form* was figured in the sensible presence of the three Divine Persons of the Blessed Trinity in whose Name the Sacrament is conferred : the voice of the Father was heard, the Son was present in the flesh, the Holy Ghost descended in the form of a dove; and the *fruit* of the Sacrament was shown by the heavens opening as they are opened to us by Baptism. But whether Baptism was instituted then or later, it is certain that its reception as a necessary means of salvation was not binding till our Saviour, after His Resurrection, said to His disciples: " Going therefore, teach ye all nations, baptising them in the name of the Father, and of the Son, and of the Holy Ghost" (Matt. xxviii. 19).

The Baptism of St. John was not a Sacrament, but an external profession of penance, to which the baptised added an external or oral confession of sins: " And they were baptised in the Jordan, confessing their sins " (Matt. iii. 6). But, although they confessed their sins and were baptised, the Baptism did not, it would seem, remit sin, as may be gathered from the words of John himself: " I baptise you with water unto penance, but He who is to come after me . . . shall baptise you with the Holy Ghost " (Matt. iii. 11). This he said to show that he did not baptise with the Holy Ghost, without which there is no remission of sin. John's Baptism, then, was only figurative of the cleansing of the heart, and those who came to him, weeping and confessing their sins, gave to it, by their penitence, an efficacy which it had not in itself. Nay, we even find it mentioned in the Acts, that those who had received the Baptism of John were afterwards baptised with the " Baptism of Christ " (Acts xix.).

The Baptism of John.

The *matter* of the Sacrament of Baptism is water together with its application: " Unless a man be born again of water and the Holy Ghost, he cannot enter into the kingdom of God" (John iii. 5). The water may be any natural water, such as rain-water, spring-water, water from the river or from the sea ; but any liquid which can be regarded as no longer retaining the quality of water would not suffice. Baptismal water, however, or water

Matter.

blessed for the purpose, is used in conferring Baptism solemnly, that is, with all the appointed ceremonies.

Water represents very vividly the effect of Baptism: it serves to remove from the body the stains and defilements that disfigure it, and thus expresses in a sensible manner the effect of Baptism upon the soul, which it purifies from the stains of sin.

The Church recognises three different ways of applying the matter: by *immersion*, *i.e.*, by dipping the person in the water; by *aspersion*, or the sprinkling of the water; and by *effusion*, which is the pouring of the water on the head of the person to be baptised; and the water must flow on the skin of the head.

The *form* consists of the words, " I baptise thee in the name of the Father, and of the Son, and of the Holy Ghost." Here we have expressed the action of the Minister who baptises; the person who is being baptised; and the distinct invocation of the three Persons of the Blessed Trinity in whose name the Sacrament is administered: " Going therefore, teach ye all nations, baptising them in the name of the Father, and of the Son, and of the Holy Ghost" (Matt. xxviii. 19). The water must be poured in sufficient quantity to flow; and the words must be said *at the same time* as the water is being poured, and by the person who pours it.

Form.

The *ordinary* Minister of Baptism is a Priest. Deacons also are Ministers, but only *extraordinary* Ministers, since they cannot baptise solemnly unless for a just cause and with the permission of the Bishop or the parish Priest. Yet anyone, be he cleric or lay, believer or infidel, Catholic or non-Catholic, man or woman, can *validly* administer the Sacrament, *and even lawfully in case of necessity*, when a Priest cannot be had. The person who baptises must, however, observe the prescribed form, and have the intention of

Minister.

doing what the Church does. If this intention on the part of the Minister is wanting, the Sacrament is null.

Since God wills that all men be saved, and has made Baptism a necessary condition of salvation, it follows that all, both children and adults, are capable of receiving Baptism.

The subject of Baptism.

In the case of infants the Sacrament should never be delayed longer than need be; for it is by Baptism that we are ranked in the number of the faithful, and, without it, none can be admitted to the enjoyment of the Beatific Vision : " Unless a man be born again of water and the Holy Ghost, he cannot enter into the kingdom of God " (John iii. 5). Yet, though children who die without Baptism are excluded from heaven, it is not supposed that they suffer actual pain, like those who have sinned of their own free will, but that they enjoy such happiness as they are capable of. In not admitting them to heaven God does them no wrong, for heaven, being a supernatural and free gift of God, is in no sense their due. When baptised children come to the use of reason they are bound to carry out the promises made in their name by their godfathers and godmothers.

Necessity of Baptism for all.

Certain conditions are required in the case of the Baptism of adults. In the first place, it is necessary, even for the *validity* of the Sacrament, that they ask, or at least that they give their consent, to be baptised. Furthermore, it is required, not for the validity, but for the lawful or *fruitful reception* of the Sacrament, that they be sufficiently instructed in the principal truths of Religion, and that they be animated with sentiments of faith, hope, and contrition for actual sins, together with a desire and resolve to lead a Christian life. " He that believeth and is baptised shall be saved ; but he that believeth not shall be condemned " (Mark xvi. 16).

Baptism of Adults.

There must be at least one godparent. If the parents

of the child desire it, there may be two; but if two be
chosen, they must not be of the same sex. If
there be only one, that one may be of either

Sponsors.

sex, irrespective of the sex of the child. Godparents,
as we have seen, contract a spiritual relationship with
their godchild which prevents them from intermarrying
either lawfully or validly. The sponsors answer in the
child's name, and take it upon themselves to see that
the baptismal promises are duly carried out. If the
parents of a godchild die, or fail to see to its Christian
upbringing, it is the duty of the sponsors, as far as possible,
to see that it receives a proper Catholic education.

When Baptism is administered privately on account of
danger of death, the Church desires the presence
of two witnesses, or one at least; but when

Private
Baptism.

there is great urgency, the Baptism must not
be delayed in order to obtain a witness.

The effects of Baptism are many and admirable, but its
principal effects are *sanctifying grace* which

Effects of
Baptism.

regenerates us in Jesus Christ, and the *character*
which it imprints on our soul. The necessity
and importance of this Sacrament may be gathered from a
full enumeration of its effects :

1. It confers on all who receive it worthily *sanctifying
grace* which purifies them entirely from sin and renders
them pleasing in the sight of God. This grace blots out
not only original sin, which all inherit from Adam, but, in
the case of adults, even the actual sins committed before
Baptism. It is the same as *habitual grace,* and is the
life of the soul.

2. It remits all punishment due to sin, so that, were a
person to die immediately after Baptism, he would go
straight to heaven.

3. It makes us Christians by uniting us to Jesus Christ
as members of the one body of which He is the Head. By
Baptism we become children of God and heirs to the
Kingdom of Heaven.

4. It makes us members of the Church, and gives us a right to the other Sacraments, which cannot be received without Baptism, and to all the blessings of the Church.

5. It infuses into the soul the Theological Virtues of Faith, Hope, and Charity, as well as the Cardinal Virtues, Prudence, Justice, Fortitude, and Temperance, in which all the Moral Virtues are included, and the gifts of the Holy Ghost.

6. It confers a sacramental grace which gives us a right to those actual graces which will enable us to fight against concupiscence, and to fulfil the duties of a Christian.

7. It imprints on our soul an indelible *character*, a spiritual sign or seal, which distinguishes us from all who are not Christians, and which prevents the Sacrament from being received more than once.

When a person is rebaptised, such as a convert to the Catholic Church, if it is doubtful whether he has been baptised at all or whether he has been validly baptised, the Baptism is given conditionally, and has no effect if the first was validly administered. In doubtful cases the words "If thou art not baptised," are pronounced before the *form*, " I baptise thee, etc."

Now although Baptism cleanses the soul from the stain of original sin, it still leaves us subject to many Concupiscence after Baptism. of the effects of original sin, such as bodily weakness, suffering, death, and concupiscence, or that rebellious principle within us, that strife between the spirit and the flesh, which remains for the trial even of the most virtuous. Yet these evil motions, although they incline us to sin, are not sinful as long as they are not voluntary and not consented to. They even increase our merit when faithfully resisted.

We will now conclude this all-important chapter by giving a short summary of the facts which Baptism a true Sacrament. go to show that Baptism possesses all that is necessary to constitute a Sacrament. It has an *outward sign* with its *matter* and *form*, viz., the pouring of the water while the words "I baptise thee, etc.," are being pronounced; an *inward grace* which is the cleansing of the soul from every stain of sin, original and actual, and which is typified by the outward sign; and its *institution by Christ*, whom we find bidding His Apostles: "Going therefore, teach ye all nations, baptising them in the name of the Father, and of the Son, and of the Holy Ghost" (Matt. xxviii. 19).

CHAPTER LXIX

THE CEREMONIES OF BAPTISM

THE ceremonies that accompany the solemn administration of Baptism are beautiful and instructive. Some of them are symbolic of the *dispositions* required in the recipient of the Sacrament; others represent its *effects*; while others again typify the *obligations* which its reception entails.

The following ceremonies precede the actual Baptism, and take place in the porch or at the door of the church, to show that Baptism alone can give the right of entrance:

Ceremonies before Baptism at the door of the church.

1. The person to be baptised is met by the Priest, who inquires what is sought, and being told "Faith," he proceeds to declare the advantages of Faith and its corresponding duties.

2. The Priest then breathes three times on the child's face to signify the breath of the new and spiritual life that is about to enter the soul by the grace of the Holy Spirit.

3. The sign of the Cross is made upon the forehead and the breast of the child to signify that he must not only cherish the doctrine of his Crucified Redeemer in his heart, but openly profess it, and never be ashamed of the Cross of Christ.

4. A few particles of blessed salt are next put into his mouth by the Priest, to denote preservation from the corruption of sin, and the savour of Christian wisdom.

5. To deliver him from the power of the devil the Priest pronounces over him the exorcisms, and, in the name of the Blessed Trinity, bids the unclean spirit go out of him.

The child is then brought into the church and carried to the font, the sponsors reciting aloud with the Priest the "I believe" and the "Our Father." The following ceremonies take place near the font:

Ceremonies before Baptism inside the church.

1. The Priest anoints the child's ears and nostrils with spittle from his own lips, saying, in imitation of our Lord when He cured the deaf and dumb man, "Ephpheta—which is, be thou opened." By this is signified that his senses are now opened to the doctrine of Christ and to its sweetness.

2. The child is now required to renounce the devil and all his works and all his pomps; after which the Priest anoints him with the oil of Catechumens on the breast and between the shoulders, to show that, to arrive at eternal life, he must fight bravely against the devil and the world.

3. The Priest asks concerning his belief in the Articles of the Creed, and if he will be baptised.

Then comes the actual Baptism.

The ceremonies that come after the act of Baptism are as follows:

Ceremonies that follow the act of Baptism.

1. The crown of the child's head is anointed with chrism, to signify that he is now a Christian and a partaker of Christ's dignity as King and Priest.

2. A white garment, the emblem of innocence, is placed on his head by the Priest, with the words, "Receive this white garment, and see thou carry it without stain before the judgment-seat of our Lord Jesus Christ that thou mayest have eternal life."

3. The Priest next gives him a lighted taper, a symbol of the light of Faith and of good example, telling him:

" Receive this burning light, and keep thy Baptism, so as to be without blame: keep the commandments of God, that when the Lord shall come to the Nuptials, thou mayest meet Him in the company of all the Saints in the heavenly Court, and have eternal life, and live for ever and ever."

He then brings the ceremony to a close with the words, " N., go in peace, and the Lord be with thee."

CHAPTER LXX

CONFIRMATION

CONFIRMATION takes the second place in the order of the Nature and definition of Confirmation. Sacraments because its great object is to confirm, or *strengthen* and complete, the life of grace received in Baptism. By Baptism we become the children of God, by Confirmation we are made strong, and receive grace to fight manfully against evil, and boldly to profess and defend the Faith that was infused into our souls at Baptism : " Confirm, O God; what Thou hast wrought in us " (Ps. lxvii. 29). Confirmation increases sanctifying grace in the soul, and gives us a title to those actual graces which enable us to advance in virtue and to lead a good Christian life. It is moreover one of the three Sacraments which imprint on us a spiritual mark or seal which can never be effaced, the mark in this case being that of soldiers of Jesus Christ.. As the Catechism has it : " Confirmation is a Sacrament by which we receive the Holy Ghost in order to make us strong and perfect Christians and soldiers of Jesus Christ."

In administering Confirmation the Bishop extends his How the Bishop administers Confirmation. hands over all those who are to be confirmed, and prays that the Holy Ghost may descend upon them with his sevenfold gifts. He next places his right hand on the head of each one individually,

and at the same time anoints his forehead with chrism
while he pronounces certain words. He then gives the one
who has been confirmed a slight blow on the cheek, saying,
" Peace be with thee." This is to remind him that he is
now strengthened, and should be ready to bear patiently
persecutions and contradictions for Christ's sake.

Confirmation, being a Sacrament, must possess the
Confirmation three essentials that go to make a Sacra-
a true Sacra- ment; *i.e.*, it must have an *outward sign*, an
ment. *inward grace*, and it must have been *instituted
by Jesus Christ* as one of the channels of grace to our soul.

The *outward sign* or visible part of the Sacrament consists in the *matter* of the Sacrament, which is
The outward the anointing with chrism together with the
sign. imposition of hands, and the *form* which is
comprised of the words used by the Bishop while he is
anointing the forehead of each individual, viz., " I sign
thee with the sign of the Cross, and I confirm thee with the
chrism of salvation, in the name of the Father, and of the
Son, and of the Holy Ghost. Amen." The Bishop performs the ceremony by placing his right hand on the head
of each one to be confirmed, while with the thumb of the
same hand he makes the sign of the Cross with the chrism on
the forehead when he pronounces the above-mentioned words.

A few formerly held that the matter of the Sacrament
consists in the general imposition of hands at the beginning
of the rite ; still fewer held that both it and the anointing
are equally necessary ; but the generally accepted opinion
is that the signing of the forehead with chrism by the
Bishop also includes at the same time the imposition of
hands and constitutes the essential matter.

On Maundy Thursday three oils are blessed by the
Bishop. Besides the *oil of Catechumens*, with
The Holy Oils. which those are anointed who are about to
receive Baptism, and which is used in certain other anoint-

18

ings also, there is the *oil of the sick*, used in administering
Extreme Unction, and *chrism*, used in Confirmation as well
as at other times.   Chrism is a mixture of the oil of olives
and balsam, and is figurative of what takes place in Confirmation.   Oil represents the fulness of grace; it easily
flows, spreads, and penetrates, softens, nourishes, and
strengthens, and thus signifies the inward effects of the
Holy Ghost on the soul.   Balsam, by reason of its fragrance,
fittingly indicates the sweet odour of virtue which those
ought to spread who have been confirmed.   It also possesses the power of preserving things from corruption, and
thus signifies that he who has been confirmed receives
from the Sacrament the grace to preserve himself from
the corruption of the world.   By the intermingling of the
oil and balsam is represented the diversity of the gifts of
the Holy Ghost communicated to us in Confirmation.

The inward grace, signified and represented by the outward sign, is the plenitude of the Holy Spirit
adorning and enriching our souls with those
interior graces with which the Apostles were
sanctified and strengthened on the Day of Pentecost.

The inward grace.

Although the exact time of the institution of this
Sacrament is not mentioned in Scripture, the
fact that it was instituted by our Lord is
clearly shown from the practice of the Apostles
themselves, who administered it as a means of grace.   We
read in the Acts: "When the Apostles, who were in
Jerusalem, had heard that Samaria had received the word
of God, they sent unto them Peter and John; who, when
they were come, prayed for them, that they might receive
the Holy Ghost. . . . They were only baptised in the
Name of the Lord Jesus.   Then they laid their hands
upon them, and they received the Holy Ghost"
(Acts viii. 14-17).

The institution by Christ.

The administration of Confirmation is a function
generally reserved to a Bishop, who alone is the *ordinary*

The Minister. Minister, as he is the successor of the Apostles to whom this right belonged. In the preceding paragraph we have seen that it was St. Peter and St. John, both Bishops, who went down to Samaria to confirm those who had recently been baptised.

A Priest may, as an *extraordinary* Minister, and with special power from the Pope, administer Confirmation in urgent cases; but even then he must have chrism blessed by a Bishop. Were he to attempt to administer Confirmation without the express consent of the Vicar of Christ the Sacrament would be null.

Necessity of Confirmation. The Sacrament of Confirmation is not necessary as an essential means of salvation, as it was not established as a means of reconciling the sinner with God; but it is so far necessary from the necessity of precept that it would be a sin if one were to refuse or neglect to receive it when a suitable opportunity arose—unless he were prevented by some reasonable cause. We all need grace and strength faithfully to practise our Religion, and we could not through contempt or negligence refuse this great grace without rendering ourselves guilty of sin before God.

Subject. All who have been baptised, both children and adults, are capable of receiving Confirmation; however, it is not now customary, unless for some grave motive, to administer it except to those who have come to the use of reason, so that they may know and understand the fruits to be derived from so great a Sacrament, and may be the better instructed and prepared for its reception.

Preparation and dispositions required. Certain dispositions are required to receive Confirmation worthily. The aspirant should be instructed in its nature and effects, and in all that has regard to the Sacrament. He should know the fundamental truths of Religion, the " Our Father," the " I believe," and the Commandments. He should heartily desire and pray for the grace of the Holy Ghost: " Your heavenly Father will give the good Spirit to them that ask Him " (Luke xi. 13). And, as Confirmation is one of the Sacraments of the living, and must be received in the state of grace, he will naturally prepare himself by a good Confession : " For Wisdom will not enter into a malicious soul, nor dwell in a body subject to sins " (Wisd. i. 4). If a person were to receive Confirmation in mortal sin, he would commit a great sacrilege, and would not receive the grace of the Sacrament till he removed the obstacle thus put in its way by a good Confession or an Act of perfect Contrition.

In Confirmation, too, a new name is taken, that of some Saint whom we wish to set before us as our further model and as our protector ; and, as in Baptism, sponsors are employed.

Sponsors. Parents cannot stand as sponsors for their own children, and the sponsors in Confirmation must, unless there be a reasonable cause to be decided by the minister, be different from the sponsors in Baptism ; they must, moreover, be Catholics who themselves have been confirmed, and be of good character. In Confirmation a godfather stands for the males and a godmother for the females. They become the spiritual parents and guardians of those for whom they stand as sponsors, by placing a hand on the right shoulder of the person who is being confirmed, while the Bishop is anointing the forehead ; and they should, as far as possible, see that their god-children live up to the practice of their religion. There also arises in Confirmation the same spiritual relationship, only however between the sponsors and the one confirmed, but not the same impediment of marriage, as in Baptism.

Effects of Confirmation. The principal effects of Confirmation have already been named while we have been treating of the Sacrament, but we may conveniently sum them up as follows :—

1. Confirmation increases sanctifying grace, and perfects in us the graces received at Baptism.

2. To sanctifying grace it joins a sacramental grace which renews within us the marvellous effects wrought by the Holy Ghost when He descended upon the Apostles. It gives us a claim to receive new strength and light, and courage to confess our Religion in the midst of persecutions. From being like timid children we become soldiers of Jesus Christ.

The seven gifts particularly attributed to the Holy Ghost are *wisdom, understanding, counsel, fortitude, knowledge, piety,* and *the fear of the Lord;* and these, though infused into the soul at Baptism, are received in their plenitude in Confirmation. The gift of tongues and of prophecy which often accompanied the Sacrament in the early Church continued as long as these were necessary for the good of the Church; but, since they were meant not for the good of those who received them, but for others, they ceased when they became no longer necessary.

3. Confirmation imprints on our soul a character, a spiritual mark or seal marking us out as soldiers of Christ. It can never be effaced, and hence prevents the Sacrament from being repeated.

CHAPTER LXXI

THE HOLY EUCHARIST—AS A SACRAMENT

Of all the Sacraments instituted by our Lord, the Character of the Holy Eucharist. Blessed Eucharist is the greatest and the most holy, for not only does it give grace to those who receive it worthily, but it contains the Author and Source of all grace, Jesus Christ Himself. The other Sacraments exist only while they are being administered, the Blessed Eucharist is something lasting and substantial, and continues to exist as long as the

species remain essentially unchanged. The Blessed
Eucharist, moreover, is not only a Sacrament, but has a
two-fold quality, that of Sacrament and Sacrifice. It is a
Sacrament when we receive it in the Holy Communion,
and when it is reserved and exposed for our adoration ; it
is a Sacrifice when it is offered to God by the Priest in the
Holy Mass. It is the great central object of Catholic
worship : " He hath made a resemblance of His wonderful
works, being a merciful and gracious Lord ; He hath given
food to them that fear Him " (Ps. cx. 4, 5).

Although the Blessed Eucharist exceeds in dignity all the
other Sacraments, it is placed third in the order of the
Sacraments because its great object is to feed and nourish
our souls, so that the supernatural life of grace received in
Baptism and strengthened in Confirmation may be perfected
and preserved by it: "If any man eat of this bread, he
shall live for ever ; and the bread that I will give is My
flesh for the life of the world " (John vi. 52).

Various names are given to this Sacrament—a fact
which helps us to realise its importance. The
first Christians spoke of it as the *Breaking
of Bread*. We frequently call it the *Holy
Eucharist* (Holy Thanksgiving) because at its institution
our Lord gave thanks to His Eternal Father, and
because by it we are enabled to render such thanks to
God as are worthy of His acceptance, and a homage of
infinite value for all the benefits we have received from Him.
It is also termed *Holy Communion* because, in an especial
manner, it unites the faithful to Jesus Christ, and to one
another as members of the mystical body of which Christ
is the head. It is by our communicating with Christ and
with one another in this Blessed Sacrament that we are
really formed into one mystical body, and made, as it were,
one bread, compounded of many grains of corn closely united
together : "For we being many are one bread, one body,

Different names of the Blessed Sacrament.

all who partake of one bread " (1 Cor. x. 17). Wè speak of it as the *Holy Viaticum* (Provision for a journey) because at the end of our pilgrimage through life it prepares us for our passage to etcrnity: formerly it was so called from its being also the spiritual food of the faithful during their pilgrimage. We call it, too, the *Most Holy Sacrament of the Altar* because the mystery of the Blessed Eucharist, which is at once a Sacrament and a Sacrifice, is effected on our Altar. It is on account of this two-fold character of the Sacrament that our subject naturally divides itself into two parts. In the first part we shall treat of the Holy Eucharist as a Sacrament, in the second as a Sacrifice.

" The Sacrament of the Holy Eucharist," the Catechism tells us, " is the true Body and Blood of Jesus Christ, together with His Soul and Divinity, under the appearances of bread and wine." It is a Sacrament because it combines within itself all the essential conditions for a Sacrament—it has an outward sign, and an inward grace, and it was ordained by Jesus Christ.

Defined as a Sacrament.

The outward sign, as in the other Sacraments, consists of the *matter*, which, in the Holy Eucharist, is Bread and Wine—wheaten bread and the wine of the grape ; and the *form*, or the words of consecration pronounced over the Bread and Wine by the Priest in the Mass, "This is My Body . . .," " This is My Blood. . . ." These words bring about *Transubstantiation*, or the changing of the substance of Bread and Wine into the Body and Blood of Jesus Christ ; so that, after consecration, although the *accidents*, that is, the species or all the outward appearances that belong to bread and wine, remain, the *substances* of these two elements have been changed into the true Body and Blood of Christ.

The Outward Sign.

The Inward Grace conferred by the Sacrament of the

Holy Eucharist—in which Christ gives Himself to us to be the life and food of our soul—is strikingly typified by the Outward Sign; for, as food and drink form the perfect nourishment of the body, so the outward appearances of bread and wine, which, as we have seen, remain even after the consecration, signify the spiritual nourishment effected in the soul by the Inward Grace of the Sacrament. "My flesh is meat indeed, and My blood is drink indeed. He that eateth My flesh, and drinketh My blood, abideth in Me, and I in him" (John vi. 56, 57).

The Inward Grace.

The Holy Eucharist was moreover instituted by Jesus Christ as a Sacrament. We read that our Lord, knowing that His hour was come when He should pass out of the world to His Father, having loved His own who were in the world, loved them to the end. Yet, wishing to remain with His faithful even till the end of time, He instituted the Sacrament of the Holy Eucharist to prove to us the excess of His love, and to continue in His Church the sacrifice which He was about to offer on the Cross. It was on the eve of His Passion, and after He and His Apostles had come to the end of the Last Supper, that He instituted the Holy Eucharist. While they were yet at table, He took bread into His sacred and venerable hands, and blessed, and broke, and gave to His Apostles, saying: "Take ye, and eat; this is My Body." In like manner, taking the chalice, He gave thanks, and bade them all drink of it, saying: "Drink ye all of this. For this is My Blood of the New Testament, which shall be shed for many unto remission of sins" (Matt. xxvi. 26-28). He then added: "Do this for a commemoration of Me."

Instituted by Jesus Christ.

It is of faith that, after the consecration, the Sacred Species contain truly, really, and substantially, the Body, the Blood, the Soul, and the Divinity of our Saviour; and thus

The Real Presence.

under the appearances of Bread and Wine there are present
the true Body and Blood of Jesus Christ, and not merely a
figure or a sign representing them.

Moreover, Christ is wholly and entirely present under
either kind alone, because His Sacred Body, which is
now a living and immortal body, cannot be separated
from the Soul and the Blood. Jesus Christ, then, is wholly
and entirely where His Body is, and wholly and entirely
where His Blood is; and, as the Hypostatic Union extends
to every part of His Human Nature, it follows that, wherever
any part of the Human Nature is, there is the Person of
God the Son, His Body and His Blood being inseparable
from His Divine Person : " Christ rising again from the
dead dieth now no more " (Rom. vi. 9). Furthermore,
by reason of the fact that our Lord's existence in the
Holy Eucharist is not in the gross, natural, and sensible
manner of ordinary bodies, but in the state of a glorified
body, *i.e.*, *something* after the manner of a spirit, or as
the soul is in the body and all its members, His Sacred
Presence fills every particle, even when the Sacred Host is
divided. No division takes place except in the sacramental species : the Body of Christ cannot be divided,
because it is incorruptible; nor is it the substance of the
bread that is divided, seeing that the substance of bread
no longer remains. He is no greater in the larger Host,
nor less in the smaller, or even in the smallest perceptible
particle : never broken, never divided : *non confractus*,
non divisus, integer accipitur (Lauda Sion). By His Real
Presence in the Blessed Sacrament our Saviour renews, as
it were, for each one of us, the wonderful mystery He
wrought in taking to Himself our human nature, and
hence we can now understand the meaning of the Fathers
when they speak of the Holy Eucharist as " the extension
of the mystery of the Incarnation."

The Real Presence, under either species alone, is clearly

shown from the words of St. Paul: "Whosoever shall eat

Christ really present under either species. this bread, or drink the chalice of the Lord unworthily, shall be guilty of the body and of the blood of the Lord " (1 Cor. xi. 27). We see from the conjunction or, which St. Paul uses, that for one to be guilty of the Body and of the Blood of Christ it is enough to communicate either under the appearance of bread, or under the appearance of wine ; from which we are to learn that the Body and the Blood are contained under either species.   This also follows from the fact that the Body of Christ is now a living body, and in a living body the flesh and the blood cannot exist apart.   In spite of this fact, however, it is most fitting that two separate consecrations should be made.   In the first place the death of Christ, in which the Blood was separated from the Body, is more strikingly shown and represented by the separate consecration of the Bread and of the Wine ; and then, as this Sacrament was to be the nourishment of our souls, it is fitting that it should be established under the form of food and of drink ; for the species of bread and wine together signify a complete spiritual repast, just as food and drink together supply the perfect nourishment of the body.   Although, then, in the consecration there is a two-fold matter and form, yet these constitute but one Sacrament.

The Sacred Scriptures furnish us with *three* distinct

Three proofs of the Real Presence. proofs of the Real Presence of Jesus Christ in the Sacrament of the Altar: the *first* we take from the sixth chapter of St. John's Gospel, in which we find unmistakably expressed the promise of our Saviour to give us His Flesh to eat and His Blood to drink ; the *second* from the words of the institution of the Blessed Sacrament; and the *third* from the words of St. Paul regarding the Holy Communion.

Our Lord, after having given a most striking image of

the Blessed Eucharist in the multiplication of the loaves, announced to His followers that He would give them a more excellent Bread still, a living Bread, the true Bread of Life that cometh down from heaven, of which the manna was but a figure, and He spoke of the great mystery that He was one day to accomplish: "Labour not," He said, "for the meat which perisheth, but for that which endureth unto life everlasting, which the Son of Man will give you" (John vi. 27). He then went on to tell them of the nature of this spiritual food, which He declared to be none other than His own Flesh: " I am the living bread which came down from heaven. If any man eat of this bread, he shall live for ever; and the bread that I will give, is My flesh for the life of the world" (John vi. 51, 52). Here our Saviour promised what He afterwards instituted and gave us at His last supper; He promised to give us His Body and Blood, the same Body, though given in a different manner, that He was to offer on the Cross for the redemption of the world.

First proof, from St. John.

The Jews took scandal at His words, and asked: "How can this man give us His flesh to eat?" They evidently believed that it was a question of a real eating of the flesh of Jesus Christ; the promise of a figurative eating, purely symbolic, would have made no impression upon them.

Notwithstanding their murmurs, and the offence which His words had given even to many of His disciples, our Lord was so far from recalling His words, or of suggesting that He had spoken only in a figurative sense, that He even confirmed His first words, and the sense in which they had taken them, in the clearest and strongest terms: " Amen, amen I say unto you: Unless you eat the flesh of the Son of Man, and drink His blood, you shall not have life in you. He that eateth My flesh and drinketh My blood hath everlasting life; and I will raise him up at the last day. For My flesh is meat indeed, and My blood is drink indeed. He that eateth My flesh, and drinketh

My blood, abideth in Me and I in him. As the living Father hath sent Me, and I live by the Father, so he that eateth Me, the same also shall live by Me. This is the bread that came down from heaven. Not as your fathers did eat manna, and are dead ; he that eateth this bread shall live for ever " (John vi.). Our Saviour then, by confirming the notion they had formed of a real eating of His body, meant His words to be taken literally. Had they been used metaphorically, they would have been understood at once, since, in the language of the Jews, " to eat one's flesh " simply means " to calumniate."

Not knowing how He would or could fulfil His promise, His hearers would listen to Him no more, but left Him, as likewise did many of His disciples, murmuring : " This saying is hard, and who can hear it ?" Yet they could never have been scandalised if they had understood His words in a figurative sense. They must, then, have taken them in the sense of a real eating.

And did our Lord attempt to correct this view ? Far from it ! He appealed to His Divine power to be displayed in the Ascension : " Does this scandalise you ? If then you shall see the Son of Man ascend up where He was before ?" As though He would have said : " When you see Me ascending into heaven, you will know that I am God and can therefore do what I have just promised ; and you will have learnt that My glorified Body has the qualities of a Spirit, and this will help you to understand in a measure that it can be present under the species of bread and wine."

When our Lord saw so many of His disciples leave Him to walk no more with Him, He turned to the twelve, and asked : " Will you also leave me ?" At once St. Peter, in the name of all, answered : " Lord, to whom shall we go ? Thou hast the words of eternal life." They understood what He had said in the same literal sense ; they believed that He was going to give them His Flesh to eat and His Blood to drink, yet they could not understand *how* His promise was to be accomplished until they saw it fulfilled on the night of the Last Supper.

Jesus, knowing that His hour was come when He should **Second proof of the Real Presence.** pass out of this world to the Father, having loved His own who were in the world, loved them to the end. Yet wishing to remain with His own even to the end of time, He instituted the Sacrament of the Holy Eucharist to testify to us the excess of His love, to continue in the Church the Sacrifice which He was about to offer on the Cross, and to apply to our souls the fruits of His Passion principally by giving Himself to us in the Holy Communion. It was on the eve of His Passion, at the end of the Last Supper, that He instituted the Sacrament of the Eucharist.

After He had washed the feet of the Apostles, and while they were sitting with Him at table, He took bread into His hands, and blessed, and broke, and gave to them, saying : "Take ye, and eat: This is My Body." In like manner, taking the Chalice, He gave thanks, and bade them all drink of it, saying : " Drink ye all of this. For this is My Blood of the New Testament which shall be shed for many unto remission of sins " (Matt. xxvi. 26-28).* Thus, by the Divine power of His word, Christ changed what was before bread and wine into His own Body and Blood. The elements of bread and wine were truly, really, and substantially changed into the substance of His Body and Blood.

We cannot desire words more exact or more precise in favour of the dogma of the Real Presence of the Body and Blood of our Lord Jesus Christ in the Blessed Eucharist than the words of consecration given above. Taking them in their literal sense they unmistakably prove the Real Presence; nor can they be taken in any other sense: " This *is* My Body : This *is* My Blood." And our Lord

* See also Mark xiv. 22-24 ; Luke xxii. 19, 20 ; St. Paul, I Cor. xi. 24, 25.

knew when He uttered them that they would be taken in their literal sense, and that, by the great body of the faithful, Divine worship would be paid to this heavenly gift to the end of time.

Again, if the words of our Lord, " This is My Body, etc.," were to be understood in a metaphorical or figurative sense only, is it probable that St. Paul, writing twenty-four years afterwards to the newly converted Gentiles at Corinth, would have used words which also clearly express a true and real presence of Christ's Body and Blood in the Holy Eucharist, without one word to signify that they were to be understood in a figurative sense only ?   "For I have received of the Lord that which also I delivered to you, that the Lord Jesus, the same night in which He was betrayed, took bread, and giving thanks, broke and said : 'Take ye, and eat : this is My body, which shall be delivered for you : this do for the commemoration of Me.' In like manner also the chalice, after He had supped, saying : 'This chalice is the New Testament in My Blood : this do ye, as often as you shall drink, for the commemoration of Me.'" St. Paul then goes on to add : " Therefore whosoever shall eat this bread, or drink the chalice of the Lord unworthily, shall be guilty of the body and blood of the Lord. But let a man prove himself ; and so let him eat of that bread, and drink of the chalice. For he that eateth and drinketh unworthily, eateth and drinketh judgment to himself, not discerning the body of the Lord" (1 Cor. xi. 23, etc.).   This demonstrates that the Real Presence of the Body and Blood of Jesus Christ in the Blessed Sacrament is quite independent of the dispositions of the communicant; otherwise the unworthy recipient could not be guilty of the Body and Blood of Christ, or justly condemned for not discerning the Body of the Lord. The enormity of the crime, too, in profaning the Blessed Sacrament here portrayed, clearly points to the Real Presence.

Third proof of the Real Presence.

Moreover, the constant teaching of the Church from the earliest times; the decrees of her Councils; the testimony of the Fathers and of ecclesiastical writers.; all combine to prove the universality of her belief in Christ's Real Presence in the Blessed Sacrament. And what the Universal Church believes and has always believed can only come from the Apostles, and consequently from Christ Himself.

Proof from the constant teaching of the Church.

Not only is this belief held by the Latins, and the Greeks, and the Easterns who are in communion with the Holy See, but it is important to remark .that the doctrine of the Real Presence is still held by the Schismatic Greeks, and the different sects of the East, some of which —as the Nestorians and the Eutychians—separated from the Roman Church as far back as the fifth century.

Christ, whose Divine power is acknowledged by all true Christians, could not have made use of plainer words than those given us by St. Matthew, St. Mark, St. Luke, and St. Paul in his first Epistle to the Corinthians: " *This is My Body: This is My Blood:* Do this for a commemoration of Me"; and that the bread and wine, at the words of consecration, are changed, by the power of God, into the Body and Blood of Christ, has been the constant teaching of the Catholic Church in all ages, as we have seen, both in the East and in the West; both in the Greek and in the Latin Churches. Although the outward appearances, or *accidents*, sight, touch, taste, etc., remain the same as before consecration, yet faith teaches us that the substance of the bread and wine is really and truly changed into the substance of Christ's Body and Blood. This change is what we mean by *Transubstantiation.*

Transubstantiation.

Some Protestants, while admitting the Real Presence, pretend that the substance of bread and wine is not destroyed, but that Jesus Christ is in the Eucharist either by *Impanation—i.e.,* not by a

Impanation and Consubstantiation.

change of substance, but by the *union* of the Body of our Saviour *with* the bread ; or by *Consubstantiation*, by which they imply. that the Body of Christ is present with the substance, or under the substance, or in the substance of the bread.   Both of these teachings have been condemned by the Church.

. After considering what is meant by Transubstantiation,
Devotion to   ·   we are in a position to understand the meaning
the Blessed   of Catholic devotion to the Blessed Sacrament ;
Sacrament.   for it is on the fact of Transubstantiation alone   .
that it rests.   It is of faith,.and follows from what has been said, that we owe to the Blessed Eucharist the worship that is due to the Person of Jesus Christ ; viz., the highest degree of worship—the worship of *latria*, the adoration, respect, devotion, and love which belong to the One True God. Our worship is given directly to Jesus Christ, the Son of God, consubstantial with the Father, and equally God with the Father.

Those who reproach Catholics with adoring merely a "bit of bread " fail to understand our belief, seeing that we hold that, after the consecration, there remains no longer bread, but that, under the outward appearance of bread, Jesus Christ Himself is really and truly present.   It is not the species that we adore, but our Lord Jesus Christ under these outward appearances.   The species serve but to veil His Sacred Person.

· The Blessed Sacrament is preserved in our churches for
                   the adoration of the faithful, that it may be
Jesus on our   received by them, and that it may be ever
Altars.   ready to be taken to the sick.   Whenever
the Blessed Sacrament is reserved in the tabernacle, a lamp is kept burning day and night before it as an emblem of our faith and love.   The Real Presence of Jesus in the Blessed Sacrament invites us frequently to visit Him, to speak to Him, humbly to adore Him, and to offer Him
. our love and gratitude.   Solemn adoration is paid to our

Lord especially during Benediction of the Blessed Sacrament; but another and still more solemn form of adoration
takes place during the Prayer of the Forty Hours, or
"Quarant' Ore," and again in solemn processions of the
Blessed Sacrament, as on the Feast of Corpus Christi.

CHAPTER LXXII

THE HOLY EUCHARIST—AS A SACRAMENT (*continued*)

"Do this for a commemoration of Me" (Luke xxii. 19).
By these words Christ gave the precept and the
The Minister of the Conse-cration. power to the Apostles and their successors,
the Bishops and Priests of His Church,
to do as He Himself had done; viz., to change bread
and wine into His own Body and Blood.   Hence
Bishops and Priests, lawfully ordained, and no others,
can validly consecrate.   The power of consecrating is
so inherent in the Priesthood that every Priest, however
unworthy he may be—be he heretic, schismatic, suspended,
or excommunicate—validly consecrates when in the Mass
he pronounces the sacramental words over the matter of
the Sacrament.

The consecration takes place about the middle of the
Mass; and the very instant the words of consecration, "This
is My Body: This is My Blood," are pronounced, the bread
and wine are changed into the Body and Blood of
Jesus Christ.   The change is made in the name and by
the power of Christ, who is the principal Priest and
Offerer, and whose Person, as we see from the very words
of consecration, the Priest represents.

The Bishops and Priests, too, are alone the *ordinary* Ministers charged with dispensing the Blessed Sacra-
The Minister of the Dis-pensation. ment in Holy Communion.   In the early ages
of the Church, deacons were commonly delegated
to administer this Sacrament and to carry it to those who

19

were unable to be present at the Holy Sacrifice of the Mass, but, as the number of Priests increased in the Church, the deacons gradually ceased to exercise this function. In the present discipline of the Church, a deacon is not permitted to administer Holy Communion, except for a grave reason and with the permission of the Ordinary or the parish Priest. He then becomes the *extraordinary* Minister of the Sacrament.

The Subject of the Holy Eucharist.

All the faithful who have come to the use of reason, and who are sufficiently instructed and in the proper dispositions, can, and must, be admitted to Holy Communion. Infidels, seeing that they are not baptised, are incapable of participating in the effects of the Sacrament; and the Church, as far as she can, prevents from approaching the Sacred Table even those of her children who are unworthy to partake of this Divine food.

How early should we Communicate?

Children, as soon as they have come to the use of reason and have sufficient knowledge to understand what they are receiving, can approach Holy Communion, and must be admitted thereto. There is moreover an obligation for them to make their Easter Communion. Hence the obligation of Confession and that of Communion begin to bind at the same time. . To make his first Communion, however, a child need not have an extensive knowledge of Christian doctrine; but he should at least be instructed in the chief mysteries of Faith, and should know that what he receives in Holy Communion is not common bread, but that, under the appearance of bread, our Lord Himself comes to dwell within him. Hence if, in a particular case, a child comes to the use of reason earlier than at the age of seven years, and is capable of understanding what he is receiving, the obligation arises at that earlier age.

Necessity of receiving Holy Communion.

The Sacramental reception of the Blessed Eucharist is *not a necessary means* of salvation, and one can be saved without having received it. It was not instituted to confer first grace or to remit mortal sin; but, being a Sacrament of the living, it supposes a state of grace in the recipient; and a soul in the state of sanctifying grace is always pleasing to God. Yet, for adults, it is necessary by Divine and ecclesiastical *precept* : " Except you eat the flesh of the Son of Man, and drink His blood, you shall not have life in you " (John vi. 54). According to this precept, then, Catholics, as soon as they are capable of being instructed in this sacred mystery, are bound to receive Holy Communion—(1) When they are in probable or approximate danger of death; and (2) by the command of the Church, at least once a year, and that at Easter or thereabouts.

Those, however, who wish to lead a good Christian life will not be content with a yearly Communion, but will approach the Sacred Table frequently. Indeed, by a decree of the holy Pontiff, Pius X., the faithful are exhorted to revert to the early Christian practice of daily Communion. No one, says the decree, who is in a state of grace, and who approaches the Holy Table with a right and devout intention, can lawfully be hindered therefrom. This right intention implies that one must not act out of mere routine, or vain-glory, or human respect, but for the purpose of pleasing God, of being more closely united to Him by charity, and of seeking this Divine remedy for one's weaknesses and defects.

Frequent and even daily Communion.

To receive Holy Communion properly, it is necessary, in the first instance, to be free from mortal sin; and although it is not strictly required that the frequent, or even the daily, communicant should be free from all attachment to venial sin, yet to be so is most profitable; and as all deliberate venial sin ought to be avoided by every earnest Christian, much more should it be shunned by the daily communicant. In order that more abundant fruit may be gained, diligent preparation should precede, and suitable thanksgiving follow, our reception of Holy Communion.

The Priest who celebrates the Mass must communicate under both species, because Communion under both belongs to the integrity of the Mass. The faithful receive only under the appearance of bread ; but it must be remembered that Christ is present wholly and entirely under either kind alone; and that thus His Body and Blood, Soul and Divinity are present under either species just as much as under both.

Communion under one species.

Although the custom prevailed in the early Church of communicating under both species, the Church, using the power given to her by Christ of regulating the administration of the Sacraments, has, for just and grave reasons, forbidden the custom, and approved the practice of communicating under one species only. Although our Lord made use of the words : " Unless you eat the flesh of the Son of Man, and drink His blood, you shall not have life in you," He also said : " The bread that I will give is My flesh for the life of the world " (John vi.). And St. Paul : " Whosoever shall eat this bread, or drink the chalice of the Lord unworthily, shall be guilty of the body and of the blood of the Lord " (1 Cor. xi. 27).

Some reasons for receiving only under the one species.

The custom of receiving under both species was stopped for many reasons. There was the danger that the Precious Blood might be profaned, since under the appearance of wine it was easily spilt; and it was especially difficult to avoid such an accident when the Blessed Sacrament had to be administered to many of the faithful. Then there was the difficulty of procuring wine in the more northern countries which were later converted to the Faith. Under the appearance of wine, moreover, the Blessed Sacrament could not well be reserved on account of the danger of the species turning sour. While perhaps the greatest reason of all is that it proves to heretics the belief of the Church that Christ is present whole and entire under either species.

As the Blessed Eucharist is the greatest and most
Dispositions for receiving. sublime of all the Sacraments, it calls for great and becoming dispositions on the part of the recipient. These dispositions have regard both to the soul and to the body.

The first and most necessary disposition of the soul is purity of conscience; that is, it must be free from
Regarding the soul. mortal sin and pleasing to God. Were a person to receive Holy Communion while conscious to himself of being in mortal sin, he would commit a terrible sacrilege by making himself " guilty of the Body and of the Blood of the Lord " (1 Cor. xi. 27). Food cannot benefit a body that is dead, neither can the Holy Communion, the Divine food of the soul, profit a soul that is in conscious mortal sin, and thus dead to the grace of God. " Let a man *prove* himself," said St. Paul, " and so let him eat of that bread, and drink of the chalice.   For he that eateth and drinketh unworthily, eateth and drinketh judgment to himself, not discerning the body of the Lord " (1 Cor. xi. 28, 29).   This *proving* himself means that, before approaching the Sacred Table, he must examine the state of his soul, and, if he is conscious to himself of mortal sin—no matter how contrite he may believe himself to be—he must first have recourse to the Sacrament of Penance and make a good confession.

Yet venial sin unrepented of is not an obstacle to Com-
Effect of venial sin. munion; that is, it does not render our Communion unworthy and sacrilegious; but an affection for venial sin, by depriving us in part of the fruits of the Sacrament, would diminish the graces we should otherwise receive from our Communions.

But, in order to receive the graces of Holy Communion
How to receive grace abundantly. in all their abundance, the soul should be free not only from all sin, but from every affection even to venial sin.   We should approach the Sacred Banquet with lively sentiments of faith and piety,

reverence and devotion, contrition and humility, ardent charity and a longing desire to be united with Jesus Christ. It may be noted, however, that these sentiments are not feelings : we may have real devotion without any feeling of devotion. God regards the heart and the will, not the feelings.

As regards the body, we are commanded to observe the sacramental fast ; that is, from the mid-night preceding our Communion we are required to abstain from everything in the way of eating or drinking, even if the food or drink be taken as medicine. This command of the Church, which cannot be broken under pain of grievous sin, has been given out of respect and reverence to the Blessed Sacrament ; and hence it is that the Church requires that, on the day of our Communion, this spiritual food of the soul shall be the first food to be received. She makes an exception in the case of those who are dangerously ill, and who receive the Blessed Sacrament by way of *Viaticum*, that is, as an immediate preparation for their passage into eternity. People, moreover, who have been laid up through illness for a month, without any certainty of a speedy recovery, may, with the advice of their confessor, be allowed to receive once or twice a week after taking medicine or liquid food when they find it difficult to fast strictly. There are a few other cases still more rare when the Blessed Sacrament may be consumed by those who are not fasting : for example, if a Priest at Mass has consecrated, and is unable to finish the Mass, any other Priest who can be summoned, although he has broken his fast, must finish the Sacrifice. Again, if the Blessed Sacrament is in danger of being profaned, it may be consumed by a Priest or a layman, even though he is not fasting.

Nothing, then, *in the way of food or drink* must be taken between midnight and our receiving Communion ;

Regarding the body.

but if, while cleaning the teeth, one were unintentionally to swallow a drop of water; or were accidentally to inhale a flake of snow or a drop of rain; or to swallow blood coming from the lips or the gums, the fast would not thereby be broken.

As regards our outward demeanour, this should be modest and respectful, and our dress becoming, although poverty should never prevent one from approaching the altar. Our Lord had a special love for the poor while He was on earth, and His love for them is equally intense when they receive Him devoutly in the Holy Communion.

Outward demeanour.

After Communion we should not hurry out of church, but should spend some time in recollection, prayer, and thanksgiving. It is then that our Lord is most lavish of His graces, and gratitude is always pleasing to Him. In St. Luke we read how, when He had cured the ten lepers, and only one came to return thanks, He asked pathetically: "Were not ten made clean, and where are the nine? There is no one found to return and give glory to God, but this stranger" (xvii. 17, 18).

Thanksgiving.

As the Blessed Eucharist contains the very Author of grace, its effects are naturally numerous and admirable; nor does it ever fail to produce grace in those who receive it worthily. Our Saviour instituted it to be the food of our souls, and promised life to all who approach it with proper dispositions. What bread and wine do for the body this Sacrament does, in an infinitely more perfect manner, for the well-being of the soul. Its principal effects then are:

Effects of the Holy Eucharist.

1. It gives us an increase of sanctifying grace and preserves the life of the soul: "He that eateth Me, the same also shall live by Me" (John vi. 58).

Increases grace.

2. And just as natural food not only preserves the
body, but causes it to grow, and produces
feelings of sweetness and pleasure, so, too, this
Divine food not only sustains the soul, but
strengthens it, and gives it a taste for spiritual things.
Even the manna, which was but a figure of the Blessed
Sacrament, contained within itself all sweetness, and filled
the mouths of those who partook of it with the most
delightful taste.

Sustains the soul.

3. It unites us more closely to Jesus Christ; and by this
union our Saviour wishes not only to make
Himself loved by us, but to make us partake of
His life: "I live, now not I; but Christ liveth
in me" (Gal. ii. 20). It is not the Sacrament, then, which
is changed into our substance, as bread and wine are
changed into the substance of the body, but it is we who
are, as it were, changed into the nature of the Sacrament:
"He that eateth My flesh, and drinketh My blood, abideth
in Me, and I in him" (John vi. 57).

Unites us to Christ.

4. It remits venial sin. Just as our bodily food in-
sensibly repairs what we lose by daily wear and
tear, so likewise is this Divine food a remedy
for the spiritual infirmities of each day. But,
it must be remembered, it is a remedy for those venial
sins only for which we no longer retain an affection.

Remits venial sin.

The Blessed Eucharist, however, is not a Sacrament of
the *dead*, but a Sacrament of the *living*, and supposes
spiritual life in those who receive it. It does not *ordinarily*
give *first grace*, nor is it intended to put the soul in the
state of grace, but to preserve it in that state. It belongs
to Baptism and Penance to purify the sinner by blotting
out mortal sin. Yet many believe that it may *accidentally*
confer first grace on one in mortal sin who, unconscious of
his state, approaches the Holy Sacrament in sincere sorrow
for sin.

5. It preserves us from future sin. One of the effects

of the Sacrament is to preserve us in the state of innocence
by acting on our soul as a Divine antidote
A preservative against all infection and corruption arising
against sin. from the deadly poison of the passions.

6. It is a pledge of a glorious resurrection. The peace
and tranquillity of conscience produced by
A pledge of this Sacrament is but a foretaste of that ever-
immortality. lasting joy and happiness for which God
has created us. As the everlasting life of the just consists
in the possession of God for ever in heaven, so Christ, in
giving Himself to us in this Sacrament, has given us a
pledge of this glorious immortality.

7. It has an effect even on the body, not only
Effects on the by cooling the passions, but by making us like
body. our Lord in the outward ways of humility,
meekness, modesty, and sweetness.

The blessed fruits, then, of Holy Communion may be
summed up by saying that this Sacrament is a most
powerful aid to the securing of everlasting glory : " He that
eateth My flesh, and drinketh My blood, hath everlasting
life ; and I will raise him up in the last day" (John vi. 55).

CHAPTER LXXIII

THE HOLY EUCHARIST—AS A SACRIFICE

THE Holy Eucharist is not only the greatest of all the
Sacraments, it is also a true Sacrifice, and this is what we
mean when we speak of the Sacrifice of the Mass.

Sacrifice. Now a *Sacrifice*, in general, is an offering
made to God in token of our dependence upon
Him, and of our submission to Him, and may be either
interior or *exterior*.

Interior Sacrifice consists in offering our hearts
and our good works to God, and is exercised by faith,
charity, and other acts of Religion. *Exterior* Sacrifice, or Sacrifice properly so called, is the oblation made,

by a lawful minister, to God alone, of some exterior sensible thing which, by a mystical rite, is destroyed or changed, as an acknowledgment of the Divine majesty of God, and of His sovereign dominion over all things. In the words of the Catechism it is "the offering of a victim by a Priest to God alone, in testimony of His being the Sovereign Lord of all things": the term *victim* being used here in a wider sense than the offering of a *living* object merely.

Thus we see that, to constitute a true sacrifice, there

Requisites for a true Sacrifice. must be immolation or destruction of the thing offered, or at least a consecration which changes its nature, its state, or its natural form; the sacrifice must be performed by a lawful minister, and be accompanied with certain rites; its end must be to acknowledge God's absolute dominion over us and our entire dependence upon Him, and to render to His Divine majesty the homage which is His due. The minister of the Sacrifice is a Priest, and to God alone can sacrifice be offered. Nay, He requires sacrifice to be offered to Him in token of His dominion over life and death, and not from any advantage He Himself derives from our sacrifices.

The idea of sacrifice was spread among all the great

Antiquity of Sacrifice. nations of antiquity, and has existed from the beginning of the world. In the times of the Patriarchs and of the Old Law Sacrifice was strictly enjoined by God Himself. "*Abel* offered of the firstlings of his flock . . . and the Lord had respect to Abel and to his offerings"(Gen. iv. 4). "And *Noe* built an altar unto the Lord; and taking of all cattle and fowls that were clean, offered holocausts upon the altar " (Gen. viii. 20). *Melchisedech,* who was a Priest of the most High God, offered in sacrifice bread and wine, a striking figure of Christ's Sacrifice in the Mass. *Abraham's* Sacrifice, too, and the *Paschal Lamb* vividly prefigured the great Sacrifice of the New Law, of which all the Sacrifices of the Old Law were but the shadows, and from reference to which they derived all their efficacy, since it was in the faith and hope of the future merits of the Redeemer that sacrifice was offered. The blood of animals was powerless in itself to take away sin, which could only be washed away by the Blood of which the ·blood of the victims offered was but a figure: "For it is impossible that with the blood of oxen and goats sin should be taken away " (Heb. x. 4).

In the Sacrifices of the Old Law God required that the victim should be without blemish, and should **The Sacrifices of the Old Law.** be slain with certain ceremonials. The *holocaust*, or whole burnt-offering—so called because the whole victim was consumed with fire—was offered, as it were, purely and solely for God's honour and glory without any part of it being reserved for the use of man. The other sacrifices of the Old Testament were either *offerings for sin*, or *peace-offerings ;* and these latter again were offered either in *thanksgiving* for blessings received, or by way of *prayer* for new favours and graces. Thus we see that Sacrifices were offered to God for four different ends or intentions, corresponding to the different obligations which man has towards God : (I) For God's honour, praise, and glory ; (2) by way of thanksgiving for all His benefits ; (3) by way of confessing and asking pardon for sin; and (4) by way of prayer for grace and help in all our necessities. In the New Law we have but one Sacrifice, that of the Body and Blood of Jesus Christ ; yet this one Sacrifice perfectly answers all the four ends named above. And just as the Blood of Christ was offered on the Cross, so we have an altar on which the unbloody Sacrifice of the Mass is daily offered to God.

Now all the Sacrifices of the Old Law, which were but **The perpetual Sacrifice of the New Law.** figures of the great Sacrifice of the New Law, ceased when the Old Law came to an end, and were replaced by the one and only Sacrifice of Jesus Christ, which embraced in the most perfect manner all the figurative sacrifices of the Old Law. In the New Law there was to be a *perpetual* Sacrifice which was to represent for all time the Sacrifice of the Cross, and to apply the fruits of it to our souls.   This Sacrifice was prefigured by the Sacrifice of Melchisedech, who was a Priest of an order different from that of Aaron, since he offered in sacrifice *bread* and *wine*, a figure of Christ's Sacrifice in the Mass.   If Christ, then, be a Priest for ever according to the order of Melchisedech, whose Sacrifice was not bloody, as those of Aaron were, what other Sacrifice does He now offer but that of His own Body and Blood, under the appearances of bread and wine, through the ministry of His Priests in the Holy Mass?   "The Lord hath sworn, and He will not repent : Thou art a priest for ever according to the order of Melchisedech "; which prophecy St. Paul clearly applies to our Blessed Lord (Heb. v. 5, 6).   But Jesus Christ can be considered as a Priest according to the order of Melchisedech only in as much as He offered to His Father the Sacrifice of His own Body and Blood under the appearances of bread and wine; and He is a Priest for ever by renewing this Sacrifice upon our altars even to the consummation of the world.

It was this same Sacrifice which was foretold by Malachias when he said to the Priests of Israel :
Foretold by Malachias. "I have no pleasure in you, saith the Lord of Hosts, and I will not receive a gift of your hand ; for from the rising of the sun even to the going down of the same, My name is great among the Gentiles, and in every place there is sacrifice, and there is offered to My name a clean oblation " (Mal. i. 10, 11).   It is not a question here of the Sacrifice of the Cross, which was offered *once* and *upon Calvary*, whereas the pure oblation of which the Prophet speaks is to be made *at all times* and *in every place*.   Neither is it a question of a sacrifice of praise, which consists in prayer and in good works, for the Prophet speaks of a particular Sacrifice, of an exterior visible Sacrifice which is to

glorify the name of the Lord among the Gentiles; of a new Sacrifice destined to replace the Sacrifices of the Old Law. The very words employed by our Lord in the institution of the Blessed Eucharist prove that He insti-

The Eucharist a true Sacrifice. tuted not only a Sacrament, but also a Sacrifice: "Taking bread, He gave thanks, and brake, and gave to them saying: This is My body which is given for you: do this for a commemoration of Me. In like manner the chalice also, after He had supped, saying: This is the chalice, the new testament in My blood, which shall be shed for you" (Luke xxii. 19, 20); or, as St. Matthew has it: "which shall be shed for many unto remission of sins" (xxvi. 28).

The word translated "do" constantly has a sacrificial meaning. Here we have, then, an offering, an oblation of the Body and Blood of Christ, which shows that the Blessed Eucharist, besides being a Sacrament, is also a true Sacrifice.

CHAPTER LXXIV
THE SACRIFICE OF THE MASS *

WE have already seen what is meant by a Sacrifice; it remains yet to show how the Mass corresponds to all the requirements laid down for a true Sacrifice.

"The Holy Mass"—to use the words of the Catechism —"is the Sacrifice of the Body and Blood of

The Holy Mass. Jesus Christ, really present on the altar under the appearances of bread and wine, and offered to God for the living and the dead." It is the perpetual Sacrifice of the New Law in which Christ, under the

* The origin of the word Mass is probably from the Latin noun *missio*, later *missa*, meaning a "dismissal." *Missa fit*, or *missa est*, was a form used in discharging or releasing from service, etc. Thus "*Ite, missa est*" would literally mean "Go, the assembly is dismissed."

appearances of bread and wine, continues to offer Himself in an unbloody manner on the altar through the ministry of His Priests, as He once offered Himself a bleeding Victim on the Cross to His Heavenly Father. It is essentially the same Sacrifice as that of the Cross, but differs in the manner of offering.

And the Mass, which is a real Sacrifice, has all the conditions required for a true Sacrifice :

The Mass a real Sacrifice.   1. There is an exterior visible oblation of the Body and Blood of Jesus Christ, really present under the appearances of bread and wine. It is Jesus Christ Himself who is the Victim,—the same Jesus Christ who once offered Himself in a bloody manner on the altar of the Cross now being offered in an unbloody manner. The species of bread and wine which veil the Body and Blood of Christ belong to the Sacrifice and render it sensible ; but they do not constitute it; nor are they the oblation which is made to God.

2. It is offered to God alone. Even when it is said in honour of the Saints, we are not to understand that it is offered to the Saints; but a commemoration is made of them in the prayers of the Mass, and their protection and intercession are sought on our behalf. The Mass is also offered to thank God for the benefits He has conferred on them.

3. It is offered by a Priest, who is the only lawful Minister. The Priest, however, is but the Minister and visible representative of Jesus Christ, who Himself is both Priest and Victim—a fact clearly shown by the words of consecration which are uttered by the Priest, not in his own name, but in the name of Jesus Christ : " This is My Body : This is My Blood."

4. There is the mystical *destruction* of the Victim, represented by the separate consecrations, which places Christ on the altar as it were dead. It is the consecration which renders the Victim present on the altar, and puts it

in a state of apparent death by the seeming separation of the Body and the Blood of Christ from each other: "This is My Body: This is My Blood." Thus Christ offers Himself to His Father under the appearance of death. Yet, although by virtue of the words of consecration the Body is *represented* as separated from the Blood, in reality Christ, who having died once, can die now no more, is present in His entirety under either species alone. Here we see the difference between the *Sacrament* of the Holy Eucharist, which is full and entire under *either* species, and the *Sacrifice* of the Mass, which is accomplished only by the consecration of *both* species.

The essence of the Sacrifice of the Mass is commonly believed to consist in the consecration. The other actions of the Priest before and after the consecration are not necessary for the Sacrifice, with the exception, however, of the Priest's Communion, which belongs to the integrity of the Sacrifice. The three principal parts of the Mass are the *Offertory*, the *Consecration*, and the *Priest's Communion*.

The Essence of the Mass.

But the Mass is not only a representation of, it has also a certain substantial identity with, the Sacrifice of the Cross. In both cases the Priest and the Victim are the same : Jesus Christ is the visible Priest on Mount Calvary, He is hidden in the Priest at the altar; Jesus Christ, the visible Victim on Mount Calvary, is the hidden Victim in the Mass under the appearances of bread and wine. Yet the Sacrifice of the Mass differs in the manner of offering from that of the Cross:

The Mass a continuation of the Sacrifice of the Cross.

1. On the *Cross* Christ was offered in a bloody manner; on the *Altar* He is offered in an unbloody and mysterious manner, the two separate consecrations merely representing the separation of the Blood from the Body. On the Cross and on the Altar His Blood cries to His Heavenly Father for mercy.

2. On the *Cross* Christ offered Himself without the ministry of another Priest ; on the *Altar* He offers Himself through the ministry of His Priests.

3. On the *Cross* Christ was offered in His own true form ; on the *Altar* He is offered under the appearances of bread and wine.

4. On the *Cross* Christ made full atonement for sin, and purchased Redemption for all mankind *in general;* on the *Altar* the merits of that general Redemption are applied to *individual* souls.

5. On the *Cross* Christ was immolated but once ; the Sacrifice offered on the *Altar* is offered daily, and is destined "to show the death of Christ until He come" (1 Cor. xi. 26).

The Mass, then, is not another Sacrifice distinct in substance from the Sacrifice offered on Calvary, but it is the Sacrifice of the Cross applied to our souls.

But if the Sacrifice of the Cross is of infinite value, how

Is the Mass a propitiatory Sacrifice? can the Sacrifice of the Mass be propitiatory ? We might answer that the propitiatory merits of the Sacrifice of the Cross are applied in the Sacrifice of the Mass; and that the Sacrifice of the Mass, which is hence of infinite value, since it is substantially the same as the Sacrifice of the Cross, is itself renewed in every place, not to add anything to the Sacrifice of the Cross, but to apply to us the fruits of this Sacrifice. Now this application is made, and can be made, only in a finite manner, and proportioned both to the dispositions of those for whom the Mass is offered, and to the merciful designs which God has over all men in general, and over each one of us in particular.

The Holy Mass, moreover, fulfils, in the most sublime

The *four* ends of the Mass. manner, the four great ends for which Sacrifice was offered in the Old Law, preserving, as it does, the very same qualities as the Sacrifice of the Cross. In offering to God the Holy Mass—

1. We render Him the supreme honour which is His
due. We offer Him a *holocaust*, a Sacrifice of
Latreutic effect, adoration and praise, the principal end of
to adore God. which is to acknowledge His sovereign dominion over all His creatures. In the Mass Jesus Christ
offers Himself wholly and entirely to the Father as a
Victim, and thus renders Him the most perfect homage
that can be paid to His Supreme Majesty. This is the
Latreutic effect of the Sacrifice.

2. We offer Him a Sacrifice of Thanksgiving for all the
Eucharistic benefits He has bestowed upon us. The Victim
effect, to thank we offer Him, being a Victim of infinite value,
God. renders Him a most adequate return for the
graces and benefits we have received, and which we are
continually receiving from His bounty and mercy. This is
the *Eucharistic* effect of the Mass.

3. We offer Him a Sacrifice of Propitiation : "This is
Propitiatory My blood of the New Testament, which shall
effect, to make be shed for many unto the remission of sins "
satisfaction. (Matt. xxvi. 28). The Sacrifice of the Mass,
however, does not remit sin directly ; it produces this effect
by obtaining for the sinner the grace of repentance. It disposes him for the Sacrament of Penance, which was instituted to take away the sins committed after Baptism. It
is offered for the living and the dead, and remits, in a direct
manner, the *temporal* punishment which often remains due
to sin even after its guilt has been forgiven. By satisfying
the Divine justice it wards off from us many afflictions,
and the scourges of God's anger which our sins deserve.
This is the *Propitiatory* effect of the Sacrifice.

4. We offer Him a Sacrifice of Impetration to obtain
Impetratory His help in all our necessities of soul and body.
effect, to obtain As Jesus Christ is our Mediator with His Father,
by petition. the Mass is the most efficacious means of obtaining from God the graces and blessings of which we stand in

20

need in the spiritual and in the temporal order. And this is what is called the *Impetratory* effect of the Sacrifice.

We have seen that Jesus Christ is at the same time both Priest and Victim in the Eucharistic Sacrifice. It is He who offers Himself to God on our altars, and who is thus the principal Minister of the Sacrifice of the Mass, even while He makes use of the human agency of His Priests. It is the Priest who alone, after Christ, is the Minister of the Sacrifice. In its institution at the Last Supper Christ said to His Apostles, and to their successors in the Priesthood: "Do this for a commemoration of Me" (Luke xxii. 19); which means to say: "The Sacrifice which I have just offered, offer you also." He thus gave them not only the power, but the precept, to do what He Himself had just done, viz., to consecrate and change the elements of bread and wine into his own Body and Blood.

The Minister.

"Let a man," says St. Paul, "so account of us as of the ministers of Christ, and the dispensers of the mysteries of Christ" (1 Cor. iv. 1). And this power to offer Sacrifice is so inherent in the Priesthood, that every Priest rightly ordained, be he sinner, apostate, or excommunicate, can *validly* say Mass. His Sacrifice is as real as that of the most saintly Priest, provided that he use the matter and form necessary, and that he celebrate with the requisite intention. But he cannot, without sacrilege, celebrate the Sacred Mysteries unless he prudently believes himself to be free from mortal sin. Yet the faithful are not allowed to assist at the Mass of one who is a notorious heretic or schismatic. It must be remembered, however, that, although it is the Priest who says the Mass, the faithful join with him in offering the Sacrifice, and that he offers it in the name of the Church. Before the preface he turns to the people and says: "Pray, brethren, that my Sacrifice and yours may be acceptable to God the Father Almighty."

To offer sacrifice belongs to the Priesthood.

The application of a Mass is the intention which the

Priest has that its benefits should go to the person or persons for whom he offers it. The fruit derived by the person who caused the Mass to be offered, or for whom it is offered, is the *principal* fruit of the Mass. A *particular* fruit, also, accrues to the Priest who says the Mass in proper dispositions. The *general* fruits go to the faithful, but especially to those who are present, and in proportion to their faith, confidence, and devotion. The Mass, moreover, may be offered—

*The applica-
tion of the
Sacrifice.*

1. For all the living, and not merely for the faithful. But, just as it can be said for the propagation of the Faith, so it may be said for the conversion of sinners, and even privately, when there is no danger of scandal, for those who are excommunicated, *e.g.*, heretics, unless they belong to the class of those " who are to be avoided," when it can be offered only for their conversion.

2. For the relief of the souls in Purgatory, that God may be pleased to shorten the time of their expiation.

3. To honour the Saints, and to obtain their intercession for us with God. We thus implore their protection, and ask them to plead for us in heaven while we celebrate their memory upon earth.

When the faithful ask a Priest to offer a Mass for their intention, it is usual to make an offering for his support. " The Lord ordained that they who preach the Gospel should live by the Gospel " (1 Cor. ix. 14).

CHAPTER LXXV

THE CEREMONIES OF THE MASS

THE Mass is a continual memorial of the Passion and Death of our Lord, for when, at the Last Supper, He instituted the Holy Sacrifice, He commanded it to be offered in remembrance of Him: " Do this for a commemoration of Me " (Luke xxii. 19), " As often as you

shall eat this bread, and drink the chalice, you shall show
the death of the Lord until He come" (I Cor. xi. 26).

Even the very ceremonies of the Mass are such as, if
carefully followed, serve to show the Passion of
Christ; and they serve moreover to awaken in
us the dispositions of devotion and reverence
with which we ought to attend this sublime act of Divine
worship. These ceremonies, added by the Church to the
Holy Sacrifice, are very ancient, and bear a sublime and
mysterious signification.

Object of the Ceremonies.

1. Look at the altar! You see that it is raised above
the general level of the church and is approached by several
steps, to remind us of the ascent to Calvary. The Priest
comes into the Sanctuary, clad in sacred vestments marked
with a Cross, to show that he is the visible minister of
Christ, the real Minister, who bore on His shoulders the
Cross on which He was about to die for our salvation.

2. The Priest begins the Mass at the foot of the altar,
where he pauses to pray; and, profoundly inclined, he
recites with heartfelt sorrow the "*Confiteor*." Christ, at
the commencement of His Passion, prayed prostrate on
the ground in the Garden of Gethsemani; and His soul
was sorrowful even unto death. "'And being in an agony
He prayed the longer. And His sweat became as drops of
blood, trickling down upon the ground" (Luke xxii. 43, 44).

3. The Priest then ascends the altar-steps and reverently
kisses the middle of the altar, which reminds us of the kiss of
Judas when he betrayed our Saviour into the hands of His
enemies. During the prayers and the Epistle which follow,
he goes to the Epistle-side and returns, and repeats the
action before he goes to the other side to read the Gospel.
Returning to the middle of the altar, on many days he
next recites the "*Credo*." So, too, our Lord passed from
the Garden of Gethsemani to the house of Annas, to
Çaiphas, to Pilate, to Herod, and back again to Pilate.
During this time He was mocked, spit upon, and treated

with scorn and derision before He was delivered up to be crucified.

4. Then the Priest, coming to the first of the three most solemn parts of the Mass, the *Offertory*, uncovers the chalice, and offers bread and wine. After this he washes his hands, to signify with what purity of heart we ought to assist at this Holy Sacrifice. Pilate also, although he ordered our Saviour to be stripped of His garments, scourged, and crowned with thorns, washed his hands before the people, pretending that he was innocent of the blood of "this just Man."

5. After bowing down at the middle of the altar, the Priest invites the faithful to fervent prayer "Pray, brethren, that my sacrifice and yours may be acceptable to God the Father Almighty." And Christ, too, on His way to Calvary, seeing that a multitude of women bewailed and lamented Him, turned to them and said: " Daughters of Jerusalem, weep not over Me, but weep for yourselves and for your children " (Luke xxiii. 28).

6. Next comes the " *Preface*," to be followed immediately by the " *Canon*,"* or that most solemn part of the Mass which includes the great act of Sacrifice, the Consecration. Here we should picture to ourselves Christ arrived at the top of Calvary, when His garments are torn from His wounded and bleeding flesh, and He is thrown down, and most cruelly nailed to the Cross.

7. This brings us to that solemn moment, announced by the simple ringing of the bell, when the Priest pronounces the mysterious words of consecration which bring the Son of God down upon the altar. After they have been uttered, he genuflects, and raises the precious Body and Blood in the sight of all the people, who bow down in silent adoration. The Elevation reminds us of Christ's being raised on the

* The Canon is so called from a Greek word, meaning "rule," and contains the rule and form of the Church's prayers for the Sacrifice. This form is very ancient.

Cross, and the two separate consecrations represent Him mystically slain on the altar.

8. After the Consecration the Priest, with hands ex-tended, offers silent prayer for God's mercy on all man-kind, and for the holy souls in Purgatory. This is followed by the Lord's Prayer, which, with its *seven* petitions, he says aloud. It is a prayer which, in substance, contains all petitions. Christ, with hands extended and nailed to the hard wood of the Cross, silently offered to the Father His sufferings as the price of our Redemption. Yet *seven times* was that silence broken by those seven utterances which were the last words of our dying Saviour.

9. Next comes the "*Agnus Dei*," which is repeated three times : " Lamb of God, who takest away the sins of the world, have mercy on us : grant us peace." Many of the Jews, too, struck with fear, returned home striking their breasts. The Roman centurion himself, filled with awe, confessed aloud : " Indeed this Man was the Son of God."

10. We are brought now to the "*Domine, non sum dignus*," and to the last of the three most solemn parts of the Mass, the *Priest's Communion*. Here we should con-sider the Body of Christ taken down from the Cross by Joseph and Nicodemus, who laid it reverently in the tomb. Those who can should communicate ; and even those who are not able to communicate sacramentally should make a fervent act of Spiritual Communion.

11. After the Communion the Priest covers the chalice, says aloud a prayer of thanksgiving on the Epistle-side, and coming to the middle of the altar, salutes the people with the words: "The Lord be with you." He utters the words of dismissal, "*Ite, missa est*," imparts his blessing, and reads the last Gospel. Christ, after His Resurrection, appeared to His Apostles, and saluted them with the words, " Peace be to you "; and on the day of His Ascension He led them to Mount Olivet, where, with

hands uplifted, He gave them His parting blessing; and as He blessed them, He raised Himself up before their eyes towards Heaven.

When we consider what the Mass is, and who it is the
The respect due to the Holy Sacrifice. Priest represents, ought we not to be filled with reverence and awe for everything connected with the Divine Sacrifice? One Mass heard well is of such inestimable value that, if we could but realise it, few of us indeed would be content with our one Mass of Obligation on a Sunday. Realising, too, that the Priest is the visible minister of Christ, who Himself is the real High Priest, we ought to show our respect for our Divine Lord by being present in our places when the Priest appears in the Sanctuary, and by refraining from leaving the church till he has withdrawn.

CHAPTER LXXVI

THE SACRAMENT OF PENANCE

If all those who have been regenerated by the waters of
Object of the Sacrament of Penance. Baptism were going to remain faithful to the graces conferred by that Sacrament, there would have been no need for our Saviour to establish another Sacrament for the remission of sins. But because He knew that many would not remain faithful, God, who is rich in mercy, and knows our weakness and our frailty, has, of His infinite goodness, provided an infallible means of reconciliation for all those who, without it, would have remained abandoned to the slavery of sin, and to the power of the devil. This means of reconciliation is the Sacrament of Penance, by which the fruits of the Passion and Death of our Lord Jesus Christ are applied to those who have had the misfortune to fall from their baptismal innocence. It is a grace very aptly

described by St. Augustine as another plank thrown out to rescue the drowning soul.

The word " Penance " is sometimes used to denote that virtue or supernatural disposition of the soul which causes it to hate the sins it has committed, and to resolve never to sin again, but rather to make satisfaction, as far as man can, to the offended majesty of God. For it is not enough to give up sin and to begin a new life ; we must, moreover, hate and detest the sins of our past life : " Cast away from you the transgressions by which you have transgressed, and make to yourselves a new heart, and a new spirit " (Ezech. xviii. 31). Penance in this sense has always been necessary for obtaining pardon for sin ; and without it no one guilty of mortal sin can be saved.

The virtue of Penance.

But in the Law of Grace, this virtue of Penance received a new character : Jesus Christ raised it to the dignity of a Sacrament, and in connection with it established a sacred rite, the exercise of which He confided to His appointed ministers. Thus Penance is a Sacrament of the New Law whereby the sins, whether mortal or venial, which we have committed after Baptism, are forgiven by the absolution of the Priest, on our confessing them with true sorrow. There is no sin, then, however great it may be, which is not remitted by the Sacrament of Penance properly received. That Penance is a Sacrament is shown by its possessing, like all the other Sacraments, an Outward Sign, an Inward Grace, and Ordination by Jesus Christ.

The Sacrament of Penance.

We read in St. Matthew how, on a certain occasion, Christ said to St. Peter : " I will give to thee the keys of the kingdom of heaven. And whatsoever thou shalt bind upon earth, it shall be bound also in heaven : and whatsoever thou shalt loose upon earth, it shall be loosed also in heaven " (xvi. 19).

Instituted by Jesus Christ.

This power of binding and loosing which, in a more eminent manner, was promised to St. Peter, was also promised to the other Apostles: "Amen I say to you, whatsoever you shall bind upon earth, shall be bound also in heaven; and whatsoever you shall loose upon earth, shall be loosed also in heaven" (Matt. xviii. 18). This power of closing or opening heaven, of binding or loosing on earth and in heaven, evidently includes the power of forgiving or retaining sins. Again, in St. John, we read how Christ, appearing to His Apostles on the day of His Resurrection, said to them: "Peace be to you. As the Father hath sent Me, I also send you: . . . Receive ye the Holy Ghost. Whose sins you shall forgive, they are forgiven them; and whose sins you shall retain, they are retained" (xx. 21-23). It was on this occasion, principally, that He instituted the Sacrament of Penance. Nor was the power which He thus gave destined to be confined to the Apostles, but it was to descend to their successors, the Bishops and Priests of the Church: " All power is given to Me in heaven and in earth. Going therefore, teach ye all nations, baptising them in the name of the Father, and of the Son, and of the Holy Ghost. Teaching them to observe all things whatsoever I have commanded you; and behold I am with you all days, even to the consummation of the world" (Matt. xxviii. 18-20). The Church has at all times taught that she possesses the power to forgive sins, and even the earliest Christian sects that fell away from her have continued to claim and to exercise this power.

Now the power of binding and loosing is never exercised except by an exterior sensible rite, that is, by the Sacrament of Penance, which is a *tribunal* of mercy and reconciliation. It is a power of jurisdiction, or power possessed by a judge, which must of necessity be exercised in a judicial manner. Those who have received this power are established judges in regard

The judiciary power of the Priest.

to our consciences, and dispense justice to sinners by pronouncing the sentence which remits or retains sin.

But they cannot pronounce their verdict arbitrarily, and without a knowledge of the cause they are called upon to judge. The sinner, then, must appear at the tribunal of Penance, and must accuse himself by making known to the Priest the grave sins at least of which he is guilty, and this with sincere sorrow of heart and with a firm purpose of amendment for the future. The sentence, too, must be understood by the penitent so that he may know whether his sins have been forgiven or retained.

Necessity of Confession.

Now the penitent's accusing himself, the sorrow he expresses for having offended God, and the words of absolution pronounced by the Priest, are an outward and sensible sign ; the rite has the power of giving grace since it was ordained to remit sin ; and it follows naturally from the power of forgiving sins granted by Jesus Christ that it is of Divine institution. Therefore our Saviour, when He gave to His Apostles and their successors the power of remitting and retaining sin, instituted what we call the Sacrament of Penance.

Penance a true Sacrament.

As in the other Sacraments, so in Penance we have the Matter and the Form. In Penance the sacramental *matter* consists in the threefold acts of the penitent, contrition, confession, and satisfaction ; and the *form* in the words of the Priest, " I absolve thee from thy sins in the name of the Father, and of the Son, and of the Holy Ghost."

Matter and Form.

The Catechism of the Council of Trent, speaking of the matter of this Sacrament, calls contrition, confession, and satisfaction the *quasi materia*, as it were the matter. By this it is merely meant that the matter of Penance is not of the same nature as the matter of the other Sacraments, which is something exterior to the person who receives

them, as water in Baptism, and chrism in Confirmation.

The Minister of the Sacrament of Penance must be
endowed with a double power, the power of
The Minister of Penance. Orders and the power of Jurisdiction, or that
licence which is given to a properly constituted
Judge·before he can exercise his authority. This double
power is given to none but Priests, who alone can administer
the Sacrament of Penance. The first power is that received
by the Priest at his ordination, the second is conferred by
his Bishop, from whom he must have received faculties or
special authority before he can administer the Sacrament of
Penance, except in the case of the dying, when, by the law of
the Church, every Priest possesses the necessary jurisdiction.

If this second power were wanting, the absolution would
not only be unlawful, but null and void; for the withholding or the granting of absolution is a sentence which
the Priest, as judge, passes in the sacred tribunal of
Penance to condemn or acquit, *i.e.*, to bind or to loose, to
retain or remit sins. Now a sentence in a court of justice
can be passed only on those who are under the jurisdiction
of him who pronounces it; and so civil judges can give
judgment only in the district assigned to them.

The Sacrament of Penance cannot be administered except
to those who have been baptised, for Baptism
Subject of the Sacrament. is, as it were, the door of the other Sacraments;
nor does the Church exercise jurisdiction except
over those who have entered her fold by Baptism. But
all who have been baptised can, when once they have come
to the use of reason, participate in the grace of the Sacrament of Penance, even though they have but venial sins of
which to accuse themselves.

The Sacrament of Penance is as necessary for those who
fall into mortal sin after Baptism, as Baptism itself is for
those who are not yet baptised; and, though Perfect Con-

trition remits mortal sin at once, whether the Sacrament of Penance can be received or not, there is an obligation, under pain of mortal sin, of confessing afterwards if this is possible. If Confession were not necessary, if there were another and easier means of recovering God's grace, then would our Saviour have given to the Church a useless commission in bestowing upon her the power of binding or loosing, of remitting or retaining sin.

Besides the *Divine* precept requiring us to have recourse to the Sacrament of Penance, there is the com-mand of the Church binding the faithful to confess *at least* once a year. All who are conscious of mortal sin would moreover be bound to approach the Sacrament of Penance if in danger of death, before going to Communion, and, unless they are able to make an Act of perfect Contrition, before performing an action which is required to be done in a state of grace.

When must we confess?

The principal effects of the Sacrament may be summed up as follows:

Effects of the Sacrament.

1. It remits the *guilt* of sin committed after Baptism: " Whose sins you shall forgive, they are forgiven them " (John xx. 23).

2. It remits the *eternal* punishment due to mortal sin, and at least some of the *temporal* punishment due to sin, if not always all of it.

3. It imparts first grace, *i.e.*, it restores sanctifying grace to one dead in sin, or increases it in one already free from mortal sin.

4. It revives in us the merits gained by performing good works in a state of grace, but lost by mortal sin.

5. It imparts Sacramental grace, or a title to *actual* grace which will enable us to shun temptation and to lead a good life.

The dispositions necessary for receiving the Sacrament worthily will be found explained in the following chapter.

CHAPTER LXXVII

THE RECEPTION OF THE SACRAMENT OF PENANCE

THERE are four things we have to do by way of preparation
for Confession: (1) We must heartily pray to
God for grace to make a good Confession;
(2) we must carefully examine our conscience;
(3) we must take time and care to make a good act of
contrition; and (4) we must resolve, by the help of God's
grace, to renounce our sins, and to begin a new life for the
future. Thus, for the worthy reception of the Sacrament
of Penance, there is required on our part: (1) Examination
of Conscience; (2) Contrition, conjoined with a Firm
Purpose of Amendment; (3) Confession; and (4) Satisfaction.

Preparation for Confession.

As we can do no good work without the help of God's
grace, it will naturally follow that our first
act on going to Confession will be to place
ourselves in the presence of God, and implore Him to give
us the grace to make a good Confession; *i.e.*, that He will
enable us rightly to know our sins, to be sorry for them,
and to confess them in all sincerity.

Pray for grace.

In order, then, to know our sins, we must make a diligent
examination of conscience; *i.e.*, we must make
a genuine attempt to find out in what we
have offended God by sins of thought, word,
deed, or omission since our last good Confession. Our
examination, moreover, must be impartial; we must not
flatter ourselves, but act in our own regard as we would in
regard to a stranger; and, if it be a question of mortal sins,
we are bound to examine ourselves on their number and circumstances. Going through the Commandments of God
and of the Church, the Seven Deadly Sins, and the obligations of our state of life, we should consider whether by

Examination of Conscience.

thought, word, deed, or omission we have failed in our duty to God, to ourselves, or to our neighbour.

When careful examination has revealed the state of the conscience, it will then be the care of the penitent to make an act of Contrition for his sins.

Now Contrition, the most important of the acts of the penitent, is a hearty sorrow for our sins because by them we have offended so good a God, together with a firm purpose never to sin again. It involves not merely the giving up of sin and the resolve to begin a new life for the future, but detestation of the sins we have committed : " Cast away from you the transgressions by which you have transgressed, and make to yourselves a new heart, and a new spirit " (Ezech. xviii. 31). We distinguish two kinds of contrition, *Perfect Contrition* and *Imperfect Contrition*, which is also called Attrition.

Contrition.

Perfect Contrition is sorrow for sin proceeding from perfect charity, from that charity by which we love God *above all things for His own sake*, as being infinitely perfect. On account of His infinite perfections, that is, because He is infinitely good, holy, merciful, lovable, and true—over and above the mere consideration of what He has done for us—we love Him above everything else, and for this reason we are grieved for having offended Him. Such Contrition, joined with the desire and the resolution to receive the Sacrament of Penance, is sufficient to remit our sins at once, even before we confess them ; but, if our sins are mortal, we are strictly bound to confess them in our next Confession.

Perfect Contrition.

Imperfect Contrition, or Attrition, is sorrow for sin which proceeds from an inferior motive to that of perfect charity. It may arise from the consideration of how good and bountiful God has always been *towards us ;* from the thought that our sins have merited the chastisements of God ; from the fear of

Imperfect Contrition.

hell and the loss of heaven; or it may be the heinousness which faith shows us in sin itself that causes us to hate our sins above all things, and to resolve never to offend God again. To repent of our sins merely because, through them, we have lost our good name or our peace of mind is not contrition. God is the person offended, and true sorrow must necessarily have reference to the one offended.

Attrition joined to the Sacrament is sufficient to restore us to God's favour, and hence it is good in itself, and suffices when we go to Confession, if, with the hope of pardon, it excludes the will to sin again; for this supposes a beginning of the love of God. But merely to fear the loss of heaven or the being condemned to hell does not constitute Attrition; there must also be repentance for our past sins and a resolution to begin a new life for the future.

Contrition, whether perfect or imperfect, must possess
Qualities of
true Contrition. *four* necessary qualities: it must be *interior, supernatural, universal,* and *sovereign.*

Interior. Contrition must be *interior,* that is, it must be a sorrow of the heart or will. As it is from the heart that sin proceeds, so it is from the heart that our repentance and detestation of sin must also arise. Sorrow that is expressed merely by the lips, or that exists only in the imagination, is no true sorrow.

Supernatural. Our Contrition must be *supernatural;* it must be produced by the grace of the Holy Spirit, and founded on motives which faith makes known to us; for without the grace of God we can do no good work towards our salvation. Yet to him who is willing to do his part this grace is always given. We should hate sin because it is displeasing to God, because it is an offence committed against Him.

If our sorrow for our sins arose from natural motives, from the consideration of their natural evil consequences,

such as shame or the chastisements we have to fear
from men, or from the temporal evils they have brought
in their train—for example, loss of health, property, or
reputation—such sorrow would be but natural sorrow, and
would not merit for us the pardon of our sins.

We must be sorry at least for *all our mortal sins* without
exception. It is impossible truly to hate a
Universal. single mortal sin as being an offence against
God, without at the same time hating whatever offends
Him mortally. There can be no true sorrow if we enter-
tain an affection for a single mortal sin.

We are not bound to confess what we know to be only
venial sins; but if a penitent has only venial sins to confess, he must be truly sorry for at least one of them, or
his Confession would be null and void; and only those
venial sins would be forgiven for which he was truly sorry.

Since Contrition is an essential part of the Sacrament
of Penance, it is well for those who have only venial sins
to confess to accuse themselves again of some grievous
sin, or at least of some greater venial sin, of their past life,
which they have already confessed, in order to ensure true
sorrow for at least one sin in their confession.

Our Contrition must also be *sovereign* or supreme, that
is to say, we must be more sorry for sin than
Sovereign. for any other evil. We should be prepared
to sacrifice everything rather than offend God mortally;
we should hate mortal sin with a supreme hatred, since
it deprives us of the greatest of all blessings, God
Himself.

Yet it does not follow that our sorrow is to be more
sensible or keener than the sorrow which may arise from
temporal evils. The loss of a father, a mother, or a friend
may affect us more deeply than the evil of sin; but if we
are disposed to suffer any loss rather than commit sin, it
is proof sufficient that our hatred of sin is supreme, and

that the love of God holds the first place in our hearts. We hate sin above all other evils when we are resolved never to commit a wilful sin for the love or fear of anything whatsoever. '

Our Contrition, moreover, to be of any value, must be accompanied with a Purpose of Amendment, or **Firm Purpose of Amendment** a resolution, as the Catechism has it, to avoid, by the grace of God, not only sin, but also the dangerous occasions of sin. This Purpose of Amendment must also possess certain qualities: it must be *sincere, firm, universal,* and *efficacious.*

There must be a *sincere* wish to amend our life and to sin no more, and a *firm* or set determination of the will to avoid sin for the future. Our resolution is *universal* when we are determined to avoid not only the mortal sins of our past life, but every mortal sin for the time to come ; and if we have only venial sins to confess, we must firmly resolve to correct these venial faults, or, at least, one of them: it is *efficacious* when it leads us to adopt the necessary means for the avoidance of sin. The penitent must forsake entirely not only sin, but everything which leads him to sin, or which is a dangerous occasion of sin to him; for example, if a man knows that going to a certain public-house causes him to commit sin, then he must give up going there ; or if a child is generally led into sin by certain companions, must keep away from them.

Confession, which forms part of the Sacrament of **Confession.** Penance, is accusing ourselves of our sins to a Priest approved by the Bishop, with a view to receiving absolution from them. In the case of one who is in danger of death any Priest may give absolution.

Qualities of a good Confession. We should remember, too, that there are certain qualities that belong to a good Confession: it ought to be *clear, sincere, humble, prudent,* and *entire.*

21

1. Our Confession must be *simple* or *clear : i.e.,* we ought
to express clearly what is necessary for making
the state of our conscience known to our Confessor, who is bound, under pain of grievous sin, never to
reveal anything he has heard in Confession.

Clear.

2. It must be *sincere.* We should mention our sins just
as they are, without hiding anything or vainly
excusing them, without detracting from them or
adding to them; giving as certain what is certain, and as
doubtful what is doubtful.

Sincere.

3. It should be made with great *humility,* seeing that it
is an accusation of guilt against ourselves that
we are making.

Humble.

4. It must be *prudent : i.e.,* we must not confess the sins
of others, nor must we make known any person
who may chance to be concerned in our sins.

Prudent.

5. And, finally, it must be full and *entire.* We must
confess, at least, all the mortal sins we remember
after a careful examination of conscience, as
well as their number, and such circumstances as may change
the nature of their guilt.

Entire.

Before pronouncing the words of absolution the Priest
assigns the *Sacramental Penance* to be performed
by the penitent; and this, if it is reasonable,
the penitent is bound to accept and faithfully to accomplish. It is the performing of the Sacramental Penance
that constitutes the third part of the Sacrament, viz.,
Satisfaction, which, as the Catechism tells us, is doing the
Penance given us by the Priest.

Satisfaction.

When we make a good Confession, God always remits
the eternal punishment due to mortal sin, but not always
all the temporal punishment. In fact, there generally
remains some temporal punishment due to sin even after
its guilt has been forgiven; and this must be expiated
either in the next world by the pains of Purgatory, or in

this world by our good works. It is for the expiation of this temporal punishment that the Priest imposes a Sacramental Penance.

Both Contrition and Confession are necessary for the

Is satisfaction necessary for the Sacrament? validity of the Sacrament of Penance, but Satisfaction, or the fulfilling of the Sacramental Penance, though belonging to the Sacrament, does not form an absolutely necessary part of it. If the penitent, after Confession, were wilfully to neglect to perform the Penance which he had accepted with the intention of performing, his Confession would not be invalid, that is, his past sins would still be forgiven, but he would commit a fresh sin by his neglect.

In its effects the Penance imposed by the Priest in Confession is more powerful, owing to its Sacramental efficacy, in expiating the temporal punishment due to sin than our corresponding voluntary good works. Of the three ways of cancelling the temporal punishment due to sin, viz., (1) *Sacramental Penance,* (2) *Good Works,* such as prayer, fasting, and alms-deeds, and (3) *Indulgences,* we shall make this last the subject of our next chapter.

CHAPTER LXXVIII
INDULGENCES : PLENARY AND PARTIAL

WE have seen that the penance given us by the Priest does not always make full satisfaction for our sins. To make up this deficiency, we are recommended to perform other good works and penances, and to try to gain Indulgences.

Now the Catechism defines an Indulgence as a remission,

The meaning of Indulgence. granted by the Church, of the temporal punishment which often remains due to sin after its guilt has been forgiven. It is, then, a remission or forgiveness granted outside the Sacrament of Penance, through the merits of Jesus Christ and of the Saints, of

the temporal punishment due to our sins; but Indulgences neither remit the sin itself nor the eternal
punishment.

. The merits of Christ were infinite, and more than enough
for the redemption of all mankind; and when we
speak of gaining Indulgences, we mean the application to the faithful of the superabundant
satisfactory merits of Christ and of His Saints,
particularly His Blessed Mother. If one who does a good
work has no sins to expiate, like our Saviour and our Lady,
this good work serves to expiate the temporal punishment of
those who gain Indulgences. It is the superabundant merits
of the Saints, and the infinite satisfaction of Christ, that
form the inexhaustible treasure of the Church, the dispensing of which, through Indulgences, is confided to the
Church, and forms part of the power of the keys. Christ
then gave to His Church the power of granting Indulgences
when He said to His Apostles: "Whatsoever you shall
bind upon earth shall be bound also in heaven; and whatsoever you shall loose upon earth shall be loosed also in
heaven" (Matt. xviii. 18). These words confer not only
the power of forgiving sins, but also of remitting the
temporal punishment due to sin.

What we mean by gaining Indulgences.

The right to grant Indulgences throughout the whole
Church belongs to the Pope, to whom Christ
gave "the keys of the Kingdom of Heaven";
yet Bishops also have power to grant partial
Indulgences in their own diocese.

The right to grant Indulgences.

This power the Church has always made use of. St.
Paul (2 Cor. ii. 10), *in the person* and by the authority
of Christ, granted an Indulgence to the incestuous
Corinthian, whom he had before put under a severe
penance, by remitting part of the temporal punishment
due to his sin. In the times of persecution it was the
practice of the Church to shorten, at the request of the

confessors and martyrs, the period of penance inflicted on sinners on their showing themselves truly penitent ; that is to say, she granted Indulgences.

Indulgences may be Plenary or Partial. By a *Plenary* Indulgence we mean the remission of the whole debt of temporal punishment due to our sins ; and, by a *Partial* Indulgence, the remission only of a part of the debt.

Plenary and Partial Indulgences.

According to the ancient discipline of the Church, those who had committed great sins were subjected to long and severe penances, in some cases extending over years, or even lasting to the end

Canonical Penances.

of their life. Now when we speak of an Indulgence of forty days or of seven years, we do not mean that one's purgatory will be shortened for so many days or so many years, but we mean the remittance of as much temporal punishment as would have been atoned for by the performance of forty days' or seven years' canonical penance according to the former discipline of the Church.

Most Indulgences are applicable, *by way of suffrage*, that is, by the mediation and prayers of the Church, to the holy souls in Purgatory. The Church exerts a direct control over the Church militant, so that when she absolves from sin, or

How Indulgences can be applied to the Holy Souls.

removes censures, or remits the debt of temporal punishment due to sin, the effect is certain if only the person is in proper dispositions : " I will give to thee the keys of the kingdom of heaven. And whatsoever thou shalt bind upon earth, it shall be bound also in heaven ; and whatsoever thou shalt loose upon earth, it shall be loosed also in 'heaven " (Matt. xvi. 19). But in regard to the holy souls in Purgatory the case is different; her authority does not extend to them as it does to the faithful on earth. She does not remit their debt directly, but offers to God a satisfaction equal to the debt they owe, and this satisfaction is always accepted either on behalf of the souls for whom it is intended, or for the benefit of others as God may choose; it will always produce its effect.

Among Plenary Indulgences there is one in particular, called the Indulgence of the Jubilee, to which are attached many special privileges. The word Jubilee, from a word denoting *remission*, *deliverance*, *liberty*, is borrowed from the Old Testament, where we find it among the ordinances enumerated in Leviticus, and given by God to Moses: "Thou shalt sanctify the fiftieth year, and shalt proclaim remission to all the inhabitants of thy land; for it is the year of Jubilee" (Levit. xxv. 10).

Jubilee Indulgence.

In the Christian dispensation the Jubilee denotes a time of Indulgence in consequence of the power left by Jesus Christ to His Church. The first Jubilee was granted, in the year 1300, by Pope Boniface VIII., who appointed it to be held every hundred years. Subsequent Popes shortened the period to fifty, then to thirty-three years, in memory of our Lord's life upon earth, and finally to twenty-five years, so that all generations of the faithful might share in its benefits. To this period it has remained fixed down to our own time, and is called a greater or ordinary Jubilee, to distinguish it from other extraordinary Jubilees which may be granted by the Pope to commemorate special occasions. For example, it is customary for a new Pope to proclaim a Jubilee to celebrate his accession to the Papacy. The greater Jubilee, or Jubilee of the Holy Year as it is called, is usually celebrated first of all in Rome, and after a year is extended to the rest of the world.

Its origin.

The conditions to be observed for gaining an ordinary Jubilee Indulgence are Confession and Communion, and a fixed number of visits to certain specified churches, where prayers are to be offered for the Pope's intention. In addition to the

Conditions for gaining the Jubilee Indulgence.

above, other conditions, such as fasting and alms-deeds, are generally prescribed in the case of an extraordinary Jubilee.

During the time in which the ordinary Jubilee is being celebrated in Rome, *i.e.*, during the Holy Year, other Plenary and Partial Indulgences granted in favour of the living are suspended. There are, however, a few exceptions ; *e.g.*, the Plenary Indulgence at the hour of death. Yet all these Indulgences can, during this year, be gained for the souls in Purgatory.

Certain conditions are always required to gain an Indulgence :

1. We must be members of the Catholic Church ; *i.e.*, we must be baptised and free from excommunication.

Conditions for gaining an Indulgence.

2. We must have the intention of gaining the Indulgence, although the intention need not be renewed with each pious act to which an Indulgence is attached. It is advisable that a *general* intention be made each morning of gaining all the Indulgences we can that day.

3. We must be in the state of grace, *i.e.*, we must be free from mortal sin, at least at the time of fulfilling the last condition. It is impossible to gain an Indulgence so long as we are in mortal sin. To gain the full effect of a Plenary Indulgence we are required to be free not only from mortal sin, but from venial sin also, since it is impossible for the temporal punishment of an unforgiven venial sin to be remitted. Yet such Indulgence is even then of great value, as it removes all punishment due to those sins whose guilt has been forgiven.

4. We must perform exactly the good works prescribed for gaining the Indulgence. The prayers and good works to which a Partial Indulgence is attached are various ; but, generally, for the gaining of a Plenary Indulgence, we are required to approach the Sacraments of Penance and Holy Communion, and to pray for the Pope's intention. Those, however, who are in the habit of going to Confession once a

fortnight can gain all the Indulgences, except the Jubilee, occurring during the fortnight, for which Confession is a condition. Daily Communicants, or such as make it a practice to go to Holy Communion almost every day, may gain any Indulgence, except the Jubilee, for which Confession is required without actually fulfilling the condition of fortnightly Confession.

The use of Indulgences is beneficial for several reasons:

1. They are a great aid to the discharge of the temporal punishment due to our sins.

2. Easy acts of piety taking the place of the long canonical penances—for such are Indulgences—induce us more readily to make our peace with God.

3. They are an incentive to us to practise frequently those acts of piety to which Indulgences are attached, and hence to approach the Sacraments regularly.

CHAPTER LXXIX

EXTREME UNCTION

EXTREME UNCTION is a Sacrament instituted by our Lord for the solace, both bodily and spiritual, of the sick. Though throughout our life the devil goes about like a roaring lion, seeking whom he may devour, yet there is no time when he strives more for our ruin than when we are nearing our end. It is then that he makes the most determined efforts to get us into his power by redoubling his temptations, more especially the temptation to despair, by which he would have us abandon all trust in the mercy of God. This is why our Saviour, in His infinite goodness, instituted a Sacrament to enable us to overcome these malicious attacks of the evil one. This Sacrament is called Extreme Unction because it is the *last anointing* of the Christian, several other anointings, as in Baptism and Confirmation, having already preceded it. It is regarded by the Fathers as the completion of the Sacrament of Penance.

Object of Extreme Unction.

Extreme Unction is defined in the Catechism as "The
anointing of the sick with holy oil, accompanied with
Extreme   prayer." Like all the other Sacraments, it
Unction de-   possesses an outward sign of an inward grace,
fined.
and institution by Jesus Christ, or the three
qualities that go to the making up of a Sacrament.

The outward sign, consisting of the matter and form, is
Outward sign.   the anointing of the sick person with holy oil,
and the words pronounced by the Priest as he
anoints the different senses. The oil used is oil of olives
blessed by the Bishop on Maundy Thursday. The anointing, too, is accompanied with prayer, to show that the effect
produced in the Sacrament is due not to any natural virtue
which the oil may possess in itself, but to the power of God.

As natural oil soothes and even heals our wounds, and
strengthens our bodily members when weakened, so it is
appropriate that holy oil should be used as the Sacra-
méntal sign of Extreme Unction to indicate the spiritual
effects of the Sacrament.

The *Form*, as we have seen, consists in the prayers
which the Priest uses during the several anoint-
The words of   ings. He anoints with the holy oil the organs
the Form.
of the different senses, eyes, ears, nostrils, lips,
hands, and feet, that the sins of which they have been the
instruments may be expiated. " By this holy anointing," he
says, anointing the eyes, " and of His most tender mercy,
may the Lord forgive thee whatever thou hast committed
by thy sight." With each anointing the self-same words are
used, except that " by thy sight " becomes "by thy hearing,"
etc., according to the sense that is being anointed. In
case of urgent need the Priest anoints the forehead, and
then, if there is time, the organs of the different senses.

The outward anointing with oil admirably represents
the inward grace imparted at the same moment
The Inward   by the Holy Spirit; and what this grace is we
Grace.
find explained at length in the fifth chapter of

St. James's Epistle: "Is any man sick among you? Let him bring in the priests of the Church, and let them pray over him, anointing him with oil in the name of the Lord. And the prayer of faith shall save the sick man; and the Lord shall raise him up; and if he be in sins, they shall be forgiven him" (v. 14, 15).

The words of St. James, moreover, show us the Divine institution of this Sacrament, for who, but God, could give to an outward sign the power to forgive sin and to impart grace? The Apostle also enjoins the constant use of the Sacrament, which he here explains to us fully and in the clearest terms, giving us at the same time the *subject* of the Sacrament, the *Minister*, the *Matter* and *Form*, and the *Effects*.

Institution by Christ.

"Is any man sick among you?" This Sacrament, then, is to be administered to every Catholic who has come to the use of reason, and who is in danger of death from sickness; but not to such as, being in health, are merely exposed to the danger of death. It is for this reason that Extreme Unction is sometimes spoken of as the *Sacrament of the infirm, or of the dying.* If a person, after receiving Extreme Unction, regains his health, he is not debarred from receiving the Sacrament again. In every dangerous illness it may be received once; and if a person so far recovers as to be out of danger, but has a relapse after the danger has been passed, he may again receive Extreme Unction.

Subject of the Sacrament.

"Let him bring in the Priests of the Church, and let them pray over him, anointing him with oil in the name of the Lord." Here we see not only the matter and form to be employed in the administration of the Sacrament, but who are its Ministers also: "Let him bring in *the Priests* of the Church." Every Priest, then, can validly administer Extreme Unction; but no one below a Priest, not even a deacon, can confer this Sacrament.

The Minister.

Extreme Unction produces three great effects on the soul: (1) It confers a special grace upon the dying Christian, which comforts and strengthens him in his last and dreadful conflict, when the devil is using his utmost efforts to ruin his soul.

Effects on the soul.

(2) But, besides this, it increases sanctifying grace, remits venial sin, and, under certain circumstances, even mortal sin. Although Extreme Unction was not directly instituted to take away mortal sin—for this belongs to Baptism and Penance—yet it is commonly believed that the Sacrament of the dying indirectly accomplishes this end; for example, when the dying person has the disposition to confess, and has at least attrition in his heart, but is unable to go to Confession. But the Sacrament of Penance being the only regular means for obtaining pardon for mortal sin committed after Baptism, a person must have recourse to this Sacrament, if he is able, as a necessary preparation for the Sacrament of Extreme Unction.

(3) Extreme Unction completes the purification of the soul by destroying the *remains of sin* already forgiven. By remains of sin we mean the temporal punishment due to sin, the inclination of the heart to evil, spiritual weakness, and that languor of soul which prevents it from raising itself to God. These results of sin are called the remains of sin because, being the consequences of sin, they generally remain even after the sins have been forgiven. They are removed entirely or in part according to the dispositions of the sick person.

One of the effects of Extreme Unction is to soothe the pains of the sick person, and even to restore him to health if God sees it to be expedient for the good of his soul. It is not by a miracle that this last effect is produced; but, as Extreme Unction brings calmness to the mind, and resignation to God's will, these effects have such a consoling influence on

Effects on the body.

the sick person that they may even bring about his restoration to health by enabling natural remedies to produce their effect. How foolish, then, it is to defer receiving this Sacrament till one is almost, or quite, beyond all natural hope of recovery.

Extreme Unction, being one of the *Sacraments of the living*, should be received in the state of grace. We ought to prepare for it by a good Coufession, but if it so happens that we are unable to do so, we must stir up in our hearts as perfect an act of sorrow as possible for all our sins; for there is no forgiveness of sin, even of venial siu, without sincere repentance.

Dispositions for Extreme Unction.

CHAPTER LXXX

HOLY ORDER: ITS MEANING AND DEGREES

WHEN our Lord, at the Last Supper, changed bread into His Sacred Body, and wine into His most precious Blood, He bade His Apostles, " Do this for a commemoration of Me" (Luke xxii. 19). Having come on earth to found His Church, He here establishes an order of Ministers, whom He not only empowers, but commissions, to offer Sacrifice ; to continue this Sacrifice and Sacrament in the Church to the end of the world, and thereby show forth the death of Christ till He come.

Sacrifice to be offered.

In the Gospel of St. John we read how our Lord, when speaking of His *Mission*, extended a Divine power and mission to His Apostles, to be handed down also to their successors in the Ministry even to the end of the world : " As the Father hath sent Me, I also send you. When He had said this, He breathed on them, and He said to them : Receive ye the Holy Ghost : Whose sins you shall forgive, they are forgiven them ; and whose sins you shall retain, they are retained " (John xx. 21-23).

Commission to forgive sins.

Here we have our Lord showing His commission, and giving power to His Apostles to forgive and to retain sins.

Again, when He commissioned them to preach and baptise throughout the world, He made mention of His authority : " All power is given to Me in heaven and in earth. Going therefore, teach ye all nations ; baptising them in the name of the Father, and of the Son, and of the Holy Ghost. Teaching them to observe all things whatsoever I have commanded you : and behold I am with you all days, *even to the consummation of the world* " (Matt. xxviii. 18-20). Here, again, we have a clear warrant and commission given to the Apostles and their successors, the Bishops and Priests of the Church, to continue their Master's work. Christ received from His Father all power in heaven and in earth, and in virtue of this power He sends them, even as His Father had sent Him, to teach and preach, to administer the Sacraments, to guide the faithful, and to govern the Church. Whoever denies these powers to the Apostles must at the same time deny that Christ, as man, possessed them. Moreover, as the Church was to continue to the end of time, the power that He gave to His Apostler was to be extended to their successors in the Ministry : " Behold I am with you all days, even to the consummation of the world." It is by the Sacrament of Holy Order that Christ perpetuates in His Church the sacerdotal character which He bestowed upon His Apostles.

Commission to teach and baptise.

" Holy Order," as defined in the Catechism, " is the Sacrament by which Bishops, Priests, and other Ministers of the Church are ordained, and receive power and grace to perform their sacred duties." It was instituted to enable all men, even to the end of the world, to partake of the graces and blessings purchased for us in the Passion and Death of our

Holy Order defined.

Lord, and to preserve and direct the Church by supplying her with a succession of Ministers. "For this cause I left thee in Crete, that thou shouldst set in order the things that are wanting, and shouldst ordain priests in every city, as I also appointed thee" (Tit. i. 5).

There exists, then, in the Church, according to the institution of Jesus Christ, a visible Priest-
Seven different Orders. hood, a body of Ministers whose duty it is to see to all that has reference to the Divine worship; a hierarchy comprising different degrees, all of which have more or less relation to the Priesthood. These degrees are *seven* in number, viz., the *Priesthood*, the *Diaconate*, and the *Sub-diaconate*, called the *major*, that is greater orders, or Holy Orders; and those of *Acolyte*, *Exorcist*, *Lector*, and *Porter*, called the *minor*, or lesser orders. The *Tonsure* is, properly speaking, not an Order, but rather an initial rite to prepare the candidate for the reception of Orders.

The Priesthood is the highest of the
The Priest-hood. Orders, and is divided into two degrees, the Episcopate and the Priesthood proper.

The Episcopate is the complement and the plenitude of the Priesthood. The functions of the Priest are to offer the Sacrifice of the Mass, to bless the faithful, and certain pious objects for the use of the faithful, to preach, to baptise, and to administer such Sacraments as are not reserved to the Bishop. But a Priest cannot lawfully exercise his powers except by the authority, and under the direction, of his Bishop; since it belongs to the Bishops, as the successors of the Apostles, to govern the Church of God. The *power of Orders* can never be taken away from the Priest, but the *power of jurisdiction* is conferred upon him by a lawful *mission*, that is, by his being sent or appointed by the Bishop of a diocese.

Bishops are superior to simple Priests, for in addition

to the powers that belong to the latter, they have power
to govern the Church, to administer the Sacraments of
Confirmation and Holy Order, and to perform several other
functions which cannot be performed by Ministers of any
inferior order.

But, *in the matter of jurisdiction* or authority, even the
Episcopate is not the highest degree in the hierarchy of the
Church. If Bishops are, according to the order established
by God, superior to Priests, they are themselves inferior to
the Pope. The Bishop of Rome, the Pope, who is the
successor of St. Peter, has, by Divine right, jurisdiction
over all the other Bishops: " Feed My lambs : Feed My
sheep " (John xxi. 16, 17).

The second of the Major Orders is the Diaconate. " At
The Diaconate. the commencement of Christianity," says
Calmet, " the faithful generally received the
Holy Eucharist after a repast, which they took together
in imitation of our Saviour, who instituted the Sacrament
after supper. Now the Deacons, who presided over the
first tables, after having distributed the corporeal food to
the assembly, ministered also the food of life, which they
received from the hands of the Bishop. Thus they were
Ministers both of the common and the sacred tables.
Afterwards they had assistants, called Sub-deacons, and as
among the Gentile converts there did not exist that community of goods as at Jerusalem, their chief employment
became to serve the Bishop in the oblation of the Holy
Sacrifice."

To-day the duties of the Deacon are to serve the Bishop
or Priest at the altar, to sing the gospel, to present the
bread and wine for consecration, and to dismiss the
faithful with the words: " Ite, missa est." If he be
delegated to preach, he must not speak from an elevated
position.

The lowest of the Major Orders is the Sub-diaconate.

The principal office of the Sub-deacon, as the name denotes, is to serve the Deacon at the altar. During the **The Sub-diaconate.** Mass he presents the chalice and the paten to the Deacon, hands him the wine, but himself pours the water into the wine destined for the Sacrifice; he also sings the epistle. To him, too, belongs the care and the washing of the altar-linen. At their ordination Sub-deacons bind themselves to recite daily the Divine office, and, according to the more common opinion, implicitly take a solemn vow to lead a life of perpetual chastity.

The *four Minor Orders* also have reference, but in a less degree, to what pertains to the Holy Mass.

It belongs to the office of the Acolytes to carry lighted **Acolyte.** candles, and to hand the cruets containing wine and water to the Sub-deacon during the Holy Sacrifice.

The Exorcist receives power to invoke the name of the **Exorcist.** Lord, and to impose his hands on those who are possessed by unclean spirits. This power, however, may no longer be exercised except by Priests, and even then only when they have the special and express leave of the Bishop.

The Lector has power to read to the faithful, during **Lector.** certain services of the Church, portions of the Sacred Scriptures.

In the early days of Christianity the Porter had the **Porter.** care of opening and closing the doors of the church to the faithful; of announcing, by ringing the bell, the hour of the Divine services; and of seeing that silence and due decorum were preserved in the House of God. To-day the office of Porter, as well as of the other Minor Orders except that of Exorcist, is commonly entrusted to the laity.

The ceremony of the *Tonsure* has been established in the Church for the purpose of separating from the world those who are preparing for Holy Orders; and of inspiring them to attain to the virtues of their state.

The Tonsure a preparation for Orders.

The period between the reception of the Tonsure and that of the Major Orders is, as it were, a novitiate for testing whether those who, by this ceremony, are raised to the dignity of clerics will prove themselves worthy of being ranked as Ministers of the Altar.

It must be remembered that, although there are different grades or steps in the Sacred Ministry, Holy Order is one Sacrament, and that the different ranks of the clergy share in it in different degrees: hence it is that we speak of the Sacred Orders.

CHAPTER LXXXI

HOLY ORDER (*continued*) : ITS NATURE AND EFFECTS

WE have already seen that our Lord, in instituting the Priesthood, gave to His Apostles and their

Meaning of the Priesthood.

successors the power to offer the Sacrifice of His Body and Blood in memory of His death, as well as the power to forgive and retain sins. This two-fold power is conferred by the Sacrament of Holy Order. Here then we see in the Priesthood two distinct kinds of power; power over Christ's natural Body, and the power of jurisdiction over His mystical Body, the Church. Among the functions of the Priesthood, therefore, some have refer-ence to the natural Body of our Saviour, namely, to offer the Holy Sacrifice and to communicate the Blessed Eucharist to the faithful; the others relate to the Church, or the mystical Body of Christ, such as the power to preach, to baptise, to remit sins and to administer the other Sacra-ments.

22

There **is** only one Sacrament of Holy Order, but this

One Sacrament of Holy Order. Sacrament is conferred in the Ordination of Deacons, of Priests, and of Bishops, who participate in it in different degrees.

With regard to the Sub-diaconate theologians are divided on the question whether it is a Sacrament; and while it is certain that the Episcopate, the Priesthood, and the Diaconate are of immediate Divine institution, it is more commonly held that the other Orders are merely of ecclesiastical origin.

In Holy Order we have all the characteristics of a true

Outward sign. Sacrament. In the outward part of the Sacrament we have the *matter*, which, in the case of the Deacon, Priest, and Bishop, is the imposition of hands, and perhaps the handing to them, and their touching, the symbols of their office, to signify the power that is given them over things sacred : " I admonish thee to stir up the grace of God which is in thee, by the imposition of my hands" (2 Tim. i. 6). The *form* consists in the prayer or the words used by the Bishop during the imposition of hands; perhaps also the words he uses in bestowing the symbols of office. It was by prayer and the imposition of hands that Saul and Barnabas were ordained, as we read in the Acts : " Separate Me Saul and Barnabas, for the work whereunto I have taken them. Then they, fasting and praying, and imposing their hands upon them, sent them away " (Acts xiii. 2, 3).

That the Sacrament of Holy Order confers grace we

Inward grace. gather, not only from the words of St. Paul just quoted above (2 Tim.), but also from the words he addressed to Timothy on another occasion : " Neglect not the grace that is in thee, which was given thee by prophecy, with imposition of the hands of the priesthood " (1 Tim. iv. 14).

    And when outward things or signs become the certain means of producing grace in the soul, it must **Ordained by Christt.** necessarily be by virtue of a Divine institution. Moreover the ordination of this Sacrament by our Lord is most clearly seen in His commission to His Apostles: "Do this for a commemoration of Me" (Luke xxii. 19). And again, "Whose sins you shall forgive, they are forgiven them ; and whose sins you shall retain, they are retained" (John xx. 23).

Effects. The effects of the Sacrament of Holy Order are threefold :

1. It confers sanctifying grace on him who receives it.

 2. It also imparts sacramental grace which makes the ordained more fit to exercise the duties of his sacred office.

3. It imprints an indelible character; and therefore it may not be repeated.

    Bishops, and only Bishops, are the Ministers of Holy **Minister.** Order; and they alone have power to consecrate other Bishops, as well as Priests and Deacons. With regard to the other Orders, it is commonly held that the Pope can delegate to a simple Priest authority to confer the Sub-diaconate and the Minor Orders.

    Episcopal Consecration is conferred by three Bishops, although one could validly and lawfully consecrate with faculties from the Pope.

    Only men are capable of receiving the Sacrament of Holy **Subject.** Order. The candidate for the Sacrament must have been baptised ; and, by an ecclesiastical precept, even before he can be admitted to the Tonsure, he must have received the Sacrament of Confirmation. To receive the Sacrament worthily, too, he must be in a state of grace, free from all canonical impediments, and have a Divine vocation : " Neither doth any man take the honour to himself, but he that is called by God, as Aaron was "

(Heb. v. 4). He must also have a fixed determination to remain unmarried and chaste.

. The dignity of the Priesthood is very great and surpasses all other earthly dignities. Priests are **Dignity of the** the ambassadors of Christ to men, as we gather **Priesthood.** from His own words: "He that heareth you heareth Me; and he that despiseth you despiseth Me" (Luke x. 16). They have powers which even the Angels themselves do not possess; power to forgive and retain sins, and power to change bread and wine into the sacred Body and Blood of Jesus Christ. How great, then, should be our respect for a dignity so sublime, and how attentively should we pay heed to the counsels which, in God's name, they give us!

CHAPTER LXXXII

THE SACRAMENT OF MATRIMONY

"MATRIMONY," the Catechism tells us, "is the Sacrament which sanctifies the contract of a Christian **Defined.** marriage, and gives a special grace to those who receive it worthily."

Marriage as a sacred and binding contract has ever existed among all nations, and, since **Marriage** it has God as its author, it is a holy state: **existed in all** **times.** "God created man to His own image . . . male and female He created them. And God blessed them, saying: Increase and multiply, and fill the earth" (Gen. i. 27, 28). These words, although they do not impose the obligation of marriage on all, clearly indicate the end for which marriage was instituted. Again we read: "The Lord God cast a deep sleep upon Adam; and when he was fast asleep, He took one of his ribs, and filled up flesh for it. And the Lord God built the rib which He took from Adam into a woman, and brought

her to Adam.   And Adam said: This now is bone of my
bones, and flesh of my flesh: she shall be called Woman,
because she was taken out of man.   Wherefore a man
shall leave father and mother, and shall cleave to his wife;
and they shall be two in one flesh" (Gen. ii. 21-24).   From
the above words we see that marriage was instituted by
God Himself when, in Paradise, He gave Eve to Adam
for his wife.

Till the coming of Christ marriage was but a purely
natural contract; but when Christ came into
the world, He gave to what before was a natural
contract a supernatural character by raising it
to the dignity of a Sacrament.   "If," says the
Council of Trent, "any one saith that Matrimony is not
truly and properly one of the seven Sacraments instituted
by our Saviour Jesus Christ . . . and that it does not
confer grace, let him be anathema."

Matrimony raised to the dignity of a Sacrament.

Now the Sacrament of Matrimony sanctifies the union
of man and woman, and confers on them the
grace necessary to sanctify themselves in the
married state.   Its object is threefold: (1) that
the married parties should prove a mutual help to each
other: "It is not good for man to be alone: let Us make him
a help like unto himself" (Gen. ii. 18); (2) that they should
extend God's kingdom upon earth by bringing children
into the world and training them in the knowledge and
service of God: "Increase and multiply, and fill the earth"
(Gen. i. 28); and (3) that it may prevent incontinency:
"Because of fornication, let every man have his own wife,
and let every woman have her own husband" (1 Cor. vii. 2).

Ends of Marriage.

Christ, then, raised Matrimony to the dignity of a
Sacrament as well for the sanctification of
those who enter this holy state, as for that of
their offspring.   Moreover, He Himself chose
this sacred union of man and woman as the

Marriage, the symbol of union between Christ and His Church.

symbol of that mysterious union that ever exists between Him and His Church: " Husbands, love your wives, as Christ also loved the Church, and delivered Himself up for it. . . . For no man ever hated his own flesh, but nourisheth and cherisheth it, as also Christ doth the Church " (Eph. v. 25, 29).

It was by virtue of the Divine institution that the matri-

Marriage between Christians always a Sacrament. monial contract between baptised Christians became a Sacrament; so that Jesus Christ, although He did not institute marriage, raised it to the dignity of a Sacrament of the New Law, and thus caused the marriage contract to be productive of grace. And, since Christ raised marriage to the dignity of a Sacrament, any matrimonial contract between Christians which has not the character of a Sacrament is not a real marriage, nor even a valid contract. In other words, a marriage between Christians cannot be valid, that is, a real marriage, without being at the same time a Sacrament. The purely natural contract can exist only between infidels.

Now there can be no Sacrament of Matrimony without

Outward sign of Matrimony. a contract, for it is indeed the base and foundation of the Sacrament. The contract embraces within itself both matter and form. The mutual giving over of the contracting parties to each other constitutes the matter, and the words or outward signs by which they take each other as husband and wife constitute the form.

Owing to the decree *Ne temere* of Pius X. (August 2,·

The decree *Ne temere*. 1907), no marriage contracted on or after Easter· Day, 1908, is valid, when one of the parties at least is a baptised Catholic, or a convert to the Catholic Church, unless it be contracted before the parish Priest or the Bishop of the place in which the marriage is celebrated, or before a Priest delegated by the parish Priest or by the Bishop. There must also be at least two witnesses.

But a Sacrament is essentially an outward sign of inward

Inward grace. grace. Hence those baptised persons who receive
the Sacrament of Matrimony worthily thereby
receive grace to enable them to perform as true Christians
the duties and obligations pertaining to their state of life.

The union of our Saviour with His spouse the Church

is given by St. Paul as the model of the union
Institution by
Jesus Christ. that ought to subsist between husband and wife.
Now Christ is united to His Church by a supernatural union, a union abounding in grace; and therefore
Matrimony is a sign to which is attached invisible grace;
but grace cannot be attached to marriage except in virtue
of a Divine institution. "This is a great Sacrament: but
I speak in Christ, and in the Church" (Eph. v. 32); that
is, the union of husband and wife is a notable type or sign
of the union of Christ with His spouse the Church. "He
who made man from the beginning," said our Lord, "made
them male and female. . . . For this cause shall a man
leave father and mother, and shall cleave to his wife, and
they two shall be in one flesh. Therefore now they are
not two, but one flesh" (Matt. xix. 4-6). It was most
probably when He uttered these words that our Lord
raised Matrimony to the dignity of a Sacrament.

The only *essential* sacramental rite consists in the exterior

Minister. sensible act by which the contracting parties,
in presence of the Priest and the witnesses, take
each other for husband and wife under such conditions as
God and the Church require. The parties thus become
the Ministers of the Sacrament to each other.

The effects of the Sacrament of Matrimony
Two-fold effects. are two-fold: it confers grace, and it enjoins
duties and obligations.

Being a Sacrament of the living, Matrimony, when

Grace. received in proper dispositions, increases sanctifying grace. It also confers sacramental grace
in bestowing upon the parties the right to those actual

graces which sanctify their union, and which enable them
to love and be faithful to each other, to bring up their
children in a truly Christian manner, and to carry out with
fidelity all the other duties incumbent on their state.

The mutual duties of husband and wife are beautifully
outlined by St. Paul in the example of Christ
Obligations. and His spouse the Church: "Let women be
subject to their husbands as to the Lord ; for the husband
is head of the wife, as Christ is head of the Church. . . .
Therefore as the Church is subject to Christ, so let the
wives be to their husbands in all things. Husbands, love
your wives, as Christ also loved the Church, and delivered
Himself up for it. . . . So also ought men to love their
wives as their own bodies. He that loveth his wife, loveth
himself. For no man ever hated his own flesh ; but
nourisheth and cherisheth it, as also Christ doth the
Church" (Eph. v. 22-29). But, besides these duties of
mutual love, fidelity, support, and forbearance, comes that
supreme duty of both, the proper upbringing of their
children, for whose well-being and Catholic education God
will hold them responsible.

To receive Matrimony worthily it must be approached
in proper dispositions. To this end the parties
Dispositions for should be instructed in the nature of the Sacra-
Matrimony. ment, and in the conditions and dispositions
necessary for receiving it validly and lawfully. They
should seek the guidance of their Confessor and the
approval of their parents : "My son, do nothing without
counsel, and thou shalt not repent when thou hast done"
(Ecclus. xxxii. 24). Nor should the wishes of parents be
disregarded, except when their consent is withheld purely
from selfish and unworthy motives. It is necessary to be
in a state of grace because Matrimony is a Sacrament of
the living. If a person were to receive it in mortal sin,
he would indeed receive the Sacrament validly, but he

would commit a great sacrilege and, instead of receiving a blessing, would draw down upon himself the anger of God. Hence, the best and safest immediate preparation for the Sacrament is the devout reception of the Sacrament of Penance, and, if possible, of Holy Communion. Moreover, the true Christian does not enter into the holy state of Matrimony except for his own greater sanctification, and that he may carry out with great fidelity the designs of God in his regard.

We next come to the Subjects of Matrimony, or to the persons capable of receiving the Sacrament. Now there is no Sacrament of Matrimony without a contract. It is especially necessary, then, that those about to be married should be such as are capable of making a marriage contract, and that this contract should embrace all the conditions required for the validity of contracts in general. As, therefore, there can be no contract without full consent, the marriage consent must be real, and not pretended or imaginary ; it must be mutual and externally manifested ; and it must be freely given on both sides. Every person, therefore, who is not hindered by any natural impediment, or by an impediment that may arise from the law of God or of His Church, and is capable of making such a contract, can validly receive the Sacrament of Matrimony.

Subject of Matrimony.

CHAPTER LXXXIII

THE SACRAMENT OF MATRIMONY (*continued*)

IMPEDIMENTS AND INDISSOLUBILITY OF MARRIAGE.

THE Impediments of the Sacrament of Matrimony are of two kinds: (1) those which are called *diriment* impediments, and which render the Sacrament *null*, by making it impossible, under the circumstances, for

Impediments.

the contract to be made ; and (2) *prohibitive* impediments, which render the marriage *unlawful*, but not null and void, or invalid.

The principal *Diriment Impediments,** or impediments which render the Sacrament null, are—

Diriment Impediments. 1. Consanguinity to the third degree and Affinity to the second degree, and Consanguinity or Affinity in the direct line to any degree ; also Spiritual Relationships which arise from persons acting as sponsors in Baptism, or from administering the Sacrament of Baptism—*e.g.*, in case of necessity.

2. A solemn vow of chastity, or the reception of Holy Orders.

3. One of the parties not being baptised. An unbaptised person cannot marry one baptised in the Catholic Church, or one converted from heresy or schism to the Catholic Faith. If both are unbaptised, the marriage is valid, but there is no Sacrament.

4. The marriage of a Catholic not celebrated in presence of the parish Priest, or a Priest delegated either by him or by the Bishop, and in presence of at least two witnesses.

5. Either party being already married.

6. Adultery with a promise of marriage when the innocent party dies, or adultery with attempted marriage —*e.g.*, marriage in a registry office ; or adultery with murder of the other by one of the parties ; or, even without adultery, murder committed by two people on the husband or wife of one of them.

7. Public Propriety. The impediment of public propriety arises from an invalid marriage, or from cohabitation

---

* Summary of Diriment Impediments :—

(1) Consanguinity, Affinity, and Spiritual Relationship.
(2) Solemn vows and Sacred Orders.
(3) Disparity of cult.
(4) Clandestinity.
(5) An existing marriage.
(6) Crime.
(7) Public Propriety.
(8) Fear.
(9) Impotence.
(10) Age.

without marriage, and prevents the valid marriage of either party to a blood relative of the other as far as the second degree.

8. When consent is either not free, or is given under stress of great fear unjustly brought about, and the person is compelled to choose marriage to free himself from it.

9. When a natural cause exists which prevents the end for which marriage was instituted.

10. By ecclesiastical law a man cannot marry before the age of sixteen, or a woman before the age of fourteen.

The *Prohibitive Impediments*, or impediments which render the marriage *unlawful*, but not null, are—

Prohibitive Impediments. 1. Prohibition by the Church.

2. The solemnisation of marriage within the forbidden times.

3. A simple vow of perfect chastity; or a vow to abstain from marriage.

4. The prohibition of marriage between a Catholic and a Protestant.

Certain diriment impediments which owe their origin to ecclesiastical law the Church can dispense from, but the dispensation must come from the Pope or, in certain cases, from the Bishop, who alone have power to grant it.

Banns. To remove as far as possible the danger of an impediment remaining unknown, it is ordained that notice of an intended marriage be publicly given in church at the principal Mass, on three consecutive Sundays or Holydays of Obligation. Moreover, if the parties live in different parishes, the banns must be published in both parishes. This proclamation of the banns, as it is called, besides the possibility of its leading to the discovery of some impediment in the way of the contemplated marriage, serves also to remind the faithful to pray to God to bless those who are about to enter the holy state of Matrimony. So serious is the obligation of having the banns published that it cannot be dispensed from except by the Bishop, or his delegate, *e.g.*, his Vicar General, and then only for a good reason. Anyone who is conscious of an existing impediment is strictly bound to make it known to the Priest.

And now let us say a word on the subject of mixed marriages. "A Mixed Marriage," the Cate-**Mixed** **Marriages.** chism tells us, "is a marriage between a Catholic and one who, though baptised, does not profess the Catholic Faith." Such marriages have always been disapproved of by the Church, nor does she ever permit them except on certain conditions, and for very grave reasons. Difference in religion in those who marry generally leads to countless evils. The Catholic party is in constant danger of losing the Faith, of being urged to the improper use of marriage, or of becoming indifferent to religion. Even if there are no such dangers, there is always a likelihood that difference in religion will cause quarrels; and thus, that which ought to be the strongest bond of union between husband and wife becomes a source of disunion. Moreover, when we consider the great ends of marriage, namely, mutual help, and the rearing and educating of a family, we see how difficult the attainment of all these ends is where unity of religious belief is not made the basis of the marriage union. It may be said, then, that the very nature of marriage excludes difference of religion in husband and wife.

If the Catholic Church sometimes, and then very reluctantly, grants a dispensation, she does so only on certain fixed conditions: (1) The Catholic party must be allowed the free exercise of the Catholic Faith; (2) both parties must promise to bring up all the children in it; and (3) the Catholic party must try, by prayer, example, and persuasion, to do all that is possible to gain over the non-Catholic party to the Faith. To contract a mixed marriage without a dispensation would be a grave sin.

Indissolubility of Marriage. We have seen how, according to the words of St. Paul, marriage represents, in many ways, the union of Jesus Christ with His Church. Jesus Christ is the head of the Church, He loves and protects it, and leads it to heaven. So, too, the husband should love his wife, should guard and protect her, and, by his words and example, lead her in the way of salvation. The Church loves Jesus Christ, is ever obedient to Him, and can never fall away from Him; but will remain faithful to Him, unspotted and unchanged to the end of the world; so also the wife ought to love her husband, and to be obedient and faithful to him. "As the Church is subject to Christ, so also let the wives be to their husbands in all things" (Eph. v. 24). And as Jesus Christ is ever united to His Church, so also are husband and wife joined together for life, death alone being able to sever their union.

It is the teaching of the Church, then, that the marriage of Christians, once consummated, is indissoluble, and cannot be broken except by the death of one of the parties. If for *just and sufficient reasons* they arrange to live apart, or should obtain what is called a *civil divorce*, neither party can contract a second marriage, while the other is alive, without committing adultery.

Christ restores the Original Condition of the Marriage State. We find the Pharisees asking our Lord: "Is it lawful for a man to put away his wife for every cause? Who answering, said to them: Have ye not read, that He who made man from the beginning, made them male and female? And He said: For this cause shall a man leave father and mother, and shall cleave to his wife, and they two shall be in one flesh. Therefore now they are not two, but one flesh. What therefore God hath joined together, let no man put

asunder" (Matt. xix. 3-6).   Christ then, besides raising
Matrimony to the dignity of a Sacrament, restored it as
God had originally instituted it.   Henceforth it is to be
a perfect figure of His union with His spouse the Church,
and consequently indissoluble.

To emphasise still further the binding force of the
marriage tie we give the words of our Lord in St. Mark
and St. Luke: "Whosoever shall put away his wife, and
marry another, committeth adultery against her.   And if
the wife shall put away her husband, and be married to
another, she committeth adultery" (Mark x. 11, 12).
"And he that marrieth her that is put away from her
husband, committeth adultery" (Luke xvi. 18).   St. Paul,
too, tells us that they that are married ought not to part,
or if a separation for weighty reasons can be allowed,
neither party is free to marry another: "To them that are
married, not I but the Lord commandeth, that the wife
depart not from her husband : and if she depart, that she
remain unmarried, or be reconciled to her husband.   And
let not the husband put away his wife" (1 Cor. vii.
·10, 11).

But, for a man who has lost his wife by death, or for a
woman who has lost her husband, it is lawful to marry
again : "A woman is bound by the law as long as her
husband liveth ; but if her husband die, she is at liberty:
let her marry to whom she will, only in the Lord"
(1 Cor. vii. 39).

PART V

VIRTUES AND VICES

" He that is just, let him be justified still ; and he that is holy, let him be sanctified still. Behold, I come quickly, and My reward is with Me, to render to every man according to his works" (APoc. xxii. 11, 12).

CHAPTER LXXXIV

VIRTUES IN GENERAL: THE INFUSED VIRTUES

VIRTUE, in its literal sense, means *strength, manliness,* but here we have to consider it in the sense of moral goodness, or the perseverance of the will in doing what is pleasing to God. As such we may define it as a habit or disposition of the soul which leads us to do good actions, and which renders those good who are endowed with it. It is a habit that gives a man readiness in acting according to the reason that is in him. It has vice as its opposite.

Virtue.

Vice then may be defined as a habit or disposition of the soul which leads us to do wicked actions and renders those wicked who are under its influence.

Vice.

Now virtues may be *natural* or *supernatural.* Those virtues are called *supernatural* which are exercised with the help of grace, and from motives of faith. When thus practised by one who is in a state of grace, they merit an eternal reward.

Supernatural Virtues.

Those are *natural* or *human* virtues which are practised

351

by man simply by the light of reason, and which have
reason only as their foundation. Their end
being purely natural and earthly, they can
never merit a supernatural reward in the life of the world
to come. A heathen may possess natural virtue, and the
fact of his living up to the light of reason may serve to
draw down upon him the mercy of God, and light to rise
to higher things.

Natural Virtues.

Again, virtues may be divided according to their origin
into *Infused* Virtues and *Acquired* Virtues.

When God bestows upon man the sanctifying grace of
the Holy Ghost, He at the same time infuses
into the soul certain supernatural habits or
virtues—principally the Theological and the
Cardinal Virtues. Such virtues are spoken of as *Infused*
Virtues, because they are, as it were, poured into the soul
of man directly by Almighty God Himself; and such are
all supernatural virtues. Whereas *Acquired* Virtues are
those virtues which a man gains by his own efforts, and by
the frequent repetition of suitable acts when he follows
the light of reason only. As they are acquired by constant
practice, so, too, they are preserved and strengthened by
exercise and practice.

Infused and Acquired Virtues.

But as all virtues are habits, whether they be infused
or acquired, so, too, like all other habits, they
grow and must be fed; and our acts are the
food that sustains them. If a habit is not
exercised, it pines away and dies. Our virtues also become
less active and energetic through want of practice, and may
be entirely lost by our doing such actions as are opposed
to them.

Habits sustained by practice.

Here it may be well to repeat that Virtue and Vice are
not acts but habits. Now a man is innocent or guilty
according to his acts, not according to his habits. It is
possible for him to do a good act without being virtuous,

as it is possible for him to do a wicked act without being vicious.

In describing the virtues in order, we shall here refer once again to the Theological Virtues already treated of in the earlier part of this work. The three Infused Virtues of Faith, Hope, and Charity are called Theological Virtues because, as we have seen, they relate immediately to God; that is, they have God Himself for their object, and are exercised directly upon Him. Like the other virtues, they can be lost by acts that are contrary to them: Faith is destroyed by infidelity, Hope by despair, and Charity by deliberate mortal sin.

The Theo-logical Virtues.

Faith is the foundation of Hope and Charity; indeed, Hope and Charity cannot exist, while we are on earth, without Faith. Without Charity, Faith and Hope can exist, but in an imperfect state; nor can they, without it, merit to life eternal. Faith, which is of things *that appear not*, and Hope, which is of things *that we enjoy not*, will cease in heaven; but Charity, which is the greatest of these three, will remain and be increased in heaven.

Those virtues are called *Moral* Virtues which have for their immediate object the regulation of our con. duct in the matter of right and wrong according to the will of God. They thus refer to God in an indirect way, whereas the Theological Virtues have as their immediate object God and His Divine Perfections.

The Moral Virtues.

In themselves the Moral Virtues belong to the order of nature, having been planted by God in our very nature. They are present within us as germs, but they require our own co-operation for their development. In the Christian, however, they pass into the state of Infused Virtues, and become supernatural at the moment in which sanctifying grace enters the soul. Their acts then become ennobled and assisted by the sanctifying grace that is in the Christian, and enriched by their now being founded on Faith.

23

There are many Moral Virtues, but among them are four that stand out pre-eminently as being the most necessary in our journey through life.

The Cardinal Virtues.

These are called the *Cardinal Virtues* (Lat. *cardo*, a hinge), because they are, as it were, the *hinges* on which all the other Moral Virtues turn, and whereon the entire life of the Christian is necessarily supported. They form four centres round which the other Moral Virtues naturally arrange themselves.

Among the Cardinal Virtues *Prudence* holds the first place. It is Prudence that points out the measure of Temperance, the limits of Fortitude, and the true path of Justice. Christian Prudence, grounded on faith, is a virtue which enlightens our mind, and points out the most effectual means for carrying out the work of our salvation. It is true wisdom applied to practice, since by it we readily discern what is most perfect, and most pleasing and acceptable to God: "Be not conformed to this world, but be reformed in the newness of your mind, that you may prove what is the good, and the acceptable, and the perfect will of God" (Rom. xii. 2).

(1) Prudence.

To the Cardinal Virtue of Prudence we naturally attach discretion, vigilance, circumspection, and docility in carrying out the advice of wise and prudent counsellors: "My son, do thou nothing without counsel, and thou shalt not repent when thou hast done" (Ecclus. xxxii. 24).

Opposed to Prudence are the vices of imprudence, negligence, precipitation, together with craftiness and too anxious solicitude for the things of the world.

Justice, as a Cardinal Virtue, embraces all the duties which we owe to God and to our neighbour. It may then be defined as a Moral Virtue which inclines the will to give what is due both to God and to man: "Render to Cæsar the things that are Cæsar's, and to God, the things that are God's" (Matt. xxii. 21).

(2) Justice.

To be truly just, then, we must give every one his due. In this we fulfil our duty to God by carefully keeping His Commandments : " All Thy commandments are justice " (Ps. cxviii. 172). " If you love Me, keep My command-ments." .(John xiv. 15). To our neighbour we must do what he has a right to expect of us; we must do to him as we would wish him to do to us; nor must we injure him in his person, or his reputation, or his property : "Thou shalt love thy neighbour as thyself" (Mark xii. 31).

Under Justice will naturally fall religion, by which we pay to God the honour which is His due; filial piety, by which children love, reverence, and honour their parents; obedience to lawful authority; gratitude, respect, and veracity or truthfulness.

The chief vices opposed to Justice are every kind of injustice, such as taking away or keeping unjustly what belongs to another, exaction, ingratitude, disrespect, dis-obedience, impiety, and sacrilege.

Fortitude is a virtue which enables a person to face with coolness and courage all dangers and difficulties **(3) Fortitude.** in the fulfilment of the duties which he owes to God, to himself, and to his neighbour.

The virtues attendant on Fortitude are confidence, courage, firmness, magnanimity, patience, and perse-verance.

The vices opposed to Fortitude may arise from excess or defect, such as rashness, presumption, and impatience; cowardice, inconstancy, and irresolution.

The fourth of the Cardinal Virtues, *Temperance*, enables us to moderate, according to the dictates of **(4) Temperance.** reason and religion, and to keep in due re-straint, the desires of the heart in regard to sensible -pleasures : " Refrain yourself from carnal desires, which war against the soul " (1 Pet. ii. 11).

With Temperance are associated the virtues of abstinence, sobriety, modesty, continency, and chastity.

The vices opposed to it are gluttony, drunkenness, immodesty, incontinency, and impurity.

Many qualities are infused into the soul with Sacramental Grace. Every soul in a state of sanctifying grace is enriched with all the supernatural virtues and the Gifts of the Holy Ghost.

Seven Gifts of the Holy Ghost.

Although the Gifts of the Holy Ghost are received by infusion at Baptism, it is more particularly in the Sacrament of Confirmation that we receive them in all their fulness. They are *seven* in number: viz., Wisdom, Understanding, Counsel, Fortitude, Knowledge, Piety, and the Fear of the Lord.

The gift of *Wisdom* teaches us to set a right value on the things of God, and to hold as naught everything that does not conduce to our eternal salvation.

Wisdom.

The gift of *Understanding* enables us to penetrate the mysteries of Faith and to comprehend the truths of religion, as far as our finite intellects are capable of grasping the things of God.

Understanding.

The gift of *Counsel* discovers to us and makes us choose whatever is conducive to God's greater glory and our own perfection and eternal salvation.

Counsel.

The gift of *Fortitude* enables us to stand firm in the cause of virtue and truth; it enables us, too, to fight manfully in the warfare against the devil, the world, and the flesh.

Fortitude.

The gift of *Knowledge* enlightens us to discern the difference between good and evil; makes us to know the will of God in whatever concerns our salvation, and discovers to us the dangers we must avoid.

Knowledge.

The gift of *Piety* enables us faithfully to practise our religion, and to carry out with zeal whatever relates to the service of God.

Piety.

The gift of *the Fear of the Lord* inspires us with a sovereign respect for God, and makes us avoid whatever is contrary to His holy will; and by bringing to our minds the thought of God's anger it makes us careful never to offend Him by the least deliberate sin: "The fear of the Lord driveth out sin" (Ecclus. i. 27).

The Fear of the Lord.

The precious Fruits which the Holy Ghost produces in the souls of those who are in possession of His Sevenfold Gifts we find enumerated by St. Paul in his Epistle to the Galatians, in which he writes: "The fruit of the Spirit is charity, joy, peace, patience, benignity, goodness, longanimity, mildness, faith, modesty, continency, chastity. Against such there is no law" (Gal. v. 22, 23).

CHAPTER LXXXV

THE WORKS OF MERCY : THE BEATITUDES

WE read in St. Mark how one of the Scribes, coming to our Lord, asked Him which was the first of all the Commandments, and that our Lord answered him: "The first commandment of all is . . Thou shalt love the Lord thy God with thy whole heart, and with thy whole soul, and with thy whole mind, and with thy whole strength. This is the first commandment.

The two great Precepts of Charity.

"And the second is like to it: Thou shalt love thy neighbour as thyself" (Mark xii. 29-31).

Now we have shown that we prove our love of God by keeping His Commandments: "If you love Me, keep My commandments" (John xiv. 15); and we shall see that the great Commandment of charity towards our neighbour is fulfilled in the faithful observance of the Corporal and the Spiritual Works of Mercy.

The seven Corporal Works of Mercy are—

The Corporal Works of Mercy.

1. To feed the hungry.
. To give drink to the thirsty.
. To clothe the naked.
. To harbour the harbourless.
. To visit the sick.
. To visit the imprisoned.
7. To bury the dead (Matt. xxv., Tob. xii.).

" Give alms out of thy substance, and turn not away thy face from any poor person; for so it shall come to pass that the face of the Lord shall not be turned from thee. According to thy ability be merciful " (Tob. iv. 7, 8).

Importance of the Corporal Works of Mercy.

The importance, to each one of us, of performing Works of Mercy may be gathered from the words of our Lord Himself, who tells us that it is the unmercifulness of the wicked that shall be their condemnation : " Depart from Me, ye cursed, into everlasting fire, which was prepared for the devil and his angels. For I was hungry, and you gave Me not to eat : I was thirsty, and you gave Me not to drink. I was a stranger, and you took Me not in : naked, and you covered Me not : sick, and in prison, and you did not visit Me. Then they shall answer Him, saying : Lord, when did we see Thee hungry, or thirsty, or a stranger, or naked, or sick, or in prison, and did not minister to Thee ? Then He shall answer them, saying : Amen, I say to you : as long as you did it not to one of these least, neither did you do it to Me " (Matt. xxv. 41-45).

But, to the just on His right hand, He shall say : " Come, ye blessed of My Father, possess ye the kingdom prepared for you from the foundation of the world. For I was hungry, and you gave Me to eat : I was thirsty, and you gave Me to drink : I was a stranger, and you took Me in : naked, and you covered Me : sick, and you visited Me : I was in prison, and you came to Me. Then shall

the just answer Him, saying: Lord, when did we see Thee
hungry, and fed Thee: thirsty, and gave Thee to drink?
And when did we see Thee a stranger, and took Thee in?
or naked, and clothed Thee?   Or when did we see Thee
sick, or in prison, and came to Thee?   And He answering,
shall say to them: Amen, I say to you, as long as you
did it to one of these My least brethren, you did it to Me"
(Matt. xxv. 34-40).

What greater or more forcible motive to charity can
we have than the assurance of Revelation that the Son of
God will accept all good offices done to the afflicted as done
to Himself?

But the exercise of fraternal charity is not confined to

The Spiritual   the Corporal Works of Mercy; it extends also
Works of   to relieving the wants of our neighbour's soul,
Mercy.   and shows itself in what are called the Spiritual
Works of Mercy.   These also are seven in number:

1. To convert the sinner.
2. To instruct the ignorant.
3. To counsel the doubtful.
4. To comfort the sorrowful.
5. To bear wrongs patiently.
6. To forgive injuries.
7. To pray for the living and the dead.

If, then, we are bound to do what we can for the

Importance of   relief of the pressing bodily needs of our neigh-
the Spiritual   bour, we are equally bound to do what we can
Works of   for the welfare of his soul.   The rewards,
Mercy.   moreover, promised to those who faithfully
perform acts of charity in the spiritual order ought to
make us realise the more forcibly the value of a single soul
in the eyes of God: "He who causeth a sinner to be converted from the error of his way shall save his soul from
death, and shall cover a multitude of sins" (James v. 20).

"They that instruct many to justice shall shine as stars for all eternity" (Dan. xii. 3).

As we are here treating of acts of charity both in the spiritual and in the temporal order, it may be advantageous to dwell at greater length on two of them especially, *Almsgiving* and *Fraternal Correction*.

Now *Almsgiving*, or the timely assisting of one in need, is of such moment that we cannot treat it as a matter of indifference. Nay, to give alms is a duty incumbent on all who have it in their power to do so : "He that hath the substance of this world, and shall see his brother in need, and shall shut up his bowels from him : how doth the charity of God abide in him ?" (1 John iii. 17). And in what proportion we are bound to give, we gather from the words of Tobias to his son : "If thou have much, give abundantly : if thou have little, take care even so to bestow willingly a little" (Tob. iv. 9). And St. John the Baptist taught the people that whatever they had more than their own wants required should be bestowed upon their needy brethren : "He that hath two coats, let him give to him that hath none : and he that hath meat, let him do in like manner" (Luke iii. 11).

Almsgiving an Obligation.

This obligation of Almsgiving naturally flows from that precept of charity which enjoins us to love our neighbour as ourselves ; that is, to do to others what we might reasonably wish that they should do to us. It is real charity that shows itself in action : "Let us not love in word, nor in tongue, but in deed, and in truth" (1 John iii. 18). When, therefore, our neighbour is in *extreme* need, that is, when a person is in evident danger of dying if not promptly relieved, we are bound under pain of mortal sin—if others fail to assist him—to aid him, not only from our superfluities, but even by depriving ourselves of what is not absolutely necessary for our own needs. In other cases, where our neigh-

Gravity of the Obligation.

bour's need is less pressing, we are bound more or less according to the urgency of the case. And our Lord tells us: " Whosoever shall give to drink to one of these little ones a cup of cold water only in the name of a disciple: Amen, I say to you, he shall not lose his reward " (Matt. x. 42).

Fraternal Correction also is an act of charity, a work of mercy in the spiritual order, and consists in admonishing our neighbour of his faults or of his sins, through a motive of charity.

Fraternal Correction.

In superiors this becomes a bounden duty ; and charity requires it in the case of others, when there is hope that reproof will not be in vain, in order to prevent sin. It is only obligatory, then, when it is likely to profit our neighbour, as charity is the only motive for exercising it. It should therefore be omitted when the contrary effect is likely to ensue : " If thy brother shall offend against thee, go and rebuke him between thee and him alone. If he shall hear thee, thou shalt gain thy brother. And if he will not hear thee, take with thee one or two more ; that in the mouth of two or three witnesses every word may stand. And if he will not hear them, tell the Church " (Matt. xviii. 15-17).

But Fraternal Correction must be administered with all possible prudence and meekness, since everyone has his failings and stands in need of indulgence from others : " Brethren, if a man be overtaken in any fault, you who are spiritual instruct such a one in the spirit of mildness, considering thyself, lest thou also be tempted " (Gal. vi. 1).

The great duties of *Prayer*, *Fasting*, and *Almsdeeds*, already described at length, rank as the Three Eminent Good Works, since they are especially pleasing to God, and include within themselves all the others. It is by *Prayer* that we appease the anger of God and consecrate to Him our heart with all its affec-

The Three Eminent Good Works.

tions. By *Fasting* we chastise the body and bring it into subjection, thus offering to Him a perpetual sacrifice. By *Almsdeeds* we make a sacrifice to Him of our earthly possessions by devoting them to Him in the persons of the needy and the poor.

There are *eight* Virtues, called the Beatitudes, specially pronounced blessed by our Lord in His Sermon on the Mount (Matt. v. 3-10):

The Eight Beatitudes.

I. " Blessed are the poor in spirit; for theirs is the kingdom of heaven."—Although this may be understood of such as are truly in poverty and want, and bear it willingly for the love of God, it is more commonly taken to signify the humble in mind and heart, and those whose desires are not set upon riches. Here the virtue of humility is placed first because it is the parent of every other virtue, as pride is the root of every vice.

2. " Blessed are the meek; for they shall possess the land."—The meek, the humble, and the oppressed, who are despoiled of their possessions by the powerful and the proud, shall obtain the inheritance of a better land. Meekness and gentleness under insults and injustice are the marks of the true Christian : " Learn of Me, because I am meek and humble of heart " (Matt. xi. 29).

3. "Blessed are they that mourn; for they shall be comforted."—Here not those who mourn from worldly motives are referred to, but such as, renouncing sinful pleasures, mourn for their sins: " You shall lament and weep, but the world shall rejoice; and you shall be made sorrowful, but your sorrow shall be turned into joy " (John xvi. 20).

4. " Blessed are they that hunger and thirst after justice; for they shall have their fill."—By which is meant that those who have an earnest desire of being just and holy, and of advancing daily in the path of virtue, shall be filled with every kind of good in their heavenly country.

5. " Blessed are the merciful; for they shall obtain

mercy."—It is not only the giving of alms, but the practice of all the works of mercy that is recommended here: "Forgive, and you shall be forgiven. Give, and it shall be given to you. . . . For with the same measure that you shall· mete withal, it shall be measured to you again" (Luke vi. 37, 38).

6· "Blessed are the clean of heart; for they shall see God."—That is, they shall see God face to face who are clean from sin, and who thus are pure in body and mind; they who give themselves up to the practice of purity and of every other virtue.

7. "Blessed are the peacemakers; for they shall be called the children of God."—To be peaceful ourselves and with others, and to bring together such as are at variance, will entitle us to rank as children of God. It was to bring peace to man, and to reconcile him with his offended Creator, that our Lord came down from heaven.

8. Blessed are they that suffer persecution for justice' sake; for theirs is the kingdom of heaven."—By justice are here understood truth, virtue, and piety. To all who suffer on this account Christ promises a seat in His heavenly kingdom: "And they indeed went from the presence of the Council, rejoicing that they were accounted worthy to suffer reproach for the name of Jesus" (Acts v. 41).

CHAPTER LXXXVI

VARIOUS CLASSES OF SINS: VIRTUES OPPOSED TO THE CAPITAL SINS: HOW WE MAY SHARE IN ANOTHER'S SIN

EVERY man, generally speaking, has within him some particular passion stronger than the rest, and to
The Predomi-
nant Passion. this passion, as a rule, may be traced, as to
their source, all the vicious inclinations to which
his heart is prone. This is called his Ruling or Predomi-

nant Passion.   It is to the uprooting of this evil tendency, and to the planting in its stead of the opposite virtue, that the chief work of the spiritual life must be devoted : "To him that shall overcome, I will give to sit with Me in My throne" (Apoc. iii. 21).   This Predominant Passion will be one of the Capital Sins.

Now there are seven sins which we call Capital or Deadly Sins, not that they are always mortal, but because they are the *heads* or *sources* from which so many sins take their rise, and because they bring *death* to the souls of such as are enslaved by them.   These seven Vices are—Pride, Covetousness, Lust, Anger, Gluttony, Envy, and Sloth.

The Seven Capital Sins.

Pride is an inordinate esteem of our own excellence, and a vain complacency in ourselves.   The proud man is odious to God and to his fellow-man, since pride causes him to despise his neighbour, and to refuse to give to God the honour which is His due.   It is the source of almost every vice, although there are some vices that seem to spring more directly from it.   "Never suffer pride to reign in thy mind, or in thy words; for from it all perdition took its beginning" (Tob. iv.14).

1. Pride.

The chief sins which flow from Pride are vainglory, self-conceit, vanity, hypocrisy, boasting, ambition, presumption, obstinacy, disobedience, and resistance to lawful authority.

Covetousness is an inordinate love of money and of worldly goods.   It is a vice that particularly withdraws us from God; and we have the words of our Lord for it that a man cannot serve the two masters, God and mammon: "for either he will hate the one and love the other; or he will sustain the one and despise the other" (Matt. vi. 24).

2. Covetousness.

Covetousness is the parent of fraud, theft, injustice, perjury, and treason; it makes those who are slaves to it selfish, and insensible even to the pressing wants of their neighbour.

Lust is an inordinate love of carnal or sensual pleasures,
3. Lust. and includes all sins of impurity, whether of thought, word, or deed, contrary to the sixth and ninth Commandments. It is a vice that ruins both soul and body.

Lust makes those who are addicted to it selfish, hard-hearted, and cruel; it destroys piety, produces aversion to prayer, darkens the understanding, leads to the loss of Faith and even to despair, and destroys domestic happiness.

Anger is a violent and inordinate emotion of the soul
4. Anger. excited by a real or supposed injury, and impelling us to avenge the wrong.

Yet Anger may proceed from a good motive, and be guided by reason and a pure love of justice. Then it is not a sin: "Be angry, and sin not: let not the sun go down upon your anger" (Eph. iv. 26).

Anger leads to hatred, revenge, enmity, ill-will, fighting, quarrelling, injurious words, and even to murder.

Gluttony is an immoderate indulgence in food or drink,
5. Gluttony. or an inordinate love of eating and drinking. St. Paul tells us that those whose God is their belly are the enemies of the Cross of Christ (Philip. iii. 18, 19).

Gluttony blinds the understanding, and often leads to drunkenness, angry quarrels, scurrilous talk, and impurity.

Envy is a feeling of sadness, uneasiness, or discontent,
6. Envy. excited at the sight of another's superiority or success, whether in the spiritual or in the temporal order; and this because we fancy our own merit to be lessened thereby.

Envy is not only contrary to charity, but leads to rash

judgment, calumny, detràction, hatred, and to rejoicing at another's ill-fortune.

Sloth is a languor of soul, a distaste for virtue, which

7. Sloth.   causes us to neglect, or to begin to perform carelessly, the duties of our state. "Go to the ant, O sluggard, and consider her ways, and learn wisdom" (Prov. vi. 6).

Sloth is the source of idleness, indifference, inconstancy, and lukewarmness: "Because thou art lukewarm, and neither cold nor hot, I will begin to vomit thee out of My mouth" (Apoc. iii. 16). And idleness, we are told, is one of the chief sins which lead to the breaking of the sixth and ninth Commandments.

The Virtues opposed to the seven Deadly Sins are given below, and, for greater convenience, are arranged each opposite its contrary Vice.

The Seven Capital Sins.	*The Contrary Virtues.*
Pride.	Humility.
Covetousness.	Liberality.
Lust.	Chastity.
Anger.	Meekness.
Gluttony.	Temperance.
Envy.	Brotherly Love.
Sloth.	Diligence.

Humility is a virtue which, from the consideration of

1. Humility.   the greatness and goodness of God and our own defects, gives us a true sense of our littleness, prevents us from raising ourselves up against the order of Providence, and causes us to refer to God alone all the good we can do. The man who thinks little of God is always great in his own eyes.

Humility is the guardian of all the other virtues, because it inspires in us watchfulness and distrust of ourselves, and prevents us from exposing ourselves rashly to the danger of sin. God, moreover, has promised particular graces to the humble: "God resisteth the proud, and giveth grace to the humble" (James iv. 6).

Pride, vainglory, self-conceit, presumption, disobedience, resistance to lawful authority, and the other sins which flow from Pride, are all opposed to the virtue of Humility.

2. Liberality. *Liberality* is a virtue which inclines us to make a generous use of our earthly goods for the relief of the needy, and for the honour and glory of God. By withdrawing our affections from earthly possessions, it leads us to exercise the Works of Mercy. God holds out great promises to him that shall shun covetousness, and He will abundantly reward our acts of mercy: "He that hath mercy on the poor lendeth to the Lord; and He will repay him" (Prov. xix. 17).

Covetousness, or Avarice, and its offspring, fraud, theft, injustice, and the like, are all opposed to the virtue of Liberality..

3. Chastity. *Chastity* is a moral virtue which keeps in restraint all impure inclinations and desires, and moderates within the bounds of duty the natural inclination for the pleasures of the flesh. This moderation is the fruit of the Holy Ghost called "Continency."

Chastity is necessary for salvation : all must be chaste in their state: "There shall not enter into it (*heaven*) anything defiled, or that worketh abomination" (Apoc. xxi. 27). And again: "Blessed are the clean of heart; for they shall see God" (Matt. v. 8). To guard this virtue we must keep a constant watch over ourselves, have recourse to prayer and the Sacraments, and carefully avoid all dangerous occasions that may lead us to violate it: it is only to the humble that God gives the specia grace of this virtue.

Another necessary safeguard to Chastity is *Modesty*, or

that virtuous sense of shame which causes aversion and horror for everything that may offend against holy purity. It is a most powerful restraint against vice, and against taking or allowing dangerous liberties. In young people who are not restrained by this sentiment of modesty, Chastity itself is in great danger, even if it has not already suffered shipwreck.

The sins contrary to Chastity are all such as have reference to Lust, that is, sins whether of thought, word, or deed, contrary to the sixth and ninth Commandments.

Meekness is a virtue which moderates Anger, maintains the soul in a state of calm and tranquillity, and banishes from the heart all feelings of bitterness. It causes us to behave towards our neighbour with kindness and with that charity " which endureth all things " (1 Cor. xiii. 7). Thus it is Meekness which suppresses all desire of revenge and every feeling of unjust anger and displeasure. It shows itself in patient forbearance, and especially marks out the true disciple of Christ: " Learn of Me, because I am meek and humble of heart " (Matt. xi. 29).

4. Meekness.

Meekness is for all men ; *Clemency* is the virtue of those in office. This latter virtue, which is a branch of Meekness, prompts superiors to mitigate deserved punishments, and sometimes to pardon the guilty. Yet clemency has limits that it cannot go beyond without degenerating into weakness and compromising authority.

Meekness is opposed to Anger and the kindred sins of hatred, revenge, ill-will, and the like.

Temperance, as opposed to Gluttony, is a virtue by which we exercise due restraint over our appetite in eating and drinking. It thus embraces *Abstinence,* or moderation in eating, and *Sobriety,* or moderation in drinking. In a broader sense, it is the virtue which enables us to keep in due control the inclina-

5. Temperance.

tions of fallen nature in regard to sensible pleasures, and, in this sense, is opposed to the vices of Gluttony and Lust.

As the virtues of Abstinence and *Self-denial* are associated with Temperance, we may here consider the means by which we are to put into practice that penance, mortification, and self-denial so much insisted on by our Divine Lord: "If any man will come after Me, let him deny himself, and take up his cross daily and follow Me" (Luke ix. 23). We cannot, then, be true followers of Christ except by renouncing ourselves, *i.e.*, by giving up our own will, and by going against our own inclinations and passions. We have already considered this duty in regard to Fasting and Abstinence when treating of the Commandments of the Church.

By *Self-denial* in its fullest sense we mean a general mortification not only of our external, but of our internal inclinations and passions which urge us to gratify our own will rather than submit to the will of God. "If thou give to thy soul her desires, she will make thee a joy to thy enemies" (Ecclus. xviii. 31). Not only must we abstain from all sinful pleasures, but we ought to refuse ourselves many lawful things that are dear and agreeable to us, in order that, by thus depriving ourselves of lawful gratifications, we may the more easily abstain from those that are unlawful. In this way we shall acquire habits of self-denial which will enable us more surely to resist temptations. Such mortification, moreover, is necessary for preserving our souls from sin: "If you live according to the flesh, you shall die; but if, by the spirit, you mortify the deeds of the flesh, you shall live" (Rom. viii. 13).

Brotherly Love, the contrary of Envy, is a virtue by which we wish well to everyone, by which we
6. Brotherly Love.
love our neighbour as we ought to love him for God's sake. It is also the bond of social

24

life. To its neglect must be attributed most of the disorders which afflict society and beget class hatred. It is the virtue that clearly distinguishes the true followers of Christ: " By this shall all men know that you are My disciples, if you have love one for another " (John xiii. 35). Our natural selfishness blinds us to all that does not concern our own interests, but, by this virtue, we sincerely " rejoice with them that rejoice, and weep with them that weep" (Rom. xii. 15), just as though our neighbours' good or ill had overtaken ourselves. It is that love that worketh no evil, and that is the fulfilling of the law (Rom. xiii. 10).

Diligence, as opposed to the vice of Sloth, is a virtue 7. Diligence. which enables us faithfully to carry out all the duties of our state of life, and thus to work zealously for the glory of God, the good of our neighbours, and the salvation of our soul. The diligent man surmounts all obstacles and difficulties that he encounters in the way of salvation. He is truly the faithful servant mentioned in the Gospel to whom were spoken those cheering words: " Well done, good and faithful servant, because thou hast been faithful over a few things, I will place thee over many things: enter thou into the joy of thy Lord " (Matt. xxv. 21).

Without this virtue of Diligence, final perseverance is impossible ; for it is not enough that we were once virtuous, we must do good constantly, even to the very end of our life: " He that shall persevere unto the end, he shall be saved " (Matt. x. 22).

More malicious than the Capital Sins, and more The Six Sins dangerous to salvation, are the Six Sins against against the the Holy Ghost. These do not arise from mere Holy Ghost. frailty or ignorance, but are generally accompanied with so much malice and such wilful obstinacy to the Spirit of God and the known truth that they who are guilty· of them are seldom converted; yet there is no sin which God cannot or will not forgive to such as are truly sorry.   These sins are—

     1. Presumption.
     2. Despair.
     3. Resisting the known truth.
     4. Envy of another's spiritual good.
     5. Obstinacy in sin.
     6. Final impenitence.

The last-named sin consists not only in putting off repentance till death, but in dying unrepentant, and thus its forgiveness becomes impossible.

The sins spoken of as the Four Sins crying to Heaven for Vengeance are the four dreadful crimes of Wilful Murder, the Sin of Sodom (an unnatural sin of lust), Oppression of the Poor, and Defrauding Labourers of their Wages.   They, as it were, cry to heaven for vengeance on those who perpetrate them, and call upon the justice of God to punish them not only in the next life, where all sins unrepented of are punished, but sometimes even in this life.

The Four Sins crying to Heaven for Vengeance.

Now it is possible to share the guilt of another's sin in such a way that we become as guilty before God as though we had committed the sinful act ourselves. This happens when we either cause the sin, or take part in it, through our own fault.   There are nine ways in which this can be done:

The nine ways in which we share in another's sin.

1. *By counsel;* i.e., by giving advice or direction to the evil-doer.

2. *By command;* i.e., by ordering him, or by any other means inducing him, to commit a sin on our behalf.

3. *By consent;* i.e., by approving of the sin, or by joining with others in voting to do harm.

4. *By provocation;* i.e., by inciting or urging one to commit sin.

5. *By praise or flattery* ; *i.e.*, by inciting another to sin by praise or blame.

6 *By concealment* ; *i.e.*, by inducing him to sin through helping him to hide his crime.

7. *By being a partner in the sin* ; *i.e.*, by sharing the fruits of another's wickedness or by aiding in any way the commission of sin.

8. *By silence; i.e.*, by not speaking out when we ought, or by not acting so as to prevent the sin when we are bound to do so.

9. *By defending the ill done* ; *i.e.*, by taking the part of the evil-doer, and attempting to justify his wicked action.

If in any of these ways we have been the cause of injury to our neighbour, either in his goods or in his character, we are as much bound to restitution as though we ourselves had done the wrong; but the amount of our share of the restitution will vary according to circumstances.

CHAPTER LXXXVII

CHRISTIAN PERFECTION

'BE ye perfect, as also your heavenly Father is perfect"
(Matt. v. 48). By this injunction we are
The Evangeli- bidden to imitate the Divine perfection, as far
cal Counsels. as our exertions, assisted by Divine grace, can
reach. Again, our Lord counsels us: "If thou wilt be perfect, go, sell what thou hast, and give to the poor, and thou shalt have treasure in heaven: and come, follow Me" (Matt. xix. 21). The passage just quoted shows that there is a difference between things that are of *precept* or *command*, and those that are of *counsel* only, which they are to aim at who would aspire to the greatest perfection. Now of the counsels, the three most eminent are what are called the Evangelical Counsels, viz., Voluntary Poverty, Perpetual Chastity, and Entire Obedience.

People in the world can lead a perfect life by living, not according to the spirit of the world, but according to the spirit of Christ. Christian Perfection, therefore, consists in being free from all inordinate love of the world and of ourselves, and in loving God above all things for His own sake, and our neighbour as ourselves for God's sake; in a word, in seeking God alone in all things. "What have I in heaven? and besides Thee what do I desire upon earth? . . . Thou art the God of my heart, and the God that is my portion for ever" (Ps. lxxii. 25, 26).

Now this perfect observance of God's precepts may be called *essential perfection*, since all men must observe them who hope to be saved; but there is an *accidental perfection* which is arrived at by adding the *Evangelical Counsels* to the keeping of the Commandments. Evangelical Perfection, then, consists in the perfect observance of God's Commandments conjoined with the practice of Voluntary Poverty, Perpetual Chastity, and Entire Obedience. Our Lord does not make these counsels obligatory, but leaves them to our free choice; yet all religious and all who have vowed to keep them are bound to do so by their vow.

Voluntary Poverty is the free renunciation of all temporal possessions to follow Christ more perfectly:
Voluntary Poverty. "Every one that hath left house, or brethren, or sisters, or father, or mother, or wife, or children, or lands for My name's sake, shall receive a hundredfold, and shall possess life everlasting" (Matt. xix. 29).

Perpetual Chastity consists not only in the abstaining from all impure pleasures, but in the free and **Perpetual Chastity.** lasting renunciation of marriage, in order that, with greater liberty and less encumbrance, we may devote ourselves to the service of God: "He that can receive this word, let him receive it" (Matt. xix. 12); *i.e.*, let those aspire to the glory of this state who feel them.

selves called by Heaven. Moreover, to be able to live singly and chastely is given to him who prays for the grace of God to enable him to do so. St. Paul, too, advises and prefers the state of virginity to that of the married life: "He that giveth his virgin in marriage, doth well; and he that giveth her not, doth better" (I Cor. vii. 38).

Entire Obedience is the total renunciation of our own will, in all that is not sin, to the will of our

Entire Obedience. lawful superiors, who stand to us in the place of God. This counsel our Lord has conveyed to us in the perfect obedience which He Himself paid even to His earthly parents: "He went down with them, and came to Nazareth, and was subject to them" (Luke ii. 51); by which He showed that nothing is so great and amiable in Christians as ready obedience to the directions of their superiors. "My meat is to do the will of Him that sent Me, that I may perfect His work" (John iv. 34).

To embrace the religious state is not a precept addressed to all Christians; it is a life of perfection and

The Religious Life. counsel for such as are called to it by God. Yet those who have the happiness of receiving this Divine vocation, and faithfully respond to it, can aim at no more meritorious state of life. Their reward will indeed be a hundredfold by the wealth of spiritual gifts and graces which they will receive in this life, and the inheritance of life eternal in the next. "And leaving all things he rose up, and followed Him" (Luke v. 28). We should do well always to remember the words of St. John: "If any man love the world, the charity of the Father is not in him; for all that is in the world is the concupiscence of the flesh, and the concupiscence of the eyes, and the pride of life" (1 John ii. 15, 16). And the world shall pass away, and all things that belong to it, but "He that doth the will of God abideth for ever" (I John ii. 17).

We have now considered the Virtues and Vices; we have

The four last things to be remembered.

seen what sin is both in itself and in its consequences; and as it is the one evil that the
Christian has to dread and shun, we shall bring
our work to a close by recalling the most powerful preservative against it; viz., the thought of what the
Catechism calls "The four last things to be ever remembered: death, judgment, hell, and heaven." "In all thy
works remember thy last end, and thou shalt never sin"
(Ecclus. vii. 40).

When Christ first appeared on earth, He came to take

Christ's Second Coming.

upon Himself the load of our sins; but at His
second coming He will appear not in the likeness of sinful man, not to redeem us, but with
great power and majesty to judge all mankind.   He will
then pronounce the just doom of the wicked, "Depart
from Me, ye cursed, into everlasting fire, which was prepared for the devil and his angels" (Matt. xxv. 41).   But
the just He will rejoice with the consoling words, "Come,
ye blessed of My Father; possess ye the kingdom prepared
for you from the foundation of the world" (Matt. xxv. 34).

Heaven, then, with the possession of God for all eternity,
is the reward of virtue; and the aim of virtue is the perfection of man: "He that is just, let him be justified still;
and he that is holy, let him be sanctified still.   Behold I
come quickly; and My reward is with Me, to render to
every man according to his works.   I am Alpha and
Omega, the first and the last, the beginning and the end"
(Apoc. xxii. 11-13).

INDEX

Printed in England